Models of the Teacher

CATHOLIC BIBLICAL QUARTERLY IMPRINTS
No. 6

EDITORIAL BOARD
Richard J. Bautch, General Editor

ASSOCIATE EDITORS

Bill T. Arnold
Mary Rose D'Angelo
Joachim Eck
Kristine Henriksen Garroway
Beverly Roberts Gaventa
Najeeb T. Haddad
J. Todd Hibbard
Francis M. Macatangay

Daniel Machiela
Roberto Martinez, OFM Cap.
Michael Patella
Anathea E. Portier-Young
Deborah C. Prince
Timothy Sandoval
Susanne Scholz

Models of the Teacher in Biblical Texts and Their Reception

Edited by
Bart J. Koet,
Gearard Ó Floinn,
and Archibald L. H. M. van Wieringen

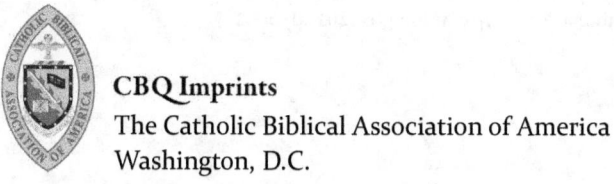

CBQ Imprints
The Catholic Biblical Association of America
Washington, D.C.

☙PICKWICK *Publications* • Eugene, Oregon

MODELS OF THE TEACHER IN BIBLICAL TEXTS AND THEIR RECEPTION

Copyright © 2025, The Catholic Biblical Association of America. All rights reserved. Except for brief quotations in critical publications or reviews, no part of this book may be reproduced in any manner without prior written permission from the publisher. Write: Permissions, Wipf and Stock Publishers, 199 W. 8th Ave., Suite 3, Eugene, OR 97401.

Pickwick Publications
An Imprint of Wipf and Stock Publishers
199 W. 8th Ave., Suite 3
Eugene, OR 97401

www.wipfandstock.com

PAPERBACK ISBN: 979-8-3852-6213-7
HARDCOVER ISBN: 979-8-3852-6214-4
EBOOK ISBN: 979-8-3852-6215-1

Library of Congress Cataloging-in-Publication Data

Names: Koet, Bart J. (Bartholomeus Johannes) editor | Ó Floinn, Gearard editor | Wieringen, Archibald L. H. M. van (Archibald Ludger Hermenigild Maria), 1963- editor
Title: Models of the teacher in biblical texts and their reception / edited by Bart J. Koet, Gearard Ó Floinn, Archibald L.H.M. van Wieringen.
Description: Washington, D.C. : The Catholic Biblical Association of America, [2025] | Series: Catholic Biblical quarterly imprints ; no. 6 | Includes bibliographical references and index.
Identifiers: LCCN 2025030961 (print) | LCCN 2025030962 (ebook) | ISBN 9780915170661 paperback | ISBN 9780915170678 ebook
Subjects: LCSH: Education in the Bible | Education--Biblical teaching | Teacher-student relationships--Biblical teaching | Bible--Criticism, interpretation, etc.
Classification: LCC BS680.E3 M63 2025 (print) | LCC BS680.E3 (ebook)
LC record available at https://lccn.loc.gov/2025030961
LC ebook record available at https://lccn.loc.gov/2025030962

Dedicated in grateful memory to Jewish teacher

Leon Mock
1968–2023
זיכרונו לברכה

Contents

Abbreviations   ix

1. "We Do Not Learn for School, but for Life":
   With the Bible in Search of the Ideal Models of the Teacher
   *Bart J. Koet, Gearard Ó Floinn, and
   Archibald L. H. M. van Wieringen*   1

2. The Book of Isaiah as a Teacher: Trajectories of Learning for the
   Text-Immanent Reader
   Archibald L. H. M. van Wieringen   14

3. Yhwh as a Teacher in the Book of Amos: An Analysis from a
   Communicative Perspective
   Bincy Thomas Thumpanathu   31

4. Ben Sira: Teacher and Pedagogue
   Panc C. Beentjes   50

5. The Teacher as Reinterpreter of Tradition: The Son of Man
   Sayings in the Gospel according to Mark
   Gearard Ó Floinn   62

6. Asking Questions as the Beginning of Being a Teacher: Jesus
   as a Student in Luke 2:46
   Bart J. Koet   76

7. Stephen and Philip: Two of the Seven, Teachers and Evangelists
   (Acts 6:1–6; 8:4–40; 21:8)
   Joke H. A. Brinkhof   88

8. Paul as a Teacher of Unity in 1 Corinthians: Some Introductory
   Thoughts about the Question of Whether Paul Is a Teacher
   Bart J. Koet   104

9. Paul as Teacher of Genesis 1:26–27 in Colossians 1:15; 3:10: A Cognitive Linguistic Approach
   Cornelia J. M. Melisse — 122

10. Moses Our Teacher: Moses as a Model for Rabbinic Teaching
    Leon Mock — 134

11. "Are We to Turn and All Listen to Her?" Mary Magdalene as Contested Teacher from the *Gospel of Mary* to *Mary Magdalene* (Garth Davis, 2018)
    Caroline H. C. M. Vander Stichele — 143

12. Job's Best Pupil: An Exploration of Gregory the Great as Teacher
    Arnold A. M. Smeets — 156

13. Francis of Assisi: Teacher as Model
    Willem Marie Speelman — 168

14. Magisterial: Thomas Aquinas as Teacher
    Henk J. M. Schoot — 187

15. The Conversation as a Space of Teaching: Pastoral-Communicative Situations within Prison Chaplaincy
    Renilde G. W. M. van Wieringen — 201

16. A Passover Gone Wrong: *BioShock Infinite* as a Teaching Model of Critical Religious Appropriation of the Bible
    Frank G. Bosman — 220

17. Epilogue: *Non scholae, sed vitae discimus*
    Bénédicte Lemmelijn — 239

Index of Ancient Sources — 247

Index of Modern Authors — 256

Personalia — 261

Abbreviations

AB	Anchor Bible
ABD	*The Anchor Bible Dictionary* (ed. David Noel Freedman; 6 vols.; New York: Doubleday, 1992)
ABS	Archaeology and Biblical Studies
ACEBT	*Amsterdamse Cahiers voor Exegese en bijbelse Theologie*
AIL	Ancient Israel and Its Literature
AJEC	Ancient Judaism and Early Christianity
AnBib	Analecta Biblica
ASNU	Acta Seminarii Neotestamentici Upsaliensis
ATD	Das Alte Testament Deutsch
AYB	Anchor Yale Bible
BBB	*Bonner biblische Beiträge*
BDF	Friedrich Blass, Albert Debrunner, and Robert W. Funk, *A Greek Grammar of the New Testament and Other Early Christian Literature* (Chicago: University of Chicago Press, 1961)
BEATAJ	Beiträge zur Erforschung des Alten Testaments und des antiken Judentums
BETL	Bibliotheca Ephemeridum theologicarum Lovaniensium
Bib	*Biblica*
BibInt	*Biblical Interpretation*
BIS	Biblical Interpretation Series
BKAT	Biblischer Kommentar, Altes Testament
BN	*Biblische Notizen*
BNTC	Black's New Testament Commentaries
BO	*Bibliotheca Orientalis*
BZAW	Beiheft zur Zeitschrift für die alttestamentliche Wissenschaft
BZNW	Beihefte zur Zeitschrift für die neutestamentliche Wissenschaft
CBC	Cambridge Bible Commentary
CBET	Contributions to Biblical Exegesis and Theology
CBQ	*Catholic Biblical Quarterly*

CBQMS	Catholic Biblical Quarterly Monograph Series
CCSL	Corpus Christianorum: Series Latina
CNT	Commentaire du Nouveau Testament
ConBOT	Coniectanea Biblica: Old Testament Series
CRINT	Compendia Rerum Iudaicarum ad Novum Testamentum
CSCO	Corpus Scriptorum Christianorum Orientalium
DCLS	Deuterocanonical and Cognate Literature Studies
EANEC	Explorations in Ancient Near Eastern Civilizations
ECL	Early Christianity and Its Literature
EHAT	Exegetisches Handbuch zum Alten Testament
EJL	Early Judaism and Its Literature
EstBíb	*Estudios Bíblicos*
ETL	*Ephemerides Theologicae Lovanienses*
FAT	Forschungen zum Alten Testament
FCB	Feminist Companion to the Bible
FOTL	Forms of the Old Testament Literature
Greg	*Gregorianum*
HS	*Hebrew Studies*
HTKAT	Herders Theologischer Kommentar zum Alten Testament
HTR	*Harvard Theological Review*
ICC	International Critical Commentary
Int	*Interpretation*
JAAR	*Journal of the American Academy of Religion*
JBL	*Journal of Biblical Literature*
JBQ	*Jewish Bible Quarterly*
JBTh	Jahrbuch für biblische Theologie
JSJSup	Journal for the Study of Judaism: Supplement Series
JSNT	*Journal for the Study of the New Testament*
JSNTSup	Journal for the Study of the New Testament: Supplement Series
JSOT	*Journal for the Study of the Old Testament*
JSOTSup	Journal for the Study of the Old Testament: Supplement Series
JTS	*Journal of Theological Studies*
KEK	Kritisch-exegetischer Kommentar über das Neue Testament
LD	Lectio Divina
LHBOTS	Library of Hebrew Bible/Old Testament Studies
LNTS	Library of New Testament Studies

LSJ	Henry George Liddel, Robert Scott, and Henry Stuart Jones, *A Greek-English Lexicon* (9th ed., with revised supplement; Oxford: Clarendon, 1996)
NA^{28}	*Novum Testamentum Graece*, Nestle Aland, 28th ed.
NCBC	New Century Bible Commentary
NEchtB	Neue Echter Bibel
NHC	Nag Hammadi Codices
NHMS	Nag Hammadi and Manichaean Studies
NIDOTTE	*New International Dictionary of Old Testament Theology and Exegesis* (ed. Willem A. VanGemeren; 5 vols.; Grand Rapids: Zondervan, 1997)
NIGTC	New International Greek Testament Commentary
NovT	*Novum Testamentum*
NovTSup	Supplements to Novum Testamentum
NPNF	Nicene and Post-Nicene Fathers
NTM	New Testament Message
NTS	*New Testament Studies*
OBO	Orbis Biblicus et Orientalis
OLA	Orientalia Lovaniensia Analecta
OTE	*Old Testament Essays*
OTL	Old Testament Library
OTM	Old Testament Message
OTS	Old Testament Studies
OtSt	Oudtestamentische Studiën
PG	*Patrologiae Cursus Completus: Series Graeca* (ed. Jacques-Paul Migne; 162 vols.; Paris, 1857–1886)
QD	Quaestiones Disputatae
RA	*Revue d'assyriologie et d'archéologie orientale*
RB	*Revue biblique*
RevQ	*Revue de Qumran*
RNT	Regensburger Neues Testament
SBLDS	Society of Biblical Literature Dissertation Series
SBS	Stuttgarter Bibelstudien
SC	Sources chrétiennes
SCS	Septuagint and Cognate Studies
SHBC	Smyth & Helwys Biblical Commentary
SJLA	Studies in Judaism in Late Antiquity
SJT	*Scottish Journal of Theology*
SNTSMS	Society for New Testament Studies Monograph Series
SubBib	Subsidia Biblica

TBü	Theologische Bücherei
TDNT	*Theological Dictionary of the New Testament* (ed. Gerhard Kittel and Gerhard Friedrich; trans. Geoffrey W. Bromiley; 10 vols.; Grand Rapids: Eerdmans, 1964–1976)
TGl	*Theologie und Glaube*
THKNT	Theologischer Handkommentar zum Neuen Testament
TSAJ	Texte und Studien zum antiken Judentum
TynBul	*Tyndale Bulletin*
VT	*Vetus Testamentum*
VTSup	Supplements to Vetus Testamentum
WBC	Word Biblical Commentary
WD	*Wort und Dienst*
WUNT	Wissenschaftliche Untersuchungen zum Neuen Testament
ZAW	*Zeitschrift für die alttestamentliche Wissenschaft*

1

"We Do Not Learn for School, but for Life":
With the Bible in Search of the Ideal Models of the Teacher

BART J. KOET, GEARARD Ó FLOINN,
AND ARCHIBALD L. H. M. VAN WIERINGEN

In this volume, a number of teachers from the Bible and its reception history are presented. Research into various models of being a teacher is part of the research program "Teaching and Tradition" of the School of Catholic Theology of Tilburg University, the Netherlands. Both notions, of "teaching" and "tradition," presuppose a dynamic unity of conservation, development, and renewal, in which the teacher has his/her own specific role. This also applies to the Bible (teachers in the biblical text and the biblical text as teacher) and its reception.[1]

As an introduction, we will briefly outline the history of the "school," after which we will summarize which teachers the reader will meet in the contributions in this volume. The authors of the contributions are senior researchers of our faculty or junior researchers who obtained their doctorate at our faculty.

---

1. Previous publications on the subject of the research program are Bart J. Koet and Archibald L. H. M. van Wieringen, eds., *Multiple Teachers in Biblical Texts* (CBET 88; Leuven: Peeters, 2017); Bart J. Koet and Archibald L. H. M. van Wieringen, eds., *Asking Questions in Biblical Texts* (CBET 114; Leuven: Peeters, 2022). See also Bart J. Koet and Archibald L. H. M. van Wieringen, eds., *Vragen staat vrij: Over vragen stellen als methode in oude en nieuwe wijsheidstradities* (Heeswijk-Dinther: Berne Media, 2020). For some first thoughts on models of being a teacher, see also Bart J. Koet and Archibald L. H. M. van Wieringen, eds., *Modellen van leraarschap: Van Jesaja tot Bioshock* (Utrechtse Studies 21; Almere: Parthenon, 2017).

■ I. The School

We do not learn for school, but for life. This was written in our classroom. This wisdom goes back to Seneca, who teaches in his *Epistulae Morales*: "Non scholae sed vitae discimus." (*Lucil.* 17–18.106.12)

In her much-praised book *Not for Profit*, philosopher Martha Nussbaum takes up this point by making a strong plea for the humanities and against market-oriented thinking in our schools and universities. Nowadays, the main goal of education seems to be to teach pupils and students to become as economically productive as possible. An underlying fear would be that countries will fall behind economically if they do not pull out all the stops to develop new technologies and business strategies. Nussbaum argues in favor of taking a much broader objective of learning: the aim should be to train people to become critical thinkers and to become empathetic and democratically minded citizens.[2]

That you learn for life was certainly evident in the ancient times, before the schools came into existence. Children learned (and still learn) primarily from their parents and guardians. In prehistoric times this was, for example, finding the way, hunting, waging war, knowing about herbs, and plants, and, at some point in history, also about agriculture. For men and women, of course, there will have been different things to learn.

Against this background, it is understandable that the son often pursued the same profession as the father and thus took over his father's job. But this father–son relationship or, more broadly, parent–child relationship is also important religiously.[3]

The narrative about the institution of the Passover meal and the liberation from the house of slavery in Egypt includes the standard exhortation to the father to teach this liberation to the son, as described in Exod 12:26–27; 13:8–10, 14; and Deut 6:20–21.[4] The verb נגד often used here is

---

2. Martha C. Nussbaum, *Not for Profit: Why Democracy Needs the Humanities* (Public Square; Princeton, NJ: Princeton University Press, 2012).

3. For general information, see Andreas Kunz-Lübcke and Rüdiger Lux, "*Schaffe mir Kinder . . .*": *Beiträge zur Kindheit im alten Israel und in seinen Nachbarkulturen* (Arbeiten zur Bibel und ihrer Geschichte 21; Leipzig: Evangelische Verlagsanstalt, 2006); Kristine Henriksen Garroway, *Children in the Ancient Near Eastern Household* (EANEC 3; Winona Lake, IN: Eisenbrauns, 2014); Kristine Henriksen Garroway, "Gendering, Engendering, and Educating the Growing Child," in Garroway, *Growing Up in Ancient Israel: Children in Material Culture and Biblical Texts* (ABS 23; Atlanta: SBL Press, 2018) 137–71.

4. Christoph Dohmen, *Exodus 1–18* (HTKAT; Freiburg: Herder, 2015), 302; Eckart Otto, *Deuteronomium 1–11*, vol. 2: *Deuteronomium 4,44–11,32* (HTKAT;

best translated as "to explain."⁵ This refers to the educational aspect of upbringing at home. To this day, this teaching continues in the celebration of the Seder meal, as *m. Pes.* 10.5 also puts it: "In each and every generation a person must view himself as though he personally left Egypt, as it is stated: 'And you shall tell your son on that day, saying: It is because of this which the Lord did for me when I came forth out of Egypt'."⁶

This father–son aspect (or, in some texts, mother–son aspect⁷) is also visible in many wisdom texts. The father gives wise counsel to the son on how to keep his path pure, including warnings against seductive women who seek to ruin the, obviously innocent, son (e.g., Prov 2:16–17; 5:1–23; 6:24; 7:5).⁸ Most life lessons consist of clichéd sayings that can be found all over the world. A famous example is Prov 26:27, כרה־שחת בה יפל וגלל אבן אליו תשוב, "whoever digs a pit, will fall into it, if someone rolls a stone, it will roll back on him" (cf. Ps 7:16).⁹ Such a father–son aspect, including what we see as misogyny, is shared with many other texts from the ancient Near East.¹⁰

Freiburg: Herder, 2012), 822–25; Richard J. Bautch, "Questions Posed in Deuteronomy 6: Learning and Teaching the Ways of God," in Koet and van Wieringen, *Asking Questions in Biblical Texts*, 35–47.

5. See especially Eduard König, *Hebräisches und aramäisches Wörterbuch zum alten Testament* (Leipzig: Dieterich, 1910) 262, s.v., נגד.

6. See also Georg Beer, ed., *Die Mischna. Traktat 3 Pesachim (Ostern): Text, Übersetzung und Erklärung: Nebst einem textkritischen Anhang* (Die Mischna; Berlin: De Gruyter, 1912) 195–96. Cf. also Baruch M. Bokser, "Ritualizing the Seder," *JAAR* 56 (1988) 443–71.

7. Proverbs 31:1–9 is about the mother–son relationship. See Carol Meyers, "Mothers' Wisdom: Technical Training and Lessons for Life," in *With the Loyal You Show Yourself Loyal: Essays on Relationships in the Hebrew Bible in Honor of Saul M. Olyan* (ed. T. M. Lemos, Jordan D. Rosenblum, Karen B. Stern, and Debra Scoggins Ballentine; AIL 42; Atlanta: SBL Press, 2021) 13–28.

8. As a counterpart, Lady Wisdom plays a very important role in Prov 8:1–9:12, positioned opposite Lady Folly in Prov 9:13–18. For recent assessments of the role of women in the wisdom literature of the Bible, see especially Roland E. Murphy, "Wisdom and Eros in Proverbs 1–9," *CBQ* 50 (1988) 600–603; Cullen Murphy, "Is the Bible Bad News for Women?," *Wilson Quarterly* 22 (1998) 14–33; Nili Shupak, "Female Imagery in Proverbs 1–9 in the Light of Egyptian Sources," *VT* 61 (2011) 310–23; Christl M. Maier, "Wisdom and Women – Wisdom of Women," in *Gerhard von Rad and the Study of Wisdom Literature* (ed. Timothy J. Sandoval and Bernd U. Schipper; AIL 46; Atlanta: SBL Press, 2022) 211–34.

9. See also Otto Plöger, *Sprüche Salomos (Proverbia)* (BKAT 17; Neukirchen-Vluyn: Neukirchener Verlag, 1984) 315–16.

10. See also John Mark Thompson, "Proverbs in the Ancient Near East," in *The Form and Function of Proverbs in Ancient Israel* (Studia Judaica 1; The Hague: Mouton, 1974) 35–58; Sara J. Denning-Bolle, "Wisdom and Dialogue in the Ancient Near East," *Numen* 34 (1987) 214–34.

4   Models of the Teacher

But when did the first teachers enter history? When a more differentiated society emerges, the role of the teacher develops. Learning together systematically, under the direction of a teacher, is probably most evident in learning to read and to write. The origin of the written characters and the emergence of the first forms of education go hand in hand. Knowledge and skills with regard to reading and writing thus become the core of the school system, the so-called "three R's" usually spoken as "reading, writing, and 'rithmatic."

The oldest writing systems were complicated, and mastery would be achieved only after years of training. The alphabet was a great advance and a relief, because learning only a limited number of characters was enough. But little changed before school training in the sense that writing—that is, learning to read and write—remained the educational core business. School and writing/reading form an unbreakable combination.

The first schools can be found in Sumer, in the delta of Mesopotamia, the oldest culture in the world, which originated in the fourth millennium before the beginning of our era. Writing exercises were repeated *ad infinitum*. Some clay tablets of the Sumerian schools have been preserved by chance. Thanks to finding those writing exercises, we know that they were instructive and playful. Famous for writing training is the wisdom riddle recovered in Ur: "One whose eyes are not open enters it; someone whose eyes are open comes out?" Fortunately, the solution is mentioned on the same clay tablet, which the student also had to write as part of the exercise: *E.DUB.A*. The *eduba* is the Akkadian word for "school," or literally, "the house of the clay tablet."[11] The learning model may have consisted of repeating, repeating, and repeating again, but an attempt was made to enliven the teaching material.

Going to school, however, was not for everyone; it was only for the rich, the elite, who could afford not to have their children participate in the necessary labor. Those who could read and write often had a prominent position in society at the time and were often in the immediate vicinity of the king.[12]

In Greek culture, too, the art of reading and writing was primarily for the elite. Our word "school" comes from the Greek word σχολή.[13] This word in Greek meant something like "leisure," the time a student did not

---

11. See Eleanor Robson, "The Tablet House: A Scribal School in Old Babylonian Nippur," *RA* 95 (2001) 39–66.
12. For a survey, see M. Civil, "Education in Mesopotamia," *ABD* 2:301–5.
13. See, e.g., Josef Pieper, *Muße und Kult* (Munich: Kösel, 1948). The title of the English translation makes Pieper's thesis clearer: *Leisure, the Basis of Culture*; including

need to work. So, it is obvious that the rich, in particular, could afford school education for their children.[14]

However, not everyone in ancient times was happy with the invention of writing. We find in Plato's dialogue *Phaedrus* 274b–275a how Socrates quotes a text in which the written word is the enemy of memory. After Socrates has treated the art of speech in the foregoing, the question remains how one can appreciate writing. Socrates then tells his audience what he has heard from ancient sages. Toth, one of the ancient Egyptian gods, was the inventor of numbers and of arithmetic, geometry, astronomy, checkers, and dice, but his most important contribution was the invention of writing. At that time, Thamos was king of Egypt. He was also worshiped by the Egyptians as the God Ammon. Toth went to present all his finds to this king. Toth presented to Thamos with writing as the key to memory and wisdom. The king disagreed. Writing will actually promote forgetting, because people no longer have to rely solely on their memory. They will use writing to support what they want to remember and in this way they will no longer exercise their memory.

From this mythical story we can distill an important purpose of writing in the earliest Greek culture. Writing was often intended as an aid to remembering oral traditions such as Homer. It is most likely that this memory of Socrates, even though Plato may have invented this myth himself, gives us some insight into the oldest way of transmitting (chokmatic) traditions: the oral tradition was passed down by learning it by heart. The epic poems attributed to Homer are its main exponents. Memorizing texts has long remained an important way of passing on traditions, even if they were also written down.

The passing on of tradition is also of eminent importance in Judaism. As a sort of prologue, the Deuteronomic version of the Ten Commandments already emphasizes that Israel must learn God's precepts—and then, of course, practice them (Deut 5:1). In the Hebrew Bible and later Jewish traditions, learning remains the basis for the covenant with God and with each other. There is debate about the percentage of people who could write among the different peoples and traditions around the

---

The Philosophical Act (San Francisco: Ignatius Press, 2009). For Pieper's outline of σχολή as "leisure," see 19–20 (German edition).

14. An overview of the history of learning can be found, for example, in William Boyd and Edmund J. King, *The History of Western Education* (London: A. & C. Black, 1972).

Mediterranean, but it is certain that, for the Jewish people, a large part of learning was learning to memorize and reproduce texts.[15]

Whereas the idea of an oral tradition is generally accepted within Old Testament exegesis,[16] it was Birger Gerhardsson who long ago started to stress the importance of memorization and oral tradition for the origin of the New Testament.[17] His point of departure was a comparison of the rabbinic teaching systems with the school of Jesus and his disciples, as presented in Luke-Acts. Gerhardsson has thus shown that it is precisely this oral tradition and the art of memory that can be a key to understanding Jesus as a teacher and to the way in which most of the writings of the New Testament originated. While his point of view was initially received with skepticism, in recent decades more and more attention has been drawn to the fact that the origin of the New Testament was preceded by a period of oral tradition. An interdisciplinary debate has arisen about fundamental questions of the way in which texts that originated in a (predominantly) oral setting are nevertheless passed on through writings.[18]

Because writing materials were expensive and large groups of people could not read or write, memorizing texts remained an important way of passing on traditions. This must certainly have been the case after the fall of the Roman Empire as well.[19] Although the status of books changed with Christianity, because they became part of the liturgy—as a matter of course comparable to Judaism—reading and writing among Christians were still limited to the elite. Consequently, there was hardly any differ-

---

15. For a survey, see André Lemaire, "Education: Ancient Israel," *ABD* 2:305–12.

16. For the problem of oral tradition and layered biblical writings, see Archibald L. H. M. van Wieringen, "A Tale of Two Worlds? A Synchronic Reading of Isaiah 7:1–17 and Its Diachronic Consequences for the Book," in *The History of Isaiah: The Formation of the Book and Its Presentation of the Past* (ed. Jacob Stromberg and J. Todd Hibbard; FAT 150; Tübingen: Mohr Siebeck, 2021) 179–95.

17. Birger Gerhardsson, *Memory and Manuscript: Oral Tradition and Written Transmission in Rabbinic Judaism and Early Christianity* (ASNU 22; Lund: Gleerup, 1961). See also publications of his students, e.g., Samuel Byrskog, "Memory and Identity in the Gospels: A New Perspective," in *Exploring Early Christian Identity* (ed. Bengt Holmberg; WUNT 226; Tübingen: Mohr Siebeck, 2008) 33–57.

18. Important publications are Werner H. Kelber, *The Oral and the Written Gospel: The Hermeneutics of Speaking and Writing in the Synoptic Tradition, Mark, Paul, and Q* (Philadelphia: Fortress, 1983); Jan Heilmann, *Lesen in Antike und frühem Christentum: Kulturgeschichtliche, philologische sowie kognitionswissenschaftliche Perspektiven und deren Bedeutung für die neutestamentliche Exegese* (Texte und Arbeiten zum neutestamentlichen Zeitalter 66; Tübingen: Narr Francke Attempto, 2020).

19. See also Guy G. Strousma, "The New Self and Reading Practices in Late Antiquity," *Church History and Religious Culture* 95 (2015) 1–18.

ence in literacy between Christians and the rest of Roman society, as a result of which, as everywhere else in antiquity, the oral medium remained the most important means for handing on tradition among Christians.[20]

Reading and writing have remained the core of education throughout the ages. Every innovation and renaissance therefore always meant a new impulse for education as well as for reading and writing. Medieval Europe can be seen as a succession of innovations in which education again and again took center stage. Regarding the Carolingian Renaissance, for example, Charlemagne promoted the establishment of schools in 787 with a special decree, although the great Charlemagne himself remained illiterate. He was not even able to write his own signature; instead, he put a small hook in the written material as proof of its authenticity. In the tenth century, the time of the Ottonian Renaissance, a revival of cathedral schools can be observed, while in the twelfth century, Cluny, where the great reform of Benedictine monastic life took shape, was a leader in the renewed momentum behind the revival of monastic schools. Learning to read and write was always regarded as the main teaching task. In this period the first universities grew out of the monastic schools.[21]

The printing press meant that reading came within the reach of much larger groups than before. Knowledge and insights were disseminated much more widely and, moreover, much faster. This also applied to the Bible, due to the greater distribution of Bible translations. In any case, an important side effect was that the accent gradually shifted from hearing to seeing texts.[22] Nevertheless, learning to read and write remained (and still remains) part of the school, but teaching it could now be done through textbooks.

■ II. The Teacher

With the rise of the school as an institution, the teacher also makes a definitive entrance on the world stage. He (or she—but there were not many female teachers in the ancient Near East and in antiquity) is the one who bears responsibility for the learning process of the class and

---

20. Strousma, "New Self and Reading Practices," 11.
21. See, e.g., Susan Wise Bauer, *The History of the Renaissance World: From the Rediscovery of Aristotle to the Conquest of Constantinople* (New York: W. W. Norton, 2013).
22. The development from spoken to written to printed to ultimately electronic writing is described, among other things, in the well-known work of Walter J. Ong, *Orality and Literacy: The Technologizing of the Word* (London: Methuen, 1982).

the students. But how should the teacher teach: drill, simplify, throw the student in at the deep end, ask questions?

Every teacher is not automatically a good teacher. Far from it. Poor and unsuccessful teachers crop up in many stories, from the inception of schools. A Sumerian clay tablet from around the year 2000 before our era bears witness to this. A schoolboy was often beaten with the cane for his poor academic performance. He proposes to his parents that they invite the headmaster for a pleasant evening with wine and food. After that evening he suddenly turns out to be a fine student.[23] Not a good model of teaching, but recognizable, even to this day.

A good teacher, who will find him/her? The search for a good teacher is quite a task. That used to be the case. Witness Flavius Josephus, for example, who speaks about his various teachers in his *Vita* 7–12. And it is still the case: the search for good teachers is perennial.

Even today, people look for good teachers. In fact, that search has led to scientists in different countries working out the competences and qualities of a teacher in detail. The European Union has even had a comprehensive overview entitled *Teachers' Core Competences: Requirements and Development* (April 2011), by the taskgroup "Education and Training 2020": Thematic Working Group "Professional Development of Teachers." Recent research, however, indicates that enthusiasm on the part of the teacher plays the most decisive role.[24]

■ III. Interpretation and Actualization: An Example from the Pentateuch

There is one aspect of biblical teachers that we would like to point out here, because this aspect is something they have in common: a biblical teacher is a teacher who actualizes Scripture(s). In New Testament texts, this is very evident in the allusions to or even formal quotations from what later came to be called the Old Testament. In fact, we already find a lot of recycling of motifs, concepts, and even texts from older writings in the Hebrew Scriptures.[25] For this there is an interesting example that we

---

23. Samuel Noah Kramer, *History Begins at Sumer: Thirty-Nine Firsts in Recorded History* (3rd rev ed.; Philadelphia: University of Pennsylvania Press, 1981) 3–13.

24. Brian C. Patrick, Jennifer Hisley, and Toni Kempler, "'What's Everybody so Excited About?' The Effects of Teacher Enthusiasm on Student Intrinsic Motivation and Vitality," *Journal of Experimental Education* 68 (2000) 217–36.

25. One of the first monographs discussing inner-biblical intertextuality is Michael Fishbane, *Biblical Interpretation in Ancient Israel* (Oxford: Clarendon, 1985).

wish to deal with briefly here, and that is the fact that two versions of the Ten Commandments are found in the five books of Moses, the Torah.

The first version of the Ten Commandments is found in the Book of Exodus. The narrative of the gift of the Ten Commandments in Exod 20:1–17 is part of the larger unit formed by chaps. 19–40.[26] It describes how God and Israel made a covenant. Chapter 24 describes the covenant-making itself. Chapters 25–31 contain a direct speech of God with a very detailed description of the ark and its accessories, as the expression of how God wants to dwell among the people. When, in Exod 32:1–6, the covenant violation occurs through the making of the golden calf and the service to it, the continuation of Yhwh's indwelling is in great danger. After Moses has averted this danger, through his intercession and through punishment of the people, Yhwh is able to march again with the people. Finally, Exodus 35–40 describes how the ark and accessories are made.

The narrative told in the Book of Deuteronomy is situated at the other side of the River Jordan. Moses tells in three large sermons (the first in 1:6b–4:40; the second in 5:1b–28:68; and the third in the collection of direct speeches in 31:2b–6, 7b–8, 10b–13, 14b, 16b–21, 23b, 26–29; 32; 33:2b–29) what happened along the way through the desert.[27] And so the Ten Commandments are also mentioned. Chapter 5 presents a second account of them, and they are further explained in chaps. 6–11. Chapters 12–28 recount the instructions that the Israelites must observe once they have settled down in the land of Canaan.

In Deut 5:1 Moses calls all Israel. At the beginning he refers to the covenant that God made with them on Horeb. Moses emphasizes that the covenant was not made with the fathers of his hearers, but with the hearers themselves. The covenant appears to be something that exists in itself and that, therefore, must be inheritable. In that sense, it becomes an act to be actualized.

Deuteronomy thus presents itself as Moses's living testament, in which Moses acts as a teacher a second time (cf. also 34:10), which in fact explains the Greek name "Deuteronomy" in the Septuagint.[28]

---

26. See also Dohmen, *Exodus 1–18*, esp. 66; cf. also Jan Assmann, *Exodus: Die Revolution der Alten Welt* (3rd ed.; Munich: Beck, 2015) 51–52.

27. S. A. Kaufmann considers the entire structure of the Book of Deuteronomy to reflect the Ten Commandments ("The Structure of the Deuteronomic Law," *Maarav* 1–2 [1978–1979] 105–58).

28. It is interesting that the Greek word δευτερονόμιον ("deuteronomy") is used in Deut 17:18, where it is mentioned as one of the king's duties that he should write a second version of the Torah, a *Mishna of the Torah* את־משנה התורה.

We focus here on just one verse in both versions, namely, Exod 20:17 and Deut 5:21. These verses read:

Exodus 20:17

לא תחמד בית רעך לא־תחמד אשת רעך ועבדו ואמתו ושורו וחמרו וכל אשר לרעך:

You shall not covet your neighbor's house. You shall not covet your neighbor's wife, nor his male or female slave, nor his ox or ass, nor anything else that belongs to him.

Deuteronomy 5:21

ולא תחמד אשת רעך ולא תתאוה בית רעך שדהו ועבדו ואמתו שורו וחמרו וכל אשר לרעך:

You shall not covet your neighbor's wife. You shall not desire your neighbor's house or field, nor his male or female slave, nor his ox or ass, nor anything that belongs to him.

What we are concerned with is comparing these versions with each other. We would like to pay attention especially to the order of the objects. In the version in Exodus, the order of object is: the house of your neighbor, the wife of your neighbor, the male and female slaves, the ox and the ass, in sum: everything that belongs to the neighbor.

Compared to the version of Exodus, a few slight changes can be noted.[29] First of all, the order is different. Now the wife comes first and possessions follow only after the wife is mentioned. There is a difference between the verb used for coveting the wife, namely, חמד, and for desiring your neighbor's possessions, namely, אוה.[30]

In the list of possessions, a new object has been added: you may not snatch your neighbor's land. This is not the place to discuss all kinds of historical reconstructions of the text and the genesis of the first or second version of the mitzvah in the Ten Commandments.[31] What is important here is that the second version can be seen as an update of the first version. Although we need not see the Deuteronomist as the first femi-

---

29. Dohmen, *Exodus 1–18*, 98.

30. See also Umberto Cassuto, *A Commentary on the Book of Exodus* (trans. Israel Abrahams; Jerusalem: Magnes, 1967; repr., Jerusalem: Magnes, 1997) 249.

31. For a diachronic comparison, see, e.g., Helen Schnügel-Straumann, *Der Dekalog, Gottes Gebote?* (SBS 67; Stuttgart: KBW, 1973) 24–38; Otto, *Deuteronomium 4,44–11,32*, 674–78; Dohmen, *Exodus 1–18*, 92–101. See also Jacques Vermeylen, "Les sections narrative de Deut 5–11 et leur relation à Ex 19–34," in *Das Deuteronomium: Entstehung, Gestalt und Botschaft* (ed. Norbert Lohfink; BETL 68; Leuven: Peeters, 1985) 174–207.

nist theologian, we can nevertheless note that here and elsewhere in Deuteronomy the position of women seems to be more "emancipated" (see also Deut 21:10–14; 22:13–19; 24:1–5).[32]

A second important difference is the fact that the first version does not mention coveting your neighbor's plot of land, whereas the second version mentions it explicitly. Here, again, it is clear that a reinterpretation has taken place that is ultimately based on an adaptation to the new situation of the people. In the promised land, the seminomads will become landowners, and the new version of this verse, therefore, is updated to take account of the new situation: in addition to not desiring other people's livestock and slaves, one should not appropriate other people's land.

The fact that we have two versions of the Ten Commandments in the Torah has implications. Ultimately, it means that actualizing Torah is already an intrinsic part of Torah itself. Thus, actualization has become one of the basic features of biblical hermeneutics of what constitutes a teacher.

■ IV. Encounters with Teachers in This Volume

The ideal teacher may be indefinable. Our volume therefore does not pretend to settle all (contemporary) discussions about teachers and teaching with the contributions presented here.

In her exposé on education, the aforementioned Nussbaum harks back to Socrates as a primeval model of a good teacher, but she also uses the poet Rabindranath Tagore from India and John Dewey from the United States of America as inspiring examples. In this way she shows that examples from the past and present can help to reflect on being a teacher and a student, and also on the purpose of learning in each case. Unfortunately, however, she ignores the entire biblical tradition and its reception.

What we offer in this volume is a series of encounters with biblical teachers and with some of those who engaged in the reception of their teaching.[33] These encounters form a multicolored palette: in their own authentic way they have given shape to the teacher's role, as a lecturer, as

---

32. Otto, *Deuteronomium 4,44–11,32*, 674–78. Cf. Athalya Brenner, "An Afterword: The Decalogue – Am I an Addressee?," in *A Feminist Companion to Exodus to Deuteronomy* (ed. Athalya Brenner; FCB 6; Sheffield: Sheffield Academic Press, 1994; repr., 2001) 255–58.

33. For an anthology of teachers throughout history, for example, see also Tobias

a writer, as a text, as a pastor, or as a computer game. All the different models can still inspire us today. We do not have to choose only one model of teaching but may be challenged by the rich variety of models of teaching that underlies our current (educational) culture.

The contributions of our volume, organized according the order of the biblical canon as used in the Catholic tradition, and the history of the reception, reveal two patterns of being a teacher: a textual character or a historical figure can function as a teacher (with which the reader therefore can identify), but the biblical text itself can function as a teacher as well (teaching the reader).

In her contribution, BINCY THUMPANATHU explains that, in the Book of Amos, a part of the character "Yhwh" includes functioning as a teacher also. A variety of pedagogical techniques is employed to convey Yhwh's lessons in fidelity to him and to his commandments. PANC BEENTJES shows the educational qualities of Ben Sira. The book becomes a *beth midrash* (literally, a "house of teaching").[34] Regarding Jesus, BART KOET shows, in the story in Luke 2:40–52, how asking questions is also a central activity of a teacher. This pericope from Luke depicts Jesus as both a teacher and a disciple. JOKE BRINKHOF discusses Stephen and Philip, two of the Seven in the Book of Acts, in their role as teachers in spreading the good news throughout the world.

BART KOET reflects on Paul as a teacher. In 1 Cor 4:17 Paul depicts himself as a teacher by using the metaphor of walking, a concept comparable to the later designation of *halakah* as a general characterization of human behavior in the rabbinic tradition. In the contribution of CORNELIA MELISSE, Paul as a teacher is also central. She focuses on Col 1:15 and 3:10, where Paul teaches Gen 1:1–2:3. Moses our teacher is important in Judaism, and LEO MOCK discusses several texts from the Jewish tradition that elaborate on this concept. CAROLINE VANDER STICHELE deals with Mary Magdalene. In the *Gospel of Mary*, Mary of Magdala acquires a teacher position, which is portrayed in the films *Mary* (2005) from Abel Ferrara, and *Mary Magdalene* (2018) from Garth Davis.

ARNOLD SMEETS studies Gregory the Great, whose teaching position moves at the intersection of monastic contemplation and worldly activity.

Georges, ed., *Bedeutende Lehrerfiguren von Platon bis Hasan al-Banna* (Tübingen: Mohr Siebeck, 2015).

34. Nowadays, in Old Testament exegesis, the commonly used designation "wisdom tradition" is seen as just a product of German exegesis. See in particular Mark Sneed, "Is the 'Wisdom Tradition' a Tradition?," *CBQ* 73 (2011) 50–71; Will Kynes, "The 'Wisdom Literature' Category: An Obituary," *JTS* 69 (2018) 1–24. The teacher in biblical wisdom books emerges late in the figures of the Qohelet and the more historically traceable Ben Sira.

Above all, however, Gregory turns out to be Job's best pupil. According to Thomas Aquinas, HENK SCHOOT explains, the learning process of the student is central. In this way, the teacher respects what God enables the student to do and shows himself a true follower of the preeminent Teacher, Christ. WILLEM MARIE SPEELMAN demonstrates that Francis of Assisi explicitly strives to imitate Jesus, his Lord and Teacher, in a physical form, which leads to learning through encounter and contemplation.

But it is not only literary characters and historical figures who are examples of teaching; the written books themselves are as well. The text becomes a teacher. We have already seen this development regarding Ben Sira, whose text becomes a *beth midrash*. The text is explicitly addressed as a teacher in the study of the Book of Isaiah by ARCHIBALD VAN WIERINGEN. The text shows two teaching lines, each with its own dynamics. GEARARD Ó FLOINN focuses on the role of the Marcan text as that which is taught by the teacher. He focuses on the pseudonymous teacher's merging of exalted Son of Man imagery from the Book of Daniel with motifs of suffering and death. RENILDE VAN WIERINGEN explains how the textual analysis of the individual pastoral conversation reveals the teaching moments of a prison chaplain. Her contribution makes clear that exegetical methods can also be used in other theological disciplines, especially to make the role of the teacher visible. Finally, FRANK BOSMAN shows how a video game, as an example of a modern text, can have as many aspects of the teacher as ancient texts. A biblical reference, such as can be found in *BioShock Infinite*, creates an exciting intertextuality, in which contemporary appropriation of the Bible raises all kinds of new questions.

The volume concludes with an epilogue by BÉNÉDICTE LEMMELIJN in her capacity as a member of the Pontifical Biblical Commission. What have all these biblical teachers and their reception taught us? The multitude of biblical teachers make it clear that teaching is an integral part of the biblical message and its reception. Tradition—and this includes the Bible itself—depends on teachers who are prepared to teach about the God of Israel in words that are ever new and always appropriate to ever new circumstances.

One of these teachers was Leo Mock, who died unexpectedly while this volume was being edited in the summer of 2023. In gratitude for his enthusiastic teaching, we would like to dedicate this volume to him.[35]

---

35. We would like to thank M. Fleur Vroege-Crijns, Tilburg University, the Netherlands, for her help in editing this volume.

2

The Book of Isaiah as a Teacher:
Trajectories of Learning for the Text-Immanent Reader

Archibald L. H. M. van Wieringen

■ I. The Call to Learn Well

Learn well! That is the motto already mentioned in the introduction (1:1–31) of the Book of Isaiah in v. 17a: למדו היטב. Learning has an important place in the Book of Isaiah.

The exhortation itself already requires a lot of attention. The majority of Bible translations, already the *versiones*, such as the Vulgate with *discite benefacere*, do not translate the Hebrew as "learn well," but as "learn to do the right thing!" This means that the infinitive absolute היטב is read as an infinitive construct that functions as an object of the verb למד ("to learn"). Grammatically, an infinitive absolute cannot have this function,[1] but the

---

1. In recent decades the verbal system of Biblical Hebrew has been the subject of research and debate. Harald Weinrich developed a linguistic theory for verbal tenses in general, in particular in his groundbreaking study *Tempus: Besprochene und erzählte Welt* (3rd ed.; Stuttgart: Kohlhammer, 1977). His theory is that verbal tenses are based on three oppositions: the difference between narrative and discursive text world, the difference between foreground and background, and the difference between a backward-looking and a forward-looking perspective. This theory has been applied to Biblical Hebrew, first, in Germany, by Wolfgang Schneider in his grammar *Grammatik des biblischen Hebräisch: Ein Lehrbuch* (Munich: Claudius, 1974; 3rd ed., 2007) now also available in English translation in a revised version, *Grammar of Biblical Hebrew* (trans. and rev. Randall L. McKinion; Studies in Biblical Hebrew 1; New York: P. Lang, 2016), and, in the Netherlands, by Eep Talstra, as he already shows in his basic publication "Text Grammar and Hebrew Bible: I. Elements of a Theory," *BO* 35 (1978) 169–74.

parallel with the preceding clause חדלו הרע ("stop doing evil"), in which the verb רעע ("doing evil") is an infinitive construct, was apparently too tempting to understand היטב in such a similar way.[2]

Or maybe there is something else going on? I think that a call to learn without specifying what has to be learned bothered the Bible translators. If you should learn well, what should you learn well? Verse 17a in the introduction to the Book of Isaiah seems to be silent about this, but in fact the Book of Isaiah as a whole is the answer.

The communicative situation in the introduction to the Book of Isaiah confirms this learning situation. Verse 17a is part of an oracle in direct speech by Yhwh starting in v. 11. The speech is addressed to a second-person plural who has to be identified as Zion. But this identification comes about in a complicated way through vv. 9–10.

Verses 1–8 discuss the situation of Zion. First, in vv. 2–4, heaven and earth, the greatest possible *décor* (stage set) and thus the greatest possible addressees, are addressed in the form of an embedded direct speech of Yhwh complaining that the sons he generated, the people of Israel, did not recognize him. Then, in vv. 5–7, with the help of a second-person plural, the inhabitants of Zion are addressed about their situation. They are already

---

See further, e.g., Eep Talstra and Constantijn Sikkel, "Genese und Kategorienentwicklung der WIVU-Datenbank, oder: ein Versuch, dem Computer Hebräisch beizubringen," in *Ad Fontes! Quellen erfassen – lesen – deuten: Was ist Computerphilologie?* (ed. Christof Hardmeier et al.; Applicatio 15; Amsterdam: VU University Press, 2000) 33–68; Eep Talstra, "Text linguistics: Biblical Hebrew," in *Encyclopedia of Hebrew Language and Linguistics* (ed. Geoffrey Khan; 4 vols.; Leiden: Brill, 2013) 3:755–60. For my view of the verbal system of Biblical Hebrew, see also *The Reader-Oriented Unity of the Book Isaiah* (ACEBT Supplement Series 6; Vught: Skandalon, 2006) 8; see also Cornelia Jacoba Maria Melisse, "De mens als beeld van God: Een cognitief semantische studie van Genesis 1:26-27 en van Kolossenzen 1:15; 3:10 en naar het gebruik van Genesis 1:26-27 in de klas" (Ph.D. diss., Tilburg University, 2020) 57–61. For the infinitive absolute as adverb, see Eep Talstra, "Text Segmentation and Linguistic Levels: Preparing Data for SESB," in *Handbuch/Instruction Manual SESB* (ed. C. Hardmeier, E. Talstra, and B. Salzmann; Stuttgart Elektronic Study Bible; Stuttgart: Deutsche Bibelgesellschaft, 2004) 23–31 (in original version in §2.4.4); see especially Scott N. Callaham, *Modality and the Biblical Hebrew Infinitive Absolute* (Abhandlungen für die Kunde des Morgenlandes 71; Wiesbaden: Harrassowitz, 2010), who unfortunately does not discuss Isa 1:17; Lutz Edzard, "Biblical Hebrew," in *The Semitic Languages: An International Handbook* (ed. Stefan Weninger; Handbücher zur Sprach- und Kommunikationswissenschaft 36; Berlin: De Gruyter Mouton, 2011) 480–514, esp. 501.

2. See also Archibald L. H. M. van Wieringen, "Leert goed! Over de Hebreeuwse *infinitivus absolutus* in Jesaja 1:16-17 en het Boek Jesaja," in *Hebreeuws in het midden: Vriendenboek van de Tilburg School of Catholic Theology aangeboden aan Piet van Midden, docent Hebreeuws, bij gelegenheid van zijn vijfenzestigste verjaardag* (ed. Archibald L. H. M. van Wieringen, Bart J. Koet, and Harm W. M. van Grol; Heeswijk: Berne Media, 2015) 139–53.

down in the dumps. The land is a wasteland, so why are they continuing on the wrong path? Finally, in a statement in v. 8, Zion's future crisis is communicated. Now there is no longer an addressee being addressed, but only the text-immanent reader,[3] who is the recipient of this communication.

Verses 9 and 10 both contain verbs in the first person plural. In verse 9, the "we"-group, which is to be interpreted semantically as the inhabitants of Zion, presents itself in a section of direct speech. The time perspective of v. 9 is in line with v. 8. In the section in direct speech, the future that is referred to appears to have already passed. The "we"-group looks back: if Yhwh had not been there for us, nothing would have been left of us. After the indications of crisis in vv. 2–8, when Zion comes to speak, the text is already beyond the crisis and, therefore, the text-immanent reader knows that the crisis does not have the last word.

In v. 10 this "we"-group is addressed. They are called to listen to תורת אלהינו ("the teaching of our God"). This means not only that the "we"-group of v. 10 is on God's side, but also that the "we"-group of v. 9 has yet to get there by means of God's teaching.

This teaching, which starts in v. 11, takes place explicitly in the now-moment of the text, following the direct speeches of the "we"-groups in vv. 9 and 10. The usual messenger formula כה אמר יהוה ("thus said Yhwh") with a *qatal*-form is not used in vv. 11b and 18c, but rather an introductory formula with a *yiqtol*-form יאמר יהוה ("Yhwh says") is employed.

This construction appeals not only to Zion but also to those who already adhere to Yhwh's teachings, such as the second "we"-group, as well as to the text-immanent reader. This participation of "we"-groups and of the text-immanent reader will appear to be important for the learning situation of the entire Book of Isaiah.

■ II. Who Are the Disciples in the Book of Isaiah?

It is not surprising that a book that presents itself as a teaching and opens with a call to learn well, implies the existence of students. The students

---

3. The text-immanent reader is not a reader of flesh and blood, but a textual one within the world of the text itself, having perfect knowledge of all the textual signs. For more methodological reflection on this, see the handbook, Frank G. Bosman and Archibald L. H. M. van Wieringen, *Video Games as Art: A Communication-Oriented Perspective on the Relationship between Gaming and the Art* (Video Games and the Humanities 12; Munich: De Gruyter Oldenbourg, 2023). See also Archibald L. H. M. van Wieringen, "Methodological Developments in Biblical Exegesis: Author – Text – Reader," *Наукові записки УКУ: Богослов'я* 7 (2020) 27–46.

appear explicitly for the first time in 8:16. The text speaks about למדי ("my students").

Since the nineteenth century, diachronic exegesis, especially in German-speaking contexts, has interpreted these disciples as being the students, that is, the disciples of Isaiah. The historical Isaiah ben Amoz apparently taught school. This Isaiah "School" continued to work on the texts of Isaiah, both in and after the Babylonian exile. Eventually this led to the creation of the Book of Isaiah in its present form.[4] But use of the concept "school" is a bit too romantic and cannot be proven historically.[5]

Moreover, in chap. 8 it is not plausible that למדי ("my students") are the disciples of Isaiah. In my opinion, v. 16 is part of a section embedded in direct speech placed on the lips of Yhwh that is introduced in v. 11 and starts in v. 12. The introductory v. 11 indicates Yhwh's action of speaking using the verb יסר ("to instruct"), which can be considered parallel to the verb למד ("to learn"). This instruction includes the concluding task of sealing Yhwh's teaching in his students. This implies that it is not Isaiah who is the teacher after all, but Yhwh. Isaiah is rather the first student of Yhwh! After Yhwh's embedded direct speech, Isaiah takes up this idea by explicitly mentioning himself and his children: "I *and* the children whom Yhwh has given me" (v. 18).[6]

This situation is thus in accordance with the introduction of the Book of Isaiah, where Yhwh as a teacher communicates his teaching to anyone who could be a student. In chaps. 6–12, however, all those potential students appear to be limited to a small group, of which Isaiah is the first member. However much Isaiah did his best to make God's message reach everyone, by writing it on a large board and putting two reliable witnesses there at Yhwh's command (8:1–2), his action unfortunately did not produce a large group of students.

---

4. E.g., Otto Kaiser, *Der Prophet Jesaja: Kapitel 13–39* (3rd ed.; ATD 18; Göttingen: Vandenhoeck & Ruprecht, 1983) 195–96; Hans-Christoph Schmitt, "Prophetie und Schultheologie im Deuterojesajabuch: Beobachtungen zur Redaktionsgeschichte von Jes 40–55," *ZAW* 91 (1979) 43–61, here 61; Manfred Görg, "Jesaja als 'Kinderlehrer'? Beobachtungen zur Sprache und Semantik in Jes 28,10(13)," *BN* 29 (1985) 12–16, here 13–14; Hugh G. M. Williamson, *The Book Called Isaiah: Deutero-Isaiah's Role in Composition and Redaction* (Oxford: Clarendon, 1994) 97–103, 240; Rainer Albertz, *Die Exilszeit: 6. Jahrhundert v. Chr.* (Biblische Enzyklopädie 7; Stuttgart: Kohlhammer, 2001) 284.

5. G. I. Davies, "Were There Schools in Ancient Israel?," in *Wisdom in Ancient Israel: Essays in Honour of J. A. Emerton* (ed. John Day, Robert P. Gordon, and Hugh G. M. Williamson; Cambridge: Cambridge University Press, 1995) 199–211.

6. See Archibald L. H. M. van Wieringen, *The Implied Reader in Isaiah 6–12* (BIS 34; Leiden: Brill, 1998) 110–13.

The word לִמּוּד ("student") returns in 50:4. This verse is the start of a description of the relationship between the Servant and Yhwh. First of all, this relationship is referred to as a relationship of learning. The "I"-figure makes clear that he is open to the teaching of God and has not turned away from it.

This creates a parallel with the I-figure in chap. 8. The Servant is, as it were, the continuation in chaps. 40–66 of the prophet figure from chaps. 1–39. This parallel is given extra relief by the fact that before 50:4 there is no I-figure who is called Servant. This identification does not occur before 50:10. Moreover, the prophet-character Isaiah in 20:3 is indicated by עֶבֶד ("servant") from the perspective of Yhwh.

Like the prophetic character Isaiah, the Servant starts as the only student. However, as the Servant becomes servants, in the same way the number of students grows as well. The transition from Servant to servants takes place in a section of direct speech in 53:1–11a. This section of direct speech is a long "we"-text, which has no introductory formula and therefore manifests itself in the now-moment of the text. It also reveals itself as an access for the text-immanent reader. In this "we"-text, it becomes clear that the Servant was not only the one who obeyed the voice of Yhwh, but also that his faithfulness to this voice cost him his life, נַפְשׁוֹ ("his soul"). Yet this is not the end of the Servant. Precisely because of this faithfulness he will see זֶרַע ("seed," v. 10). From that moment on, the text mentions only וַעֲבָדָיו ("servants" [pl.]).[7] Because of this communicative setting, this reference to seed is also the point of access for the text-immanent reader.

The servants become primarily visible at their first mention in 54:17. Jerusalem appears to be the inheritance of the עַבְדֵי יהוה ("servants of Yhwh"). Prior to this they are referred to as students, just as the Servant first appeared as a student in the text. In 54:13 all the sons of Zion appear to be לִמּוּדֵי יהוה ("students of Yhwh"). In 63:7–64:12 these servants, sons of Zion and students of Yhwh, speak their elaborate "we"-speech, using the same technique that is aimed at the text-immanent readers as the "we"-speech in 53:1–11a.[8]

---

7. See Willem A. M. Beuken, *Jesaja deel III A* (Prediking van het Oude Testament; Nijkerk: Callenbach, 1989) 440; Willem A. M. Beuken, "The Main Theme of Trito-Isaiah: The 'Servants of Yhwh,'" *JSOT* 47 (1990) 67–87.

8. See van Wieringen, *Reader-Oriented Unity*, 146.

■ III. THE FIRST TRAJECTORY OF LEARNING: TRUST IN GOD

God's teaching unfolds in the Book of Isaiah in two learning trajectories. The first is that of trust in God.[9] Considering faithfulness as a characteristic of Yhwh's students, both of the prophet-character Isaiah and of the Servant-character, this is not really a surprise.

This training in trust is taught in four successive lessons, increasing in difficulty, with a fifth lesson as its completion.

The first lesson is discussed in Isa 7:1–17.[10] This text is a remarkable narrative. It seems to start in a normal way with the opening verbal form ויהי ("and then it happened that . . ."). But already in the first verse, by using the *qatal*, the end of the narrative is revealed: ולא יכל להלחם עליה ("but he [the enemy] had not been able to fight a war against her [Jerusalem]"). The story is not completed either; it just stops after the prophet Isaiah's address in direct speech to King Ahaz. But it does not have to be completed. After all, the text-immanent reader already knows the outcome: the enemy was not able to fight a war against Jerusalem.

The narrative seems exciting, because it appears to be about an imminent siege of the capital Jerusalem, but in fact it is not, since the outcome is already proleptically present at the beginning. Of course, it is exciting for the characters in the narrative. King Ahaz does not know the outcome and, therefore, it is not easy for him to respond to the call of the prophet Isaiah to trust in God that Jerusalem will not be taken and that the Davidic royal house will be continued. With a religiously formulated excuse that he does not want to test Yhwh, he rejects the offer of a sign of deliverance, an אות (v. 12). In contrast to Ahaz, Isaiah presents a counter-image of the ideal leader who knows the difference between good and evil: the Immanu-El (vv. 14–15), which means "God with us" and thus evokes a "we"-group. Meanwhile Ahaz may count on an even more dangerous enemy: Assur (vv. 16–17). However, as exciting as all this may be for the characters in the narrative, the text-immanent reader is not shivering in the same way as the trees of the forest are moved by the wind (v. 2).

The excitement of the narrative in 7:1–17 can be found in an aside in v. 9b, which the text-immanent author addresses directly to the text-

---

9. For my first thoughts on this, see Archibald L. H. M. van Wieringen, "Jesaja 1–39: Geloof en vertrouwen," in *De Bijbel Spiritueel: Bronnen van geestelijk leven in de bijbelse geschriften* (ed. Frans Maas, Jacques Maas, and Klaas Spronk; Zoetermeer: Meinema, 2004) 351–57.

10. See also van Wieringen, *Implied Reader in Isaiah 6–12*, 61–72.

immanent reader: אם לא תאמינו כי לא תאמנו ("if you do not trust it, you will not survive").[11] This call to the text-immanent reader is made at the very moment when the character Isaiah addresses the same call to the character Ahaz. The text narrates how Yhwh commands Isaiah to communicate to Ahaz to trust in God, but does not narrate this communication itself. It is elliptically present between v. 9 and v. 10. With v. 10, the communication between these two characters continues, a communication in which it becomes clear that Ahaz says no. But what does the text-immanent reader say? It has been made very easy for him not to say no. After all, he already knows the outcome. He knows what will happen if you say yes. He has even been directly addressed about it by the text-immanent author. The first lesson of trust in God for the text-immanent reader is extremely simple.

The second lesson is a bit more difficult. It consists of chaps. 36–37. The narrative is semantically similar to that of 7:1–17, but for the text-immanent reader it is much more difficult to get through.

The semantic parallel is already explicitly visible at the beginning of the narrative (36:2) using the same location, בתעלת הברכה העליונה במסלת שדי כובס ("at the end of the conduit of the upper water basin at the way to the bleaching field").[12] This is a crucial location, since a safe and sustainable drinking water supply is indispensable for a city in the event of a siege. However, the meeting that takes place there is not between the prophet Isaiah and the king, but rather between the Assyrian commander in chief and the dignitaries of the Jerusalem king.

Moreover, the prophet gives an אות ("sign") on the part of Yhwh (37:30), which, this time, is accepted by the king. While Ahaz was an example of not trusting Yhwh, Hezekiah turns out to be an example of how things should be done.

The difficulty for the text-immanent reader, however, lies in the fact that this time the ending is not revealed at the beginning. The reader has to continue to the end to know whether trusting God is indeed a meaningful

---

11. It is hard to make a proper translation of the Hebrew wordplay with the verb אמן. The translation "survive" is a quite free translation. In my monograph *Implied Reader in Isaiah 6–12*, I translated it as "if you do not have faith, you do not stand firm" (53). See also Christoph Hardmeier, "Gesichtspunkte pragmatischer Erzähltextanalyse: 'Glaubt ihr nicht, so bleibt ihr nicht' – ein Glaubensappell an schwankende Anhänger Jesajas," WD n.F. 15 (1979) 33–54.

12. See Archibald L. H. M. van Wieringen, "Assur and Babel against Jerusalem: The Reader-Oriented Position of Babel and Assur within the Framework of Isaiah 1–39," in *"Enlarge the Site of Your Tent": The City as Unifying Theme in Isaiah* (ed. Archibald L. H. M. van Wieringen and Annemarieke van der Woude; Papers from the Isaiah Workshop / De Jesaja Werkplaats; OtSt 58; Leiden: Brill, 2011) 49–62.

attitude. As one reads the text, one finds that one is not directly addressed in an aside either. Fortunately, the reader is helped by the good example of the character Hezekiah.

This time the narrative does not conclude with an open ending, but rather with a happy ending. And it is told twice, to emphasize that trust in God pays off. First it is told that the מלאך יהוה ("messenger of Yhwh") goes forth and strikes the army camp of Assur (37:36). The verb נכה alludes here to the plagues in Egypt by Yhwh when the people were oppressed there (e.g., Exod 7:17; Pss 135:8; 136:10). The great victory on the part of Yhwh is reused in the Books of Maccabees to describe the victory over the Jew-hating Nicanor, the Seleucid general under Antiochus IV Epiphanes (1 Macc 7:41; 2 Macc 8:19; 15:22). All that remains for the Assyrian king is to call a retreat and return home. The text emphasizes the fact that he does not return to Jerusalem subsequently by saying that he remains home (37:37).

A second happy ending follows in 37:38, with even more humor.[13] The Assyrian king is murdered, remarkably in a temple to some idol, while he was celebrating a ritual there. The contrast with Hezekiah's visit to the temple of the one and only true God (37:1, 14) could not be greater. It is clear which God you can trust and which god you cannot trust.

In fact, a coup takes place in the temple, in which the Assyrian king is murdered by his sons Adrammelech and Sharezer. The perpetrators manage to escape, although they have to move even farther away from Jerusalem, toward the land of Ararat. The successor Esarhaddon does not have to be feared, because apparently he does not even take action against the two men who carried out the coup. Or would he, also as a son of the murdered king, have had a hand in the putsch himself? As part of a happy ending, humor has endless possibilities.

The third lesson is again a bit more difficult. It occurs in chap. 38.[14] The narrative has no prolepsis in which the happy ending is told in advance. Nor does the narrative contain an aside to keep the text-immanent reader directly informed. Moreover, the narrative has an open ending—and not because the ending could have been left out because the text-immanent

---

13. See also Patricia K. Tull, *Isaiah 1–39* (SHBC; Macon, GA: Smyth & Helwys, 2010) 536–37.

14. See also Peter R. Ackroyd, "An Interpretation of the Babylonian Exile: A Study of 2 Kings 20 / Isaiah 38–39," *SJT* 27 (1974) 329–52; Archibald L. H. M. van Wieringen, "The Diseased King and the Diseased City (Isa 36–39) as Reader-Oriented Link between Isa 1–39 and 40–66," in van Wieringen and van der Woude, *"Enlarge the Site of Your Tent,"* 81–93; and Archibald L. H. M. van Wieringen, "The 'I'-Figure's Relations in the Poem in Isa 38,10–20," *Bib* 96 (2015) 481–97.

reader knows about the happy ending. In the third lesson a lot is asked of the text-immanent reader for reading on to the very end of chap. 38.

The story does not start with the traditional verb form ויהי ("and then it happened ..."), but with the asyndetic time phrase בימים ההם ("in those days"). In this way the narrative of the sick king Hezekiah is connected to the siege of Jerusalem by Assur. A sick king during a siege is an immense problem because it is precisely the king who should lead the city in such a threatening situation. Since the second lesson, however, the text-immanent reader has experienced that trust in God, without knowing the ending in advance, paid off and that Jerusalem did not fall. Can he draw the conclusion that trust in God will pay off again and that the king will not fall in death?

The character Hezekiah once again supports the text-immanent reader with his good example. Isaiah announces to the king that he will die presently, upon which he prays to Yhwh in tears. Yhwh hears Hezekiah's prayer and sees his tears. He lets Isaiah know that he can tell Hezekiah that he will not die then.

As in the previous two lessons, a sign is given on the part of Yhwh (vv. 7–8). The contrast with the bad example of Ahaz is obvious: the sign is connected to a thing to which Ahaz's name is linked. All the *versiones* think of a sundial, but the precise meaning of the word is actually far from clear. What is evident is that the word is connected with shadows. When shadows grow longer, evening falls and death comes. It is exactly this line of thought that is reversed in the sign.

At first glance, the position of the text-immanent reader seems not to have changed compared to the previous lessons, but with vv. 9–20 a change comes about. These verses contain the מכתב לחזקיהו ("writing of Hezekiah"), as the heading in v. 9 indicates. Narratologically, the poem that comprises Hezekiah's writing parallels the narrative situation in the preceding verses: Hezekiah prays to Yhwh and Yhwh gives deliverance. In the poem, the "I"-figure, to be identified with Hezekiah, also develops into a "we"-figure (v. 20b). This "we"-figure, which is not defined any further, offers access to the text-immanent reader.

The poem contains an ellipsis between vv. 14 and 15. While in vv. 10–14 the "I"-figure describes the precarious situation of his impending death, in vv. 15–20 he speaks of his salvation. The turnaround, caused by Yhwh's intervention in favor of the "I"-figure, therefore, took place between v. 14 and v. 15. The subject of the ellipsis is interesting for the text-immanent reader in this third lesson. The reader has already come across an ellipsis in the first lesson in 7:1–17. This was accompanied by an aside to call the reader to trust in God. The ellipsis in the poem contains no aside, but after the ellipsis the text-immanent reader is offered access to the "I"-figure's trust in God, as already said, by means of the "we"-figure that has arisen in vv. 15–20.

And there is more. The poem has a heading. The Book of Isaiah is one of the few books of the Bible to have a heading. These headings mark larger units. The heading in 38:9 is an exception: it is marking a part of a text within a larger narrative unit, that is, chaps. 36–39. Moreover, it is the only heading in which a written product is mentioned, namely, a מכתב. It is not an aspect of the prophetic seeing as in words such as חזון ("vision") or דבר ("word"). This brings the poem to the highest communicative level of the Book of Isaiah with the text-immanent reader. Therefore, 38:9 is the last heading in the Book of Isaiah, since new headings in chaps. 40–66 do not apply.

There is still more work to be done for the text-immanent reader. Now that the reader has access to the living "we"-group and to the communication at the level of the entire Book of Isaiah, the reader is supposed to be able to deal with the open ending of the narrative in chap. 38. After all, vv. 21–22 are not to be understood as a kind of pluperfect, as many modern Bible translations have it, but as normal *wayyiqtol*-forms. They form the temporal progress after vv. 1–8. Isaiah says that Hezekiah will live (v. 21). Does the text-immanent reader believe that? On the basis of preceding passages, it should not be a problem. And if the reader does believe and reads on, they will meet Hezekiah in chap. 39 who is alive. The final question of Hezekiah in 38:22 is even more exciting: What is the sign that will indicate that he will ascend to the house of Yhwh? As there are two signs in 7:1–17: one that refuses the bad example of Ahaz and the other that is given on the part of Yhwh by Isaiah (but not to Ahaz), so there are also two signs in chap. 38. The shadow has already proven its function. But what about the new sign? If the text-immanent reader has followed the lessons properly so far, they can read on. Unfortunately, it suddenly turns out that chap. 39 does not simply confirm what has been learned so far . . .

As the fourth lesson for the text-immanent reader in this learning trajectory, chap. 39 is the most difficult one. No prolepsis. No aside. No happy ending. No completed story, but an open ending.[15]

Everything is different in chap. 39. Assur, the successor of Rezin in 7:1–17, has been replaced by Babel. While Rezin and Assur do not enter Jerusalem, Babylon does. Babel is even received hospitably and is allowed to

---

15. See also Christopher T. Begg, "Babylon in the Book of Isaiah," in *The Book of Isaiah / Le Livre d'Isaïe: Les oracles et leurs relectures unité et complexité de l'ouvrage* (Papers read at the 37th Colloquium Biblicum Lovaniense; ed. Jacques Vermeylen; BETL 81; Leuven: Peeters, 1989) 121–25; Christopher R. Seitz, *Zion's Final Destiny: The Development of the Book of Isaiah; A Reassessment of Isaiah 36–39* (Minneapolis: Fortress, 1991).

see everything: the religious value of Jerusalem as well as its financial and military resources (v. 2). And the narrative does not say that Babylon is leaving.[16]

The good example of the case of Hezekiah fails. Hezekiah does not go to the temple, the issue that the previous chapter left as an open question. At least, not to pray—and he gives the prophet an incomplete answer. What Babylon said remains uncommunicated. In 7:1–17 the words of the threatening enemies were communicated in v. 6—not directly, but through an embedded instance of direct speech on the part of Yhwh. In chaps. 36–37 the words of Assur were given in detail. But, whereas the number of words of the praying Hezekiah increased in these chapters, the number spoken by Assur decreased. In chap. 39, however, Babel's words are hidden. It is not possible for them to be less present in the text than this. Because of the parallel with 7:1–17 and chaps. 36–37, they cannot contain much good.

Isaiah rejects Hezekiah on behalf of Yhwh. He uses the expression הנה ימים באים ("days are about to come . . . ," 39:6) as he used it against Ahaz in 7:17. Nothing will remain in the exile he announces and applies to Hezekiah's sons (39:7).

And Hezekiah responds. Twice he speaks about טוב ("good"). Unlike Ahaz in the sign of 7:14–15, Immanu-El, knows what is good. This is by way of contrast to the son of Tabeal (a name that means "good–no!"), the one in 7:6 whom the enemies have in mind to make king in Jerusalem instead of the Davidic king. Does Hezekiah nevertheless continue this "good" mentioned in 7:14–15?

The text does not answer this question. The text-immanent reader is left empty-handed. Has the reader learned to have enough faith in God to continue reading on anyway?

The last lesson in this learning trajectory is formed by 40:1–11. This lesson is, as it were, the reward of learning achieved by the text-immanent reader.

While chap. 39 ended in crisis, 40:1–11 moves beyond this. The new situation opens with consolation. Zion's צבא ("service time") is over. She has done satisfaction for her sins (v. 2). This means that the crisis is found between chaps. 39 and 40. It is not recounted. It is there only elliptically.

Looking backwards, the crisis for the text-immanent reader appears to have been even greater than the reader knew. Whereas in chap. 39 it is only the sons of Hezekiah who were mentioned, in 40:1–11, however, most likely the whole people appears to have been involved. The learning situation in

---

16. For more details on this, see van Wieringen, "Assur and Babel against Jerusalem," 61–62.

chap. 39 was the most difficult one in the Book of Isaiah. The Book of Isaiah shows compassion for the text-immanent reader as a student!

A way is being created for the people to travel back to Jerusalem, and that is proclaimed without difficulty. For while it is true that a flower wilts easily, it is also true that the word of Yhwh endures (vv. 6–8).

From the beginning, the text-immanent reader is directly involved in the new, positive situation. Not only is God presented as speaking, without the mediation of a prophet-character, but the fact that God speaks is confirmed in direct speech: יאמר אלהיכם ("says your God," v. 1). Because of the *yiqtol*, this instance of direct speech is not only in the present moment of the text and thus already offering access for the text-immanent reader, but it also makes use of the second-person plural suffix *your*.[17] Thus, the text addresses itself directly to the text-immanent reader, just as such a direct address occurred in the first lesson of this learning trajectory in 7:9b.

The new situation of comfort, forgiveness, and salvation has not only arrived, but the text-immanent reader is also directly involved in it and is part of it. In addition, the reader does not have to do anything special, because it is the reader that is addressed! With this denouement the first learning trajectory through the Book of Isaiah is completed.

■ IV. THE SECOND TRAJECTORY OF LEARNING: BREAKTHROUGH TO THE WORLD OF NATIONS

The second learning trajectory is about the position of the nations. In the Book of Isaiah, the salvation of Yhwh for the people becomes accessible also for the nations. Directly after the introductory chapter, the content of this learning trajectory is discussed in 2:2–5. It describes how the small mountain of the house of Yhwh rises high above all mountains and hills (v. 2). Not only the people of God, but all nations go up there (v. 3). The materials of war are forged into farm implements so that there may be food for all (v. 4). The significance of the nations is emphasized by the fact that it is they who are mentioned first as going up to the house of Yhwh and after them the house of Jacob (v. 5).

This grand perspective at the beginning of the Book of Isaiah is presented as being in the future. With this the text-immanent reader is confronted with the question, When will its implementation take place in the Book of Isaiah?

---

17. See van Wieringen, *Reader-Oriented Unity*, 134–39.

The text helps the text-immanent reader to answer this question by mentioning a moment in time in the future from the perspective of 2:2–5: אחרית הימים ("the moment in time beyond the days," v. 2).[18] From the introduction in chap. 1, the text-immanent reader understands days as moments in time: from the ימים ("days") of the kings mentioned in v. 1. Only in 40:1–11 are we told that these days of kings appear to be over. The chaotic ending of chap. 39 already alluded to this with the word יום ("day") connected to the word טוב ("good") in Hezekiah's reaction to his rejection by Isaiah.

In five lessons, the text-immanent reader learns about breakthrough to the world of nations in the Book of Isaiah. The first four lessons are connected with five consecutive text-units in the Book of Isaiah. The fifth lesson forms the climax of this learning trajectory.

The first lesson in this second learning trajectory is found in 11:10, 11–16. In 7:1–17 the Immanu-El is depicted as a counter-image to Ahaz's failing actions. In 7:1–17, a pregnant woman is mentioned (v. 14). The Immanu-El image is further formed in the continuation of the text-unit of chaps. 6–12, namely, in the birth of the child in 8:23a–9:6 and the sprouting Shoot as the young leader in 11:1–9. To conclude this development from pregnancy to birth to young man, the expression ביום ההוא ("on that day") connects two texts, namely, v. 10 and vv. 11–16, to 11:1–9.

Verse 10, as a first elaboration, describes how the ideal leader functions as נס עמים ("a banner for the nations"). In this way he marks the place to which the nations must ascend.

However, the second elaboration in vv. 11–16 is less broad. Many nations are listed—Assur, Egypt, Pathros, Kush, Elam, Shinar, the region of the Philistines, Edom, Moab (Babylon is not mentioned)—but they are only the areas from which Yhwh gathers the people. The perspective is that of the people of God only (v. 16).

In the text-unit of chaps. 13–23, the nations are central. In two major movements, the focus is on Jerusalem: first, from the distant Babel in chaps. 13–14 through the nearby areas of Moab, Damascus, and Egypt in chaps. 15–19, the text reaches the endangered Jerusalem in chap. 20; next, through the distant Babel in 21:1–10 and the nearby areas of Edom and Arabia in 21:11–16, the text reaches again the endangered Jerusalem in chap. 22 (after which chap. 23 on Tyre forms a transition to the following text-unit of the chaps. 24–35). Jerusalem is threatened, and the nations play a negative role

---

18. See Archibald L. H. M. van Wieringen, "Reading towards the Future in the Book of Isaiah: The Beyond the Days (Isa 2,2) and the Days of the Kings," *Greg* 98 (2017) 223–26.

in this. It is not without reason that this text-unit opens with the downfall of Babel in chaps. 13–14.

The text-immanent reader should be able to interpret the role of the nations. In 10:5–19 the reader learned that the nations are only an instrument in the hand of Yhwh to get the sinful Zion on the right path. However, the nations tend to believe that they are not a mere instrument, that is, to be handled by someone, and that they can operate independently. Yet the stick does not lift up the one who raises it and the ax does not loom higher than the one who wields it (v. 15).

To keep the perspective of 2:2–5 visible, 19:16–25 is the second lesson. The text contains several elaborations connected to the oracle against the nation of Egypt in vv. 1–15. After Yhwh has revealed himself to Egypt (19:21), so that Egypt may "return" (the verb שוב) to Yhwh (v. 22), there is a road that connects Egypt and Assur. As a matter of course, a road between Assur and Egypt leads through the land of the people of God. The result of the road is that both, Assur and Egypt, "serve Yhwh" (the verb עבד in v. 23). Verses 24–25 add to this: Israel will be the third after Egypt and Assur. Thus, all three will be a blessing on earth, just as all three will be blessed by Yhwh as his people, the work of his hands, his inheritance has been blessed already.

In this way, the text-immanent reader is given a reference to the ideal of 2:2–5. However, a reader who pays close attention notices not only that it is not yet an implementation of the grand opening perspective of 2:2–5, but also, that not all nations are mentioned.

The third lesson, which takes place in the text-unit of chaps. 24–35, is formed by 25:6–10.[19] The perspective of 2:2–5 is kept open for the text-immanent reader, more than ever before.

Parallel to the expression ביום ההוא ("on that day"), the phrase בהר הזה ("on this mountain") identifies the place of an abundant feast to be established by Yhwh for all nations (25:6). It is not Godself whom God reveals, but through God the nations are revealed and the veil that covers them is destroyed (v. 7), just as Yhwh also destroys death (v. 8). The elaboration in vv. 9–10 offers a text in direct speech: on that day ואמר ("one will say"), Who is this "one"? From the preceding verses one should think not only of the people of God (עמו, "his people," in v. 8) but also of all nations. If everyone belongs to that "one," then the text-immanent reader

---

19. See Archibald L. H. M. van Wieringen, "Isa 24:21–25:12: A Communicative Analysis," in *Formation and Intertextuality in Isaiah 24–27* (ed. J. Todd Hibbard and Hyun Chul Paul Kim; AIL17; Atlanta: Society of Biblical Literature, 2013) 77–97.

also belongs to it and, therefore, learns in this third lesson to be part of the confession of faith that is pronounced.

Is the ideal there now? Apart from the fact that the perspective involving the nations is presented as a future perspective, it turns out in v. 10 that Moab is not included. Moab is trampled on and, in contrast to the mountain of Yhwh, there is nothing left of it but an ashpit. The text-immanent reader may have access to the confession pronounced by the "one" but should be aware that the realization of the ideal of 2:2–5 has not yet come to pass.

The fourth lesson takes place in the text-unit of chaps. 40–66. These chapters are introduced in 40:1–11 with the flattening of each mountain and hill (v. 4). When the heights are leveled and a flat road is built, it will be obvious that the mountain of the house of Yhwh is above all else.

The Servant of Yhwh is the first to respond to the call of God's voice, to travel on the road and to return to the land. He is the forerunner, but who follows him is the question for the text-immanent reader. From chap. 49 onward the perspective of the answer to this question is broadened, especially in 49:6. The Servant not only has the task of gathering the tribes of Jacob again and of bringing back the survivors of Israel, but he also has a task for the world of the nations. For this task, he is initiated by Yhwh לאור גוים ("to a light for the nations"). After all, God wants salvation to reach to the ends of the earth. The text-immanent reader must now ask oneself whether these nations are actually coming.

That seems to be the case, but only as couriers to bring back Zion's sons and daughters. Afterwards they bite the dust, become subordinate to the sons and daughters they brought back, or simply disappear from the text. It is true that Yhwh does raise a נס ("banner") in 49:22–23, which alludes to the "banner" in 11:10, but the nations are merely a means of transport, and not participants in Yhwh's salvation.

In chap. 60, the situation is not substantially different. In v. 3 the nations come to the אור ("light") that is Zion. In v. 4, the sons of Zion also come back, and her daughters are carried back on the hip. The text leaves unexplained whether the nations here are the couriers of Zion's inhabitants, or whether they are included among those who are returning, which would give them a place equal to that of the returning sons and daughters. In addition to the return of people, all riches are brought along with them. That the Tarshish ships are only a means of transport and disappear from the text after the transport has been completed is obvious. Although the exact role of the nations is uncertain, it is nevertheless crystal clear that an implementation of the great ideal of 2:2–5 has not come to pass: foreigners build the city wall, and the kings of the nations become subservient, as do the sons of the former oppressors (60:10, 14 and

16). Furthermore, any nation or kingdom that does not participate in this will perish (v. 12).

Isaiah 66:18–21 is the fifth and final lesson. This text is communicatively complex. The text-immanent author renders in direct speech a communication from Yhwh: אמר יהוה ("said Yhwh"). What Yhwh said is thus placed in the past. The content of this block of direct speech from Yhwh concerns the future. Has this vision of the future, pronounced in the past, already been realized in the present of the text-immanent author, and thus of the text-immanent reader?

Yhwh speaks of all nations and languages (66:18). They will bring all brethren of the people of Zion back to Yhwh's holy mountain, to Jerusalem (על הר קדשי ירושלם, "to my holy mountain Jerusalem," v. 20). The implementation that involves the nations indeed seems to have been realized in the last text-unit of the Book of Isaiah, chaps. 40–66. To emphasize this, the text-immanent author interrupts Yhwh's direct speech with a double aside: "a sacrifice for Yhwh" (66:20b) and "as the sons of Israel bring the sacrifice in clean dishes to the house of Yhwh" (66:20e).[20] In this way the author indicates how the return of the absent brethren is to be interpreted. This also makes the role of the nations clearer: they act as Israel acts when Israel goes up to the house of Yhwh. Yhwh's words in direct speech continue with the announcement that Yhwh will take priests and Levites from the nations as well.

The double aside in 66:18–21 is different from that in 7:9b, in which the text-immanent reader was addressed directly, but of course it also functions here in relation to the text-immanent reader. If the first aside is in the context of the realization of the return to Zion, as described in chaps. 40–66, in the moment of time of the text-immanent author, and thus also of the text-immanent reader, who after all cannot be earlier in time than the text-immanent author, does the same phenomenon apply in the case of the second aside?

In any case, the position of the second aside makes it impossible for the text-immanent reader to be surprised at the content of the continuation of Yhwh's speech, because it explains that the nations will act with regard to the house of Yhwh in the same way as Israel does.

In this way, at the end of the Book of Isaiah, 2:2–5 obtains its farthest-reaching implementation. The final realization of this vision lies beyond the text of the Book of Isaiah itself. The learning process of the text-immanent reader, therefore, also extends beyond the Book of Isaiah.

---

20. See van Wieringen, *Reader-Oriented Unity*, 218–19.

■ V. Learning Well

The Book of Isaiah can be understood as a school for the text-immanent reader. Isaiah is not so much the teacher as he is a character in the text of chaps. 1–39, namely the first student, as the Servant is a student-character in chaps. 40–66.

Learning is a complex process. At least two learning trajectories span the Book of Isaiah, both of which have their own character. In the first learning trajectory about trust in God, the text-immanent reader as a student gets gradually involved. Every subsequent lesson is a bit more difficult. The same text-immanent reader, as a student, is immediately and totally submerged at the start of the second learning trajectory about the nations. The first learning trajectory reaches a completion. But the second learning trajectory arrives not at a completion but at an implementation beyond the text.

These two trajectories of learning have been thoughtfully woven together. After the call to learn well in the introduction, the most difficult lesson of the second learning trajectory follows in 2:2–5. Next, the lessons of the first learning trajectory are offered, step by step, to its completion in the ellipsis between chaps. 39 and 40, while a number of lessons of the second learning trajectory pass by in the meanwhile. When the first learning trajectory is completed, the second one can open a new perspective by taking up the implementation of the involvement of nations in Yhwh's salvation. This will continue to the end of the Book of Isaiah, and even beyond it.

The learning trajectories in the Book of Isaiah are very complex. That is the reason why, at the start, the Book of Isaiah appeals to the text-immanent reader in the terms of the not superfluous call: למדו היטב, "Learn well!"

3

Yhwh as a Teacher in the Book of Amos:
An Analysis from a Communicative Perspective

BINCY THOMAS THUMPANATHU

The Book of Amos is not only a manifesto of social justice policies and a litany of divine judgments, as is widely acknowledged, but beyond that, of considerable interest throughout are the communicative elements in the Book of Amos, both internal and external, with the utterances of Yhwh being of special significance.[1] By including numerous examples of the admonitions received by the people (Judah and Israel) on account of their unacceptable behavior, the Book of Amos conveys the mood of Yhwh's engagement with them. Even when Yhwh speaks directly to them, beseeching them to mend their ways, the divine words go very much unheeded. Typical for the rebellious Israelites is the character Amaziah. In contrast, the prophet character Amos, who accepted the divine call to go and teach the word of God, and did so diligently, is presented as a model of dependability.

The Book of Amos presents its communication as an evolving process with a combination of divine exhortations and threats. On the one hand, the book presents the divine judgments as being inexorable and unavoidable, but, on the other hand, it communicates the sense of the deep bond that exists between Yhwh and the people, drawing attention to the fact that, despite all their wrongdoings and rejections of the divine commands, Yhwh continues to make repeated and earnest efforts to

---

1. This contribution is based on my Ph.D. dissertation, which was completed at Tilburg University. See Bincy Thomas Thumpanathu, *Communication and the Role of the Lord: Their Development and Their Implications for the Text-Immanent Reader* (Utrecht: Eburon, 2019).

bring them back. Wonder is a sentiment felt at both the beginning and the end of the Book of Amos, but for very different reasons. At the beginning, wonder is provoked by Yhwh roaring in anger, whereas at the end it is brought about when Yhwh, speaking in a much gentler voice, promises an abundance of good things and a restoration of the fallen booth of David. The relentless stream of condemnations and punishments that runs through the Book of Amos is suddenly replaced by blessings from Yhwh and the promise of brighter days ahead. Yhwh uses this technique to instruct and incentivize the people, just as a teacher punishes or encourages students as the situation demands. In addition, the rhetorical speech of Yhwh, as employed in the text, fulfills the same function.

In this essay, I aim to demonstrate the role of Yhwh as a teacher in the Book of Amos. I ask, How does Yhwh, the principal agent and central figure in the prophecies, communicate with the people and educate them in the ways of justice? Yhwh is shown to be their constant companion (2:10; 3:3) and the one who condemns acts of injustice, iniquities, and also the false pieties practiced by the people (3:9–10; 4:4–5; 5:7, 10, 12, 21–23; 8:7–8). Through the use of rhetoric, in several subtle lessons and instructions, the people are afforded many opportunities to return to Yhwh and to avoid the divine wrath. I explore how rhetoric is employed in the book to demonstrate Yhwh's ways of teaching. These include using words of warning, sarcasm, irony, and reversals in Yhwh's approach to getting the divine message across. Along with these are the powerful prophetic descriptions of Yhwh. Presenting Yhwh as teacher in respect of the communication in the Book of Amos, I arrange my essay as follows:

1. I will explore the engagement of Yhwh and the people as it occurs in the Book of Amos. Emphasizing Yhwh's admonitions of the people, I will explain what is communicated between (a) Yhwh and the people of Judah, (b) Yhwh and the people of Israel, and (c) Amos and Amaziah, with the focus on units 2:4–5; 2:6–13; and 7:10–17, respectively. How the relationships progress and what lessons and directions the people receive from Yhwh through these engagements are the issues under consideration here.

2. I will explore the rhetoric in the Book of Amos and its function as it pertains to Yhwh's methods of teaching. Use of rhetoric renders the instructions of Yhwh more effective in persuading the people that the warnings should be taken seriously. In addition, the powerful portrayal of Yhwh, along with the irony in the statements relating to the people's way of life are influential in convincing them to uphold the teaching of Yhwh and to escape punishments.

■ I. The Engagement between Yhwh and the People of God

From the title containing the clause חזה על־ישראל ("he [Amos] saw concerning Israel," 1:1), it is evident that the communication is addressed to the characters in Israel. What is communicated to them is not pleasing to the ear: יהוה מציון ישאג ומירושלם יתן קולו ("Yhwh roars from Zion and from Jerusalem he utters his voice," 1:2a-c). This astonishing introduction to Yhwh at the start of the book continues with the depressing picture of Israel mentioning that the pastures of the shepherds mourn (ואבלו נאות הרעים) and the top of Carmel withers (ויבש ראש הכרמל).[2] In any case, the situation depicted in the opening is distressing. The roaring, the raised voice, the wailing, and the withering all point to the tension that exists between Yhwh and the people, a tension that acts as a prelude to what follows.

A. Judah Held to Account

The engagement between Yhwh and the people recorded in 2:4 explores this tension explicitly and provides lessons for the people. Yhwh and Judah take center stage here. The accusation against Judah, details of Judah's transgressions, Yhwh's fury as evidenced in the divine decision not to revoke the punishments, and finally the pronouncement of the list of chastisements—all these portray an unsettling scene in 2:4. Unlike Damascus, Gaza, Tyre, Edom, Ammon, Moab, the first six nations in the list of the so-called prophecies against the nations, Judah is judged not for having inflicted cruelties on others, but because of the fracturing of their relationship with Yhwh.[3] It is explicitly stated in 2:4c that Judah had rejected תורת יהוה ("the teaching of Yhwh"),[4] and had not kept the

---

2. S. D. (Fanie) Snyman, "Eretz and Adama in Amos," in *Stimulation from Leiden: Collected Communications to the XVIIIth Congress of the International Organization for the Study of the Old Testament, Leiden 2004* (ed. Hermann Michael Niemann and Matthias Augustin; BEATAJ 54; Frankfurt am Main: P. Lang, 2006) 137–46, here 140.

3. Only Judah is condemned because of directly challenging Yhwh's commands; the other nations are judged on the basis of international relations. See John Haralson Hayes, *The Oracles against the Nations in the Old Testament: Their Usage and Theological Importance* (Princeton, NJ: Princeton University Press, 1964) 180.

4. By rejecting the law of Yhwh, they risk damaging their relationship with Yhwh. See Archibald L. H. M. van Wieringen, "The Prophecies against the Nations in Amos 1:2–3:15," *EstBíb* 71 (2013) 7–19, here 13.

precepts of God (וחקיו לא שמרו).⁵ By placing these semantically similar phrases directly one after the other, the text-immanent author puts the focus firmly on the central message. Neglecting תורה and חקיו means abandoning יהוה and taking alternative paths. What the people opt for becomes clear in 2:4f, where it is stated that they walked in the wicked ways of their fathers (אשר־הלכו אבותם אחריהם). The implication is that Judah neglected תורת יהוה and embraced false doctrines and was duly punished. Rejection of תורת יהוה is condemned throughout the Book of Amos. As the chosen people, Judah had a particular responsibility to uphold the divine Torah, but by purposely neglecting תורה Judah fractured its relationship with Yhwh. Yhwh, the teacher, reminds them that ultimately this will result in a breakdown in their relationships with one another.

B. *Israel Held to Account*

It is only in the reference to Yhwh's command, as it appears in the prophecy against Judah (2:4), that the word תורה is used. In the judgment against Israel, however, a detailed account of the people's wrongdoing in terms of their violations against one another is provided. This, too, amounts to a rejection of the תורה.⁶ The charges against Israel are presented in two parts, in 2:6c–8b and in 2:12a–d. In 2:6c–8b, the people stand accused of selling the righteous for silver and the needy for a pair of shoes, burdening the lowly and turning away the poor, condemning the actions of a father and son who go to the same maid, stretching out pledged garments beside every altar and drinking the wine taken as fines. Yhwh instructs them that these actions are unjust and an abuse of power.

The selling of the righteous for silver and the needy for a pair of sandals highlights the perversion of justice.⁷ Taking advantage of the needy,

---

5. See Jakob Wöhrle, "'No Future for the Proud Exultant Ones': The Exilic Book of the Four Prophets (Hos., Am., Mic., Zeph.) as a Concept Opposed to the Deuteronomistic History," *VT* 58 (2008) 608–27, here 615. Wöhrle notices that the words שמר ("to keep"), תורה ("law, torah"), חקה ("statute"), and אב ("father"), are used to catch attention in Amos 2:4 and 2 Kgs 17:13, but this particular combination of terms does not occur anywhere else in the Hebrew Bible.

6. See Thomas Renz, "Torah in the Minor Prophets," in *Reading the Law: Studies in Honour of Gordon J. Wenham* (ed. J. G. McConville and Karl Möller; LHBOTS 461; London: T&T Clark, 2007) 73–94, here 83–84.

7. Duane A. Garrett defends the innocence of the righteous, saying, "he does not deserve this." The righteous are violated by being: (i) sold into slavery for silver, (ii) sold into slavery for unpaid debts, (iii) forced to pay bribes in the law courts (*Amos: A Handbook on the Hebrew Text* [Baylor Handbook on the Hebrew Bible; Waco, TX: Baylor University Press, 2008] 56–57).

who are unable to repay their debts, is a merciless act.⁸ Equating the value of the marginalized with that of a pair of sandals is even worse. This highlights how the people belittled those in need. The people's attitude to the poor and the needy is confirmed by their acts of trampling the heads of the poor into the dust of the earth and casting the afflicted to one side.⁹ The victims of this abuse are צדיק ("the righteous," v. 6c), ואביונים ("and the needy," v. 6d), דלים ("the lowly," v. 7a), and ענוים ("the poor," v. 7b),¹⁰ who together constitute the underprivileged.¹¹ Over and over again the disrespect and disdain shown for the penniless is seen.¹² Likewise, the son and his father going to the same maid is an outrageous and degrading act, grossly offending Yhwh. The implication of these instructions is that the crimes of Israel are not only a matter of private concern but are also an insult to Yhwh and a violation of the Torah. Exploitation is further evidenced in the people's act of stretching out pledged garments (בגדים חבלים) and drinking the illegally obtained wine (יין ענושים) in the house of their god.¹³ The fact that what they gained by their unjust acts was for their own gratification rather than out of necessity adds to the gravity of their sins (v. 8b). It is clear their behavior in no way accords with the message of the Torah.¹⁴

---

8. Avi Shveka, "'For a Pair of Shoes': A New Light on an Obscure Verse in Amos' Prophecy," *VT* 62 (2012) 95–114, here 96.

9. Luciano R. Peterlevitz perceives it as physical violence against the weak, either the violence of master against slave or the violence perpetrated by the army of Jeroboam against the weak ("Amós: O Profeta, o Contexto e o Texto," *Revista Theos* 6 [2011] 1–14, here 10). That there is violence against the weak is undisputed.

10. Fred Guyette provides a concise explanation of ᵓebyônîm, ᶜănāwîm, ṣaddîk, dallîm, the words that are used in Amos to describe the plight of the poor of Israel ("Amos the Prophet: A Meditation on the Richness of 'Justice,'" *JBQ* 36 [2008] 15–21, here 17).

11. Garrett, *Amos*, 55; Aron Pinker, "Observations on Some Cruxes in Amos, Part I," *JBL* 29 (2001) 18–26, here 22.

12. Graham R. Hamborg points out that this accusation has to do with (i) an illegal act, (ii) a lack of mercy and compassion, (iii) feasting while having no thought for the poor whose garments they hold (*Still Selling the Righteous: A Redaction-Critical Investigation of Reasons for Judgment in Amos 2:6–16* [LHBOTS 555; London: T&T Clark, 2012] 212).

13. Robin Wakely explains various applications of the term חבל ("take in pledge"), in particular in regard to Amos 2:8 ("חבל," in *New International Dictionary of Old Testament Theology and Exegesis [NIDOTTE]* [ed. Willem A. VanGemeren; Grand Rapids: Zondervan, 1997] 2:6–11).

14. Archibald L. H. M. van Wieringen observes that the elite of the Northern Kingdom act against the Torah, which, as he illustrates by referencing Lev 25:39, demands support and freedom for the poor ("The Triple-Layered Communication in the Book of Amos and Its Message of Non-Appropriation Theology," in *Multiple*

In 2:12a–d, the people stand accused of tempting the nazirites to drink wine and of commanding the prophets not to prophesy. The seriousness of sin can be better grasped when vv. 11 and 12 are taken together.

2:11a	I [Yhwh] raised up prophets from your sons
2:12b–d	[but] you [Israel] commanded the prophets not to prophesy
2:11b	I [Yhwh] raised up nazirites from your young men
2:12a	[but] you [Israel] made the nazirites drink wine

The Israelites compelled the nazirites to drink wine and thus to break their vows to Yhwh (Num 6:2–3). Likewise, they commanded the prophets not to prophesy, thereby forbidding them from carrying out their divine call (Deut 18:18). A prime example of the latter can be seen in Amos 7:10–17, where Amaziah, the high priest in Bethel, forbids Amos from prophesying. The account of the Amos–Amaziah confrontation is couched in language that is pedagogical in nature, as explained below.

C. Amaziah, a Symbol of the Rebellious Israelites

Amaziah was certain that Amos was a "seer" (חזה) and addresses him as such in 7:12b; yet he refused him permission to prophesy in Bethel (7:13a–b) despite his divine commissioning: לך הנבא אל־עמי ישראל ("go, prophesy to my people Israel," 7:15c–d). This implies that Amaziah rejected not just the words of Amos the prophet but the very words of Yhwh. The order not to prophesy in Bethel is indicative of the resolute resistance to the prophetic call of Amos (7:13a–b): ובית־אל לא־תוסיף עוד להנבא ("but in Bethel, no way you ever add to prophesy"). The *hiphil* form of יסף, preceded by the negative particle (לא־תוסיף), and the adverb that follows (עוד) equally reveal that Amaziah no longer approved of Amos prophesying in Bethel. Amaziah also speaks in a formal manner, which is commanding and threatening, as confirmed by the imperative forms of the verbs הלך ("go," v. 12c), ברח ("flee," v. 12d), and אכל ("eat," v. 12e) in his polemic against Amos.

Added to that, in 7:13c and 7:13d Amaziah tries to vindicate his argument with the כי clause הוא כי מקדש־מלך ("for this is the sanctuary of the king") and ובית ממלכה הוא ("and this is the house of the kingdom"). Amaziah's attempt to secularize Bethel as the sanctuary of the king and the house of the kingdom is ironic, for Bethel is in fact the house of God.[15]

Teachers in Biblical Texts [ed. Bart J. Koet and Archibald L. H. M. van Wieringen; CBET 88; Leuven: Peeters, 2017] 89–106, here 94).

15. Paul R. Noble, "Amos and Amaziah in Context: Synchronic and Diachronic Approaches to Amos 7–8," *CBQ* 60 (1998) 423–39, here 429.

The deeds of Amaziah and the repeated terms in his assertion such as מלך ("king") and ממלכה ("kingdom") reveal his submissiveness to Jeroboam, the king, rather than to Yhwh and his docility in relation to the royal house, in contrast to his disregard for the laws of the house of God.[16] As a result, Amaziah suffers the consequences. The text teaches that the relationship between Yhwh and Amaziah should be taken as a serious warning for anyone who acts contrary to the commands of Yhwh. Other lessons this episode communicates to the rebellious Israelites are that the power of Yhwh is greater than any human power and also that Yhwh will not fail those charged with carrying out the divine instructions.

It is in this context that the faults of Judah and Israel often come in for much criticism, and, throughout the Book of Amos and through the prophetic character, Yhwh strives to convince the listeners of the error of their ways. The way in which the Book of Amos presents the development in communication and the role of Yhwh and Yhwh's efforts to instruct the people is fascinating from the point of view of the clever use of rhetoric. I will explain below how this rhetorical language is employed to ensure effective communication.

■ II. Rhetoric in the Book

Besides enhancing Yhwh's communication with the people, the rhetoric utilized in the text also has pedagogical purposes. It often serves to educate the listeners in regard to the gravity of Yhwh's communication and to motivate them to faithfully follow the divine teachings. This section analyzes the role of rhetoric in the book and how it supports the teaching of Yhwh.

A. Presenting Yhwh as the All-Powerful

Depicting Yhwh as being all-powerful adds to the sense of importance attaching to his communication. The prophet provides multiple examples of Yhwh's awesome power in 4:13; 5:8–9; and 9:5–6, each of which is designed to confirm Yhwh's divine authority over the people and over all that is in the world.

(i) 4:13: In 4:13a–g, a detailed description of Yhwh's power is provided.[17] This description is preceded by the warning לקראת־אלהיך הכון ("be

---

16. J. Blake Couey, "Amos vii 10–17 and Royal Attitudes toward Prophecy in the Ancient Near East," *VT* 58 (2008) 300–314, here 312–13.

17. In this regard, John D. W. Watts deals with all three hymns one after the

prepared to meet your God") with the tone of the announcement clearly indicating that it should not be ignored. Recalling the repeated refrain of Yhwh in 4:4a–11f, ולא־שבתם עדי ("and yet you did not return to me"), the prophet strongly advises Israel to prepare properly for its encounter with Yhwh,[18] a coming together that is both decisive and impending, and which it must not disregard. The vocabulary employed powerfully conveys the feeling of urgency in respect of this teaching regarding the situation in which Israel finds itself, but also the sense of the power and majesty of Yhwh.

The verbs יצר ("to form")[19] in 4:13a and ברא ("to create"; see Gen 1:1–2:3) in 4:13b attest the creative power of Yhwh. The one who turns the dawn to darkness (עשה שחר עיפה), the next appellation bestowed on Yhwh, introduces a negative tone to the text, as the act alluded to contradicts the act of creation.[20] A sense of hopelessness enters the situation regarding Israel, with the darkness not only symbolizing, but also heightening the level of danger inherent in the divine judgment.[21] This in turn leads to a growing belief that the encounter between Yhwh and Israel could end in failure, with dire consequences. Worthy of particular mention is the unique and elaborate divine naming יהוה אלהי־צבאות ("Yhwh, God of hosts") in 4:13f, conveying as it does the great power and glory of Yhwh, a fitting climax to the unit.

(ii) 5:8–9: A description of Yhwh as the one whose power extends not just over a tiny portion of land or over one small part of the world but over everything is found in 5:8, illustrating once again the credibility and power of Yhwh, to whom Israel is answerable for its wicked ways. Yhwh

---

other in their *Sitz im Leben* (*Vision and Prophecy in Amos: 1955 Faculty Lectures, Baptist Theological Seminary, Rüschlikon/ZH, Switzerland* [Leiden: Brill, 1958] 52–67). Stefan Paas comprehensively examines the hymns in Amos, interpreting content, setting, style, and structure, as well as their function (*Creation and Judgement: Creation Texts in Some Eighth Century Prophets* [OTS 47; Leiden: Brill, 2003] 198–326).

18. Francis I. Andersen and David Noel Freedman, *Amos: A New Translation with Introduction and Commentary* (AB 24A; New York: Doubleday, 1989) 413, 450; Aaron Schart, "The First Section of the Book of the Twelve Prophets: Hosea–Joel–Amos," *Int* 61 (2007) 138–52, here 144; Joyce Rilett Wood, *Amos in Song and Book Culture* (JSOTSup 337; London: Sheffield Academic Press, 2002) 62.

19. A. H. Konkel, "יצר," *NIDOTTE* 2:503–6.

20. Pinhas Carny observes that the upending of the laws of nature results in complete ruin ("Doxologies: A Scientific Myth," *HS* 18 [1977] 149–59, here 155–56). See also Karl Möller, *A Prophet in Debate: The Rhetoric of Persuasion in the Book of Amos* (JSOTSup 372, Sheffield: Sheffield Academic Press, 2003) 286.

21. Möller is of the opinion that they probably would not have imagined him as the one who changes the dawn into darkness (*Prophet in Debate*, 287).

is presented as the one who makes the Pleiades and Orion (5:8a), turns the shadow of death into the morning and day into night (5:8b), and calls for the waters of the sea and pours them out over the face of the earth (5:8c). The implication is that Yhwh is sovereign and has the power to change the destiny of Israel in accordance with the divine will. As Yhwh, can do all—create, save, and destroy—for "Yhwh is his name" (יהוה שמו, 5:8f). If Yhwh possesses such great powers, Yhwh can certainly prevail in one small part of the world, the land of Israel. The implication of the teaching is that Israel must take Yhwh's warning seriously and is obliged to respond positively to Yhwh's call.

(iii) 9:5–6: The description of Yhwh in 9:5–6, recorded immediately after the fifth vision, induces a sense of dread in the context of the judgments announced in the vision. The actions of Yhwh depict the deity as being furious with Israel. Yhwh touches the earth, with alarming results such as the melting of the earth (ותמוג), the lamentation of the inhabitants (ואבלו), and the rising and subsiding of the River of Egypt (ועלתה כיאר כלה ושקעה כיאר מצרים).[22] Apart from that, Yhwh calls on the waters of the sea (הקרא למי־הים) and pours them over the face of the earth (וישפכם על־פני הארץ). All these destructive actions demonstrate Yhwh's supreme power. The sovereignty of Yhwh is further shown in the expression, "Yhwh builds his staircases in the heavens [הבונה בשמים מעלותו] and establishes his vault upon the earth [ואגדתו על־ארץ יסדה]." The combination of the terms "heaven" (שמים) and "earth" (ארץ) projects the majesty of Yhwh, Yhwh of all. And finally, all these descriptions of Yhwh are sealed with the proclamation יהוה שמו, "Yhwh is his name."

B. A Blend of Divine Threats and Persuasion

Often, it seems, the repeated warnings received by the people cross the boundaries between what is reasonable and what is not when it comes to Yhwh showing mercy. Nevertheless, toward the end it becomes clear to the text-immanent reader that these rhetorical warnings are in fact salvific and are a means of instruction. It can be said that the Yhwh-Israel relationship produced a range of emotions. Because of the repeated wrongdoings, relations are strained between Yhwh and the people and communication becomes increasingly tense.

---

22. Karl Möller notes that this, the third account of Yhwh that appears in the book, brings a more powerful portrayal of Yhwh's power to bring ruin and the accompanying total grief ("'Hear This Word against You': A Fresh Look at the Arrangement and the Rhetorical Strategy of the Book of Amos," *VT* 50 [2000] 499-518, here 514).

Confirmation that the people of Israel refused to turn away from their evil ways comes in the form of the catalog of punishments, as outlined in 4:6a–11a. The recurring statement ולא־שבתם עדי ("yet you did not return to me," 4:6c, 8d, 9c, 10d, 11e) leaves little doubt as to the stubbornness of the people and their unwillingness to return to Yhwh. The punishments inflicted on them were in fact an attempt at encouraging them to act justly. However, with unfeeling hearts, the people of Israel continued leading a life of excess, while still taking advantage of the downtrodden and abusing the destitute, thus wasting the numerous chances afforded them to accept the directions of Yhwh.

Whereas, previously, Yhwh was portrayed as the one who warns and who administers punishments, in 5:4a–b Yhwh is seen as an admonisher: "seek me and live" (דרשוני וחיו). Certainly, in contrast to the dire warnings, this is a very welcome exhortation. The advice דרשוני is to be read together with the recurring statement of Yhwh, ולא־שבתם עדי, in 4:6a–11f. The contrasting messages convey how much Yhwh longed for the people to make amends.

Since the people did not mend their misguided ways, Yhwh announces that disasters (5:3b–f), wailing (5:16b–17a), exile (5:27a; 6:7b, 8e), annihilation (6:11a–12d) and invasion (6:14a–f) are about to befall the house of Israel. Importantly, among the punishments announced is that of famine in 8:11c–f. In this context, the instructions about the famine do not refer to a lack of bread and water, but rather to a longing for the word of Yhwh. Its absence indicates that communication between Yhwh and the people of Israel has ceased. Consequently, extreme tension enters their relationship, causing the people untold trauma.

Nevertheless, accepting the intercessions of the prophet, Yhwh twice revokes the decision to punish the people. The words of Yhwh לא תהיה ("it shall not be") in 7:3b and גם־היא לא תהיה ("it also shall not be") in 7:6b, testify to this. The remarkable statement נחם יהוה על־זאת ("Yhwh repented for this") in 7:3a and 7:6a confirms Yhwh's decision not to proceed with the planned punishments even though there is nothing in the text to suggest that the Israelites have repented. This decision of Yhwh, however, eases the tension. It not only brings relief to the people, but it also serves to highlight Yhwh's concern for them.

That the divine admonitions were, in fact, intended to be restorative rather than punitive is hugely significant in terms of the communication in the Book of Amos. Because of the wicked behavior of the people, it is legitimate for Yhwh to end the relationship with them. Nevertheless, their stubbornness has not diminished Yhwh's desire to bestow benevolence on them. This is confirmed by the remarkable change in the role of

Yhwh in the final section of the Book of Amos. From one who appears as the proclaimer and the administrator of punishments, Yhwh becomes the one actively engaged in ending the captivity of the people and in reinstating, repairing, and restoring Israel to its former glory. Ultimately, Yhwh's passionate love for Israel is so great that all past iniquities are forgiven. Thus, Yhwh, whose concern for the well-being of the people is unfailing, is seen as a benevolent mentor.

C. A Succession of Ironies

Irony is used to dramatic effect in the communication process in the Book of Amos and is instrumental in alerting the listeners to the seriousness of the message conveyed. It sets forth the teaching of Yhwh in making the people fully aware of the gravity of the situation in which they find themselves. This method of instruction very effectively gets across the import of the communication.

In 3:12a–d, the double use of נצל ("to rescue") appears positive. It soon becomes clear, however, that what is being rescued is insignificant.[23] Any hope of survival is well and truly dashed[24] when the comparison with the shepherd managing to salvage but a piece of an ear and two shanks is made.[25] Any thought that נצל (3:12b) promises deliverance is unfounded.[26] The way of life enjoyed by the Israelites, with all its opulence and privileges, is coming to an end.[27] They and all their possessions face utter destruction, leaving fragments so tiny as to be nonexistent.[28]

A note of sarcasm can be detected in 4:2b, as here the verb בוא ("to come") is used in a much more threatening manner than the similar verb בוא ("to bring") in 4:1g. In 4:1g the "cows of Bashan" commanded "their

---

23. Robert L. Hubbard Jr., "נצל," *NIDOTTE* 3:141–47.
24. Mark Daniel Carroll R., *Contexts for Amos: Prophetic Poetics in Latin American Perspective* (JSOTSup 132; Sheffield: JSOT Press, 1992) 198.
25. Stephen G. Dempster sees these two legs and a piece of an ear as evidence of annihilation ("Amos 3: Apologia of a Prophet," *La Revue Baptiste de Théologie* 5 [1995] 35–51, here 46).
26. Andersen and Freedman, *Amos*, 373; Gary V. Smith, *Amos: A Commentary* (Library of Biblical Interpretation; Grand Rapids: Zondervan, 1989) 122; Möller, *Prophet in Debate*, 239; Blair J. Wilgus, "Judgment on Israel: Amos 3–6 Read as a Unity" (Ph.D. diss., University of Edinburgh, 2012) 76; Åke Viberg, "Amos 7:14: A Case of Subtle Irony," *TynBul* 47.1 (1996) 91–114, here 109.
27. *Harper's Bible Commentary* (ed. James L. Mays et al.; San Francisco: Harper & Row, 1988) 722.
28. Meindert Dijkstra, "The Ivory Beds and Houses of Samaria in Amos," in *Image, Text, Exegesis: Iconographic Interpretation and the Hebrew Bible* (ed. Izaak J. de Hulster and Joel M. LeMon; LHBOTS 588; London: Bloomsbury, 2014) 192–93.

lords" (אדניהם) to bring something to drink, whereas what they actually receive is days of punishment from the real Lord (אדני יהוה), attested in 4:2a–b.[29] These days will bring grief and hardship, instead of joy and prosperity, attested by the following phrases: ונשא ("he will lift") in 4:2c, תצאנה ("you will go out") in 4:3a, והשלכתנה ("will be thrown out") in 4:3c [uncertain], בצנות ("hooks") in 4:2c, and בסירות דוגה ("fishhooks") in 4:2d.

In unit 4:4a–5f, the character of the communication is transformed from previous words of punishment to that which revolves principally around sacrifices.[30] This is well reflected in the language employed, for example, זבח ("sacrifice") in 4:4f, מעשר ("tithe") in 4:4g, קטר ("kindle"), חמץ ("a leaven sacrifice"), תודה ("praise"), all in 4:5a, and נדבה ("freewill offering") in 4:5b. Induced by the opposing themes of sin and sacrifice, a sense of sarcasm is diffused throughout the entire unit.[31] The invitation to go to Bethel, in fact Beth-El, "house of God," a holy place, and to commit sin there is laced with sarcasm.[32] The use of sarcasm effectively illustrates how Yhwh, who has been disobeyed by the people, instructs them for their faithfulness, rather than for the charade of their empty acts of public worship.[33] In a similar way, an ironic reversal of what is normally expected can be seen in unit 5:21a–23b, when the sacrifices expected to be pleasing to Yhwh are detested by him.[34] The second-person masculine suffix, "your," attached to a succession of nouns—חגיכם ("your feasts"), בעצרתיכם ("your assemblies"), ומנחתיכם ("your gifts"), מריאיכם ("your fatlings"), שריך ("your songs"), נבליך ("your harp")—indicate that the sacri-

---

29. Möller, *Prophet in Debate*, 257–58.
30. Smith characterizes these practices as proud demonstrations of piety (*Amos*, 2).
31. William Rainey Harper, *A Critical and Exegetical Commentary on Amos and Hosea* (ICC; Edinburgh: T&T Clark, 1979) 91; Andersen and Freedman, *Amos*, 434; Carroll R., *Contexts for Amos*, 206; Möller, *Prophet in Debate*, 263; Wilgus, "Judgment on Israel," 113–23; Viberg, "Amos 7:14: A Case of Subtle Irony," 110; A. Vanlier Hunter, *Seek the Lord! A Study of the Meaning and Function of the Exhortations in Amos, Hosea, Isaiah, Micah, and Zephaniah* (Baltimore: St. Mary's Seminary & University, 1982) 70.
32. Thomas Jemielity, *Satire and the Hebrew Prophets* (Literary Currents in Biblical Interpretation; Louisville: Westminster John Knox, 1992) 54.
33. By quoting the prophets Hosea and Micah, Smith highlights the message communicated: "Hosea preached God was more interested in fidelity than oblations (Hos 6:8) and Micah made it known that God required justice, charity and humility, not a thousand rams or ten thousand rivers of oil (Mic 6:6–8). God's desire is to encounter the person who finds contentment in God, not the person who is merely performing meaningless rituals" (*Amos*, 143).
34. See Mays et al., eds., *Harper's Bible Commentary*, 724.

fices were, in reality, for Israel's own gratification, and not something desired by Yhwh.[35]

Unit 5:18a–20d opens with the declaration that a woe would befall those who desire the day of Yhwh. The irony of the situation quickly becomes apparent, in that the eagerly anticipated day of Yhwh, which promised so much hope and a future filled with happiness, instead offers only darkness.[36] The repeated references to the absence of light—הוא־חשך ("it is darkness," 5:18d, 20a), לא־אור ("no light," 5:18e, 20b), אפל ("even darkness," 5:20c), לא־נגה ("no brightness," 5:20d)—serve to highlight not only the sense of hopelessness but also that this longed-for day was going to be one of retribution, when Israel would be held to account for its evil ways, and not the one it believed would bring salvation.[37]

A further woe, beginning once again with the interjection הוי ("alas!") is recorded in 6:1a–2f. The speech is directed against those at ease in Zion, who trust in their own ability to confront and defeat any enemy.[38] The term שאנן ("at ease") in 6:1b suggests that a feeling of security exists in Zion and on the hill of Samaria, a view that is challenged by the references to the fall of other kingdoms, namely, Calneh (6:2a), Hamath (6:2c), and Gath (6:2d), which were considered to be just as powerful as Israel, if not more so.[39] The irony, however, is that, given what has happened else-

---

35. Theresa Veronica Lafferty comments that "the people's celebrations are not having any positive effect on God whenever Amos calls them 'yours'" ("The Prophetic Critique of the Priority of the Cult: A Study of Amos 5:21–24 and Isaiah 1:10–17" [Ph.D. diss., Catholic University of America, 2010] 62). Aaron Schart says that the attack is on the people who worship and not on the cult ("The Fifth Vision of Amos in Context," in *Thematic Threads in the Book of the Twelve* [ed. Aaron Schart and Paul L. Redditt; BZAW 325; Berlin: De Gruyter, 2003] 46–71, here 53).

36. John Barton, *The Theology of the Book of Amos* (Old Testament Theology; Cambridge: Cambridge University Press, 2012) 62–63; Daniel E. Fleming, "The Day of Yahweh in the Book of Amos: A Rhetorical Response to Ritual Expectation," *RB* 117 (2010) 20–38, here 29.

37. See Shimon Bakon, "The Day of the Lord," *JBQ* 38 (2010) 149–56, here 151; John Barton, "The Day of Yahweh in the Minor Prophets," in *Biblical and Near Eastern Essays: Studies in Honour of Kevin J. Cathcart* (ed. Carmel McCarthy and John F. Healey; JSOTSup 375; London: T&T Clark, 2004) 68–79, here 69; Tim Bulkeley, "The Book of Amos and the Day of Yhwh," *Colloquium* 45 (2013) 145–69; Gerhard F. Hasel, *Understanding the Book of Amos: Basic Issues in Current Interpretations* (Grand Rapids: Baker, 1991) 111.

38. For a discussion on the idol of national security and the futility of trusting in military strength, see M. Daniel Carroll R., "Imagining the Unthinkable: Exposing the Idolatry of National Security in Amos," *Ex Auditu* 24 (2008) 37–54, here 46–53.

39. J. J. M. Roberts, "Amos 6:1–7," in *Understanding the Word: Essays in Honor of Bernhard W. Anderson* (ed. James T. Butler, Edgar W. Conrad, and Ben C. Ollenburger; JSOTSup 37; Sheffield: JSOT Press, 1985) 155–66, here 158–59.

where, foolishly putting their faith in their own strength will actually lead to the realization that they are indeed vulnerable and far from indestructible.

The narration of the confrontation between Amaziah and Amos, coming as it does between the third and fourth visions, conjures in the mind of the text-immanent reader images that give a glimpse of the evil practices engaged in by the people.

- Amaziah, the high priest of Bethel, reports to Jeroboam that Amos is conspiring against him. He does not, however, make any mention of Amos's intercessions on behalf of the people of Israel as indicated in the visions. The question of who is in fact conspiring, Amos or Amaziah, gives rise to a degree of irony.
- It is ironic that Amaziah, the high priest, whose duty it is to serve Yhwh, in fact serves the king.
- In 7:5c, Amos beseeched Yhwh (חדל־נא) to stop the punishment, whereas in 7:13a–b, Amaziah ordered Amos to stop prophesying. What a contrast!
- The positive response of Amos to Yhwh's command לך הנבא אל־עמי ישראל ("go prophesy to my people Israel") in 7:15c–d, contrasts sharply with his negative response to the command issued by Amaziah, לא תנבא על־ישראל ולא תטיף על־בית ישחק ("you do not prophesy against Israel and do not speak against the house of Isaac") in 7:16c–d.
- Amaziah demanded of Amos not to prophesy in Bethel, whereas Amos demanded of Amaziah to hear the word of Yhwh.
- Amaziah complains to King Jeroboam about Amos; however, there is no indication of any action being taken against him. Ironically, Amaziah is the one who suffers punishment for his endeavors to silence the agent of Yhwh.

Irony prevails in chap. 9, the climax of the Book of Amos, where it is made clear that punishment is unavoidable: there will be no escape and no hiding place.[40] Amos 9:2–4 lays stress on Yhwh's indignation, which cannot be eluded. Yhwh vows to seize the people of Israel from wherever they choose to conceal themselves. If they dig into Sheol (שאול) or climb up to heaven (שמים), Yhwh's hand will take them. All their attempts at escape, even in the remotest of places such as the top of Mount Carmel

---

40. Tchavdar S. Hadjiev, *The Composition and Redaction of the Book of Amos* (BZAW 393; Berlin: De Gruyter, 2009) 66.

and the bottom of the sea, are doomed to fail.[41] Yhwh will order the serpent to pursue and kill them. And if they are imprisoned by their enemies, they will die by the sword at Yhwh's command.[42] All these descriptions emphasize the fact that no one will escape judgment. Thus, these ironies function as a powerful communicative tool for the benefit of the text-immanent reader and provide the reader with a set of guidelines to help in abiding the instructions of Yhwh.

D. Overturned Situations

A series of reversals adds greatly to the communicative setting in the Book of Amos. The analysis below of the examples of this literary device that occur in the text demonstrates how well the reversals function as a means of communicating the messages of Yhwh.

(i) Initially, the prophecies against the other nations do not give either Judah or Israel any cause for concern. Indeed, they may well have agreed that those nations deserved to be punished.[43] It comes as a devastating blow to the people, however, to find that they also are being indicted.[44] This final stroke dealt to Israel is an inferno, whereas the prophecies against the other nations were but tiny flames. Whatever sense of superiority Israel might have harbored when they saw their neighbors being punished for their wrongdoings is well and truly shattered when they are brought to realize that their own sins are equally evil.[45] The fact that Israel and Judah are the recipients here makes this piece of communication remarkable in itself.

---

41. Hadjiev speaks about the sets of notions that give rise to the idea of a ubiquitous God from whom Israel cannot escape (*Composition and Redaction*, 64).

42. Carol J. Dempsey, *Amos, Hosea, Micah, Nahum, Zephaniah, Habakkuk* (New Collegeville Bible Commentary: Old Testament 15; Collegeville, MN: Liturgical Press, 2013) 35. See also Clarence Hassell Bullock, *Introduction to the Old Testament Prophetic Books* (Chicago: Moody, 2007) 73.

43. John Barton notes that, because the people feel that sin and judgment are rightly linked, this in turn creates for them a difficult situation from which to free themselves (*Understanding Old Testament Ethics: Approaches and Explorations* [Louisville: Westminster John Knox, 2003] 79).

44. Viberg, "Amos 7:14: A Case of Subtle Irony," 108; Ferry Y. Mamahit and Pieter M. Venter, "Oracle against Israel's Social Injustices: A Rhetorical Analysis of Amos 2:6–8," *HTS Teologiese Studies* 66 (2010) 1–11, here 10. James R. Linville observes that the teeth in the prophecies against the nations are the final two prophecies against Judah and Israel ("What Does 'It' Mean? Interpretation at the Point of No Return in Amos 1–2," *BibInt* 8 [2000] 400-424, here 408).

45. See Barton, *Understanding Old Testament Ethics*, 79.

(ii) The image of the פרות הבשן ("cows of Bashan") in 4:1 is intended to hold up to ridicule the people being addressed. This metaphorical usage evokes the meaning behind the language of the text with successive scenes suggesting, for example, being lifted by בצנות ("hooks") and by בסירות דוגה ("fishhooks") and being transported. The allusion to hooks and fishhooks conjures up unpleasant images of captives being held and painfully lifted up, unable to break free no matter how hard they struggle.[46] Hooks are used by those moving cows; therefore, a reference to the "cows of Bashan" being lifted by hooks out of their comfortable surroundings and being led out through the breaches is very apt. Contrasting scenes, such as that where the פרות הבשן, who once oppressed the poor (דלים) and the needy (אביונים) and who now suffer that same fate themselves, serve to highlight the scope and influence of the communication.

(iii) The prophet describes the יום יהוה ("day of Yhwh") in a way that is totally different from the expectation of the people. In 5:18d–e, 20a–d he describes the יום יהוה as a day shrouded in deep darkness (חשך). In addition, the comparison of a man's encounter with three animals (a lion, a bear, and a snake)[47] intensifies the terror of the sudden and unexpected disasters to come on the day of Yhwh.[48] The episode in 5:19, which shows the irony of someone escaping the jaws of a lion only to be confronted by an equally dangerous bear, and then, having evaded danger a second time, enters his house, which he considers to be a place of refuge, only to be

---

46. Cf. 2 Kgs 19:28; 2 Chr 33:11; Jer 16:16; Ezek 29:4; Hab 1:15, where captives were led away by hooks through the nose, by their victors. Archibald van Wieringen explores the use of the words "hooks" and "fishhooks" in the context of the cow imagery ("Feminized Men in Amos 4:1–3," in *The Books of the Twelve Prophets: Minor Prophets, Major Theologies* [ed. Heinz-Josef Fabry; BETL 295; Leuven: Peeters, 2018] 403–9, here 406–7). After being slaughtered cows are hung on hooks. Also, cows are transported from one place to another using hooks, this being a reference to exile.

47. In Genesis, the man had been instructed to rule over every living creature (Gen 1:28); however, in Amos 5:19 he fails to do so. Aulikki Nahkola comments that a heightening of the sense of horror is the intention of the hostile meeting with these three animals ("Amos Animalizing: Lion, Bear and Snake in Amos 5:19," in *Aspects of Amos: Exegesis and Interpretation* [ed. Anselm C. Hagedorn and Andrew Mein; LHBOTS 536; New York: T&T Clark, 2011] 83–104, here 103–4).

48. Hasel suggests that "the picture of the person, however, is to be applied to the nation and not to a single individual or group within Israel" (*Understanding the Book of Amos*, 112). In my opinion, however, the individual in the description of the day of the Lord is anonymous and functions as a representative example, rather than referring to a specific person or group. This comparison is brought forth to highlight the dangerous situation that awaits Israel on the day of the Lord.

bitten by a snake,[49] makes clear that all attempts to reach safety are ultimately futile.[50] The joyful expectation of the day of Yhwh is reversed as a day filled with darkness and danger. The lesson conveyed is that having great expectations of the day of Yhwh, despite not having atoned for previous wrongdoing, is utter folly. In short, all hope is lost, and only woe remains.[51]

(iv) In 5:16b–17b Yhwh announces lamentation, with wailing in all places (5:16b). The cry of grief "alas, alas" would be heard in every street (5:16c-d). The vineyards, places associated with yielding rich harvests, would be filled with tears and turned into places of lamentation (5:17a). The reason for the lamentation is explained by the כי-clause כי־אעבר בקרבך ("for I pass through your midst") in 5:17b, revealing the personal involvement of Yhwh in relation to it. The result of Yhwh's visit, which would ordinarily be beautiful, joyful, and blessed will, on the contrary, be full of much weeping and sorrow.

(v) The narrative of the Amos-Amaziah confrontation (7:10–17), includes reversals of fortune and notes of sarcasm. The climax comes when Amaziah himself, who tried to prevent Amos from prophesying in Israel, now faces punishment, a dramatic fall for the one who considered himself to be beyond reproach (7:17). The character Amaziah expected to receive benefits from the king for revealing the alleged conspiracy against Israel, but instead he suffers total humiliation at the hands of the one true king, Yhwh.

(vi) Further, it is interesting to note the changes in the communication strategies employed, especially when the prophet, who, as a pronouncer of divine punishments, at a certain point becomes an intercessor. On foreseeing what was about to happen to Israel, Amos twice successfully intercedes on its behalf: אדני יהוה סלח־נא ("Lord God, forgive now, please") in 7:2 and אדני יהוה חדל־נא ("Lord God, cease, please") in 7:5. On both occasions, Yhwh relents (לא תהיה, "it will not happen") in 7:3 and

---

49. This image of the biting snake in the sense of bringing destruction can be seen again in Amos 9:3; Num 21:6–9; and Jer 8:17. See Martin Beck, *Der "Tag YHWHs" im Dodekapropheton: Studien im Spannungsfeld von Traditions- und Redaktionsgeschichte* (BZAW 356; Berlin: De Gruyter, 2005) 61.

50. Viberg describes the dramatic irony scene in 5:19 as "a man manages to flee from a lion, a remarkable achievement in itself, only to come upon a bear! Somehow, he escapes the bear as well, comes home and rests his hand against the wall, only to be bitten by a snake. The point of the irony is clear; just as he thought he was safe, he was lost" ("Amos 7:14: A Case of Subtle Irony," 110).

51. James D. Nogalski mentions that, when the day comes, escape will be impossible ("The Day(s) of Yahweh in the Book of the Twelve," in Schart and Redditt, *Thematic Threads in the Book of the Twelve*, 192–213, here 204).

again in 7:6. This was short-lived, however, and he was soon to resume the role of pronouncer of doom. Likewise, Yhwh, who roars in anger, threatening and executing punishments, ultimately becomes the bestower of blessings. These reversals picture Yhwh as a compassionate instructor merciful enough to save the people from punishments. The feeling of fear and despair in the opening pages is replaced by one of joy and hope at the end.

■ III. Conclusion

In conclusion, it can safely be said that Yhwh is a competent teacher, one who adopts a variety of roles, each with a pedagogical dimension to it. These roles include judge, proclaimer and administrator of punishments, accuser, admonisher, motivator, and protector. In all these cases, Yhwh communicates the fundamental message of fidelity to the deity and to the deity's commandments. A variety of pedagogical techniques is employed in the Book of Amos to convey these lessons. It utilizes a wide range of teaching styles, the subject of this particular analysis, keeping in mind the role of Yhwh as a teacher from a communicative perspective. During the course of my analysis, many instances of persuasive rhetoric were found in the extensive discourse structures. Examples came in the form of the divine swearing of oaths, prophetic lamentations and woes, ironies and sarcastic calls, and dialogue full of twists, turns, and reversals. Together these features constitute a complex system of communication, which in turn leads to a deepening of inner meanings and a heightened awareness of existing tensions. The portrayal of Yhwh as an effective teacher is helped in no small way by the successful use of rhetoric in particular.

Throughout the Book of Amos, communication, which remains very much to the fore, reveals Yhwh to be not only the people's instructor but also their constant companion. Yhwh communicates with the people, often with a furious voice, but always with a purpose in mind. On certain occasions Yhwh instructs the people in the ways of the just and exhorts them to seek Yhwh. The issuing of threats, warnings, punishments, and judgments confirms the urgency of Yhwh's call to conversion. The beautiful image of Yhwh as teacher is found throughout the Book of Amos, and Yhwh's role as teacher, which is implied by the rhetoric used, is attested by the intensity of the engagement of Yhwh and the people.

It is evident that there is tremendous progression in regard to communication in the Book of Amos. This progression is seen in the actions of Yhwh, who goes from being the one who roars in anger, to the one who blesses. The mode of instruction changes accordingly. The Book of Amos also communicates that, when it comes to the question of Yhwh and judgment, no favoritism is shown. For example, at the very beginning, the text-immanent reader feels that, as the chosen people, Israel and Judah are exempt from divine judgments. However, this is but a fleeting thought, like bubbles on water. The people in fact will suffer greater devastation. Thus, Yhwh proves to be a just teacher who passes fair judgment on the people. Regarding the communication with the recipients, it is emphatic and compelling and delivered with great rhetorical effect. The prospects of the admonitions to return to Yhwh being successful are enhanced by the strength of the communication. The Book of Amos is not merely a catalog of punishments, as it might appear at first. Rather, the judgments and punishments are in fact rhetorical devices designed to invite the people to repent. It is quite interesting to note that, as with Judah and Israel, the text-immanent reader is also challenged to pay heed, and that the now-moment communication aspect in the Book of Amos continues to flow and develop. The communicative situation is more than just a mirror for the text-immanent reader, who learns to read the text and to develop a response.

The communication embedded in the Book of Amos is a rich source of inspiration; and, thus, discovering new dynamic methods of communication and finding innovative ways of employing them arouses great excitement. This strategy, which maintains an open-ended invitation for society to engage with the text, is perfectly sensible. The reader-oriented instances in the text provide moments that are both illuminative and educational.

4
Ben Sira:
Teacher and Pedagogue

PANC C. BEENTJES

This contribution sketches a portrait of the Jewish teacher Ben Sira, who, around 190–180 BCE in Jerusalem, published a Hebrew document that is now usually referred to as "The Wisdom of Jesus Sirach," but often also known as "Ecclesiasticus," the name according to the Old Latin translation.[1]

The fact that this teacher published his writing in Hebrew is not unimportant, and its significance is far from being self-evident, since the common language in Palestine in those days was Aramaic and, after the conquests of Alexander the Great, Greek was also spoken, certainly in Jerusalem.[2] The return to Hebrew is a clear proof that this teacher (סופר) deliberately chose to write down his message in the language of the Jewish tradition.[3]

That Jewish tradition was under a lot of pressure in his days. Around 200 BCE the Egyptian general Scopas had suffered a serious defeat against Antiochus III the Great in the battle of Paneion, so that Palestine finally came under the authority of the Seleucids, who were based in Antioch.

---

1. According to Sir 50:27 (Hebrew), the author's full name is "Simeon, son of Jeshua, son of Eleazar, son of Sira."

2. See John J. Collins, *Jewish Wisdom in the Hellenistic Age* (OTL; Louisville: Westminster John Knox, 1997) 23–41.

3. See Helge Stadelmann, *Ben Sira als Schriftgelehrter: Eine Untersuchung zum Berufsbild des vor-makkabäischen Sōfēr unter Berücksichtigung seines Verhältnisses zu Priester-, Propheten- und Weisheitslehrertum* (WUNT 2/6; Tübingen: Mohr Siebeck, 1980).

As a result, Hellenistic culture and philosophy of life accelerated their entry into Palestine, putting the Jewish identity under pressure.[4] There were also intrigues relating to the position of the high priesthood, which was granted to the highest bidder by the Seleucid monarchs.

In those turbulent and confused times, both politically and religiously, Ben Sira publishes his writing. In an attempt to put both the author and his work in sharper focus, I quote from the two autobiographical passages of the book:

> As for me, I was like a canal from a river,
>   like a water channel into a garden.
> I said, "I will water my plants,
>   and drench my flowerbeds."
> And lo, my canal became a river,
>   and my river a sea.
> I will again make instruction [παιδεία] shine forth like the dawn,
>   and I will make it clear from far away.
> I will again pour out teaching [διδασκαλία] like prophecy,
>   and leave it to all future generations. (Sir 24:30–33)[5]

Ben Sira sees it as his task to channel the Jewish tradition that has been reflected in the Torah to new ground. He even dares to place his work within a prophetic line and does not hesitate to include himself in the broad stream of Israel's tradition. His teaching, however, is intended not only for his contemporaries but also for the distant future, for Jews elsewhere in the world—not only for his own audience but also for future generations.

> Now I was the last to keep vigil.
>   I was like a gleaner following the grape-pickers.
> By the blessing of the Lord I arrived first,
>   and like a grape-picker I filled my wine press.
> Consider that I have not labored for myself alone,
>   but for all who seek instruction [παιδεία]. (Sir 33:16–18)

Ben Sira apparently considers himself to be the last in line of those who watch over the traditions of Israel. The first two lines of this passage can also be read very easily as a disguised criticism of the ever-increasing Hellenization of Jerusalem and its surroundings.[6]

---

4. This would eventually culminate in the Maccabees' revolt (167–160 BCE).
5. Biblical quotations are adapted from the NRSV, unless otherwise indicated.
6. No one doubts that Ben Sira, in 38:24–39:11, which provides a detailed description of the ideal סופר, has in fact written down his own work and ideas.

■ I. FROM GRANDFATHER TO GRANDSON

Although Ben Sira wrote his work in Hebrew, it is not the Hebrew version of this scripture that gained authority. We do not know the decisive reason(s) for the fact that this Hebrew document was not included in the list of "books that pollute the hands." It may be that the concealment of Ezra in the "Praise of the Fathers" (Sirach 44–50) caused this, or that the colophon giving the author's name and byname (Sir 50:27) stood in the way of its inclusion in the Hebrew canon.

It is the Greek translation of Ben Sira's grandson that is included in our Bibles, and which has been given the status of "deuterocanonical scripture." The grandson who provided his translation of a πρόλογος, a "Foreword," puts readers very much on the trail of the intention of the work:

> So, my grandfather Jesus, who had devoted himself especially to the reading of the Law and the Prophets and the other books of our ancestors, and had acquired considerable proficiency in them, was himself also led to write something pertaining to instruction [παιδεία] and wisdom. (Sirach Prologue)

The Greek noun παιδεία can be found a total of thirty-five times in the Greek translation of the grandson,[7] making it unmistakably a favorite word of the grandson, especially when we compare it with the "only" sixty-five times that παιδεία appears in the remainder of the Septuagint.

In his Leiden dissertation, Theophil Middendorp even tried to show that Ben Sira wanted to compose a textbook following the example of Greek models. This theory, however, is hardly considered valid anymore.[8]

The grandson explicitly describes his grandfather's writings as a work that "contained instruction" (Sirach Prologue). The autobiographical passages of his grandfather quoted above also clearly point in this direction. Are there any other indications that Ben Sira himself regarded his book as a source of instruction? To this end, we will now look at the Hebrew text to see whether we may find any evidence there to justify such a conclusion.

---

7. In addition, the verb παιδεύειν occurs nine times, the participle πεπαιδευμένος six times and the noun παιδευτής once (Rudolf Smend, *Griechisch-syrisch-hebräischer Index zur Weisheit des Jesus Sirach* (Berlin: Reimer, 1907) 176.

8. Th. Middendorp, *Die Stellung Jesu Ben Siras zwischen Judentum und Hellenismus* (Leiden: Brill, 1973).

II. "House of Teaching" and "Teaching Chair": Metaphor or Reality?

An intriguing clue as to how Ben Sira considered his work is found, in my opinion, in one of the lines in the final passage of the book: פנו אלי סכלים ולינו בבית מדרשי, "Come to me, unreasonable (ones), and stay in the house of my study/my house of study" (Sir 51:23).[9] James Crenshaw, who mentions this passage twice in his essay on education in ancient Israel, qualifies this verse as "the first explicit reference to a school," but in the same sense he also speaks of a "deficiency of hard evidence."[10]

Sirach scholars have long been debating the exact meaning of the collocation in the phrase "the house of my study/my house of study." Is this indeed the very first written proof of the existence of the phenomenon of a "house of teaching," or academy?[11] If it is, and if it is indeed a physical school or academy that is meant, then we should also take seriously the implication of the verb associated with it in Sir 51:23, thus creating an interesting case. Immediately prior to and directly linked to the collocation "the house of my study/my house of study" is the verb לין, which means "to spend the night." If we take the second half of 51:23 literally, it means that the pupils of this school or study house were staying at school, that is, receiving education from Ben Sira at a kind of boarding school. Although it cannot be completely ruled out, this possibility seems rather unlikely to me.

It is therefore more correct to interpret the formulation "house of my study/my house of study" as a metaphor for Ben Sira's activities as a teacher of wisdom. "The house of my study/my house of study" then functions as a metaphor for his book.[12]

---

9. The Greek text reads: ἐγγίσατε πρός με, ἀπαίδευτοι, καὶ αὐλίσθητε ἐν οἴκῳ παιδείας.

10. James L. Crenshaw, "Education in Ancient Israel," *JBL* 104 (1985) 601–15, here 601.

11. See Rudolf Smend, *Die Weisheit des Jesus Sirach* (Berlin: Reimer, 1906) 508: "Der Ausdruck ist geschichtlich wichtig als Bezeichnung des Hauses des Weisheitslehrers"; John G. Snaith, *Ecclesiasticus, or the Wisdom of Jesus Son of Sirach* (CBC; Cambridge: Cambridge University Press, 1974) 261: "school"; R. A .F. MacKenzie, *Sirach* (OTM 19; Wilmington; Glazier, 1983) 196: "'house of learning,' a technical name for the place where students assembled for instruction in the Law."

12. Norbert Peters, *Das Buch Jesus Sirach oder Ecclesiasticus* (EHAT 25; Münster: Aschendorff, 1913) 451: "Hier meint der Autor übrigens sein Buch"; see also Peters, "Ein übersehendes Zeugnis für die literarische Art des 'Midrasch' in unserer Bibel," *TGl* 3 (1911) 143: "Dieses 'Midraschhaus' meint aber in übertragener Bedeutung das Buch des Jesus Sirach, nicht den Ort, an dem der Autor lehrte."

Some authors, however, want to keep both options open.¹³ There are also those who consider the collocation בית מדרשי as not authentic and—partly because of the Greek (ἐν οἴκῳ παιδείας) and Syriac translation (ܒܝܬ ܝܘܠܦܢܐ)—plead for the collocation בית מוסר.¹⁴ The main argument used is that, while it is correct that the grandson represents מוסר with παιδεία here, this combination of words is not the usual one employed by him, since it applies in only six of the thirty-five cases.¹⁵

Since Sir 51:13–30 is, moreover, constructed as an acrostic, many scholars want to change פנו at the beginning of 51:23 to סורו, so that, in this way, the order of the letters in the Hebrew alphabet will be respected. Thus, one may postulate a wordplay between the verbs סור ("to turn") and מוסר ("to instruct").¹⁶

The acrostic also contains data that need to be taken into account. These are the opening words of Sir 51:29: תשמח נפשי בישיבתי, "my soul rejoices in my sitting," a reference to the seat on which the teacher sits.¹⁷ In parallel with 51:23, one could argue that the *hapax* בישיבתי is not about "education," but about a physical יְשִׁבָה. But, given the phrase in 51:28, "Hear my teachings,"¹⁸ I advocate in 51:29, as in 51:23, for an interpretation of the Hebrew phrase that favors an abstract meaning, such as education or instruction, over a physical one that would refer to the building where that education could have taken place.¹⁹

---

13. Burkard M. Zapff, *Jesus Sirach 25–51* (NEchtB 39; Würzburg: Echter, 2010) 398: "Wiewohl 23b hier auch rein metaphorisch verstanden werden kann, so ist es doch ein früher Beleg für die Existenz von weisheitlichen 'Lehrhäusern.'"

14. Israel Lévi, *L'Ecclésiastique, ou, La sagesse de Jésus, fils de Sira* (2 vols.; Bibliothèque de l'École des hautes études: Sciences religieuses 10e; Paris: Leroux, 1898–1901) 2:229: "בית מדרשי serait un néologisme un peu prémature. Il y avait probablement בית מוסר."

15. Sir 34:17; 35:14; 41:14; 42:5; 42:8; 50:27.

16. E.g., Celia Deutsch, "The Sirach 51 Acrostic: Confession and Exhortation," *ZAW* 94 (1982) 400–409, here 403; Eric D. Reymond, "Sirach 51:13–30 and 11Q5 (= 11QPsª) 21.11–22.1," *RevQ* 23 (2007) 207–31, here 223; W. Th. van Peursen presents a number of arguments that lead him to conclude that Sir 51:13–30 can only be a retranslation from Syriac ("Sirach 51:13–30 in Hebrew and Syriac," in *Hamlet on a Hill: Semitic and Greek Studies Presented to Professor T. Muraoka on the Occasion of His Sixty-Fifth Birthday* [ed. M. F. J. Baasten and W. Th. van Peursen; OLA 118; Leuven: Peeters, 2003] 357–74, here 366, 369–70).

17. According to *Dictionary of Classical Hebrew* (ed. David J. A. Clines; 9 vols.; Sheffield: Sheffield Academic Press, 1993–2016) 4:332: "sitting of teacher, i.e., teaching."

18. The Greek has παιδεία.

19. Van Peursen, "Sirach 51:13–30," 366–67: "The original Hebrew text may have read תשמח נפשכם בישועתו, 'may your soul rejoice in His salvation' (cf. Isa 25:9) . . .

Finally, an additional argument in favor of the metaphorical option should be pointed out. In Cave 11 of Qumran, a part of an alphabetical song has been found that corresponds with Sir 51:13–20, 30 on a number of points and appears to be a much more authentic version with a strongly erotic character.[20] In that acrostic, a young man who has entered into a relationship with a young woman is speaking. The young woman—Wisdom—is presented as his teacher and lover. So, this acrostic is certainly an allegory, which, reinforced by the Sirach passage, could be considered additional evidence in favor of the metaphorical interpretation of "house of teaching" and "teaching chair."

■ III. Whom Is Ben Sira Addressing Anyway?

Like the Book of Proverbs, Ben Sira's writing is addressed to בני ("my son"). In Proverbs, the address בני appears twenty-three times, and one could easily maintain that it is a word that should be interpreted in the context of the family.[21] That is to say, the content of the book comes from the mouths of a father and a mother. In relation to the Book of Ben Sira, this is very unlikely to be the case. For in that document, there are twenty-one unmistakable references to the disciple who is addressed and instructed by the wisdom teacher.

Strikingly enough, this is indirectly confirmed by the Greek translation of both Proverbs and Sirach. First of all, the possessive pronoun "my" in the Hebrew form of address בני is not copied in the Greek translation of either work. As a result, the family relationship is already somewhat diluted. Then it is telling how the noun בן is represented. In the Greek translation of the Book of Proverbs this appears as υἱέ ("son"), while, in

---

'from a reconstructed בישועתו we can explain both the reading in G (ἔλεος being a translation equivalent for ישועה also elsewhere in Ben Sira) and the reading in B (as a textual corruption, be it via Syriac or not)."'

20. For recent, extensive studies with full bibliography, see Reymond, "Sir 51:13–30"; and Émile Puech, "La Sagesse dans les Béatitudes de Ben Sira: Étude du texte de Si 51,13–30 et de Si 14,20–15,10," in *The Texts and Versions of the Book of Ben Sira: Transmission and Interpretation* (ed. Jean-Sébastien Rey and Jan Joosten; JSJSup 150; Leiden: Brill, 2011) 297–329.

21. R. N. Whybray, *Proverbs: Based on the Revised Standard Version* (NCBC; Grand Rapids: Eerdmans,1994) 37, with reference to Prov 1:8; 6:20; 31:1: ". . . the reference to the mother's teaching side by side with that of the father . . . makes a family setting plausible."

the translation of Jesus Sirach's grandson it is τέκνον ("child").²² The first is more specifically masculine compared to the second, which has a common gender.²³

Thus, the writings of Jesus Sirach fit into the long and venerable traditions of the ancient Near East in which it is primarily the student rather than the blood relative who is addressed as "my son."²⁴

▪ IV. Moving to a Representative Passage

It is now high time to show, by means of a continuous passage from the Book of Ben Sira, the way in which the Jerusalem scholar works. An illustrative example can be found in Sir 6:18–37, which—coincidentally or not—has twenty-two lines, exactly the same number as the acrostic in Sir 51:13–30, with which it also has a remarkable number of connections.²⁵ A problem is immediately apparent, however. Only the last two words of Sir 6:18 have been preserved in Hebrew (חכמה תשיג, "you will gain wisdom"). Further, and rather strangely, there is no v. 34 in the Greek translation, to correspond to the Hebrew text of this verse.

Here we come across a phenomenon that is constantly present in the study of the Book of Jesus Sirach. Only about 70 percent of the work has been preserved in the Hebrew form, so that the oldest complete Ben Sira text is available only in Greek translation.²⁶ But this oldest Greek text (the so-called *Greek I*) has been expanded over the course of the first two centuries on a number of points (the so-called *Greek II*) with verses that either wanted to give a meaning or nuance different from the original translation, on the one hand, or, on the other, that wanted to draw more

---

22. Υἱέ occurs twenty-seven times as a form of address in Proverbs; τέκνον eighteen times as a form of address in Jesus Sirach.

23. This is, however, denied by Georg Fohrer, "υἱός," *TDNT* 8:353.

24. Otto Plöger, *Sprüche Salomos (Proverbia)* (BKAT 17; Neukirchen-Vluyn: Neukirchener Verlag, 1984) 14: "Die Anrede 'Mein Sohn,' in altorientalischen Weisheitstexten des Nillandes und Mesopotamiens ebenfalls bezeugt, hat einen fiktiven Adressaten im Auge, gleichsam das Modell eines Schülers, aber sie ist der Wirklichkeit abgelauscht."

25. See especially Franz Böhmisch, "Ein Liebesgedicht eines jüdischen Weisheitslehrers auf seine Jugendliebe (Sir 30-51,13)," *Biblisches Forum: Zeitschrift für Theologie aus biblischer Perspektive* 1 (2000) 1–19, esp. 9–11.

26. For details of the Hebrew manuscripts and their location, see Pancratius C. Beentjes, *The Book of Ben Sira in Hebrew. A Text Edition of all Extant Hebrew Manuscripts and a Synopsis of all Parallel Hebrew Ben Sira Texts* (VTSup 68; Leiden: Brill, 1997; Atlanta: Society of Biblical Literature, 2006) 13–19.

attention to a certain theme, for example, that of individual eschatology, than was the case in the original Hebrew.[27] Since, moreover, the grandson's Greek text is not a meticulous translation but is, at times, rather free, it is impossible to translate missing verses or passages back into Hebrew.[28]

Moreover, in the Hebrew text between 6:22 and 6:23 we find two verses that may be identified as Sir 27:5–6 and have no corresponding translation in the Greek text.[29] Finally, it should be mentioned that some small fragments from 6:13–31 have been found at Qumran (2Q18 [2QSir]), which may indicate the importance of this particular passage.

■ V. The Pedagogue Takes the Floor

A passage that, in my opinion, provides a representative portrait of Ben Sira as an educator, may be found in Sir 6:18–37. It is a passage that could certainly be described as characteristic. It consists of three parts (vv. 18–22, 23–31, and 32–37), each of which opens with the address "my son/child," thus creating three explicit moments of attention.[30]

> 18 [My child, from your youth choose discipline [παιδεία]
>   and when you have grey hair] you will attain Wisdom.[31]
> 19 As ploughing and reaping, draw near to her
>   and await the abundance of her crops,
>   because in her cultivation you will work a little,
>   and tomorrow you will eat her fruit.
> 20 A steep path is she to the fool.
>   The one who lacks understanding will not persevere in her.

---

27. A fine example is Conleth Kearns, *The Expanded Text of Ecclesiasticus: Its Teaching on the Future Life as a Clue to Its Origin* (ed. Pancratius C. Beentjes; DCLS 11; Berlin: De Gruyter, 2011).

28. The most comprehensive study on this subject is from Benjamin G. Wright, *No Small Difference: Sirach's Relationship to Its Hebrew Parent Text* (SCS 26; Atlanta: Scholars' Press, 1989).

29. This insertion also leads to confusion in comments on the counting of the verses after 6:22–23.

30. The literature on Sir 6:18–37 is enormous. See, among others, the bibliography at Johannes Marböck, *Jesus Sirach 1–23* (HTKAT; Freiburg: Herder, 2010) 116; Jesse Rogers, "As Ploughing and Reaping Draw Near to Her: A Reading of Sirach 6:18–37," *OTE* 13 (2000) 364–79.

31. Text in square brackets is a translation from the Greek text in the absence of a Hebrew text. Translation of the Hebrew of 6:18b–22, 25, 27–31, 32–37 is from Rogers, "As Ploughing and Reaping Draw Near," 370–71.

> 21 She will be like a burdensome stone upon him
> and he will not hesitate in casting her aside.
> 22 For Discipline [מוסר], as her name, so she is,
> and she is not obvious to many. (Sir 6:18–22)

In the final verse of the first section (v. 22) it is striking that the Hebrew (and Syriac) text talks about discipline (מוסר) and education (ܡܪܕܘܬܐ), while the Greek translation gives σοφία ("wisdom"). The line in the Greek text runs from παιδεία (v. 18a) to σοφία (v. 22a), while the Hebrew text apparently wants to emphasize an *inclusio* on the term מוסר. The Greek translator is most likely guided by the conclusion of v. 18 (wisdom) and the metaphor in v. 19 (harvests, fruits) which will be fully developed in chapter 24:19–22.[32] It is also possible that the conclusion of v. 22 ("not easily accessible") played a role in this, as the same word in Prov 8:9 can be heard from the mouth of Our Lady Wisdom. It seems that the grandson uses παιδεία and σοφία as interchangeable terms here, something that will be the case again later on in the text.

> 23 [Listen, my child, and accept my judgment;
> do not reject my counsel.
> 24 Put your feet into her fetters,
> and your neck into her collar.]
> 25 Stoop your shoulder and carry her
> and do not be vexed at her bonds.
> 26 [Come to her with all your soul,
> and keep her ways with all your might.]
> 27 Search out and seek, look for and find,
> and when you grasp her, do not let her go,
> 28 For in the end you will find her resting place
> and she will be transformed into delight for you.
> 29 Her net will become your strong foundation
> and her rope, garments of fine gold.
> 30 Her yoke will be an ornament of gold
> and bonds a purple cord.[33]
> 31 As garments of glory you will wear her
> and put her on as a crown of splendour. (Sir 6:23–31)

---

32. See Pancratius C. Beentjes, "'Come to me, you who desire me . . .': Lady Wisdom's Invitation in Ben Sira 24:19–22," in *Weisheit als Lebensgrundlage: Festschrift für Friedrich V. Reiterer zum 65. Geburtstag* (ed. Renate Egger-Wenzel, Karin Schöpflin and Johannes Friedrich Diehl; DCLS 15; Berlin: De Gruyter, 2013) 1–11.

33. The Hebrew word for chain (מוֹסָר) creates a beautiful word game with the central theme of discipline (מוּסָר).

After Ben Sira has made it clear in the first part that it is really not easy to submit to discipline/teaching, but that it will lead to great results, he then urges the student in the second part to take his advice fully to heart and to put all his efforts into finding Lady Wisdom and to come all the way into her sphere of influence, literally, to be weighed down by her.

And what is promised after all these efforts, does not fail to materialize: not only pleasure but also the most beautiful scenes. The description of these beautiful clothes, on the one hand, reminds us of passages in the Old Testament about the king and the high priest (Exod 28:28), and, on the other, a formulation like a purple cord (v. 30b) acts as an echo of Num 15:38—that thread on the hem of their clothes is a visible sign to remind the Israelites of all the commandments of Yhwh and to observe them.

Moreover, it is certainly no coincidence that a crown of splendor (v. 31b) returns once more in Ben Sira's book, in the description of Aaron (45:12). This high priest plays an extremely important role in the work, because, according to Ben Sira, the royal rule (in addition to the priestly one?) has also passed to Aaron and his descendants.[34]

Didactically, this argument has so far been very cleverly put together. It illustrates that it does indeed pay to have to endure unpleasant things sometimes. In the end, it is argued, they are the perfect fit for the most beautiful panoramas.

> 32 If you wish, my son, you will become wise[35]
>   and if you set your heart on it you will become prudent.
> 33 If you are willing to listen [you will gain]
>   and incline your ear, you will be instructed.[36]
> 34 [Stand in the company of the elders.
>   Who is wise? Attach yourself to such a one.]
> 35 Be eagerly inclined to hear every meditation,
>   and let no wise proverb escape you.
> 36 If you see someone with understanding, seek him diligently;
>   let your feet wear away the threshold.
> 37 Attend to the fear of the Most High
>   and on his commandments meditate continuously.

---

34. For detailed information on this, see P. C. Beentjes, "The Book of Ben Sira: Some New Perspectives at the Dawn of the 21st Century," in *Goochem in Mokum: Wisdom in Amsterdam: Papers on Biblical and Related Wisdom Read at the Fifteenth Joint Meeting of the Society of Old Testament Study and the Oudtestamentisch Werkgezelschap, Amsterdam, July 2012* (ed. George J. Brooke and Pierre Van Hecke; OTS 68; Leiden: Brill, 2016) 1–19, esp. 2–11.
35. The Greek text has παιδευθήσῃ.
36. The Greek text has σοφὸς ἔσῃ.

> Then he will instruct your heart
> and he will give you the wisdom you desire. (Sir 6:32–37)

The third part is in fact the practical implementation: listen and look carefully, make sure you are present in the right place, deal with the right people. And, as always in his writings, this passage ends by emphasizing the fear of the Most High, the central theme of the wisdom book with no fewer than fifty-two places where it may be found.[37] The English noun "fear," however, has a very negative connotation, which is completely absent in the setting of Ben Sira's book. In addition, the alternative "awe for God" does not really reflect the essence of this biblical expression. Perhaps "sincere faith in God" is the best description.[38]

The passage that gives by far the best explanation of what the fear of the Lord/awe for God means, may be found almost at the beginning of the book, in Sir 1:11–30:[39]

> 11 The fear of the Lord is glory and exultation,
>   and gladness and a crown of rejoicing.
> 12 The fear of the Lord delights the heart,
>   and gives gladness and joy and long life.
> 13 Those who fear the Lord will have a happy end;
>   on the day of their death, they will be blessed.
> 14 To fear the Lord is the beginning of wisdom;
>   She is created with the faithful in the womb.
> 15 She made among human beings an eternal foundation,
>   and among their descendants she will abide faithfully.
> 16 To fear the Lord is fullness of wisdom;
>   she inebriates mortals with her fruits;
> 17 She fills their whole house with desirable goods,
>   and their storehouses with her produce.
> [...]

---

37. The most extensive treatment of this subject is that of Josef Haspecker, *Gottesfurcht bei Jesus Sirach: Ihre religiöse Struktur und ihre literarische und doktrinäre Bedeutung* (AnBib 30; Rome: Pontifical Biblical Institute, 1967).

38. Renate Egger-Wenzel, "'Faith in God' rather than 'Fear of God' in Ben Sira and Job: A Necessary Adjustment in Terminology and Understanding," in *Intertextual Studies in Ben Sira and Job: Essays in Honor of Alexander A. Di Lella, O.F.M.* (ed. Jeremy Corley and Vincent Skemp; CBQMS 38; Washington, DC: Catholic Biblical Association of America, 2005) 211–26.

39. Alexander A. Di Lella, "Fear of the Lord as Wisdom: Ben Sira 1:11–30," in *The Book of Ben Sira in Modern Research: Proceedings of the First International Ben Sira Conference, 28–31 July 1996, Soesterberg, Netherlands* (ed. Pancratius C. Beentjes; BZAW 255; Berlin: De Gruyter, 1997) 113–33.

25 In the treasuries of wisdom are wise sayings,
   but godliness is an abomination to a sinner.
26 If you desire wisdom, keep the commandments,
   and the Lord will lavish her upon you.
27 For fear of the Lord is wisdom [σοφία] and discipline [παιδεία],
   fidelity and humility are his delight. (NRSV)

With this contribution I wanted to outline how a Jewish teacher in the second century BCE works to educate young people in the spirit of Israel's wisdom traditions. It is therefore hardly surprising that the church father Clement of Alexandria (ca. 150–215 CE) in his book *The Pedagogue* (*ΠΑΙΔΑΓΩΓΟΣ*) explicitly qualifies Jesus Sirach as παιδαγωγός a number of times.[40] And on the basis of the above analysis, it seems to me that this qualification is more than justified.[41]

---

40. Clemens Alexandrinus, *ΠΑΙΔΑΓΩΧΟΣ* II, 10.84, 85, 87 (Migne, *PG* 8:516, 517, 528). The reference "*Pedagog.* II. 10.99" by Francesco Vattioni (*Ecclesiastico: Testo ebraico con apparato critico e versioni greca, latina e siriaca* [Testi 1; Napoli, 1968] xii) is incorrect. In Peters, *Das Buch Jesus Sirach*, xxvi, the references to Migne are also incorrect.

41. The following publications deal with the theme of "Teaching at Ben Sira": Beate Ego, "Im Schatten hellenistischer Bildung: Ben Siras Lern- und Lehrkonzeption zwischen Mündlichkeit und Schriftlichkeit," in *Die Textualisierung der Religion* (ed. Joachim Schaper; FAT 62; Tübingen: Mohr Siebeck, 2009) 203–21. Martin Ebner, "Weisheitslehrer" – eine Kategorie für Jesus? Eine Spurensuche bei Jesus Sirach," in *Der neue Mensch in Christus: Hellenistische Anthropologie und Ethik im Neuen Testament* (ed. Johannes Beutler; QD 190; Freiburg: Herder 2001) 99–119; Benjamin G. Wright, "From Generation to Generation: The Sage as Father in Early Jewish Literature," in *Biblical Traditions in Transmission: Essays in Honour of Michael A. Knibb* (ed. Charlotte Hempel and Judith M. Lieu; JSJSup 111; Leiden: Brill, 2006) 309–32 [reprinted in Benjamin G. Wright, *Praise Israel for Wisdom and Instruction: Essays on Ben Sira and Wisdom, the Letter of Aristeas and the Septuagint* (JSJSup 131; Leiden; Brill, 2008) 25–47]; Benjamin G. Wright, "Ben Sira on the Sage as Exemplar," in Benjamin G. Wright, *Praise Israel for Wisdom and Instruction: Essays on Ben Sira and Wisdom, the Letter of Aristeas and the Septuagint* (JSJSup 131; Leiden: Brill, 2008) 165–82; Katja Tesch, *Weisheitsunterricht bei Ben Sira: Lehrkonzepte im Sirachbuch und ihre Relevanz für heutiges Lernen im Religionsunterricht* (BBB 169; Göttingen: V&R Unipress, 2013); Benjamin G. Wright, "Torah and Sapiential Pedagogy in the Book of Ben Sira," in *Wisdom and Torah: The Reception of "Torah" in the Wisdom Literature of the Second Temple Period* (ed. Bernd U. Schipper and D. Andrew Teeter; JSJSup 163; Leiden: Brill, 2013) 157–86.

5
The Teacher as Reinterpreter of Tradition:
The Son of Man Sayings in the Gospel according to Mark

GEARARD Ó FLOINN

The activity of teaching comprises four separate and interlinked elements: teacher, student(s), subject matter, and methodology. Narrative analysis provides the interpreter with the opportunity to look at a text through the lens of teaching and learning by thinking about who is teaching, who is being taught, what is being taught, and how it is being taught. A narrative-critical reading of the Gospel according to Mark, enables us to imagine the implied author as teacher and the implied readers and hearers as students or learners. The narrative itself becomes the means of communication between these two groupings. It contains within it both the content of what is being taught and the method(s) whereby it is taught. In this contribution, the focus on Mark as teacher directs attention to the teacher as interpreter of tradition, who in the process, expands, adapts, and changes his teaching material to meet the needs of his learners. This essay will show how Mark accomplishes this task in the way he deals with the Son of Man sayings, where his initial impulse is to reiterate the tradition and then to juxtapose it with other, often different, even contradictory material. It was Werner H. Kelber who drew attention to Mark's strategic placing of the Son of Man sayings throughout his Gospel.[1] Second, juxtaposition has been identified by

---

1. In the words of Werner H. Kelber, Mark "in part adopted, in part shaped and created, and above all strategically placed the Son of Man sayings throughout the Gospel" ("The Hour of the 'Son of Man' and the Temptation of the Disciples [Mark

Elizabeth Struthers Malbon as a crucial element of Marcan rhetoric. I pay particular attention to this practice in the interpretation of 9:9–13.[2] Mark's approach amounts to a radical re-presentation of the tradition relating to the Son of Man in a way that, for the first time in the New Testament, integrates that tradition with Jesus's fate of crucifixion and death. We may extrapolate that, by adopting this approach, Mark as teacher made it possible, or easier, for his audience to accept a messiah who had suffered and died.

Joel Marcus postulates that in Mark, as in Daniel 7 and the Similitudes of Enoch (*1 Enoch* 37–71), the term "the Son of Man" is a designation for a heavenly apocalyptic figure who functions as revealer, redeemer, and judge.[3] It is easy to see how this one-sided presentation of the Son of Man, untainted by references to suffering and death would have posed a difficulty for the early communities of disciples who may have been scandalized by the fate of Jesus and who, for the same reason, may have resisted accepting him as Messiah. A good teacher will present his or her material in ways that address the needs of the students. If the author of Mark has expanded the traditional portrayal of the Son of Man and rearranged it skillfully to include the concepts of failure and of being treated with contempt, we may assume that this was in line with his judgment of what would be of benefit to his hearers and readers.

In this essay, I investigate the role of teacher as interpreter of tradition. I focus exclusively on Mark's Son of Man sayings as his reworking of traditions received by him. I begin with some preliminary remarks on the term "the Son of Man" by way of background. I then categorize the occurrences of the term in Mark into three groups: first, where the expression is spoken of in terms of exaltation only; second, where glory and rejection are presented side by side; and third, where Jesus's ominous fate is referred to without mitigation. I identify two elements of Mark's teaching method: first, the expanding of the traditional teaching to include the new elements of failure and death; and, second, the judicious

---

14:32–42]," in *The Passion in Mark: Studies on Mark 14–16* [ed. Werner H. Kelber; Philadelphia: Fortress, 1976] 41–60, here 51). Summarizing the discussion on the Son of Man and the identity of Jesus, John R. Donahue concludes, "The 'Son of Man' Christology as it is found in Mark is then in a real sense a Markan creation" (*Are You the Christ? The Trial Narrative in the Gospel of Mark* [SBLDS 10; Missoula, MT: Society of Biblical Literature, 1973] 182).

2. Elizabeth Struthers Malbon, "Teaching Mark's Narrative in a Markan Narrative Way," in *Communication, Pedagogy, and the Gospel of Mark* (ed. Elizabeth E. Shively and Geert Van Oyen; Atlanta: Society of Biblical Literature, 2016) 29–43, here 30.

3. Joel Marcus, *Mark: A New Translation with Introduction and Commentary* (2 vols.; AB 27 [New York: Doubleday], AYB 27A [New Haven: Yale University Press], 2000–2009) 1:530.

juxtaposing of old and new elements in a narratively skillful way. I show how these two methods are used to effect in 9:9–13 by way of an object lesson. I finish with some concluding remarks on the content and method of Mark's teaching.

■ I. Preliminary Remarks on the Title "the Son of Man"

Researchers into the term "the Son of Man" are faced with an initial paradox: on the one hand, there is an extensive body of literature dealing with the origins and meanings of the term and its usage in biblical and extrabiblical locations from the postexilic period to the end of the New Testament.[4] On the other hand, a relatively recent German trend displays a good deal of skepticism about the existence of an ancient Jewish Son of Man tradition.[5] The resolution of the paradox may in all probability be explained by the fact that much of the literature has been occasioned by the prominence of the term in the New Testament, which is out of proportion to the place it occupies in the Hebrew Bible and contemporaneous apocryphal literature.

---

4. See Edward Adams, "The Coming of the Son of Man in Mark's Gospel," *TynBul* 56.2 (2005) 39–61; Maurice Casey, *Aramaic Sources of Mark's Gospel* (SNTSMS 102; Cambridge: Cambridge University Press, 1998) 138–92; Maurice Casey, *The Solution to the "Son of Man" Problem* (LNTS 343; London: T&T Clark, 2009); Harry L. Chronis, "To Reveal and to Conceal: A Literary-Critical Perspective on 'the Son of Man' in Mark," *NTS* 51 (2005) 459–81; James D. G. Dunn, "The Danielic Son of Man in the New Testament," in *The Book of Daniel: Composition and Reception* (ed. John J. Collins and Peter W. Flint; 2 vols.; VTSup 83; Leiden: Brill, 2001) 2:528–49; Morna D. Hooker, *The Son of Man in Mark: A Study of the Background of the Term "Son of Man" and Its Use in St Mark's Gospel* (London: SPCK, 1967); J. C. Naluparayil, "Question of Jesus' Identity and the First 'Son of Man' Logion in Mark 2.10," *Bible Bhashyam* 29 (2003) 251–77; Jens Schröter, "The Son of Man as the Representative of God's Kingdom: On the Interpretation of Jesus in Mark and Q," in *Jesus, Mark and Q: The Teaching of Jesus and Its Earliest Record* (ed. Michael Labahn and Andreas Schmidt; JSNTSup 214; Sheffield: Sheffield Academic Press, 2001) 34–68; Christopher M. Tuckett, "The Present Son of Man Sayings," *JSNT* 14 (1982) 58–81.

5. Scholars have argued that the use of the term "the Son of Man" in the Gospels is a major instance of the influence of the early church on the New Testament. See also Stefan Beyerle, "One Like a 'Son of Man': Innuendoes of a Heavenly Individual," in *Enoch and Qumran Origins: New Light on a Forgotten Connection* (ed. Gabriele Boccaccini; Grand Rapids: Eerdmans, 2005) 54–58, here 54. Beyerle cites as a prime example Matthias Kreplin, *Das Selbstverständnis Jesu: Hermeneutische und christologische Reflexion, historisch-kritische Analyse* (WUNT 2/141; Tübingen: Mohr Siebeck, 2001).

It is likely that the literary dependence of Mark on Daniel 7 goes beyond the use of the term in the former to include the literary device of *post eventum* prediction. In Mark, the expression is found exclusively on the lips of Jesus, a phenomenon that highlights its importance for the evangelist.[6] Malbon sees in this phenomenon further evidence of Mark's skill as a teacher. She argues that, since Jesus never states explicitly that he is the Son of Man, the conclusion must be drawn by the implied audience.[7] When this happens, it is a successful outcome for any teacher.

A significant number of the Marcan occurrences of the term (nine of fourteen) occur in the context of this device.[8] The eschatological impetus of Daniel 7 may be behind what Jens Schröter has characterized as the subordination of the titles "Christ" and "Son of God" in Mark to the designation "the Son of Man."[9] That it plays a crucial role in Mark's narrative is beyond doubt.

II. The Son of Man in Mark

Kelber's view that Mark's is the primary influence in the way the Son of Man sayings are created, shaped, and located is shared by Joel Marcus.[10] Whether Mark was the first to make the connection between Jesus and the second of the two superior beings, the one "like a son of man" in Dan 7:13 is difficult to say with certainty. Whether it was in circulation when he was writing is a question for historical critics to address.[11] What we

---

6. See Brian Han Gregg, *The Historical Jesus and the Final Judgment Sayings in Q* (WUNT 2/207; Tübingen: Mohr Siebeck, 2006) 181–82.

7. Elizabeth Struthers Malbon, "Narrative Christology and the Son of Man: What the Markan Jesus Says Instead," *BibInt* 11 (2003) 373–84, here 375.

8. For an account of *ex eventu* prophecy as a literary device, see John J. Collins, *Daniel: With an Introduction to Apocalyptic Literature* (FOTL 20; Grand Rapids: Eerdmans, 1984) 11–12.

9. Schröter concludes that the Christology of Mark (and of Q) is oriented to the expectation of the return of the currently absent Son of Man, Jesus, who commands his disciples to continue his activity in the intervening time ("Son of Man as the Representative," 34–68).

10. Marcus, *Mark 1–8*, 528–32.

11. Adela Yarbro Collins reminds readers that ὁ υἱὸς τοῦ ἀνθρώπου ("the son of the human being") is not a Greek idiom (*Mark: A Commentary* [Hermeneia; Philadelphia: Fortress, 2007] 187–88). She suggests a number of Semitic antecedents for the term, including, in Hebrew, בן אדם and, in Aramaic, בר נשא or בר אנשא. She argues that the use of the term in relation to Jesus implies that he was recognized as the chief agent of God, the Messiah, prefigured in Daniel 7. While in the narrative context of the Gospel the use of the term is ambiguous, especially for gentile Christians, for the informed it would have had the force of acclaiming Jesus as Messiah.

know is that Mark's Gospel is the earliest New Testament document to do so, and that there the linking of both plays a seminal role in the unfolding of the narrative. There the term occurs fourteen times.[12]

The occurrences may be divided into three categories with overlapping membership. In the first one, five occurrences of the expression attest to the exalted status of Jesus without reference to suffering and death (2:10, 28; 8:38; 13:26; 14:62). He has authority on earth to forgive sins (2:10). He is lord of the Sabbath (2:28). Three times he is spoken of in the language of the vision of judgment before the Ancient of Days in Daniel 7 (8:38; 13:26; 14:62) in the so-called three eschatological predictions. In the second category, four occurrences integrate suffering and resurrection (8:31; 9:9, 31; 10:33). The first, third, and fourth of these instances form the three "passion predictions." The remaining occurrence states simply that he will rise from the dead, thereby implying prior death (9:9). The third category comprises five occurrences of the expression where suffering is mentioned without mitigation (9:12; 10:45; 14:21 [2x], 41). Linking the concept of the Son of Man with suffering and death is a central contribution of the Gospel according to Mark to the understanding of Jesus in early Christianity. It is also a crucial element of what he, as teacher, wishes to convey about Jesus. The failure of Jesus on a human level, as we have noted, may have posed difficulties for disciples to accept him as having a God-given role. The failure of the disciples themselves is taken up by Suzanne Watts Henderson as compounding the "failure" of Jesus and potentially causing resistance on the part of some early converts to Christianity.[13] Mark's skillful weaving of antithetical destinies in his treatment of the Son of Man sayings is one way in which it is likely that such early fears where calmed.

■ III. MARK'S STRATEGIC NARRATIVE SEQUENCING OF THE SON OF MAN SAYINGS

Following Kelber's identification of the significance of the strategic placing by Mark of the Son of Man sayings in the Gospel we shall investigate the order in which the sayings are presented in the narrative

---

12. Mark 2:10, 28; 8:32, 38; 9:9, 12, 31; 10:33, 45; 13:26; 14:21 (2x), 41, 67.
13. Henderson argues that any "apparent" failure, whether it is in relation to the disciples, in terms of incomprehension, desertion, or denial or, in relation to Jesus, especially the rejection and humiliation of death on a cross, "becomes subsumed within God's triumphant claim upon the world" (*Christology and Discipleship in the Gospel of Mark* [SNTSMS 135; Cambridge: Cambridge University Press, 2006] 261).

as a lens through which Mark's teaching method may be more fully examined.

The first two times that the reader encounters the title the Son of Man (2:10, 28), it is predicated of him that he has authority to forgive sins and is lord of the Sabbath, respectively. These two occurrences stand apart from the rest on several counts. They are the only two sayings that fall into the Galilean section of the Gospel. In portraying the subject in the terms they do, they are notably in keeping with the traditional teaching on the subject found in Daniel 7 insofar as they attest to this figure's exalted status. Craig A. Evans points out that the combination of ἐξουσία ("authority") and ὁ υἱὸς τοῦ ἀνθρώπου ("the son of the human one") provides an intertextual link between them.[14] Adela Yarbro Collins sums up the author's achievement in the use of the phrase thus: ὁ υἱὸς τοῦ ἀνθρώπου may be said to mean that Jesus had the authority to forgive sins on earth, "because he is the chief agent of God, the Messiah prefigured in Daniel 7."[15] These sayings are sometimes referred to as present sayings, since they are spoken about in the present tense and refer to Jesus's current status.[16] However, the elevated language employed in them would appear to anticipate the glory of the exalted Jesus of the future. From the narrative perspective, the initial impression made in the first of these sayings and reiterated in the second is that the author is familiar with the traditional imagery of the Son of Man and is happy to confirm it. From the pedagogical point of view, we may claim that the author, as teacher, is beginning with what is already known (and presumably shared) by his students.

The third and fourth sayings (8:31, 38) may be considered together here, not least because they occur in the same literary unit (8:27–9:1). Each occurs as part of a prediction, the third as an element of the first so-called passion prediction and the fourth as a constituent of the first so-called eschatological prediction. The third saying predicts the suffering

---

14. Craig A. Evans, *Mark 8:27–16:20* (WBC 34B; Nashville: Thomas Nelson, 2001) 202.

15. Yarbro Collins, *Mark*, 189.

16. Christopher M. Tuckett distinguishes between those sayings that have a present frame of reference and those with a future one ("The Present 'Son of Man' Sayings," *JSNT* 14 [1982] 58-81, here 70). He places these two sayings in the former category. He argues, nevertheless, that they contain a hint of the future suffering of Jesus. He bases this claim on his assumption that most of the present Son of Man sayings in Q, as in Mark, are not so much about the present authority of Jesus as about rejection and suffering. While this contention has some validity since the other three present sayings (14:21 [twice] and 14:41) are couched in ominous language, I am not convinced that this applies to these first two.

and death of the Son of Man preceding resurrection; the fourth foretells his return in the glory of his Father. They are the first two of seven Son of Man sayings that are situated in the short section of Mark's Gospel (8:22–10:52) that divides the Galilean and Jerusalem halves of the work. From the narrative point of view, the first passion prediction has a bombshell effect on the reader despite the familiarity of the Gospel text. Pedagogically, being the effective teacher that he is, the author moves from the known to the not-yet known. Although the ultimate glorious destination of the Son of Man is affirmed in this saying, for the first time, the audience is confronted with imagery that sharply contrasts with the Danielic tradition. For the first time in Mark and most likely, for the first time in the tradition, the Son of Man is linked with the threefold ominous fate of suffering, rejection, and death. Resistance to this new teaching is present in the text itself. It is not entirely clear whether Peter is objecting to the idea of suffering and death in relation to Jesus on a personal level or to the combining of the concept of the Son of Man with suffering and death, albeit in a fusion that ends in resurrection.[17] The fact that these three images contain references to suffering juxtaposed with resurrection gives us an insight into Mark's teaching method. That method of juxtaposition is applied once again in the fourth saying in 8:38 with its unadulterated image of glory and its clear verbal evocations of the vision of Daniel 7.

The third pairing of sayings (9:9, 12) continues Mark's pattern of combining death and resurrection, both within and between sayings. The first of these, which is the fifth occurrence of the term "the Son of Man" in Mark speaks explicitly about rising from the dead in a subordinate temporal clause. While semantically the emphasis is on resurrection, the author's phrasing joins rising and death in a symbiotic relationship. The sixth saying is introduced with exquisite skill by Mark. This occurrence will be investigated more thoroughly in the final section of this essay. It speaks only of the suffering of the Son of Man. It is the first occurrence

---

17. For examples of scholarship that reflects the former notion, see Daniel J. Harrington, "Mark," in *The New Jerome Biblical Commentary* (ed. Raymond E. Brown, Joseph A. Fitzmyer, and Roland E. Murphy; Englewood Cliffs, NJ: Prentice Hall, 1990) 596–629, esp. 657; C. E. B. Cranfield, *The Gospel according to Saint Mark* (Cambridge Greek Testament for Schools and Colleges; Cambridge: Cambridge University Press, 1959) 280. The alternative position is taken by Wilfrid J. Harrington (*Mark* [NTM 4; Dublin: Veritas, 1979] 122) and Ezra P. Gould (*A Critical and Exegetical Commentary on the Gospel according to St. Mark* [ICC; Edinburgh: T&T Clark, 1922] 155). For Edward J. Mally, it is not a matter of either/or, but rather of both/and ("Mark," in *The Jerome Biblical Commentary* [ed. Raymond E. Brown, Joseph A. Fitzmyer, and Roland E. Murphy; Englewood Cliffs, NJ: Prentice Hall, 1968] 21–61, here 53).

of the term that is not mitigated by reference to resurrection or glory. It has taken the author of the Gospel five earlier sayings before he presents the term "the Son of Man" in ominous terms only. Granted, in this instance, the saying occurs during the descent of the mountain where the events portrayed there have been described as an enthronement,[18] and it is found in proximity to the reference to rising from the dead. The author's incremental placing of references to death and resurrection side by side is evidence of the consistency of his pedagogical methodology.

The seventh and eighth sayings (9:31; 10:33), namely, the second and third so-called passion predictions, both contain references to death and resurrection as the first one did. The ninth saying (10:45) explicitly speaks about the Son of Man's giving his life, in terms that could be translated as to give up his life (in death).[19] If the latter interpretation is preferred, the saying reiterates the sixth saying (9:12) in that it speaks about death without mentioning resurrecting. However, there is a difference here that is significant. The protagonist gives or gives up his own life in a reflexive sense, which identifies him as the subject of the verb.[20] From a narrative perspective, the incremental nature of the author's juxtaposing of suffering and death reaches its climax in this saying.[21] His pedagogical methodology has been evident in the last seven occurrences of the term "the Son of Man," all of which occur with a notable level of concentration in the short transitional or middle section of the Gospel narrative.

The final five Son of Man sayings occur in the second half of Mark's narrative, which is set in Jerusalem against the background of the last

---

18. Adrian Wypadlo, *Die Verklärung Jesu nach dem Markusevangelium: Studien zu einer christologischen Legitimationserzählung* (WUNT 308; Tübingen: Mohr Siebeck, 2013) 41. See also Philipp Vielhauer, "Erwägungen zur Christologie des Markusevangeliums," in Vielhauer, *Aufsätze zum Neuen Testament* (TBü 31; Munich: Kaiser, 1965) 199–214.

19. The expression δοῦναι τὴν ψυχήν ("to give the/one's life") is also found in 1 Macc 2:50; 6:44. In a Jewish context, it usually refers to the death of martyrs, and in a Greek milieu to the death of soldiers. See Vincent Taylor, *The Gospel according to St. Mark: The Greek Text with Introduction, Notes, and Indexes* (London: Macmillan, 1963) 444.

20. The sublimity of this action is captured beautifully by Saint Thomas Aquinas (1225–1274) in his hymn *Verbum supernum prodiens* for the Office of Lauds of the Feast of Corpus Christi, by means of the wordplay involved in the verbs *tradere*, and *se tradere*, "to betray" or "to hand over" and "to hand oneself over" or "to give oneself," respectively.

21. Bruce J. Malina and Richard L. Rohrbaugh confirm this interpretation (*Social-Science Commentary on the Synoptic Gospels* [2nd ed.; Minneapolis: Fortress, 2003] 193). They draw attention to the fact that a ransom could take place only if the person being accepted as a ransom were of a higher honor status than those being set free.

days of the life of the protagonist. The first (13:26) and the last (14:62) of these take the form of eschatological predictions with intertextual links to the apocalyptic vision in Daniel 7 and are framed in terms of glory only. Mark 13:26 is situated in a context replete with apocalyptic predictions. The tone of eschatological fear present in many of these predictions stands in contrast to that of exaltation in 13:26.[22] In that sense, it is possible to speak of a juxtaposition of current and future omens, on the one hand, and the splendor of the return of the Son of Man, on the other. The final occurrence of the term in the Gospel contrasts the current captive state of the protagonist with a reiteration of the return of the Son of Man at the right hand of the power and coming with the clouds of heaven ἐκ δεξιῶν καθήμενον τῆς δυνάμεως καὶ ἐρχόμενον μετὰ τῶν νεφελῶν τοῦ οὐρανοῦ, "seated, and from the right of the power, coming with the clouds of heaven" (Mark 14:62). Here, too, the juxtaposition is between the current, weak, and despised state of Jesus and his future majestic state. While the prediction itself is free from any reference to suffering and death, these themes envelop him at this point in the narrative.

The other three references to the Son of Man (14:21 [twice], 41), which are sandwiched between the two just considered, take place while Jesus is eating with the Twelve. All three refer only to suffering and exclude any element of glory. They speak of the Son of Man's going to his ominous destiny, and twice of his betrayal. In all three instances, the present tense is employed with the sense of an imminent future. These last five Son of Man sayings place side by side, in an *a b b b a* arrangement, his glory and his ignominious fate. Mark very skillfully weaves the narrative in a way that combines, for the first time in the New Testament, the rejection by human beings of the Son of Man and his vindication by the divine person at the center of the vision of Dan 7:13–14.

■ IV. MARK 9:9–13: AN OBJECT LESSON IN MARK'S TEACHING METHOD

In this section I take a close look at Mark's content and the teaching method applied by him in his treatment of the term "the Son of Man." I begin by providing a literal translation of the Greek.

---

22. See Gearard Ó Floinn, *The Motif of Containment in the Gospel according to Mark: A Literary-Critical Study* (London: St Pauls, 2018) 109.

And as they were coming down from the mountain
he ordered them
that to no one the things they had seen they should relate
until the son of man from dead ones had arisen.
And the word they grasped to themselves
seeking together what it is the rising from dead.
And they interrogated him saying
that the scribes say
that it is necessary that Elijah first come;
and he spoke to them:
"Elijah is coming first to restore all things.
Indeed, and Elijah is coming first to restore all things.
And how is it written about the Son of Man
that he will suffer many things and be despised?
But I say to you that Elijah has indeed come
And they did to him whatever they wished
as it is written about him." (Mark 9:9–13)

A. *Context of Mark 9:9–13*

Mark 9:9–13 occurs in Mark's middle section (8:22–10:52), which divides the Gospel into two main sections, 1:1–8:21 and 11:1–16:8. The travel narrative, which begins and ends with the healing of a blind man, presents Jesus and his disciples heading toward Jerusalem. They travel first to Bethsaida and then to Caesarea Philippi in northern Galilee, where Peter's confession of Jesus as the Messiah occurs (8:27–30). The pattern of prediction (8:31; 9:31; 10:32–34) and misunderstanding (8:32–33; 9:32–37; 10:35–41) gives this middle section of the Gospel its literary unity. Within this structure a variety of incidents occur, including the transfiguration (9:2–8); teachings on different subjects, especially discipleship (8:34–38; 9:42–49) and the coming of Elijah and the dire fate of the Son of Man (9:9–13). The immediate context of the last-mentioned section is that it is the second of two pericopes that depict the scene on the top of a high mountain and the dialogue during the descent, respectively. It is this latter pericope that is the precise focus here.

B. *Literary Unity of Mark 9:9–13*

The beginning of the literary unit 9:9–13 is signaled by the transition from the summit of the mountain to the descent. The unit consists of a dialogue between the protagonist and his disciples in the form of predictions, questions, and answers. The end of the unit is flagged by the arrival of the party at another place

C. Structure of Mark 9:9–13

Transition → 9:9a → Indication of a spatial change
    9:9b → *First prediction*: Jesus predicts the resurrection of the Son of Man.
    9:10 → Response: the hearers seek its meaning, together.
    9:11 → *Second prediction*: The disciples reiterate the scribes' prediction that Elijah must first come.
    9:12a → Jesus confirms the prediction is being fulfilled.
    9:12b → *Third prediction*: Jesus claims that a written prediction (for which there is no evidence) has foretold that the Son of Man will suffer and be despised.
    9:13 → Jesus confirms that the prediction about Elijah's coming is fulfilled.
    Jesus corroborates that the ominous fate of Elijah has been the subject of a written prediction (for which there is no evidence) and that it has been fulfilled.
Transition → 9:14 → Indication of a spatial change

D. Content of Mark's Teaching on the Son of Man in 9:9–13

The pericope 9:9–13 is an account of a dialogue between Jesus and three of his disciples, Peter, James, and John, as they descend a mountain. It is a tightly organized unit, whose structure provides an insight into Mark's teaching method. It contains three predictions. The first prediction (v. 9) spoken by the protagonist about the Son of Man foretells his death and resurrection, so it is an example of a saying where both suffering and exaltation are spoken of side by side. It is an oral prediction whose fulfillment is still in the future. The second prediction (v. 11) referring to the coming of Elijah, is repeated by the disciples, and its origin is attributed by them to the scribes. This prediction is confirmed by Jesus as being fulfilled in the present time. The protagonist speaks the third prediction (v. 12b), which foretells the suffering and derision of the Son of Man without any redeeming features. It is claimed by him to be the subject of a written prediction. By all accounts, there is no evidence for such a prediction, and it is therefore likely that it has been composed by the author for this occasion. The status of a prediction is enhanced when it is identified as a written prediction. The pericope continues with a confirmation by Jesus that the second prediction foretelling Elijah's return has already been fulfilled. It ends with a new claim, namely, that it was foretold that Elijah would meet a frightful fate, that that prediction has now been fulfilled, and that it had the additional status of having been committed to writing.

E. Mark's Teaching Methodology in 9:9–13

This passage illustrates Mark's teaching methodology perhaps more than any other passage in the Gospel. At its center is the juxtaposing of the scriptural prediction of the return of Elijah with another prediction foretelling the suffering of the Son of Man, totally at variance with the tradition that has most likely been composed by the evangelist. By using the expression ἐκ νεκρῶν ἀναστῇ ("from dead [ones] will have arisen") in 9:9, the author confirms that the Son of Man will die. This is the second time such an outcome is foretold in the Gospel. It is a reiteration of the first passion prediction in 8:31, and, like that first reference, it also includes the element of resurrection. The clear emphasis here is on the final word ἀναστῇ ("[he] will have arisen"). The fact that it occurs in a subordinate clause makes it easy to miss the significance of what is happening. The author clearly intends to communicate that fulfillment is certain. The expression εἰ μὴ ὅταν ("until after") indicates a temporal rather than a conditional formulation. The prohibition from speaking about the transfiguration will be removed when, not if, the Son of Man rises from the dead. The allusion to the Son of Man in 9:9 is sandwiched between two references to Elijah, the first in 9:5 on the mountain and the second in the prediction at 9:11 as precursor of another person or event.[23]

Because of the stature of Elijah in Jewish tradition, the juxtaposition by Mark of the prediction of the death and resurrection of the Son of Man with the prediction of Elijah's return enhances the status of the former. In this way, the second reference in the Gospel to the Son of Man's death is mitigated. The expectation of a return of Elijah is articulated in Mal 4:5 (3:23 LXX): "I will send you Elijah, the prophet, before the great and terrible day of the Lord comes." James D. G. Dunn suggests that the popularity of the return of Elijah in Ben Sira and the Gospels may connect with the belief that he was translated to heaven without having

---

23. Bart J. Koet refers to the fact that the verb συζητέω ("to examine together") is used in Mark always in the context of a deliberation about the meaning of Scriptures ("Markus 12,28–34: Übereinstimmung über das Wichtigste," in *The Scriptures in the Gospels* [ed. Christopher M. Tuckett; BETL 131; Leuven: Peeters, 1997] 513–23). Here that is also the case. It is likely that this usage is an antecedent of the use of דרש in later Rabbinic Hebrew.

died.[24] Jesus's confirmation that this prediction is currently being fulfilled increases the status of the former prediction by association.

No text from the Hebrew Bible refers directly to the suffering of the Son of Man.[25] In making his claim in 9:12a, the author puts a new teaching into Jesus's mouth. While it is only the second time in the Gospel where the negative fate of the Son of Man is flagged, it is the first time where this fate is presented in terms unadulterated with references to glory or resurrection. We could almost say that, by enveloping this newly composed prediction between two confirmations that the foretelling of Elijah's return is being and has been fulfilled, respectively, the author wishes to play down the explosive nature of what he has put on the lips of Jesus about the ominous fate of the Son of Man. By conferring on this saying the status of a written prediction with the words πῶς γέγραπται ("how is it written?"), Mark deftly alters the accepted teaching on the status and destiny of the Son of Man, thereby presenting a teaching that is of central importance for his Gospel. By his strategic positioning of this prediction, Mark makes it easier for his audience to accept the teaching of a Messiah who suffered, was rejected, and rose from the dead.

■ V. Conclusion

In this essay I argued that the lens of teaching and learning was a useful one from which to examine the Gospel according to Mark for the insight it provides into the author's dealing with the traditional teaching about the Son of Man that he had inherited. There is formal evidence that the apocalyptic vision of Daniel 7 and some of the Son of Man sayings are linked intertextually. In the former text, the one "like a son of man" is depicted in terms of exaltation. He is the second of two heavenly beings, who stands beside the other one who possesses divine-like status. From this link we may conclude that at least one of the strands of the teaching about the Son of Man that was handed on to the author involved glorification. Two elements of Mark's teaching method may be observed. The first involves presenting the traditional teaching about the Son of Man and expanding it with new elements. In this regard, we may say that the

---

24. James D. G. Dunn, *Did the First Christians Worship Jesus? The New Testament Evidence* (Louisville: Westminster John Knox, 2010) 86–87. The implication is that Elijah was keeping himself in readiness to return at a time that God would choose.

25. Yarbro Collins observes that scholars are divided about whether γέγραπται is intended to refer to a specific text, and those who concur that it does are divided about which text (*Mark*, 413).

author is reinterpreting the tradition to meet the needs of a new situation. This is what Mark does in a series of strategically placed movements. He begins with reiterating the tradition in the first half of his Gospel set in Galilee, which contains the first two sayings. The Son of Man has power on earth to forgive sins and is lord of the Sabbath. In the middle section of the Gospel, with the journey motif as backdrop, a change occurs. This glorified image of the Son of Man is expanded to include the themes of suffering and death, themes that in the first instance appear to contradict the tradition. In a judiciously arranged concentration of seven occurrences of the expression, four contain combinations of death and glory, two refer to an ominous fate without mitigation, while one is phrased in terms of resurrection only. In the second half of the Gospel, which takes place against the background of the final days of Jesus's life, the ratio of glory to rejection is reversed: three sayings speak of suffering only, and two of glorification only.

The second element in Mark's teaching method is the device of juxtaposition. It may be observed particularly clearly in the 9:9–13, where for the first time in the Gospel, suffering and contempt are predicated of the Son of Man without any reference to exaltation. The rhetoric of juxtaposition is so skillfully accomplished that this happens almost imperceptibly as far as the audience is concerned. It occurs in the narrative without any observable response. A prediction whose fulfillment lies in the future is placed beside an already fulfilled prediction, thereby encouraging the audience to expect that the former will be brought about with equal certainty. A prediction that has been composed by the author for his own literary purposes is placed beside a prediction that enjoys the status of having been committed to writing and, so to speak, basks in the reflected glory of the latter. A prediction prefiguring the suffering and rejection of the Son of Man ends on a word of resurrection.

The content of Mark's teaching is the inclusion of references to Jesus's passion and death in the exalted tradition of the Son of Man that he had received. He expresses this combination as a divine necessity, communicated by the impersonal δεῖ ("it is necessary") of the first passion prediction in 8:31 and of the return of Elijah in 9:11. Interpreting tradition and, in the process, expanding and altering the teaching he had inherited, as a good teacher does to meet the needs of his students, reveal the author of Mark to be a teacher of skill whose teaching would have made it easier for his audience to integrate the failure of Jesus on a human level and, by extension, the failure of his disciples, and their own failure with the kingdom of God.

6

Asking Questions as the Beginning of Being a Teacher:

Jesus as a Student in Luke 2:46

BART J. KOET

If you are a parent, and your child comes home from school, what do you ask your child? It turns out that Dutch parents mainly ask whether it was fun. Chinese mothers would ask whether the child had achieved high grades. According to German friends, they would ask whether a child had been good. A student from England told me that in the U.K. they might ask a child whether they had fought. And what would—we shall move to another category—Jewish parents ask? They would inquire whether the child had asked good questions.[1] Although these are caricatures somewhat, posing the question does help to shed new light on a passage from the New Testament, namely, the one about Jesus as a child in the Jerusalem temple (Luke 2:40–52): Jesus asking questions is part of a Jewish tradition.

The purpose of this contribution is to investigate whether the passage in which Jesus sits in the temple as a child among the teachers in Luke 2:40–52 says anything about his later teaching. Does the way Jesus is presented as a disciple in that passage also say something about how he

---

1. For an example of this in the contemporary Jewish tradition, see Jonathan Sacks, "The Necessity of Asking Questions" (blog online; https://rabbisacks.org/covenant-conversation/bo/the-necessity-of-asking-questions/, last modified January 30, 2017; accessed December 12, 2024) and Jonathan Sacks, "Pesach" (blog online; https://rabbisacks.org/ceremony-celebration-family-edition/pesach-family-edition/, last modified April 12, 2022; accessed December 12, 2024).

will be as a teacher? In the first section, I outline briefly the way in which "teacher" is one of Jesus's most important titles. Then I go into the issue of whether the child Jesus is a teacher or a disciple in the temple. In the last two paragraphs, I elaborate on how in the Gospel of Luke an organic development in the asking of questions may be traced. It begins with the portrayal of Jesus as a disciple who asks questions and ends with the asking of questions becoming a characteristic feature of Jesus the teacher.

■ I. Gospel as Narrative Pedagogy

Another important aspect of Jesus's teaching is the way he learns. The Gospels sometimes explicitly say something about Jesus's teaching. There is no extensive discussion, however, about the pedagogy of Jesus. A caveat in a reconstruction of Jesus's teaching is the distance in time and therefore also of presuppositions in teaching and tutorship between the time of Jesus and the twenty-first century.[2] Nevertheless, we can reconstruct some of his pedagogical principles with some caution, by identifying and considering the phenomenon of narrative pedagogy. In an earlier work, I typified narrative pedagogy as an approach to teaching and learning that uses story to provide insights and to resolve dilemmas.[3]

This is in fact a rather classical way of teaching. Plato talks about Socrates and shows how the latter unfolds his teaching in his encounters. It is obvious that a story evokes very different reactions from a scientific treatise or a textbook.[4] Moreover, sometimes it is easier to address the different sides of a problem in a story than in another way.

The Gospel is a story about Jesus in which it is made clear by means of a narrative how Jesus is a teacher.[5] That story, however, also shows

---

2. Samuel Byrskog says that the Gospels are not pedagogy, but above all revelation history ("Das Lernen der Jesusgeschichte," in *Religiöses Lernen in der biblischen, frühjüdischen und frühchristlichen Überlieferung* [ed. Beate Ego and Helmut Merkel; WUNT 180; Tübingen: Mohr Siebeck, 2005] 191–209, here 192). I think it can be both.

3. I have written about this more extensively in Dutch; see Bart J. Koet, "Theo Thijssen en de mythe van het 'Nieuwe Leren,'" *Tijdschrift voor Humanistiek* 9 (2008) 75–82. Theo Thijssen was a Dutch teacher and novelist who was influential in the study of pedagogy in the Netherlands. An English-speaking counterpart is Frank McCourt, *Teacher Man: A Memoir* (New York: Scribner, 2005).

4. I cannot elaborate on this in this context. In philosophy, Martha C. Nussbaum advocates considering literature as a special form of philosophy (*Love's Knowledge: Essays on Philosophy and Literature* [Oxford: Oxford University Press, 1990]).

5. Rainer Riesner even states that the didactics of Jesus is one of the origins of the

that Jesus himself tells stories to make his teachings clear. Storytelling is one of the ways Jesus teaches (see Luke 15:3–7, 8–10, 11–32; 16:1–13; and so forth). Another way is to give summaries (Mark 12:28–34). Jesus also teaches by presenting proverbs or collections of proverbs to people (Matthew 5–7; Luke 6:20–38).[6]

In the Gospels, there are also all kinds of teaching situations that can be further investigated. We could see, for example, the places where Jesus teaches—in the temple, on the mountain, in the field, in the synagogue, but also at the table. By showing how to eat together, Jesus elucidates something of his doctrine. An interesting perspective could also be the investigation of the relationship between teaching or proclaiming, on the one hand, and healing, on the other At various places in Luke-Acts we encounter discussions about the relationship between learning and doing.[7] This relationship becomes an important theme in the later rabbinic tradition.[8]

In this contribution I will focus on just one element of Luke's vision of Jesus as a disciple and as a teacher, namely, the asking of questions.

■ II. LUKE 2:41–52

As I have discussed before, the structure of Luke 1–2 is clear.[9] There is a remarkable parallel between the announcement (1:5–25, 26–38), the birth,

---

Jesus lore (*Jesus als Lehrer: Eine Untersuchung zum Ursprung der Evangelien-Überlieferung* [WUNT 2/7; Tübingen: Mohr-Siebeck, 1988] 499–500).

6. Not only is Jesus a teacher, but John the Baptist is also meant—even from birth—to be a teacher. See my "Elijah as Reconciler of Father and Son: From 1 Kings 16:34 and Malachi 3:22–24 to Ben Sira 48:1–11 and Luke 1:13–17," in *Rewriting Biblical History: Essays on Chronicles and Ben Sira in Honour of Pancratius C. Beentjes* (ed. Jeremy Corley and Harm W. van Grol; DCLS 7; Berlin: de Gruyter, 2011) 173–90.

7. For an example of this discussion in Luke-Acts, see Bart J. Koet, "Luke 10:38–42 and Acts 6:1–7: A Lucan Diptych on Diakonia," in *Studies in the Greek Bible: Essays in Honor of Francis T. Gignac, S.J.* (ed. Jeremy Corley and Vincent Skemp; CBQMS 44; Washington, DC: Catholic Biblical Association of America, 2008) 163–85.

8. Following Jesus is an example of the ideal that the life of the teacher is shared with the disciples. In *b. Ber.* 62a it is recounted that even a joint toilet visit with the teacher is learning Torah because one can learn from the example of the teacher how to do this best.

9. See Bart J. Koet, "Simeons Worte (Lk 2,29–32.34c-35) und Israels Geschick," in *The Four Gospels, 1992: Festschrift Frans Neirynck* (ed. F. Van Segbroeck, Christopher M. Tuckett, G. Van Belle, and J. Verheyden; 3 vols.; BETL 100; Leuven: Peeters, 1992) 3:1549–69; now also published in Bart J. Koet, *Dreams and Scripture in Luke–Acts: Collected Essays* (CBET 43; Leuven: Peeters, 2006) 99–122.

circumcision, and naming of John the Baptist and the events in the life of Jesus (1:57–80 and 2:1–40). There is, however, no parallel for the pericope that tells of Jesus's stay in the temple of Jerusalem (2:41–52). Although there may be some discussion as to where the pericope begins (Is v. 40 a conclusion of the previous pericope or is it the beginning of the next one, so that v. 40 together with v. 52 includes the whole passage?), the narrative at least commences in v. 41. Although Joseph A. Fitzmyer, in his commentary, claims that this passage does not fit in well with the previous one, one could also argue for the opposite position.[10] After all, both in the preceding passage and in this one, Jesus is situated in an environment faithful to the Torah (Luke 2:22, 23, 24, 27, 39). It is precisely this faithfulness to the Torah that brings the parents to Jerusalem at Passover, and which is indicated by the custom (vv. 41 and 42).[11] The pericope can easily be divided in two. In vv. 41–45 there is the separation of Jesus from his parents. As usual, Luke tells us at Καὶ ἐγένετο ("and it happened," v. 46) that there is a new beginning. There it is revealed that the parents find him (= Jesus) in the temple. In the past, this passage has been examined mainly historically-critically. Important questions were: Does this story go back to a source, or did Luke write the whole passage himself? If Luke used a source, could there be a historical core in this story? Related to this are the questions about possible historical circumstances: Where in the temple would Jesus have spoken with the teachers?

In an important article, Henk Jan de Jonge showed that most of the story betrays the hand of the writer/editor of Luke-Acts.[12] In his survey about Jesus as a teacher, Rainer Riesner tries—against de Jonge—to save a number of elements of the story as being historically reliable.[13] He claims that 2:46–47 fits well with account of models of teaching and

---

10. Joseph A. Fitzmyer, *The Gospel according to Luke: Introduction, Translation, and Notes* (2 vols.; AB, 28, 28A; Garden City, NY: Doubleday, 1981–1985) 1:434.

11. Here is not the place to elaborate on this term, but in Josephus ἔθος is often used to refer to the Jewish halakah. See Bernd Schröder, *Die "väterlichen Gesetze": Flavius Josephus als Vermittler von Halachah an Griechen und Römer* (TSAJ 53; Tübingen: Mohr Siebeck, 1996); see also Bart J. Koet, "Ethics or Halacha? 'Calling' as a Key to the Dynamics of Behaviour according to Paul in 1 Cor. 1:1–11," in *Biblical Ethics and Application: Purview, Validity, and Relevance of Biblical Texts* (ed. Ruben Zimmermann and Stephan Joubert; WUNT 348; Tübingen: Mohr Siebeck, 2017), 243–57.

12. Henk J. de Jonge, "Sonship, Wisdom, Infancy: Luke ii. 41–51a," *NTS* 24 (1978) 317–54. For a short assessment of this passage as part of Luke's pedagogy, see Reinhard Feldmeier, "Before the Teachers of Israel and the Sages of Greece: Luke-Acts as a Precursor of the Conjunction of Biblical Faith and Hellenistic Education," in *Religious Education in Pre-Modern Europe* (ed. Ilinca Tanaseanu-Döbler and Marvin Döbler; Numen Book Series 140; Leiden: Brill, 2012) 77–95, here 84–85.

13. Riesner, *Jesus der Lehrer*, 233–36.

learning as these relate to younger Jewish children at the time and which he outlined on an earlier occasion.[14]

Other elements are also highlighted in the exegetical literature. There are scholars who believe that there is a relationship between the presentation of Jesus here and in wisdom literature.[15] A second point to which scholars pay a lot of attention is the question of Jesus: v. 49 is often seen as the center of the story. Who the real Father is seems to be the plot. Another point of attention is the incomprehension of the parents.[16]

However, I would especially like to look at the earlier verses, namely, vv. 46–47, because they describe a learning situation.[17] The question is how Luke intends this learning situation to be understood. In a short but interesting article, John Kilgallen points out that the story about Jesus in Jerusalem can be seen as a story that offers a preview of Jesus the teacher.[18] Kilgallen believes that, given the whole context, Jesus's questions relate to the Torah. The admiration of bystanders for Jesus's understanding of the Torah that was given to Israel is a foretaste of his later work as a teacher.

The interpretation that Jesus is presented here as a teacher is not so new, because some classical commentaries already made this claim.[19] There were also dissenting voices, who said that this passage is about presenting Jesus as a disciple. In his influential commentary Alfred Plummer takes this view: he claims that Jesus is portrayed here as a disciple.[20]

I think that in 2:40–52, Luke presents Jesus as a disciple, but in such a way that we can find traits here of the way in which Jesus will act as a teacher later. Verse 47 tells us that his parents are surprised by his answers. Plummer points out, however, that there is a certain climax in Luke's

---

14. Ibid., 196–97.

15. For references, see Fitzmyer, *Gospel according to Luke*, 1:436–37.

16. Chris A. Frilingos, "Parents Just Don't Understand: Ambiguity in Stories about the Childhood of Jesus," *HTR* 109 (2016) 33–55.

17. De Jonge points out that the current form of the passage is constructed more or less concentrically, and that therefore the accent is on Jesus's presence among the teachers ("Sonship, Wisdom, Infancy," 339). In this way, the emphasis is on being a student.

18. John J. Kilgallen, "Luke 2,41–50: Foreshadowing of Jesus, Teacher," *Bib* 66 (1985) 553–59, here 553.

19. See, e.g., Marie-Joseph Lagrange, *Évangile selon saint Luc* (Paris: Gabalda, 1921) 96.

20. For example, Alfred Plummer (*A Critical and Exegetical Commentary on the Gospel according to St. Luke* [5th ed.; ICC; Edinburgh: T&T Clark, 1960] 76): as a learner, not as a teacher.

presentation of Jesus: he is characterized as a child (v. 43) who listens and asks questions (v. 46) and who also gives answers (v. 47). It is exactly this sequence that typifies him as a student, according to Plummer. It is precisely the asking of questions that makes Jesus an ideal disciple, but consequently also an ideal teacher. To explore this in more detail, I will now look at how the asking of questions, an activity that began in this story returns in the rest of the Gospel.

■ III. JESUS ASKING QUESTIONS

Martin Copenhaver wrote a popular book entitled *Jesus Is the Question: The 307 Questions Jesus Asked and the 3 He Answered*.[21] It contains a list of all the questions Jesus asked in the Gospels. In the more scientific exegetical literature, however, little systematic attention is paid to questions as part of Jesus's way of learning.[22] In all three Synoptic Gospels, Jesus repeatedly asks questions, both in the traditions that the three have in common and in other traditions. In this essay, I will discuss only the Lucan material.[23] Below, I consider some examples based on an inventory I made of questions in the Gospel of Luke. In this study, there is no room to examine systematically all the questions or to identify categories of questions that occur in the Gospel. The inventory shows that it is not only Jesus who asks questions. Zechariah is the first person to open his mouth in the Gospel: he asks a question of the angel who promises him a son (1:18). After that, it is Mary who speaks also to the angel. She too

---

21. Martin B. Copenhaver, *Jesus Is the Question: The 307 Questions Jesus Asked and the 3 He Answered* (Nashville: Abingdon, 2014).

22. Extensive literature research on my part and a consultation with fellow Luke experts did not lead to new secondary literature. I remembered one exception: David Daube, *The New Testament and Rabbinic Judaism* (1956; repr., University of London Press, 2011), especially the chapters "Socratic Interrogation" (141–57) and "Four Types of Questions" (158–69). Daube compares passages from the Jesus traditions with both Greco-Roman and rabbinic stories. See also Deborah T. Prince, "'Why Do You Seek the Living among the Dead?' Rhetorical Questions in the Lukan Resurrection Narrative," *JBL* 135 (2016) 123–39. Moreover, Jesus's questions in Luke 2:46 have already been linked to questions as part of the Jewish teaching method. For this thesis and some references, see Hermann L. Strack and Paul Billerbeck, *Kommentar zum Neuen Testament aus Talmud und Midrasch* (6 vols.; Munich: Beck, 1922–1961) 2:150–51.

23. Space does not permit a systematic description of where Luke follows earlier traditions and how he uses questions as part of the teaching of Jesus.

poses a question (1:34). And after she has greeted Mary, Elizabeth also asks a (rhetorical?) question (1:43).

When Jesus's parents find him in the temple, it is once again Mary who poses a question (2:48). Jesus responds, and it is the first time in the Gospel that he takes the floor (v. 49). He answers the question with two counterquestions: (literally) "What is it, that you have sought me? Did you not know that I must be in the things of my Father?" (my translation).

We saw above that immediately prior to this encounter, Luke had just characterized Jesus as a child who impressed the bystanders by listening and asking questions. In the continuation of the Gospel of Luke, Jesus remains a questioner. There are a lot of situations where Jesus poses questions to his audience to make his teaching clear. For example, in the Sermon on the Plain (Luke 6:20–49), we encounter a whole series of questions that can make the audience think (see 6:39 [in the form of a parable], 41, 42, 46). Most notably, Jesus often asks questions in response or as an answer to the implicit or explicit questions that play a role in the lives of his audience.

A special category of question posed by Jesus is where he repeatedly asks about the thoughts of characters in his audience, in a particular scene. In Luke 5:17–26, we hear about the healing of a paralyzed person. The Pharisees and Torah teachers ask each other two questions: the first one about Jesus, and the second about whether it is not God alone who can forgive (v. 22). Jesus perceived their intentions and was aware of their discussion, and he asks two questions ("Which is easier, to say, 'Your sins are forgiven you,' or to say, 'Stand up and walk'?," v. 23 NRSV). (The Greek and Latin say that he answers them with these two questions.)

At a dinner in his house (7:36–50), Simon, a Pharisee, asks himself something about Jesus (v. 39). Jesus responds (again, Greek and Latin say that Jesus answers) to Simon's thoughts with a parable, followed by a question about the parable (v. 42). Then Jesus asks whether Simon sees the woman (v. 42: "Which of the two will the creditor love more?" And v. 44: "Do you see this woman?"). So here Jesus responds to an implicit question from Simon with an explicit question. In Luke 2:46–49 Jesus answers the explicit question of Mary with an equally explicit counterquestion. This feature also occurs regularly in the rest of the Gospel of Luke. The question about fasting posed by John's disciples is answered by Jesus with a counterquestion (5:34).

We often find counterquestions in discussions about the Sabbath, for example, in Luke 6:1–11; 13:10–17. In Luke 6:1–11 we find another conversation between Jesus and some of the Pharisees about the Sabbath.

The Pharisees ask the disciples about their behavior. Is this really halakically justified (v. 2)? It is not the disciples but Jesus who answers this explicit question. He does so with counterquestions.

> Jesus said to them in reply, "Have you not read what David did when he and those [who were] with him were hungry? [How] he went into the house of God, took the bread of offering, which only the priests could lawfully eat, ate of it, and shared it with his companions." (Luke 6:3–4)

Questions also play an important role in the next section of the text (6:6–11), Jesus's instruction in the synagogue, in the context of which the healing of a man with a "withered" right hand takes place. Now it is the scribes and Pharisees whose thoughts are disclosed to the reader before anything else happens (6:7). As in Luke 5:23 and 7:40, Jesus knows their reflections. He first asks the man to stand in the middle (6:8), and then he opens the interaction with a question about interpreting the Sabbath. Only then will he heal the hand of the man.

Also, in Luke 13:10–17 we find Jesus teaching on a Sabbath in a synagogue. In vv. 13–15 there is a conversation about the Sabbath. In response to an act of healing by Jesus, the leader of the synagogue reacts, this time openly, by issuing a command to the crowd. Jesus once again answers with a question in v. 15: "Hypocrites! Does not each one of you on the sabbath untie his ox or his ass from the manger and lead it out for watering?"

There are always questions about Jesus's identity. Sometimes these are questions from others, as in 8:25, when the disciples among themselves pose the question of who it is that can command the winds and the waves (see also 7:49, where the people sitting at Simon's table ask themselves who this Jesus really is). A further example is the question of Jesus's identity, posed by John the Baptist by means of messengers to Jesus (7:19). This question leads to a further question from Jesus about John the Baptist by way of reply to the disciples of John. Herod too wonders who this person is about whom he hears so much (9:9). In 9:18, however, Jesus also asks his disciples about what people think about him: "Who do the crowds say that I am?" A little later, in v. 20, he asks his disciples, "But you, who do you say I am?" Sometimes, too, Jesus asks about the identity of someone who is being healed. "What is your name?" he asks the man possessed by demons in the Gerasene region (8:30). When the woman with the blood flow touches him, he asks in 8:45: "Who is it that touched me?"

Several times Jesus answers a question with a counterquestion. In response to a question from someone who asks him to persuade his brother to share the inheritance, Jesus responds with a counterquestion in 12:14: "Man, who has asked me to be a judge or arbitrator about you?" It does not stop with a question, for it is followed by advice (v. 15) and a parable (vv. 16–21). Jesus then advises the select group of his disciples not to worry, and this lesson too is interspersed with questions (12:24, 25).

Yet another example of a counterquestion in answer to a question is found in 18:18–19. A leader asks Jesus, "Good teacher, (after) having done, what shall I do to inherit eternal life?" (my translation). Jesus immediately responds with a counterquestion: "Why do you call me good? No one is good, but One, namely God." Another example can be found in 20:1–7. This time Jesus is teaching in the temple (v. 1). The (high) priests and scribes stand together with the elders and ask for Jesus's credentials (v. 2). Jesus answers very explicitly with a counterquestion. In 20:21–23, Jesus answers another question with a counterquestion.

In Luke 13:2 and 14:3, it is Jesus himself who asks the first question, and shortly thereafter a parable (13:6–9; 14:7–10) follows, explaining the question in one way or another. Questions and counterquestions are therefore a very striking part of Jesus's acting as a teacher. By responding to questions with questions, Jesus presents himself as a teacher who repeatedly entices his audience to think for themselves. Answering negative questions with a counterquestion ensures that the ball is firmly back in the questioner's court and indicates that Jesus apparently does not want to be drawn into a conflict that way.

■ IV. Questions as a First Step on the Path to Learning Together: En route to Emmaus (Luke 24:13–35)

We have seen above that Jesus keeps asking questions. In this last section we look closely at a particular example, namely, Jesus's last performance in the Gospel of Luke and the role that questions play in that scene. In earlier publications I pointed out that the two disciples who are on their way from Jerusalem to Emmaus are working on the Scriptures while walking.[24] Often this is no longer apparent from our translations, but when the Greek text is taken into consideration, the scriptural effort of the disciples may be clearly seen from the first words. Their communica-

---

24. For a more extensive introduction to the semantic field of interpretation in Luke 24:13–35, see my "Some Traces of a Semantic Field of Interpretation in Luke 24,13–35," *Bijdragen* 46 (1985) 59–73, also published in my book: *Five Studies on the Interpretation of Scripture in Luke–Acts* (Studiorum Novi Testamenti Auxilia 14; Leuven: Peeters, 1989) 56–72.

tion along the way is described with the verb ὁμιλέω (v. 14). In the Greek of the Fathers of the Church, the noun from this verb, ὁμιλία, means "a sermon," a very special form of communication (and so, the derivation of our word "homily" becomes apparent). Although the Greek verb in v. 14 will still mean "to be in communication with," "to communicate with," when the same word is used again a little later in v. 15, this communication will be strongly linked to the exposition of the Scriptures.

In v. 15, besides ὁμιλέω, a second verb is used to describe their communication: συζητέω. The King James Version translates it as "to reason," while the New American Standard Bible has "to discuss." This verb is used ten times in the New Testament and in almost every case in the context of those contacts of Jesus with people where explanations of the Scriptures play a role. For example, there is the reference to learning in the synagogue (Mark 1:27; see 1:21).[25] In Liddell and Scott's *Greek-English Lexicon*, the first meaning of συζητέω is "to examine together."[26] The Vulgate translates the verb thus: *secum quaerent* (from *quaero*, "to desire," "to research," "to question," "to seek"). Given the context, in these places the Scriptures are the object of this examination. In fact, we have thus arrived at the discovery of the concept that has come to play such an important role in the later rabbinic thinking: the midrash. That concept is derived from the Hebrew word דרש, which means "to search." The midrash initially has the Scriptures as its object. Back to Luke 24:15. The verb συζητέω was probably used there as well to suggest that the discussion the two students were having was (at least, partly) about the Scriptures.[27]

In this essay, however, I want to show that Jesus deals with the problems of the disciples in a special way. In line with many other places in the Gospel, Jesus begins the conversation with a question. Jesus asks about their words. It might be that implicit in his question is the fact that they throw Scriptures at each other (ἀντιβάλλω) and the characterization of walking in v. 17 as περιπατέω calls for the disciples to be concerned with philosophical questions of life. The pupils react with a counterquestion. Jesus responds to the counterquestion with one word: "Which?" (v. 19). This question leads the disciples to speak about their problems

---

25. For the use of it in Mark, see my "Markus 12,28–34: Übereinstimmung über das Wichtigste," in *The Scriptures in the Gospels* (ed. Christopher M. Tuckett; BETL 131; Leuven: Peeters, 1997) 513–23.
26. LSJ, s.v. συζητέω, "search" or "examine together with," τινι.
27. The fact that the Greek συζητέω is used here also says something about the relationship between Jesus as a teacher and his disciples. Perhaps it presupposes a certain equality. However, this aspect cannot be further examined here.

concerning the present moment. In response to their recounting of their problems, Jesus asks two counterquestions.

Fitzmyer shows that this pericope is full of Lucan theological motifs.[28] It may be added that in this pericope the pedagogical theme of Jesus as questioner also returns. In his relationship to the disappointed disciples, the Jesus of this story retains somewhat the character of a disciple. He asks questions, and this is the onset of a learning process which he starts in the company of the disciples.

From the above considerations, a certain image emerges. We see how the disciples struggle with the meaning of the Scriptures in the light of current events, especially in terms of what happened to Jesus. Jesus behaves in this conversation as an ideal teacher because he connects with the questions of the disciples themselves. The story of the Supper at Emmaus can be seen as a blueprint of a pastoral encounter and perhaps also as a prototype of a pastoral learning situation. The pupils have become frustrated in their interpretation of the Scriptures and in their understanding of the current situation. They do not grasp how these two things are compatible. This also prevents them from recognizing Jesus. Jesus does not solve this misunderstanding by directly revealing himself. He does not allow himself to be praised for anything. Instead, all he does is to ask. Only after their stories have been discussed in detail (vv. 19–24) does Jesus move to center stage. Once again it becomes clear that in Moses and the Prophets the explanation of Jesus's life can be found. Then the disciples can return to Jerusalem, from where they had departed.

Yet there is another element to this story that is important for the whole concept of the disciples and their teacher in Luke–Acts. Because of Jesus's explanation, the disciples rediscover themselves, as disciples. From that moment on it is they, disciples and teachers at the same time, who become co-responsible for the interpretation of the Scriptures in word and deed.

In the beginning of the Gospel, Jesus is characterized as a disciple who asks good questions, and throughout the course of that Gospel one of his most important pedagogical methods appears to be the asking of questions. He has been considered and examined from the image of the student in Jerusalem to that of the teacher on his way to/in Jerusalem. His questions, however, can often function as the stimulus for the initiation of the students and as their first steps toward their identity and role as teachers. And then it will become true that the student will be equal to the teacher (Luke 6:40).

---

28. Fitzmyer, *Gospel according to Luke*, 2:1557.

■ V. CONCLUDING REMARKS

In this essay I outlined Jesus's method of asking questions as an integral part of his pedagogy. A more systematic examination of the different ways in which questions function in the Gospel of Luke or, more broadly, in the Synoptic traditions could reveal even more about Jesus's teaching strategy according to Luke, Matthew, or Mark. For example, it would be good to compare Jesus's way of asking questions with similar material in sources that are contemporaneous with the Gospels. Our first probing, however, shows that questions about the way Jesus is a teacher provide new insights into the manner of his being a teacher. Luke's presentation of Jesus as a twelve-year-old child in Jerusalem shows that the way he was a disciple is an anticipation of his way of being a teacher. Asking questions in all different contexts and in all different ways is an intrinsic part of Jesus's pedagogy according to Luke's presentation of him.

7

Stephen and Philip:

Two of the Seven, Teachers and Evangelists
(Acts 6:1–6; 8:4–40; 21:8)

JOKE H. A. BRINKHOF

The evangelist Luke provides us in the Acts of the Apostles with one of the oldest sources of the origin and the life of the first Christian communities. Although Paul's letters are even older than Acts, they are mostly addressed to special communities with their own features, customs, and problems, while Acts tends to provide a more general overview. That is why we consider Acts to be a historical monograph,[1] which, though written from a subjective perspective, reliably describes, to a certain extent, the way the life of the disciples developed after Jesus's life, death, and resurrection and shows how the apostles shaped their mission to spread the gospel. In this context, we should understand "description" not in our current way of presenting facts and data but in the way in which Luke himself announces it in his prologue: as a trustworthy account for his addressee Theophilus, to show him "the certainty of those things wherein he has been instructed" (Luke 1:3–4). At the same time, however, the author seems to build on existing traditions of the Christian communities of his day, just as we read in Paul's letters.

As Luke tells us: the apostles who remained in Jerusalem after the resurrection and ascension of Jesus faced a considerable challenge. Not only the increase in the number of adherents, but also the fact that their

---

1. See Joseph A. Fitzmyer, *The Acts of the Apostles: A New Translation with Introduction and Commentary* (AYB 31; New Haven: Yale University Press, 1998) 55–60.

work was soon no longer confined to Jerusalem, required organization of some kind. They energetically took this responsibility in hand. In the way the expansion of the "Christian movement" is described, there are, besides the apostles, other authoritative disciples in the foreground. This essay looks at one of them, Philip, who is known as "one of the Seven," particularly in his activities as proclaimer, preacher, and teacher.[2] He is the only one in the New Testament who is called "evangelist" (Acts 21:8). The story about the appointment of these seven men for the table service has been seen, since the second century, as the founding of the ordained ministry of deacons (6:1–6). In this study, I do not focus on the historical reality of Philip, deacons, or the development of this ministry in churches; I see Philip as a narrative character, portrayed by the author of Luke–Acts.

First, in section I, I will consider the appointment of these seven by the apostles. After this, in section II, the focus will be on Stephen and Philip, two of the Seven to whom the author devotes special attention. The second one, Philip, is the main subject of this study. Following section III, on Stephen in Jerusalem, in section IV we get a closer view of the activities of Philip, who preaches and teaches outside the familiar surroundings of Jerusalem and lays the foundation for preaching to non-Jews (Acts 7–8). After these narratives about Stephen and Philip, the latter emerges again many chapters later when he is called "one of the Seven" and "evangelist" and when he is the host of Paul (21:8). Embedded in the story about Philip, there is the meeting of Peter and Simon, a man practicing magic. This may be seen as a prolepsis of the turn to the nations in section V. In the concluding section (VI), it will emerge that the Seven, and especially Philip, who is also a teacher, show how they bridge the gap between the apostles and the nations, and between Peter and Paul, so that the good news spreads to the ends of the earth.[3]

---

2. Regarding Philip, see also Joke H. A. Brinkhof, "Philip, One of the Seven in Acts (6:1–6; 8:4–40; 21:8)," in *Deacons and Diakonia in Early Christianity: The First Two Centuries* (ed. Bart J. Koet, Edwina Murphy, and Esko Ryökäs; WUNT 2/479; Tübingen: Mohr Siebeck, 2018) 79–90.

3. In the last decades, several monographs about Philip have been published: F. Scott Spencer, *The Portrait of Philip in Acts: A Study of Roles and Relations* (JSNTSup 67; Sheffield: JSOT Press, 1992); Axel von Dobbeler, *Der Evangelist Philippus in der Geschichte des Urchristentums: Eine Prosopographische Skizze* (Texte und Arbeiten zum neutestamentlichen Zeitalter 30; Tübingen: Francke, 2000); Patrick Fabien, *Philippe "l'évangéliste" au tournant de la mission dans les Acts des Apôtres: Philippe, Simon le magicien et l'eunuque éthiopien* (LD 232; Paris: Cerf, 2010).

■ I. The Seven Chosen

Just before his ascension, Jesus commands his apostles to be his witnesses in Jerusalem, in all Judea and Samaria, and unto the ends of the earth (Acts 1:8). This will be the red line in the story about the adherents. They go all over the world to spread the message and attract a lot of followers.

First of all, after Jesus has departed to heaven, Acts continues with the selection of a new apostle, to complete the Twelve. The death of Judas, the traitor (ὁ προδότης, Luke 6:16), caused an empty place. Peter, referring to the Book of Psalms (Pss 69:26; 109:8), notes that, because Judas had a share in the ministry (ἡ διακονία) of the apostles and was numbered among them (Acts 1:14–20), he should be replaced. Therefore, someone else has to receive the share of this ministration and the apostleship of Judas. Just as Jesus chose his apostles from a larger group of followers (see Luke 6:13), the believers now can choose from several candidates. Peter sets out the criteria for the choice of a new apostle. It must be someone who, like the other apostles, can be a witness to Jesus's resurrection, because he was with the apostles from the baptism by John until the ascension (Acts 1:21–22).

The number of apostles, twelve, matters. Twelve is the number of the tribes of Israel, according to the twelve sons of Jacob (Gen 49:28; Num 17:16–17; Deut 1:23; Josh 3:12; 4:2).[4] "Twelve" symbolizes completeness. That is why, after the death of Judas, the number of apostles must be replenished, by the choice of Matthias, to exactly twelve (Acts 1:15–26). The symbolic value of the number twelve is underlined by the fact that from this point on most of the apostles as individuals are never mentioned again, but, as in the Gospel of Luke, there are references to them as "the apostles"[5] or "the Twelve" (οἱ δώδεκα).[6] They have this latter title once in Acts (6:2). As a full dozen, the apostles are equipped for their ministry of witnessing.

---

4. Besides the number of the tribes of Israel and the number of the apostles, twelve is also the number of the parts of the abused wife of the Levite (Judg 19:29); of the water wells at Elim (Num 33:9); of the stones in the river to the promised land (Josh 4:1–8); of the years of illness of a woman and the age of the daughter of Jairus (Matt 9:20; Mark 5:25, 42; Luke 8:42–43); and of the age of Jesus when he is found in the midst of the teachers (Luke 2:42).

5. Luke 6:13; 9:10; 17:5; 22:14; 24:10; Acts 1:2, 26; 2:37, 42, 43; 4:33, 35, 36, 37; 5:2, 12, 18, 29, 40; 6:6; 8:1, 14, (18); 9:27; 11:1; 14:4, 14; 15:2, 4, 6, 22, 23; 16:4.

6. Luke 8:1; 9:1, 12; 18:31; 22:3; Acts 6:2.

Used for the group of apostles, the expression "the Twelve" creates a connection to a second group of ministers, "the Seven." Like the number twelve, the number seven has symbolic value as a sign for completeness, as it is, for instance, the number of days of the creation.[7] Seven is the number of men who constitute this group, and they too are organized for their ministry. All of them are introduced in 6:1–6 by their Greek names: Stephen, Philip, Prochorus, Nicanor, Timon, Parmenas, and Nicolaus. Although their number is seven, they are not mentioned as such in this pericope. That will happen only in 21:8, where Philip, the second one on the above list, is called "the evangelist, one of the Seven" (Φιλίππου τοῦ εὐαγγελιστοῦ ὄντος ἐκ τῶν ἑπτά).

The formation of this group is due to the growth of the circle of disciples (μαθηταί) in Jerusalem. Though Luke, like the other evangelists, uses "disciples" regularly in the Gospel, in Acts this is the first time he uses the word to indicate the followers of Jesus (Acts 6:1). An interesting development is that the disciples now are an independent group, because the master is no longer physically among them. In Jewish tradition, making disciples is seen as a goal for a teacher (*Pirqei Avot* 1:1), and so Jesus succeeded. It may be owing to the Greek influence on the New Testament tradition that the term "disciples" is invoked to describe the relationship between Jesus and his followers.[8] The Gospels employ the word "disciples" (μαθηταί) liberally for those who follow Jesus. However, the Old Testament never uses "disciple," for example, to designate Elisha as a follower of Elijah or to name Baruch as someone following Jeremiah. Just as Sophists or Stoics were called disciples (μαθηταί), as students of an eminent teacher, so also is Jesus's relationship with his followers viewed as that of a teacher and his disciples. There is murmuring among these disciples because the Hellenists complain that their widows are overlooked in the daily ministration. In response, the Twelve act as teachers. "The Twelve," not mentioned by their individual names or as "apostles," suggest that seven men would be chosen to fulfill that necessity. They also formulate the profile that these seven men[9] must meet: they must be men

---

7. Seven is the number of the days of the creation of the world, the Sabbath included (Gen 2:2); the pairs of clean beasts and birds Noah takes with him into the ark (Gen 7:2–3); the years Jacob works for Laban to earn Leah and another seven for Rachel; the years of abundance and of famine in Egypt (Gen 41:53); the daughters of the priest of Midian (Exod 2:16); the days of unleavened bread (Exod 12:15–20); the days of cleansing (Leviticus 14); the years of the Sabbath for the land and for the jubilee after seven times seven years (Leviticus 25).

8. Fitzmyer, *Acts of the Apostles*, 346.

9. Paul refers to Phoebe, a woman (sister) as deacon (Rom 16:1).

of the brethren, well testified, and full of the Holy Spirit and wisdom (Acts 6:3).[10] They will be in charge of serving at tables (διακονεῖν τραπέ- ζαις). At the same time, Peter defines the task of the apostles, the Twelve. Their main occupation and responsibility are prayer and the ministry of the word (ἡ διακονία τοῦ λόγου, Acts 6:4).

"Ministry of the word" happens to be a new formula describing the mission of the Twelve. At the end of the Gospel of Luke, Jesus explains that repentance and remission will be proclaimed in the Name of the Messiah. He orders his apostles to stay in Jerusalem until they are filled with power from above. That will strengthen them to be witnesses "of these things" (Luke 24:48). Peter, in his plea for the choice of a new apostle, profiles the apostles as the ones who can testify to the resurrection. Now, in front of the needs of a growing community, Peter indicates what witnessing means, not only for the apostles but also for others who take care of the community. It is also a matter of praying, of the ministry of the word, as of serving at table, or, in other words, praying, preaching, and teaching with words and deeds, about Jesus, his life, death, and resurrection, and the proclamation of him as the Messiah.

The tasks of the Twelve and the Seven have been distinguished in this joint assignment. Their mutual relationship is also taking shape. The calling of the apostles by Jesus and the way the twelfth apostle (Matthias) was included in the group of apostles are simple and inconspicuous events. Now, a more solemn ritual is performed for the appointment of the seven men. The Twelve, having prayed, lay their hands upon the seven men chosen by the multitude. The way in which the Twelve share their guiding function and their role as teachers with the Seven presupposes a hierarchical relationship.

Note that the laying on of hands is not combined with the gift of the Spirit: these seven men were already filled with the Spirit (Acts 6:3).

■ II. Stephen and Philip, Two of the Seven

After this introduction of the Seven, Acts follows two of them, Stephen and Philip. The other five will not be mentioned again. Their "fate" is similar to that of most apostles, the majority of whom are no longer mentioned after their number has been reconstituted. This seems to underline the symbolic value of the numbers twelve and seven. The actions of some

---

10. "Wisdom" (σοφία) in the Septuagint is often used as a translation of חָכְמָה. For example, wisdom like Solomon's (1 Kgs 4:29).

individuals of the Twelve or the Seven represent the entire group to which they belong. By telling about the first two of the Seven, Stephen and Philip, Luke sketches what he considers to be a complete portrait of all of them. They are, so to speak, the prototypes of the Seven.

Luke often tells two similar stories about characters who are more or less parallel, such as the birth and beginning of Jesus and John, or about Peter and Paul in Acts.[11] As we will see, he does the same with Stephen and Philip.

One would expect the first thing the Seven would take in hand after their election and the task they received would be to start waiting at tables (διακονεῖν τραπέζαις, Acts 6:1–3). But the author focuses on another aspect: since the growth of the community is the reason for expanding the group of ordained ministers, this expansion, in turn, is also the cause of a further growth of the group of followers (6:1, 7; see 2:47; 4:4; 5:14, 16). Thereafter we hear that, instead of serving at tables, Stephen and Philip successively perform miracles and signs and act as teachers, first Stephen before the Sanhedrin (6:8–8:2), and, second, Philip in Samaria and on the way to Gaza (8:1–40; 21:8).

■ III. Stephen

Stephen is well known as the first martyr among the disciples of Jesus. Before his martyrdom he gave an impressive speech to the Sanhedrin. Just as the apostle Peter was the first to take over the role of Jesus as a

---

11. See Joop F. M. Smit, "The Function of the Two Quotations from Isaiah in Luke 3–4," in *The Scriptures of Israel in Jewish and Christian Tradition: Essays in Honour of Maarten J. J. Menken* (ed. Bart J. Koet, Steve Moyise, and Joseph Verheyden; NovTSup 148; Leiden: Brill, 2013) 42–55; David P. Moessner, "The Christ Must Suffer: New Light on the Jesus–Peter, Stephen, Paul Parallels in Luke-Acts," in *The Composition of Luke's Gospel: Selected Studies from "Novum Testamentum"* (ed. David E. Orton; Leiden: Brill, 1999) 117–53; Henry J. Cadbury, *The Making of Luke–Acts* (2nd ed.; London: S.P.C.K., 1958; orig., New York: Macmillan, 1927) 232. Peter and Paul both heal people, even if they are not present themselves (Acts 5:12–16 // 19:11–12). Both healed a paralytic (Acts 3:1–10 // 14:8–10). The raising of Tabitha by Peter (Acts 9:36–41) has a parallel in the resurrection of Eutychus by Paul (Acts 20:9–10). Both Peter and Paul are given the opportunity to be freed from prison (Acts 12:6–10 // 19:23–40). Both are called by a double name: "Simon, Simon" (Luke 22:31), "Saul, Saul" (Acts 9:4); see Marc Rastoin, "Simon-Pierre entre Jésus et Satan," *Bib* 89 (2008) 153–72, here 163. The gift of the Spirit in Ephesus to twelve men after Paul had imposed his hands (Acts 19:1–7) is reminiscent of Pentecost, where Peter is present (Acts 1:26 [twelve] –2:4), and there is parallelism between Peter's encounter with Simon from the world of "magic" (Acts 8:14–24) and Saul with the magician Bar-Jesus (Acts 13:6–12).

teacher who explained Scripture (Acts 1:15–22; 2:14–36; 3:12–26; 4:8–12), so Stephen is the first of the next circle of disciples, the Seven, to do the same.

Stephen is described as a man of grace and power who does great wonders and signs (τέρατα, σημεῖα) among the people. That causes discussion (συζητέω)[12] with certain (Greek-speaking) groups in the community. Yet they are unable to resist the wisdom of Stephen. Before the Sanhedrin they accuse Stephen of blasphemous words against Moses, God, and the temple (6:14). This development illustrates that the harmonious congregation as presented in 2:42–44 and 4:32–37 is divided, as was already announced by the problems with Ananias and Sapphira (Acts 5). The witnesses brought up against Stephen are false (ψευδής, 6:13), as were those against Jesus in Mark 14:56–57. By reworking the material of Mark, Luke creates a parallelism between Stephen and Jesus (see also the parallelism between the shedding of the blood of Stephen and Jesus, ἐκχύννομαι; Acts 22:20 // Luke 22:20).[13]

In reaction to these untruthful accusations, Stephen teaches the Sanhedrin the whole of Jewish history in the light of Jesus. It is a well-outlined discourse, with resemblance to other biblical retellings of Israel's history.[14] The most striking in this context is that Stephen's words evoke the preaching of Peter at Pentecost and to the Sanhedrin (Acts 2:14–36; 4:8–11), and so Stephen follows in the footsteps of Peter. Stephen does not defend himself against the charges leveled against him by the false witnesses by denying them. Instead, he refutes the charges with an exegetical account of the history of Israel. So, he emerges as a teacher, a servant of the word who explains Scripture, like the apostles. The Sanhedrin, however, does not want to listen to Stephen's teaching (7:57). Unlike what happened to Peter after he delivered his speeches (when the Sanhedrin had feared unrest among the people [4:21] or had been convinced by the positive intervention of Gamaliel [5:39])—but in a way similar to what happened to Jesus—Stephen's words bring about his death by stoning. Just as the apostles said, when they were confronting the Sanhedrin, that they could not be silent about what they had seen and heard, neither can Stephen. He adds a final testimony just before his death and a plea,

---

12. Bart J. Koet notes that this discussion concerns the interpretation of Scripture (*Five Studies on Interpretation of Scripture in Luke–Acts* [Studiorum Novi Testamenti Auxilia 14; Leuven: Leuven University Press, 1989] 58–60).

13. As in Acts 6:14, the alleged quotation of Jesus that he would destroy the temple and rebuild it in three days is found in Mark 14:57.

14. Joshua 24; Ezek 20:5–40; Neh 9:7–57; Pss 78; 105.

like Jesus, for forgiveness for his murderers. Saul witnesses and approves of Stephen's death (Acts 7:58–60 // Luke 23:34, 46; 8:1).

So Stephen, the first one of the seven men chosen for service at the table of the widows of the Hellenists, is not portrayed as a waiter for the Greek widows. He works miracles and signs among the people and gets into a discussion with Greek-speaking Jews. They do not act against the miracles, but precisely against the words of spirit and wisdom that he speaks. It leads them to take him to the Sanhedrin, where Stephen speaks again and explains Scripture. The way in which his trial and death are presented him as parallel to Jesus, while his speech makes him look like Peter. Thus, he is in line with these earlier teachers. The unrest created by the Greek speakers in the community seems to end with Stephen's death. At the same time, a new divisive issue has come to light: his death is the result of the Sanhedrin's unwillingness to listen to him.

An important character is introduced to the events surrounding Stephen's death: Saul, later Paul. He is a witness of the execution of the first martyr, just as the apostles were witnesses to the death of Jesus. In Acts, we will hear a lot more about Saul after the story of the second member of the Seven: Philip.

■ IV. PHILIP

The death of Stephen is not enough to temper the anger of the antagonists. On the same day, violent persecution broke out against the congregation (ἐκκλησία) in Jerusalem. Saul, who saw Stephen's death happen before his very eyes, takes it seriously and drags people out of their homes and imprisons them (Acts 8:1, 3). As a result, the followers of Jesus, except for the apostles, flee Jerusalem and become scattered abroad in the regions of Judea and Samaria, proclaiming the good message (εὐαγγελίζομαι). So it is that Philip, the second of the Seven, comes to Samaria (8:5).

A. Philip as a Teacher in Samaria

After the introduction of the Seven in Acts 6 and the lengthy speech by Stephen and his death, the narrator's perspective now turns to a second man of the Seven: Philip. There are some similarities between him and Stephen. They are both chosen for service at table (Acts 6) but are not described as table servants. They show great "signs"; it was said of Stephen that he "performed great wonders and signs among the people" (Acts 6:8) and of Philip that "great signs and miracles took place" (Acts

8:13). And as Stephen goes around and disputes with some of the Jews, Philip wanders around Samaria and proclaims "the good message" in that region (8:4). But there are also differences. For example, Stephen delivers his teaching speech before the Sanhedrin, in the Jewish setting of Jerusalem, while Philip leaves Jerusalem and enters less familiar Samaria. Thus, a beginning is made on the farther spread of the gospel, according to the command of Jesus to the apostles that it should be brought to "all Judea and Samaria, and to the ends of the earth." Philip goes even farther, for after Samaria (8:5) he appears on the southern road from Jerusalem to Gaza, the desert (8:26), and later in Azotus and Caesarea (8:40; 21:8). Moreover, we get a verbatim account of Stephen's teaching before the Sanhedrin, while Philip's message is expressed in more general terms. But no less telling, Philip is the preacher of "the good news" (εὐαγγελίζομαι) and proclaims Jesus as "the Messiah" (8:4–5).

After Stephen's death, a two-part story follows about Philip. Later we will meet Philip one more time, in Caesarea. He receives Paul and is himself called an evangelist (εὐαγγελιστής). He then has four prophesying daughters (21:8; see 2:17). The title "evangelist" for Philip is related to the events in Acts 8. Philip, as one of the seven wise men, known and filled with the holy Spirit, is a preacher of "good news" (εὐαγγελίζομαι, 8:12, 35, 40) like the people who fled the city because of the persecutions in Jerusalem (8:4). Philip brings the good news of the kingdom of God and proclaims that Jesus is the Messiah (8:5). He is the first in Acts to "proclaim" (κηρύσσω, 8:5). He is also the first who, after the apostles, calls Jesus "the Christ" (ὁ Χριστός, 8:5). In the Gospel of Luke, "proclaiming" is the responsibility of John the Baptist, Jesus, and the apostles.

Thus, Philip follows very closely in the footsteps of the apostles, who were previously said to be teaching and bringing the good news that Jesus is the Messiah (5:42), showing even more understanding than the apostles themselves of the "good news" about the kingdom of God, for they, the apostles, have not spoken of this kingdom since their conversation with Jesus about the restoration of Israel (1:6).

The "good news" proclaimed by Philip is accompanied by signs and healings, and examples are given of these blessings: unclean spirits are cast out, and people who are paralyzed and lame are healed (πνεῦμα ἀκάθαρτον, παραλελυμένος, χωλός, 8:7). It is not so much Philip's signs, however, as it is the good message he taught about God's kingdom and the name of Jesus Christ, which leads the Samaritans to believe and to be baptized (8:12). Philip baptizes. That is not said of his colleague Stephen, but it was told about the apostles. The apostles have been promised baptism with the holy Spirit, and Peter pledged the Spirit to the followers who would be baptized after his long speech (1:5; 2:41). Another time Philip is a successor to the apostles, because in Samaria people believe as a result of his teaching and preaching (8:12–13).

It is not told how baptism works. That follows later. In the next story of Philip with the Ethiopian eunuch, baptism, along with scriptural interpretation and catechesis, forms the plot of the story, with a special emphasis being placed on the act of baptism itself (8:26–39).

In Acts, little is spoken about baptism ($\beta\alpha\pi\tau\acute{\iota}\zeta\omega$). From the beginning there is a difference between baptism with water and baptism with the Spirit. The baptism of the disciples with the Spirit manifests itself in the Pentecost story with the sound of wind and tongues of fire and speaking in tongues (2:1–4). Here, in Samaria, it is mentioned almost casually, similar to the way the apostles baptize (8:3–14; cf. 2:38–41). But afterwards, the apostles came to Samaria from Jerusalem because the baptized did not receive the holy Spirit (8:14–17). After prayer and the laying on of hands by the apostles, the Samaritans accept the holy Spirit ($\lambda\alpha\mu\beta\acute{\alpha}\nu\omega$, 8:15, 17).

We see that Philip's teaching is followed by baptism, the same sequence that occurred after Peter's sermon at Pentecost. The apostles add an extra dimension with the laying on of hands, after which the Samaritans receive the Spirit. The laying on of hands is ritually similar to the "ordination" of the Seven. Thus, Philip's preaching and baptism are associated with the apostles and the gift of the Spirit.

So, in this episode, the Twelve and the Seven do not differ that much in their tasks, at least not to the extent suggested in Acts 6.[15] The subsequent story of Philip (8:27–39) further nuances the strict distinction between the two groups, as Philip's journey is inspired and guided by an angel and the holy Spirit. They act as the authorization of Philip from heaven.

B. Philip Teaching the Ethiopian

After their visit to the Samaritans, Peter and John return to Jerusalem, while they send the good news to many villages in Samaria. Philip also departs from Samaria because an angel asks him to leave for Gaza. On the way he meets an Ethiopian official, returning after a pilgrimage to

---

15. Saul/Paul also is baptized not by an apostle but by Ananias (see Acts 9:17–18; 10:44–48; 13:12, 48; 22:16). Acts 19:2–7 refers to the baptism of John (see Acts 1:5). This baptism is not associated with the holy Spirit and is renewed by Paul's baptism, including laying on hands and the receipt of the holy Spirit (see Acts 8). Paul also baptizes Lydia (Acts 16:15) and a jailer (Acts 16:33).

Jerusalem, who reads the prophet Isaiah in his carriage. When Philip hears this, he asks the man whether he understands what he is reading (Acts 8:30). The man replies that he cannot, unless someone will guide him, teach him, show him the way (ὁδηγέω). The verb "to guide" is rarely used in the New Testament. It is what is said about a blind person, who cannot be guided by another blind one (Matt 15:14; Luke 6:39) and about the holy Spirit and the Lamb as guides for Jesus's followers (John 10:13; Rev 7:17). The Ethiopian invites Philip to be his guide in reading several verses from the prophet Isaiah about the servant of the Lord who, like a lamb, is mute before its slaughter (Isa 53:7–8). After reading, the Ethiopian asks Philip about whom this is said, the prophet himself or someone else? This gives Philip the opportunity to teach the man. It is explicitly mentioned that Scripture is the starting point. Philip explains the Scriptures, responds to his pupil's question, and is a teacher, a guide for him.

Philip turns out to be a different kind of teacher from Peter or Stephen. That is not surprising. Both Peter and Stephen could presume that their listeners would have knowledge of the Scriptures. What they do in their proclamation is to interpret biblical texts and explain that they are about Jesus. It was not different for Philip in Samaria, where he could tie in what he was saying with what he supposed was known to his audience. In guiding the Ethiopian, Philip uses more or less the same learning model as Jesus employed in his post-resurrection conversation with the two disciples on the way to Emmaus, who were leaving Jerusalem like the Ethiopian. Jesus asks them what they are talking about and after their explanation he explicates from all the Scriptures for them what pertains to himself, starting with the Law and the Prophets. This activity, along with the breaking of the bread, makes the two recognize him. They themselves interpret it as opening the Scriptures to them (Luke 24:13–35). But even now Jesus used and explained the scriptural knowledge present, which led the disciples to realize that he had risen.

In the same Gospel, Jesus starts his public life in the synagogue of Nazareth. He reads texts from Isaiah and declares before his audience that these texts apply to him (4:16–30). Of course, the people in the synagogue know the Scriptures. Jesus and these Scripture readers engage in different interpretations, such as in other conversations about the Scriptures (see also 6:6 and 10:26).

Philip must take a dissimilar approach to his interlocutor, who, because of his pilgrimage to Jerusalem and his reading of the Scriptures, is clearly curious and eager to learn; but, given his origin and question, he needs a guide in his interpretation of what he is reading. It is remarkable that, just as a text of Isaiah was central to the beginning of the public life of Jesus, such a text is the beginning of the proclamation to those who are not familiar with the Scriptures from birth.[16]

As in Samaria, the teaching by Philip leads to baptism. It seems to be a somewhat accidental occurrence. The two arrive at water, and the man asks whether there is anything preventing him from being baptized. Philip baptizes the Ethiopian, who is, like the Samaritans, filled with joy and who then continues his journey.

Immediately after this baptism, Philip is taken away by the Spirit of the Lord and is found at Azotus, and passes through there, proclaiming good news (εὐαγγελίζομαι) till his arrival at Caesarea. That is where, later, he hosts Paul and is called "evangelist" and "one of the Seven" (Φιλίππου τοῦ εὐαγγελιστοῦ ὄντος ἐκ τῶν ἑπτά, Acts 21:8).

Like Stephen, Philip is not depicted as a waiter at table for the widows of the Hellenists. Whereas Stephen is portrayed as one looking like Jesus, Philip resembles more the apostles: healing, baptizing, and bringing good news. He is the first one who goes out of Jerusalem and turns to the nations, starting in Samaria, and he is a guide and teacher to them in interpreting Scripture. He also shows himself to be a creative teacher. By taking an inquisitive student by the hand he builds a bridge to the proclamation of the good news to the nations.

V. Philip, Simon, Peter, and Paul

In Samaria, Simon, a man who practices magic, is a celebrity.[17] Both he and Philip perform impressive signs. Yet Simon begins to believe and is baptized, like the other Samaritans. This is not because he rates Philip's signs more highly (cf., e.g., Exod 7:8–12). It is the very message that Philip teaches about the kingdom of God and the name of Jesus Christ that make the difference (Acts 8:12). Thus, this scene can be interpreted as a victory for Philip's teaching over the world of magic. However, when the apostles from Jerusalem come to Samaria to lay hands on the new believers, a different picture emerges. Philip is no longer mentioned. The matter is between Peter and Simon. Simon's request to Peter and his offer to pay money to participate in the laying on of hands are strongly rejected.

---

16. Bart J. Koet, "Isaiah in Luke–Acts," in Koet, *Dreams and Scripture in Luke–Acts: Collected Essays* (CBET 42; Leuven: Peeters, 2006) 51–79.

17. Joke H. A. Brinkhof, *Zicht op de Volkeren: Een Portret van Simon in Handelingen 8:5–24* (Bergambacht: Uitgeverij 2VM, 2015) 148–52, esp. 152.

Peter condemns Simon as a wizard, one who engages in the customs of the foreign peoples, the gentiles, customs forbidden to Israel.

Philip and Simon's meeting thus ends in a serious confrontation between Peter and Simon, between an apostle and a former, perhaps pagan, stranger. Did Philip made a mistake by baptizing Simon? Does Peter see anything that Philip has overlooked?

The author offers us some tools to understand this scene better. The first is a parallel representation of Simon and Philip.[18] They are both impressive and receive approval from the Samaritans (προσέχω, Acts 8:6, 10, 11). They also both cause surprise (ἐξίστημι, Acts 8:9, 11, 13). The verb "to say" (λέγω) is used with regard to both Philip and Simon (see 8:6, 9, 10). There is also a subtle play on the words "great" and "magic" (Μέγας // μάγος, μαγεύω, 8:7, 9, 10, 11, 13). The parallelism between Philip and Simon works to show how they differ. Thus, this episode ends with the superiority of Philip's word to the magic and great power of Simon (8:9, 13). Simon remains loyal to Philip after his baptism. "Loyal" is the translation of προσκαρτερέω, a verb previously used in Acts only in a positive sense for the truthfulness and loyalty of the faithful (1:14; 2:42, 46; 6:4). Philip has acquired a faithful, loyal follower.

A second tool offered by the author to the reader about a possible assessment is that Philip does not play any part in the next scene. Peter and Simon face each other. Simon, and not Philip, is corrected. So, the point is not to put Philip in his place, as if his preaching and teaching had not been done properly. By winning Simon over, Philip made no miscalculation, and his decision to baptize Simon is vindicated.

Philip is just one of the first disciples to fulfill the mission that Jesus gave them: to preach and teach repentance and forgiveness of sins in Jesus's name among all nations (Luke 24:47; see Acts 1:8). Philip goes to the nations uninhibited and takes them with all their quirks and details. Peter is not that open-minded. He seems to shun the consequences of teaching the nations outside of Jerusalem. That could be the reason for his pertinent refusal to give Simon a part or lot (κλῆρος; cf. Acts 1:17, 26) in an area (λόγος) that belongs to the apostles (8:21).

---

18. This parallelism is often noticed; see, e.g., Von Dobbeler, *Der Evangelist Philippus*, 50–67; Spencer, *Portrait of Philip*, 88–127; Fabien, *Philippe*, 80–83; Patrick Fabien, "La conversion de Simon le magicien (Ac 8,4–25)," *Bib* 91 (2010) 210–40, here 220; Hans-Josef Klauck, *Magic and Paganism in Early Christianity: The World of the Acts of the Apostles* (Edinburgh: T&T Clark, 2000) 17–19; Andy M. Reimer, *Miracle and Magic: A Study in the Acts of the Apostles and the Life of Apollonius of Tyana* (JSNTSup 235; London: Sheffield Academic Press, 2002) 1.

To guide the reader in this direction, Luke provides a third tool: the name "Simon." The only characters in this scene are Simon and Peter. Peter is also called Simon, as in Luke 22:31-32, where Jesus calls Peter "Simon, Simon" and commands him to strengthen his brothers after he repents, or turns back (ἐπιστρέφω). Now that Peter is standing before Simon, in Samaria, this name "Simon" has a signaling function. This point is strengthened because, in a second confrontation of Peter with a stranger from outside Jerusalem, Cornelius, another character is named Simon: Simon the tanner (9:43). Simon Peter must turn to the gentiles. Leaving Jerusalem constitutes the first step. The "turn to the nations" is worked out in Acts 10, and, as Acts 15:7-11 demonstrates, Peter convinces the brothers to welcome the gentiles (see Luke 22:32).

Finally, for the fourth tool, we take Peter's meeting with a man who practices "magic'" (Acts 8:9). The confrontation between Simon and Peter occurs after Philip has completed his mission. In this scene, therefore, the reader learns about both Peter and Simon. Simon's request to Peter (8:24) to pray for him that the curse pronounced (8:20) may not become true reveals a surprising degree of humility on the part of a man used to being successful. At the same time, Simon thus confirms and engages Peter's spiritual authority.

An encounter with a magician is also reported about Saul, who in Acts, embodies the "turn to the nations." Earlier we mentioned Saul as a witness to Stephen's death and to the violent persecutions that led Philip to Samaria (7:58; 8:1, 5). These persecutions continue after Philip's story, but Saul is confronted by the Lord himself on the way to Damascus. He becomes a follower of Jesus and is baptized by Ananias. On one of his later journeys, he meets Bar-Jesus, a magician at the court of Sergius Paul (13:6-12). Remarkably, after this his name changes from "Saul" to "Paul." This confrontation with a magician and the scene of Peter and Simon is one of the parallels in the description of Peter and Paul in Acts.[19] Two encounters with magic, one by Peter, one by Paul. Embedded in the story about Philip, the meeting of Peter and Simon is like a prolepsis or preview of the turn to the gentiles and the transfer of the main character from Peter to Paul. An additional indication to take this episode as an example is that the teaching of the kingdom of God, started by Philip (8:12), is taken up exclusively by Paul.[20]

---

19. For example, healings: Acts 5:12-16 // 19:11-12; Acts 3:1-10 // 14:8-10; raising of Tabitha and Eutychus: Acts 9:36-41 // 20:9-10; opportunity to escape from prison: Acts 12:6-10 // 19:23-40. See Moessner, "Christ Must Suffer," 117-53.

20. Acts 14:22; 19:8; 20:25; 28:23, 31.

■ VI. The Seven, Agents of the Apostles, Ministers of the Word

In the stories about Stephen and Philip we see that the task of the Seven is not limited to the service at tables (διακονεῖν τραπέζαις). While the Twelve, giving the Seven a share in their duties, distinguish between the ministry of the word and the ministry of the table, both Stephen and Philip are in fact, ministers of the word. They preach the kingdom, teach about Jesus, and do signs and wonders like the apostles. Both the apostles and the Seven are filled with the holy Spirit, and both groups reveal Jesus through their preaching, teaching, signs, and healings.

The difference between the Twelve and the Seven is mainly in their relationship to Jesus. Apostles are direct witnesses of Jesus and of his resurrection (Luke 24:45–49; Acts 1:8, 21–22). The Seven form a kind of next generation. That is not to say that the apostles stop teaching and preaching, leaving it to the Seven. On the contrary, they just get on with it. Instead, we see that the circle around Jesus is expanded with a new circle, which also takes on the proclamation and extends the work area beyond Jerusalem. The Seven have a bridging function. They form the connection between Jerusalem and the rest of the world, as well as between the Jews and the nations. They are the agents of the apostles to the world. Not only do they speak the words of the apostles, but they also have an independent role as witnesses of the word, like Philip in his teaching to the Ethiopian. So, they create a smooth transition to other leading people in the Christian movement.

After the Seven, we see others sharing and acting in this ministry like the Twelve, for example, Ananias baptizing Saul. Most notable is Saul himself, who is not wrongly called the apostle of the gentiles. He proclaims his message all over the earth. The transition from apostles to other teachers, from Peter to Paul, is also narratively shaped in the description of Stephen and Philip. Just as Paul, the persecutor in the story of the Seven, converts immediately afterwards and becomes a devoted teacher, so Peter, in Samaria, starts to convert to turn to the nations.

The scenes about Stephen and Philip are embedded in a transitional episode of Acts: from Jerusalem to the ends of the earth, from the apostles to others, from Jews to the nations, and from Peter to Paul.

In Philip's story, all these bridges are constructed. He shows that "bringing the good news" (εὐαγγελίζομαι) is not only a matter of preaching and miracles, but also of teaching and guiding the ones you find on your way. Therefore, Philip, sharing in the tasks of the apostles, is rightly given the title "evangelist, bringer of good news." In Acts 21:8–9, he receives Paul, the former persecutor and the successor of Peter, in his house in Caesarea where his four prophesying daughters are also mentioned. Thus, the title "evangelist" is not a "slip of the pen" by Luke, but represents his vision that, like the apostles, the Seven in teaching and acting spread the good news of the kingdom of God and the name of Jesus Christ all over the world.

8

Paul as a Teacher of Unity in 1 Corinthians:
Some Introductory Thoughts about the Question of Whether Paul Is a Teacher

BART J. KOET

In chap. 11 of his famous *Tractatus Theologico-Politicus,* Baruch Spinoza discusses the question of whether the apostles wrote their epistles as apostles and prophets, or as teachers.[1] Although that philosopher was of course very much at home in Jewish traditions, he also made interesting observations about the New Testament writings.[2] It is not unlikely that that very question comes to him precisely because it is with his knowledge of Jewish traditions that he is looking at the New Testament and thus he sees more quickly the Jewish matrix of learning that one can find in the New Testament.

> This contribution and this book are dedicated to my deeply mourned Judaica colleague, Rabbi Dr Leo Mock (1968–2023), who passed away much too soon. As connoisseurs of Judaism of the Second Temple period, he and his predecessor as our colleague, Dr Chana Safrai (1946–2008), who also passed away much too soon, knew so much about the New Testament that it felt like a homecoming for me to study and teach with them. That this was also accompanied by great hospitality and great humor made it a pleasure and joy to work with them. Both showed me the importance of *m. Avot* 1:6. I miss them very much. I am glad that Prof. Ze'ev Safrai, Chana's brother, was willing to comment on this contribution.
>
> 1. Baruch Spinoza, *Tractatus Theologico-Politicus* (Gebhardt edition, 1925) (trans. Samuel Shirley; introduction by Brad S. Gregory; 2nd ed.; Leiden: Brill, 1991).
> 2. That Spinoza knew and actively practiced the Jewish matrix of learning from experience is clear from Steven Nadler's standard biography: *Spinoza. A Life* (2nd ed.; Cambridge: Cambridge University Press; 2018).

In asking that question, Spinoza focuses first on the most important letter writer of the New Testament—the "apostle" Paul.³ Spinoza argues that Paul, like Moses and Jesus, was a prophet, but that he was certainly also a teacher. Although Paul's being a teacher is clear for Spinoza, it is less explicit than in the case of Jesus, who is quite often called and typified as a teacher in the Gospels. When one examines more extensively the differences in word usage between the Gospels and the Acts of the Apostles, on the one hand, and the letters of Paul, on the other (I limit myself in this contribution to those letters that are generally seen as authentic), it is striking that in the former a word like "disciple" is one of the most frequently used words and that this very word is missing in Paul's letters. We also find a word like διδάσκαλος ("teacher") very regularly in the works of the evangelists, but hardly at all in Paul's writings.⁴ That raises a question about the nature of those letters and about the author: it is abundantly clear that Jesus and John the Baptist are characterized as teachers, but what about Paul?

When one reads older literature on Paul, attention is directed mainly to Paul and his theology and less on Paul and his being a teacher.⁵ It is therefore striking that in recent decades a few books have appeared that, based on Paul's letters to the Corinthians, give explicit attention to Paul as a teacher. For example, in 2012 Claire Smith published a book in which she examined the semantic field of teaching in 1 Corinthians, 1 and 2 Timothy, and Titus.⁶

A few years later, Devin White broadened the focus. He begins by showing that, in the reception of Paul, the image of him being a teacher arises early on, and in this respect he can refer to the reception of Paul both in Acts (15:35; 18:11) and in 1 and 2 Timothy (2:7 and 1:11 respec-

---

3. Paul calls himself an apostle, but, for example, in the Acts of the Apostles, "apostle" becomes the designation for one of the Twelve (see 1:22–23). Yet, in the later traditions, Paul is called quite systematically "apostle," for example, by Augustine and Thomas Aquinas.

4. Thus, the focus of Devin L. White (*Teacher of the Nations: Ancient Educational Traditions and Paul's Argument in 1 Corinthians 1–4* [BZNW 227; Berlin: De Gruyter, 2017] 53) is more on educational motives and imagery.

5. See, e.g., an older work like Adolf Deissmann, *Paulus: Eine kultur- und religionsgeschichtliche Skizze* (Tübingen: Mohr, 1911), but even in a book like E. P. Sanders, *Paul and Palestinian Judaism: A Comparison of Patterns of Religion* (2nd ed.; London: SCM, 1981) there is no explicit attention to Paul as a teacher.

6. Claire S. Smith, *Pauline Communities as 'Scholastic Communities': A Study of the Vocabulary of 'Teaching' in 1 Corinthians, 1 and 2 Timothy and Titus* (WUNT 2/335; Tübingen: Mohr Siebeck, 2012).

tively). He can also point, for example, to *1 Clement* 5:5–7, *Acts of Paul and Thecla* 16–17, and Tertullian (see, e.g., *Adversus Marcionem* 4.2.4).

White notes that the way the early church remembered Paul as a teacher is now being slowly rediscovered by contemporary scholars.[7] After a sketch of Greek, Roman, and Jewish educational institutions,[8] he first examines the presence of educational language like μανθάνω ("to learn") in 1 Cor 4:6 and διδάσκω ("to teach") in 4:17 (see also a topos of the rod as "tool" of a teacher/magister in 4:17). He also investigates a less obvious type of evidence: the educational motifs in 3:1–4:21, where one can find the highest concentration of explicitly educational ideas. He mentions the metaphor of milk and solid food (3:1–4), an agrarian metaphor (3:5–9a), a construction metaphor (3:9b–17), Paul's framing of himself and Apollos as stewards (4:1–2), the contrast between pedagogue and father (4:14–15), and mimesis as an educational strategy (4:16).[9] Subsequently, he assesses the less obvious but equally significant educational motifs in 1:10–2:16.[10] White concludes halfway through his book that "[p]erhaps the most prominent function of the educational motifs is to depict Paul as a teacher."[11]

The above-mentioned authors and a number of other recent scholars[12] examining Paul's role as a teacher mostly focus (at least also) on 1 Corin-

---

7. White, *Teacher of the Nations*, 5; and see 8–24 (an overview of previous scholarship on educational discourse in 1 Corinthians), 10–16 (on Paul as a Greco-Roman teacher), and 16–18 (on Paul as a Jewish teacher).

8. Ibid., 27–57.

9. Ibid., 58–101.

10. Ibid., 102–25.

11. Ibid., 100.

12. See, e.g., Robert S. Dutch, *The Educated Elite in 1 Corinthians: Education and Community Conflict in Graeco-Roman Context* (JSNTSup 271; London: T & T Clark, 2005). This book suffers from a remarkable one-sidedness: Dutch does not pay much attention to the fact that, in examining first-century Corinth, one must also take into consideration the Jewish backgrounds of some of the populace. Although in his discussion of 1 Cor 1:22–24 (pp. 55–56) he says that Paul mentions Jews and Greeks, he only discusses what is meant by Greeks. The same thing happens on p. 60. Dutch quotes an article on education in Jewish and Greco-Roman context and then discusses only the latter. Especially curious is his statement that in 1 Corinthians we find "a racially [*sic!*—The origin and precise meaning of the term "race" are controversial, and the concept seems to me to be an anachronism with complicated connotations here] mixed church!" When he brings up Apollos in Acts 18:24 as a model of a Jew who belongs to a gymnasium (p. 163), he ignores the fact that Acts 18:24 mentions that this Apollos was at home in the Scriptures. What is going on here? Is this a systematic avoidance of certain elements in the text? Is it a blind spot? In any case, it makes his whole research a little bit dubious.

thians.¹³ To present Paul as teacher in this volume, I join that trend. I will focus on 1 Cor 4:17. In the authentic Pauline epistles, it is the only place where Paul himself is the subject of the verb διδάσκω and where he thus explicitly presents himself in the role of teacher.¹⁴ On closer investigation, we will see that Paul portrays himself not so much as a teacher of the nations (1 Tim 2:7), but as a teacher of unity.

An older but still relevant article is Wilhelm Wuellner, "Paul as Pastor: The Function of Rhetorical Questions in First Corinthians," in *L'Apôtre Paul: Personnalité, style et conception du ministère* (ed. A. Vanhoye; BETL 73; Leuven: Leuven University Press, 1986) 50–72.

13. Peter J. Tomson suggests in his highly lucid article that, in Protestant scholarly theological and exegetical circles, people often relied mainly on Romans and Galatians in formulating Paul's theology ("Paul as a Recipient and Teacher of Tradition," in *Multiple Teachers in Biblical Texts* [ed. Bart J. Koet and Archibald L. H. M. van Wieringen; CBET 88; Leuven: Peeters, 2017] 184–205). This does not bring into focus that Paul uses traditions he received. One then relies mainly on Gal 1:13 (see also 1:1), where there is so much emphasis on the fact that Paul would not have received his gospel through the mediation of humans, but through divine revelation. As a result, in speaking about Paul, the perspective of 1 Corinthians, where Paul does appeal to tradition, was often neglected. Incidentally, Tomson shows that Paul, even in Romans and Galatians, operates within the framework of Jewish *and* apostolic traditions. As we will see below, like some other scholars, Tomson shows that Paul in 1 Corinthians deals with issues that are recognizably akin to the halakic discussions of the rabbis. It therefore emerges that in 1 Corinthians Paul places much less emphasis on relativizing Jewish law. Tomson argues that, when one studies Paul and his thought, it is (sometimes) necessary to start with 1 Corinthians because there, Paul as teacher of tradition, rather than the dogmatic Paul, emerges! For his assessment of halakic material in this Pauline letter, see Peter J. Tomson, *Paul and the Jewish Law: Halakha in the Letters of the Apostle to the Gentiles* (CRINT 3.1; Assen: Van Gorcum; Minneapolis: Fortress, 1990). Benjamin L. White also stresses Paul's appeal to tradition in 1 Corinthians and blames Protestant tradition for the neglect of that aspect of Paul ("The Traditional and Ecclesiastical Paul of 1 Corinthians," *CBQ* 79 [2017] 651–69).

14. For διδάσκω and related words, see Frans Neirynck and Frans van Segbroeck, *New Testament Vocabulary: A Companion Volume to the Concordance* (BETL 65; Leuven: Peeters, 1984) 93. For the use of διδάσκω in the seven Pauline letters, see Rom 2:21; 12:7 (about the teachers in the body of Christ more in general); 1 Cor 4:17; 11:7 (about the "nature" as teaching); Gal 1:12 (about Paul's stressing that he received "the gospel" not from a human and that no one taught him, but he received it through a revelation of Jesus [the] Christ). In 1 Tim 2:7 (διδάσκαλος ἐθνῶν ἐν πίστει καὶ ἀληθείᾳ, "a teacher of the gentiles in faith and truth") and 2 Tim 1:11 (διδάσκαλος ἐθνῶν), Paul explicitly calls himself a teacher, namely, a teacher of the non-Jews. Nowhere in the letters commonly seen as authentic does he use that word to characterize himself; cf. Eph 4:21, where διδάσκω is used to describe the Christ as teaching the audience of this letter.

■ I. Paul as a Teacher?

1 Corinthians 4:17 is part of a larger whole: 1:10–4:21.[15] Joop Smit, after studying the divisions of that passage by a number of exegetes, observes that this section is similarly divided by them into smaller segments: 1:10–17, 18–25, 26–31; 2:1–5, 6–16; 3:1–4, 5–17, 18–23; 4:1–5, 6–13, 14–21.[16] In order to assess Paul's use of διδάσκω in 4:17, I will, in the first instance, focus on its role in 4:14–21. Like many other exegetes, Smit regards this passage as a coherent whole. After Paul focuses again on his audience in 4:6 (ἀδελφοί, "brothers [and sisters]") he returns to his previously discussed collaboration with Apollos. That collaboration becomes his basic argument for two appeals to his hearers: the audience has to learn from them not to think of men as above that which is written of them, and that none of them should exalt himself (literally "be puffed up") over and against another.[17]

Earlier in this passage, Paul had outlined how the cooperation between him and Apollos was complementary: Paul as the one who planted and Apollos as the one who watered (3:5–8). They are, according to Paul, διάκονοι ("deacons"/"go-betweens," 3:5) and thus each other's συνεργοί ("collaborators," 3:9). In 4:6, the theme of "learning" is raised for the first time in 1 Corinthians: Paul's audience should be able to learn from that example of Apollos and Paul (KJV: "that ye might learn in us not to exceed what is written").[18] As in 1 Corinthians 3, Paul is not playing Apollos and himself off against each other, but rather presenting their joint action as something his audience can learn from.

In the sequel, in 4:7–13, Paul plays ironically with the self-aggrandizement that can be found in the community and asks them to consider what things they have that they have not been given (4:7). From whom? From the apostles! And yet those very apostles are accounted as fools

---

15. Joop F. M. Smit, "Epideictic Rhetoric in Paul's First Letter to the Corinthians 1–4," *Bib* 84 (2003) 183–201, here 200–201.

16. Joop F. M. Smit, "'What Is Apollos? What Is Paul?' In Search for the Coherence of First Corinthians 1:10–4:21," *NovT* 44 (2002) 231–51, here 232; for the criteria used by Smit for his delimitation and divisions, see 235.

17. "Puffed up"/"blown up" is based on the funny Greek word φυσιόω, which occurs seven times in the New Testament: 1 Cor 4:6, 18, 19; 5:2; 8:1; 13:4; and Col 2:18. We see here that Paul is able to describe the state of affairs somewhat ironically and sarcastically. His playfulness is too often ignored.

18. It is not possible to assess this sentence here with any degree of sufficiency. In this contribution I regularly use the King James Version because it preserves the metaphor of (walking) the way slightly more consistently than many other translations.

(4:10). They are hungry and thirsty, naked and beaten, and without a home (4:11).

In 4:14, a final subsection of this larger passage begins, and it is here that Paul says for the first and only time in his letters that he "teaches" (καθὼς πανταχοῦ ἐν πάσῃ ἐκκλησίᾳ **διδάσκω** ("as everywhere, in every *ecclesia*, I teach," 4:17). In 4:14, he stresses that, by his statements in 4:6–13, he did not mean to shame his audience but rather to admonish them (or possibly to instruct them)[19] and that is because they are his beloved children. In the next verse, he explains that his fatherhood is more important than having ten thousand pedagogues. He has fathered his audience like a father through the gospel in Christ Jesus (διὰ τοῦ εὐαγγελίου ἐγὼ ὑμᾶς ἐγέννησα, "through the gospel it is I who have begotten you," 4:15). As in 1:10, Paul appeals to his audience (Παρακαλῶ οὖν ὑμᾶς, "therefore, I call you in," 4:16) and asks them to become μιμηταί ("imitators") of him (μιμηταί μου γίνεσθε, "become imitators of me," 4:16). For the purpose of their becoming his imitators, he has sent them Timothy, who is also a beloved child of Paul. However, Timothy is not only loved, but he can also be trusted (πιστός, "trustworthy," 4:17).

It is this Timothy, who will "remind you of my [= Paul's] ways in (the) Christ, as everywhere in every *ecclesia* ["assembly"] I teach" (ὃς ὑμᾶς ἀναμνήσει τὰς ὁδούς μου τὰς ἐν Χριστῷ καθὼς πανταχοῦ ἐν πάσῃ ἐκκλησίᾳ διδάσκω, 4:17). The remarkable thing is that, while Paul does characterize himself here as one who teaches, he does so through an intermediary. He is outlining a process of tradition here as, for example, in 1 Cor 11:23.

So, what and how does Paul teach here? The question now is, What is the content of his teaching? What is Paul referring to when he speaks about "my ways which be in Christ, as I teach everywhere in every church" (4:17 KJV)? In her book on Paul, Smith also addresses this question.[20] She argues that Paul taught doctrinal truths, ethical standards and

---

19. The verb νουθετέω occurs eight times in the New Testament, meaning "to put in mind," "to admonish," "to warn," but also "to instruct" (LSJ, s.v. νουθετέω). It is possible that it is sometimes translated a little too much in a moral sense. The verb can thus also be related to the verb "to learn."See, for example, the fact that in Col 1:28 and 3:16 it is used in the context of teaching activities. Claire Smith discusses this verb and its derivatives (*Pauline Communities as 'Scholastic Communities'*, 325). She observes that there is at least an element of instruction in the meaning of this verb, but she tends to pick out the admonitory element in particular as more important, understanding it as a paternal admonition: "The dual elements of fatherly love and the threat of punishment provide the motivational force to this didactic warning." There is no room here to weigh up comprehensively the various possibilities, but see, e.g., Job 4:3 LXX.

20. Smith, *Pauline Communities as 'Scholastic Communities'*, 55–57.

a lifestyle that flowed from the gospel, but she stresses that "those ways" cannot be narrowed down to doctrine, conduct, and demeanor or moral standards.[21] In that context, she notes that this verse is not about halakic interpretation of the Old Testament.[22]

Here she seems to mix up two forms of Jewish genres; and, because it is about the only place where Paul so explicitly uses the word "teaching" to signify his own work, it is appropriate to examine this comment more closely, precisely because it is also about how Paul can or cannot be related to Jewish and rabbinic traditions of learning.

Smith rejects the notion that in 4:17 there is "halakhic interpretation of the OT."[23] This remark requires some explanation. After all, interpretation of Scripture (of course the term "Old Testament" is not used in a Jewish context) is typified in the Jewish tradition with *midrash* (searching for the meaning of texts from the Tanakh), while "halakah" is the term used in the later rabbinic tradition for the ways of life of the Jewish people and the fixed laws that emerged from the thought and study of the Pharisaic tradition and other circles within Jewish society.[24] Halakah somehow connected to biblical laws as purity and Sabbath regulations.[25] Halakah was developed based on everyday problems,[26] and establishing a relationship between a halakic rule and a scriptural word was in the Mishnah the exception rather than the rule.[27]

Smith's rejection seems to be based on a lack of knowledge of what halakah is. The question does arise where she found the idea that the concept of halakah would come into play here. In a footnote, she mentions two commentaries.[28] Examination of a representative number of commentaries in different languages shows that there is a tradition of more than 120 years of referring τὰς ὁδούς ("the ways") in this verse to halakah. The oldest reference I found was by Johannes Weiss, but he

---

21. Ibid., 56.
22. Ibid.
23. Ibid.
24. Shmuel Safrai, "Halakha," in *The Literature of Jewish People of the Second Temple and the Talmud* (ed. Shmuel Safrai and Peter J. Tomson; CRINT 2.3; Assen: Van Gorcum; Philadelphia: Fortress, 1987), 121–209, here 121.
25. Ibid., 123–25.
26. Ibid., 128–29.
27. See the comment in Pierre Lenhardt and Peter von der Osten-Sacken, *Rabbi Akiva: Texte und Interpretationen zum rabbinischen Judentum und Neuen Testament* (Arbeiten zur neutestamentliche Theologie und Zeitgeschichte 1; Berlin: Institut Kirche und Judentum, 1983) 34. This book is a beautiful presentation of a dialogue between rabbinic texts and New Testament texts.
28. Smith, *Pauline Communities as 'Scholastic Communities'*, 56 n. 37.

refers in a footnote to an even older commentary and does not address why one might make that comparison.[29] Interestingly, although some commentaries do mention it, the justification is sometimes only a reference to an earlier commentary, and over the years the reference becomes more and more superficial and, in Smith's case, simply incorrect.[30]

It is time to take a closer look at whether the comparison of what Paul says here about his human behavior as an example for the human conduct of his audience(s) with halakah has any merit. Answering that question may also contribute to the increasing interest in Paul's ethics. In recent decades we find quite a few scholars assessing Paul's ethics, although I have argued that this term is not one used by Paul.[31]

Thus, in this essay, I wish to assess whether a concept such as halakah can help us to understand Paul's views on human behavior. I am not making any claims about genetic relations, but the first goal is to assess four features in 1 Corinthians which can be compared with similar features in the concept of halakah.[32] First, I look at whether the metaphor of walking that underlies the term "halakah" can shed light on 1 Corinthians 4:17. Next I treat the way halakah can be seen as Jewish law and whether Paul's way of addressing themes can be compared to it. Thereafter I

---

29. Johannes Weiss, *Der erste Korintherbrief* (KEK 5; Göttingen: Vandenhoeck & Ruprecht, 1910) 119. See the references in n. 1 on that page.

30. See, e.g., Jean Héring, *La première épitre de saint Paul aux Corinthiens* (CNT 7; Neuchâtel: Delachaux & Niestlé, 1949) 38: "Le pluriel oi odoi désigne les principes moraux, un peu comme le mot halacha en hébreu (cp Actes 14. 16; Jacques 1. 8; Apoc. 15. 3)." See also C. K. Barrett, *The First Letter to the Corinthians* [BNTC; London: Adam & Charles Black, 1968] 117): "The word *way* may suggest Paul's Jewish, rabbinic background (cf. the word *halakah*); it seldom has a moral significance in Greek." Also Roy E. Ciampa and Brian S. Rosner, *The First Letter to the Corinthians* (Pillar New Testament Commentary; Grand Rapids: Eerdmans, 2010) 189: "'Ways' (the term is in the plural literally) reminds us of the Jewish metaphor of 'walking,' common also in Paul's letters, to encompass the whole life lived out in obedience to God, *halakah*." These authors do not reflect on this association.

31. See Bart J. Koet, "Ethics or Halacha? 'Calling' as a Key to the Dynamics of Behavior according to Paul in 1 Cor 1:1–11," in *Biblical Ethics and Application: Purview, Validity, and Relevance of Biblical Texts in Ethical Discourse* (ed. Ruben Zimmermann and Stephan Joubert; WUNT 384; Tübingen: Mohr Siebeck, 2017) 243–57.

32. For some methodological reflections about comparing Paul with movements more or less contemporaneous with him, see Stanley K. Stowers, "Does Pauline Christianity Resemble a Hellenistic Philosophy," in *Paul beyond the Judaism/Hellenism Divide* (ed. Troels Engberg-Pedersen; Louisville: Westminster John Knox, 2001) 81–102. Stowers rightly warns, "Similarity is not sameness!" (89). He also stresses that similarities are not exclusive and that it is necessary to compare Pauline groups to Judean communities. This also applies to our theme, *mutatis mutandis*.

explore the theme of tradition chain, and, finally, I compare Paul's goal in 1 Corinthians with an important motive for defining halakah.

II. THE METAPHOR OF "WALKING IN THE WAYS OF THE LORD"

We see here that Paul uses the metaphor of walking for law-abiding behavior, which is familiar from the biblical tradition but also features prominently in later Jewish writings.[33] Walking can be a metaphor for living, for living in a good way (expressed biblically, for example, in the combination of walking in the the way of the Lord) or in a bad way (expressed biblically, for example in Ps 1:1, as not walking in the counsel of wicked). The rabbinic term "halakah" is also an example of this metaphor.

The question, however, is whether in Paul's time a term like "halakah" or a related expression could have been used as a technical term, more or less, for this concept of moving as an indication of lifestyle. Or, more specifically, can the transmission of a "lifestyle" which Paul teaches through Timothy to his audience in Corinth be compared to the halakic discussions as recorded in Jewish traditions such as the Mishnah (and the Tosefta) and both Talmudim?

A first step to test such an assertion might be to take a closer look at the term "halakah" itself. Shmuel Safrai states, "As is the case with other technical terms, nowhere in rabbinic literature from the Talmudic period do we find any attempt to define, or even to interpret, the word halakha."[34] In the famous standard work on exegetical terminology in Jewish literature, Wilhelm Bacher notes that "halakah" is an Aramaic word from whose basic meaning of walk, step, path, an expansion occurred to include the concepts of custom, usage, statute.[35]

---

33. I deliberately use "law-abiding" here and not a term like "moral," because the latter term is too limited; the issue is not just moral righteousness, but also following rules that contribute to Jewish identity and thus are community-forming. In halakah, sometimes that community-forming is important.

34. Safrai, "Halakha," 121.

35. See already Wilhelm Bacher, *Die exegetische Terminologie der jüdischen Traditionsliteratur* (2 vols.; Leipzig: Hinrichs, 1905; repr., Darmstadt: Wissenschaftliche Buchgesellschaft, 1965) 1:42: "Ein dem Aramäischen entnommen Wort, aus dessen Grundbedeutung – Gang, Schritt, Weg – sich die Bedeutung: Brauch, Sitte, Satzung entwickelte."

The question can be asked whether one can use that Aramaic word to describe the way Paul teaches his audience about his "precepts." Isn't that too rabbinic a term? However, the term "halakah" seems to be in line with the fact that the concept of "going along the road" is often related to the notion of right behavior.

Already in the Torah, the five books of Moses, the verb הלך is associated with right action in several places. For example, in Exod 18:20 it is said, "And thou shalt teach them ordinances and laws, and shalt shew them the way wherein they must walk, and the work that they must do" (KJV). In Lev 18:3–4, two ways of going are contrasted: walking/going according to the commandments of the land of Canaan (compare Lev 20:23 and 26:21, 23, 27, 40) and going according to the statutes of Israel's God (compare Lev 26:23). According to Deut 5:33, going in the ways of Yhwh (see also 8:6; 10:12; 11:22; 19:9; and so forth) will also result in the people doing well and being allowed to live. The verb הלך is also used elsewhere to express a way of life, as, for example, in Pss 26:1, 3, 11; 119:1, 3; 128:1 and in other, especially prophetic texts such as 1 Kgs 6:11; Hos 14:9; and Ezek 11:20.

The metaphor of walking can also be found, for example, in a wisdom writing like Ben Sira, where the word ὁδός in the Greek version very often denotes a person's lifestyle in both a negative and a positive sense (for the ways of the Lord in the positive sense, see Sir 2:6, 15 and 48:22: Hezekiah remaining faithful to the ways of David, his father). In Acts, the metaphor of walking becomes one of the designations of the community of disciples after the ascension, as can be found in 9:2; 19:9, 23; 22:4; 24:14, 24. See also 2:28 (the metaphor of walking in the Psalm quotation); 13:10 ("the straight ways of the Lord"); 16:17 ("the way of salvation"); 18:25 ("the way of the Lord"); and 18:26 ("the way of God"). A Mishnah tractate like *Pirqei Avot* talks about the straight path (e.g., 2:1, 9 דרך ישרה).

In 1 Cor 4:17 the metaphor of (walking) the way(s) is combined with two other elements often related to this phenomenon, namely, remembering and an act of tradition, handing on the lessons you received. In Mark 7:1–23 there is a dialogue between Jesus and Pharisees and some of their γραμματεῖς ("scribes") on the issue of the interpretation of lore regarding the washing of hands.[36] This leads to the question posed by the Pharisees and their companions. In this context, the metaphor of walking is combined with a word indicating the process of handing on

---

36. It is not the place here to go into the precise role of these *grammatikoi*, but it seems that they were the beginners in the study of Torah.

the tradition.³⁷ Also in Col 2:6, we find the metaphor of walking combined with the theme of handing on: "as you therefore have received Christ Jesus the Lord, *so* walk in Him" (2:6 NASB).

This brief sketch of the metaphor of walking in biblical traditions shows that we find the concept in the various biblical traditions, in the Old Testament, in the New Testament, and certainly in later rabbinic Judaism. With 1 Cor 4:17, Paul fits into that tradition.³⁸ In the later rabbinic tradition, the concept of halakah will become the main characterization of the Jewish way of interpreting the tradition of Moses in daily practice.

■ III. HALAKIC DISCUSSIONS IN 1 CORINTHIANS?

A second angle to see if Paul's comment in 1 Cor 4:17 can somehow be related to halakah is to examine whether the problems Paul wants to solve in 1 Corinthians can be compared to halakic problems in Second Temple Judaism and later.

In recent years, there has been a growing interest in what is called "Paul's ethics." Ethics is seen as a somewhat systematic reflection on the nature of the good or the right. As I have argued elsewhere, one may wonder whether it is appropriate to speak about Pauline ethics, since in the Pauline writings we cannot find a systematic reflection on human behavior. Furthermore, the use of the word "ethic" does not really fit with those terms that Paul *himself* uses for describing human behavior.³⁹ Since the term "ethic" is not used in the Pauline letters, but is used in the scholarly exegetical literature on Paul anyway, the term "halakah" could also be used to describe the precepts that Paul teaches through his "son/disciple" Timothy—and all the more so since Paul does use the metaphor of the ways in Christ that one time.

One of the authors who uses the term "Christian halakah" to characterize Paul's regulations in 1 Corinthians 7 is Stephen Barton, but he does

---

37. The verb here is περιπατέω ("to walk around"), a word familiar from the philosophical tradition, but according to a yet-to-be-published thesis this word in quite a few Greek Jewish writings is the Greek equivalent of halakah. See also 1 Cor 7:17, where Paul uses this verb to refer to the metaphor of walking.

38. We can find the metaphor of the ways also in early Christian literature; see *Didache* 1:1–2; 6:1.

39. For an assessment of ἔθος in the New Testament and in Flavius Josephus, see Koet, "Ethics of Halacha," esp. 246–48. In Luke and in Josephus, ἔθος is used to describe ethical behavior as well as a way of acting related to religious institutions as an identity marker and thus as quite an elaborate term.

not justify this position at length.⁴⁰ One of the most extensive attempts to show that halakah can be a key to approaching Paul's writings and especially 1 Corinthians is found in Peter Tomson's book *Paul and the Jewish Law*.⁴¹ Tomson (re-)introduces the term "halakah" to typify some of Paul's discussions about specific human behavior. In doing so, he typifies halakah as "practical law tradition"⁴² or "Jewish law."⁴³ Tomson stresses the fact that in 1 Corinthians practical paraenesis has a prominent place and within that framework there are quite a few positive appeals to "the Law" and "tradition." That is one of the reasons that Tomson uses "halakah" to typify Paul's practical regulations for his audience. Tomson mentions several Pauline rules that can be typified as *halakot*: 5:1 (a rule prohibiting non-Jews from cohabiting with their stepmothers); 7:3–6 (regarding marital obligations); 9:9–10 (concerning the wages of field laborers); 10:24–29 (discussing eating food of unknown status, but possibly offered to idols); and 14:16 (regarding community benedictions).

In this essay, I will go into a little more detail on only one of the most recent attempts to connect the term "halakah" with Paul's First Letter to the Corinthians. This is an article by Yonder Gillihan.⁴⁴ Gillihan argues that there is no "handbook information" about ideas regarding sexuality and the social status of men and women in the Corinthian *ecclesia* or in Corinth itself. He turns to ancient Jewish *halakot* as a key to understanding 1 Cor 7:12–16. One argument in support of this attempt is that there

---

40. Stephen C. Barton, "Sanctification and Oneness in 1 Corinthians with Implications for the Case of 'Mixed Marriages' (1 Corinthians 7:12-16)," *NTS* 63 (2017) 38–55, here 43–51. See also White, *Teacher of the Nations*, 94. However, White does not explain what he means when he uses the word "halakic."

41. Tomson, *Paul and the Jewish Law*, 55–95.

42. Peter J. Tomson, "Paul's Practical Instruction in 1 Thess 4:1–12 Read in a Hellenistic and a Jewish Perspective," in *Not in the Word Alone: The First Epistle to the Thessalonians* (ed. Morna D. Hooker; Benedictina: Biblical-Ecumenical Section 15; Rome: Benedictina, 2003) 89–130, here 91.

43. Peter J. Tomson, "Halakah in the New Testament: A Research Overview," in *The New Testament and Rabbinic Literature* (ed. Reimund Bieringer, Florentino García Martínez, Didier Pollefeyt, and Peter J. Tomson; JSJSup 136; Leiden: Brill, 2010) 135–206, here 135: "Instead of 'halakhah' we could simply say 'Jewish law.'" See also Tomson, "The Term Halakha," in Tomson, *Studies on Jews and Christians in the First and Second Centuries* (WUNT 418; Tübingen: Mohr Siebeck, 2019) 3–7; and, in the same volume, Tomson, "Halakhic Letters in Antiquity: Qumran, Paul, and the Babylonian Talmud," 21–40. For a recent assessment of the halakah in the Gospels, see Ze'ev Safrai, "Halakha in the Gospels," in *Ashrēch Ziqnāti* (*Blessed Are You, My Old Age*): *Studies in Honor of David Bivin's 85th Birthday* (ed. Joshua N. Tilton; Jerusalem: Jerusalem Perspective, 2024) 182–268.

44. Yonder M. Gillihan, "Jewish Laws on Illicit Marriage, the Defilement of Offspring, and the Holiness of the Temple: A New Halakic Interpretation of 1 Corinthians 7:14," *JBL* 121 (2002) 711–44.

is enough literary and archaeological evidence to conclude that there was a sizable and influential Jewish community in Corinth.⁴⁵

Gillihan claims that 1 Cor 7:12–16 is clearly halakic: "Paul's goal in writing the instruction in 1 Cor 7:12–16 is to apply the commandment of the Lord against divorce casuistically to 'mixed' marriages in which one partner is a believer and the other not."⁴⁶ Gillihan notes that two different types of authority are in play here: on the one hand, there is a "command" of the Lord (7:10–11), but, on the other hand, there is an interpretive application of Paul's own general rule (7:12–16). This difference of authority reminds him of the difference in 4QMMT between what is written and "what we think"⁴⁷ and the difference the rabbis in the Mishnah make between their interpretations and key verses in the Torah. He emphasizes that this is a difference between the self-evident authority of the Lord (7:10) and Paul's authority.⁴⁸

The gist of Paul's decision is that in 7:14 he argues that the unbelieving spouse is sanctified by the believing one and that the key word here is "to sanctify." That very term is the title of a Mishnah tractate that deals with the relationship between a man "acquiring" a woman: *Mishnah Qiddushin*. M. Qid. 2:1 is often translated as follows: "A man may betroth a woman either by his own act or by that of his agent; and a woman may become betrothed either by her own act or by that of her agent."⁴⁹ Gillihan stresses that another translation of the particular verb here is actually more appropriate: "betroth" should be replaced by "sanctify" and then it becomes immediately clear that Pauline thought articulated in 1 Cor 7:12–16 is akin to similar arrangements in later rabbinic halakah as articulated in *Mishnah Qiddushin*.

Incidentally, there are also differences: the text from the Mishnah is about making the act of a new relationship legal, while in Paul's case it is about justifying the legitimacy of an existing relationship and thereby also about establishing the legal status of children.⁵⁰

There is no need in this essay to go further into this passage and its very extensive discussion of various halakic perspectives in the Pauline

---

45. Gillihan, "Jewish Laws on Illicit Marriage," 712–13.
46. For this and the following, see Gillihan, "Jewish Laws on Illicit Marriage," 713–14.
47. Gillihan refers to 4QMMT B 27–29, 64–66, 70, 76–77 ("Jewish Laws on Illicit Marriage," 713 n. 8).
48. Ibid., 714 n. 9.
49. For this and the following, see ibid., 717–19.
50. Incidentally, the legitimacy of children also plays a role in *Mishnah Qiddushin*. Gillihan discusses *m. Qid.* 3:12 for this purpose ("Jewish Laws on Illicit Marriage," 719).

passage and in earlier arrangements such as a Qumranic text like 4QMMT and later rabbinic texts in *Mishnah Qiddushin*.

Here, it is enough to note that, when Paul uses a walking-the-way metaphor in 1 Cor 4:17, 1 Cor 7:12–16 can be an example of Paul making halakic-like rules as it happened in the community of 4QMMT and in the rabbinic tradition.

IV. Paul as Teacher Is Part of a Tradition Chain

When Paul talks about his teaching in 1 Cor 4:17, he explicitly says that it is Timothy who is his mouthpiece. Even though he calls Timothy his son here, it is abundantly clear that Timothy is also his disciple. Tomson has pointed out that Paul positions himself as the bearer of a tradition in 1 Corinthians more than in his other letters, and on that point his teaching again becomes comparable to similar teachers among the Jews of the Second Temple period and later.[51]

Here it is appropriate to refer again to the presence of the metaphor of walking in the Torah and, specifically, in Exodus 18. In this passage, Moses, the leader of the Jewish people, the עבד־יהוה ("servant of Yhwh"), receives a beautiful lesson in leadership and self-regulation from his father-in-law, Jethro. Moses is told that he cannot solve the problems of the people on his own and that he needs assistants. Jethro says to Moses that, since he is a teacher, he should teach his people: "And thou shalt testify to them the ordinances of God and his law, and thou shalt shew to them the ways in which they shall walk, and the works [in Hebrew מעשה; LXX ἔργα] which they shall do" (Exod 18:20 KJV; I prefer the translation *deeds* instead of *works*).[52] Here, the similarity is not only in the metaphor of the way but also in the context: Exod 18:20 speaks about the appointment of judges and leaders under the auspices of Moses when God bestows his Spirit on them, and Moses gives them his authority, making them his

---

51. Tomson, "Paul as Recipient and Teacher of Tradition." The fact that in 1 Corinthians tradition is important is also emphasized by White ("Traditional and Ecclesiastical Paul," esp. 655–63).

52. For the importance of this verse in later rabbinic tradition, see, e.g., the Midrashim of the Tannaim: *Mekilta de-Rabbi Yishmael*, Yitro, Nas. De-Amalek ii; *Mekilta de-Rabbi Shimon Bar Yochai* Exod 18:20 and *b. B. Meṣ.* 30b. According to these works, this verse includes all branches of the law, as well as "good deeds." For the importance of Exodus 18 in Acts 6:1–7, see David Daube, "A Reform in Acts and Its Models," in *Jews, Greeks, and Christians: Religious Cultures in Late Antiquity; Essays in Honor of William David Davies* (ed. Robert Hamerton-Kelly and Robin Scroggs; SJLA 21; Leiden: Brill, 1976) 151–63.

representatives and also agents of God. This, too, is the position of Timothy toward the Corinthians (and maybe also the position of Paul himself).

Moses the lawgiver (and later the source of halakah) appoints assistants and thus hands over his teaching to the next generations. Handing over is also quite important in early Christian tradition like the apostolic writings as well as in the rabbinic tradition. We can find the concept discussed, for example, in the final chapter of Amran Tropper's book on *Pirqei Avot*, where he compares *Avot*'s chain of transmission with early Christian models.[53] He outlines how early Christianity and rabbinic Judaism were formed within the cultural environment of the early Roman Empire. He suggests that since *Avot* is a literary work, early Christian literature probably contains features relevant for a comparison between contemporary Christianity and *Avot*. Amram Tropper argues that the hypothetical collection Q resembles the wisdom collection in *Avot*.[54] He then examines the theme of apostolic succession from *First Clement* onwards and compares it with the concept of the chain of tradition in rabbinic Judaism. However, one can already find traces of such chains of tradition in the New Testament.

Long ago, Birger Gerhardsson, in his attempt to compare the early Christian tradition as presented in Luke-Acts and in Paul's writings with the later rabbis, wrote about the semantic field of learning and tradition in Paul.[55] What is especially important for us here is that Gerhardsson shows that terms like διδαχή ("teaching") and παραδίδωμι ("to hand on") belong to the Jesus-tradition in the various New Testament books. It is especially so in 1 Corinthians, that Paul presents himself as standing in a didactic tradition and that traces of a chain of *tradentes* ("those who hand on") can be found. In 1 Cor 4:17 Paul says that Timothy will call to mind ("let them remember!") Paul's ways in Christ as he teaches them everywhere, in every ecclesia.[56] Just as in 1 Cor 11:23–25 ("For I have received of the Lord that which also I delivered unto you" [KJV]) Paul speaks about a tradition that he received and passed on, it seems that here also Paul is portraying himself pre-

---

53. For this and the following, see Amram Tropper, *Wisdom, Politics, and Historiography, Tractate Avot in the context of the Graeco-Roman Near East* (Oxford Oriental Monographs; Oxford: Oxford University Press, 2004).

54. Tropper, *Wisdom, Politics, and Historiography*, 210.

55. Birger Gerhardsson, *Memory and Manuscript: Oral Tradition and Written Transmission in Rabbinic Judaism and Early Christianity* (ASNU 22; Lund: Gleerup, 1964).

56. In 2 Cor 1:19, Paul will refer to Timothy as one who proclaims his message in line with Paul's proclamation.

cisely as the *tradent* of his teaching—using the metaphor of the ways—
to the Corinthians through Timothy.[57]

V. RULES/HALAKAH AS A MEANS OF FORGING UNITY

There is another observation to make, which is important for our assessment of the term "halakah" as an apt description of Paul's views on human behavior. Halakah provides rules for the sake of the unity of the Jewish people. It is an identity marker. Halakic behavior as the right way to pray, to eat, or to have festivals is much more than a matter of ethical behavior. Kosher eating is not in the first place an ethical issue. It is, rather, aimed at building a community and thus a unity. Having rules that are made for promoting the unity of the community is another point of agreement between Paul and Jewish halakic thinking.[58]

What is the purpose of Paul's precepts in 1 Corinthians, and is it comparable to the purpose of halakah in Jewish tradition? To start with the latter: it is of course impossible to distil a single purpose in that vast sea of texts of Jewish tradition. But we can identify motives and concerns that are comparable to Paul's reasoning. Here, I picked just one.

In *b. B. Bat.* 60b, we find a conversation among several rabbis about whether meat could still be eaten and wine drunk after the destruction of the temple. After that destruction, there were many in Israel who abstained from eating meat and drinking wine.

This question is taken up by Rabbi Yehoshua. He answers that surely it is no longer possible to eat meat where once meat was sacrificed on the no longer existing altar, and he asks how one can still drink wine where

---

57. In Homily 15 of his series of sermons on the two letters to the Corinthians, John Chrysostom notes that Paul does not say "shall teach," but that he says that Timothy shall help them to remember. John Chrysostom explains that the Corinthians were used to Paul's teaching and that thus Timothy's task was to help them to remember those lessons. The different purposes of tradition (to teach and to stimulate people to remember the teaching of somebody) are also noted by W. Schrage, "Das apostolische Amt des Paulus nach 1 Kor 4:14–17," in *L'Apôtre Paul: Personalité, style et conception du ministère* (ed. A. Vanhoye; BETL 73; Leuven: Leuven University Press, 1986) 103–19, here 117. Although Schrage very briefly mentions the walking metaphor (115), he sees this mainly as a reference to commandments. He very easily (too easily!) connects Paul's ways with the proclamation of a *theologia crucis* (116).

58. That Paul's aim is to encourage unity is seen also by Barton ("Sanctification and Oneness," 39): "So Paul's holiness language and holiness theology represent a *pedagogy* (italics added) for competing factions with the aim of encouraging a common mind and shared practice."

once libations were made. There follows a whole exchange on different ways of expressing mourning over the temple.

In that context, a baraita is quoted (see *t. Sotah* 15.10) with an important argument that I would like to quote here as an example of how in Jewish tradition the importance of the majority is kept in mind: "It is taught: Rabbi Ishmael ben Elisha says: From the day the temple was destroyed, it is right that we decree over ourselves not to eat meat and not to drink wine. But one proclaims an ordinance over a community only when the majority of that community is able to bear it."

Rabbi Ishmael shows in his own way that halakah is all about the community. Perhaps we may even say that he shows that in cases of disagreement, decrees should be made in such a way that the majority can bear it. Even if at first glance this does not seem to be about the unity of the community, ultimately it is. You can never get a community in which all the members are of the same opinion on any matter, but you can try to create as much unity as possible.

In 1 Corinthians, Paul goes out of his way to shape that unity. That unity is the goal of this letter he makes clear in the epistolary opening 1:10–11. In 1 Cor 1:12–4:21, he tries to frame the contrasts between the various groups in such a way that they are complementary. In the following chapters, he tries to keep the community from practicing all sorts of abuses.

There is a remarkable parallel here with halakic thinking about unity. In the above discussion, the critical issue is about the majority being able to do it. We also find that the majority is important in *b. B. Meṣ.* 59.[59] 1 Corinthians 10:1–11:1 is also about unity (see the emphasis on that unity in 10:1–15). There is a reference, however, to the fact that the majority failed to sustain that unity (10:6–11). Paul encourages the Corinthians to be mindful of one another. In doing so, Paul also provides a kind of criterion: "Even as I please everyone in all *things*, not seeking my own profit, but the *profit* of many, that they may be saved" (10:33). Apparently, saving the majority is already a goal.

---

59. See, in relation to the importance and the difficulties of deciding by majority, *b. B. Meṣ.* 59. I discuss that passage in Bart J. Koet, "Words as Weapons? Listening to Four Voices from Antiquity: Cicero, Tacitus, Jesus and Rabbi Eliezer" (forthcoming).

VI. Concluding Remarks

While Paul in Gal 1:14–15 uses a prophetic text to depict his prophetic mission, in 1 Cor 4:17 he depicts himself as a teacher of the metaphor of the ways, which was common in the Tanakh and which will be so important in rabbinic tradition.[60]

In this contribution, I have tried to assess that, when using the word "teacher" to depict Paul's view of human behavior, one could use a term like "halakah" to describe that view. I juxtaposed various concepts that can be found in biblical and later rabbinic traditions with elements from 1 Corinthians. Paul's remark in 1 Cor 4:17 about his ways can be compared with the metaphor of walking in other biblical writings, and with the later designation of halakah as a general characterization of human behavior in the rabbinic tradition. Assessing Paul's view of human behavior, the comparison made in this essay makes it clear that both Paul and the rabbis give directions for community unity, and in both we also find the importance of standing in the tradition of receiving and handing on. Albeit that in 1 Corinthians there is not much mention *of* Paul being a teacher, we do find fine examples of *how* Paul teaches. He acts as one who wants to teach his audience *koinōnia*.[61] Morality for Paul is part of a bigger picture; it is not just about right behavior, but also about the unity of the community. Therefore, it seems appropriate to typify Paul's view of human behavior not only with an "extern" term like "ethics," but also with a term like "halakah." Paul presents himself in 1 Cor 4:17 as a teacher and, even more, as a teacher of unity. The way he does so is certainly similar to the manner in which later rabbinic thinking elaborates the emergence and development of halakah.

---

60. Prof. Ze'ev Safrai mentions that, from the point of view of the Sages, prophecy is a historical phenomenon that has passed, and, in their opinion, there are no more prophets in their days. Sages see themselves as a category separate from prophets, as more authoritative than prophecy when it comes to determining halakha. However, as is known, Josephus talks about prophets at the end of the Second Temple period. Safrai argues that this is a possible indication that in that era there was the beginning of a certain tension between the figure of the prophet and the emerging sage. This is possibly the background for the fact that in Gal 1:15–16 Paul depicts himself as someone with a prophetic mission, while in 1 Cor 4:17 he assumes a profile like that of the later Sages. This is not the place to elaborate on that subject.

61. See Koet, "Ethics or Halacha?," 256–57.

9
Paul as Teacher of Genesis 1:26–27 in Colossians 1:15; 3:10:
A Cognitive Linguistic Approach

CORNELIA J. M. MELISSE

Students always find themselves within a certain starting situation, namely, their own context. What they already know is part of this context. This knowledge is referred to in education as "prior knowledge." As a result of this initial situation, learning cannot be regarded as an objective, contextless activity. Students are not passive, empty objects that can be filled with knowledge by a teacher. On the contrary, learning is an active practice by students in which they interpret new information, based on their prior knowledge. They test new teaching material against what they already know, and new teaching material can influence the meaning they give to material previously taught. In this way, new knowledge arises. If teachers wish to teach their students something, it is therefore important that teachers determine which prior knowledge their students have and that teachers activate this prior knowledge to start the learning process.[1]

Readers of the Letter to the Colossians, too, make use of their prior knowledge, of which—ideally—the Old Testament is a part. In Col 1:15 and 3:10, Paul[2] explicitly activates prior knowledge about Genesis by

---

1. Cok Bakker, "Levensbeschouwelijk leren in de beginsituatie van de leerling: Bouwstenen voor een didactiek van interreligieus leren," in *Religieus opvoeden in een multiculturele samenleving* (ed. Bert Roebben; Leuven: Davidsfonds, 2000) 105–20, here 109–10.

2. In Col 1:1, Paul and Timothy introduce themselves as the text-immanent

alluding to Gen 1:26–27.³ The fact that Paul alludes to Genesis in these verses makes clear that he wishes to refer to this source and believes that the readers can recognize and understand this reference. Otherwise, it would not have made sense to include such an allusion in the text. Paul uses the prior knowledge of the readers, his students, to address them and make them sensitive to the message he wishes to convey. In this message, the source—in this case Genesis—and the new context—faith in Christ—come together.⁴ In this essay, I would like to describe how Paul acts as he teaches Gen 1:26–27 to his students and what he wishes to make clear to them about Christ.

Genesis 1:26–27, the source text, is part of the pericope 1:1–2:3, which narrates the creation. Verses 26–27 describe the creation of the human. In v. 26b, God says, "Let us make man בצלם כדמות." God creates the human בצלמו in v. 27a and בצלם of God in v. 27b. In the Septuagint, the Hebrew word צלם ("image") in Gen 1:26–27 is translated by εἰκών ("image"), and this word is also used in Colossians. In the new context of Col 1:15 and 3:10, Christ is described as the εἰκών of the invisible God, the firstborn of all creation (1:15) and as εἰκόνα of God (3:10).⁵

It is, therefore, important to start by asking what the words צלם and דמות ("likeness") mean in the context of the Genesis text and then how this meaning—the prior knowledge—is activated by Paul the teacher to

---

authors, the authors present in the text of the letter. From 1:23 onwards, Paul appoints himself as the author. See Lukas Bormann, *Der Brief des Paulus an die Kolosser* (THKNT 10.1; Leipzig: Evangelische Verlagsanstalt, 2012) 6. I therefore take the text-immanent author Paul as my starting point. In my opinion, however, the text was not actually written by the historical Paul, but by one of his followers. This author shares with Paul the cognitive worldview of the first Christians of Asia Minor. For some arguments why the letter was probably not written by Paul himself, see Arthur G. Patzia, *Ephesians, Colossians, Philemon* (New International Biblical Commentary 10; Peabody, MA: Hendrickson, 1995) 9; Markus Barth and Helmut Blanke, *Colossians: A New Translation with Introduction and Commentary* (trans. Astrid B. Beck; AB 34B; New York: Doubleday, 1994) 57–59.

3. This contribution is based on my thesis: Cornelia Jacoba Maria Melisse, "De mens als beeld van God: Een cognitief semantische studie van Genesis 1:26–27 en van Kolossenzen 1:15; 3:10 en naar het gebruik van Genesis 1:26–27 in de klas" (Ph.D. diss., Tilburg University, 2020).

4. For explanation of allusions, see also Christopher A. Beetham, *Echoes of Scripture in the Letter of Paul to the Colossians* (BIS 96; Leiden: Brill, 2008) 16–21; Jerry L. Sumney, "Writing 'in the Image' of Scripture: The Form and Function of References to Scripture in Colossians," in *Paul and Scripture: Continuing the Conversation* (ed. Christopher D. Stanley; ECL 9; Atlanta: Society of Biblical Literature, 2012) 185–229, here 186–88.

5. Melisse, "De mens als beeld van God," 65, 104, 290, 554, 632–33, 636.

connect to new information—that which Paul wishes to convey in his letter. Therefore, I will first look at what Gen 1:26–27 means; then, explore how Paul takes up this meaning in a new context; and, finally, identify which point he wishes to make clear by doing so.

■ I. Cognitive Grammar

To determine what the words צלם and דמות in Gen 1:26–27 mean, I use *cognitive grammar* in relation to semantic Bible research. This can be referred to as cognitive semantics. The term "cognitive" is used to indicate that language should be regarded as an integral part of a person's ability to know and think.[6] Our interaction with and in the world in which we live takes place based on the information structures in our thinking ability. Language plays an important role in this process: language ensures that the information we receive is ordered, processed, and interpreted. The meaning of words is determined by their users and depends on their own context, namely, the world in which they live and how they interpret this world (their cognitive worldview).[7] A word should be regarded as a mental idea or concept: a principle of categorization.[8] For example, if you know the concept "island," you can describe exactly what is and what is not an island.

In researching word meanings by using cognitive grammar, the conceptual approach—that is, the idea that a word represents a concept—is central. In a noun, a "profile," the most important aspect, is profiled against a "base," which constitutes the configuration of knowledge that provides the context to make a conceptualization. Together, profile and base form the meaning of a word. In addition, a word is conceptualized against one or more domains that relate to general background knowledge.[9] In the word "island," for example, a "piece of land" is profiled against the base "surrounding water." An island differs from other pieces of land precisely because it is surrounded by water.[10]

---

6. Dirk Geeraerts and Hubert Cuyckens, "Introducing Cognitive Linguistics," in *The Oxford Handbook of Cognitive Linguistics* (ed. Hubert Cuyckens and Dirk Geeraerts; Oxford Handbooks; Oxford: Oxford University Press, 2007) 3–4.

7. Ellen van Wolde, *Reframing Biblical Studies: When Language and Text Meet Culture, Cognition, and Context* (Winona Lake, IN: Eisenbrauns, 2009), 23, 34–35, 53–54.

8. John R. Taylor, *Cognitive Grammar* (Oxford Textbooks in Linguistics; Oxford: Oxford University Press, 2002), 42–43.

9. Ibid., 192–95.

10. Ibid., 198–99; van Wolde, *Reframing Biblical Studies*, 57.

Verbs, conjunctions, prepositions, adjectives, and adverbs do not profile things (in contrast to nouns), but relations. To describe these relations, the terms "trajector" and "landmark" are used. The trajector is the most important element within the relation and receives the most attention. The landmark, the other part of the relation, receives less attention.[11] For example, in the sentence "Ann reads a book" the verb "to read" profiles a temporal relation—a relation that is profiled within a certain time period[12]—between the trajector "Ann" and the landmark "a book." If we look at the word "book," we see a bundle of papers with letters on them profiled against the base that these letters form a consistent whole that wishes to make something clear. The word "book" can be used within the domains "education," "relaxation," and "holidays."

■ II. THE WORD צלם IN GENESIS 1:26–27

To determine what the words צלם and דמות mean, it is necessary to define the base against which the word צלם is profiled and the domain(s) in which this conceptualization takes place. In addition, this should be established for the word דמות. Since cognitive grammar is based on the principle that the meaning of words is determined by the language user and by the context in which he or she lives, it is important to research all the attestations of these words and, consequently, all the pericopes in which these words occur. In this way, all contexts and domains come into focus. By studying the domains in which a word is used, the entire context of the word in question can be mapped out, and more information about this context can be obtained by studying other (biblical) texts and their material culture.[13]

Profile and base are defined by analyzing each pericope from a syntactic, semantic, and cognitive point of view and comparing these analyses with one another. On this basis, it can be established that both the word צלם and the word דמות can profile different things against different bases and in different domains. Four forms of use can be distinguished for both words.[14]

1. Research into the word צלם makes clear that, in seven pericopes, the word profiles "one or more objects" against the base "worship." In

---

11. Taylor, *Cognitive Grammar*, 205–6, 216. See (a)temporal relationships for more explanation (ibid., 205–21).
12. Ibid., 210.
13. Melisse, "De mens als beeld van God," 55, 153, 193.
14. Ibid., 186–87.

three pericopes the base "specific shape" can also be found.[15] In all these pericopes the domain "cult" is important. The word can best be translated by "image." There is an image (profile: "object") that is venerated (base: "worship") and that sometimes reflects the appearance of the one, or the thing that is venerated (base: "specific form").[16]

2. In three pericopes the profile can be described as "one or more objects" or as "a two-dimensional representation," against the base "specific shape."[17] These pericopes are not about cult images but about other types of images or about two-dimensional images.[18]

3. Furthermore, the word צלם can profile a "material or immaterial object" (Ps 39:2–7) or "immaterial entity" (Ps 73:13–20), against the base "volatility." The word צלם refers to a mental idea with a fleeting character and can also be translated by "image."[19]

4. Finally, a fourth form of use can be distinguished, namely, the way the word צלם is used in Gen 1:1–2:3; 5:1–5; and 9:1–7. In 1:26–27 the word צלם profiles a "characteristic or feature" against the base "the trajector of the temporal relation." This trajector is God. God makes the human בצלמו ("in his image") and בצלם ("in the image") of God. The word צלם is therefore always associated with God and, both in v. 26a and in v. 27a–b, God thus forms the trajector of the temporal relationships profiled by the verbs "to make" and "to create." The word צלם can be translated by "image": the human has a characteristic that connects one to God; the human is God's image. The preposition ב-, which precedes the word צלם, can be understood both as a *beth normae*, which leads to the translation "in the image of God," and as a *beth essentiae*, which leads to the translation "as the image of God." In fact, the Genesis text uses the latter interpretation: God does not need an example or model to create the human, so the human is not created in God's image, but as God's image.[20]

---

15. In Num 33:50–56; 2 Kgs 11:1–20; Dan 3:1–30; 2 Chr 23:1–21 only the base "worship" can be discerned. In Ezek 7:10–22; 16:1–19; Amos 5:21–27, the bases "worship" and "specific form" are found. In Dan 3:1–30, in v. 19, the word צלם is used in a unique way to refer to the emotion on the face of King Nebuchadnezzar.

16. Melisse, "De mens als beeld van God," 188, 190–91, 204.

17. It concerns 1 Sam 6:1–11; Ezek 23:1–20; Dan 2:24–35.

18. Melisse, "De mens als beeld van God," 189, 191, 208.

19. Ibid., 189, 191–92, 209.

20. See, e.g., Ute Neumann-Gorsolke, "Reigning within the Limits of Creation: A Contribution to Old Testament Anthropology Using the Example of Psalm 8, Genesis 1 and Related Texts" (Ph.D. diss., Eberhard-Karls-Universität, 2002) 193–96; Ernst Jenni, *The Hebrew Prepositions*, vol. 1: *The Preposition Beth* (*Die hebräischen Präposi-*

Although the word צלם has different profiles and bases, and is therefore used in different ways, these forms of use are nevertheless interrelated. This is exactly the reason why the word צלם is used in these Old Testament texts. If we study this in more detail, it is striking that the domain "cult" is important. The domain is central to the first form of use, as the word צלם refers to cult images that are worshiped or venerated. The domain "cult" is also assumed in the second form of the use of the word צלם.[21] In the cognitive worldview of the time, cult images were considered representations of the deity depicted. The deity in question initiated the making of an image for him/herself, in which he/she would really be present. The statue represented the physical, anthropomorphic form of the deity.[22] That a certain reality could be present in a statue is applied to the statues of the mice and the tumors produced in 1 Sam 6:1–11. The third form of use may be associated with cult statues as well.[23] In Israel's polemic against cult statues, which came about through the imposition of the image ban, they were considered the result of a human and not of a divine act. The divine was not present in an image, and images were meaningless and without power.[24] This also applies to the mental images indicated by the word צלם.[25]

The meaning of the word צלם cannot therefore be seen in isolation from the domain "cult"—more specifically, the veneration of images. This also applies to the use of the word צל in Genesis. The pericopes from Genesis are part of the Priestly source (P)[26] and were probably written down during or shortly after the Babylonian exile, that is, at the same time that the ban on images was imposed.[27] The pericopes should be understood

---

tionen, Band 1: Die Präposition Beth; Stuttgart: W. Kohlhammer, 1992) 71, 79, 84. See Melisse, "De mens als beeld van God," 140, 190, 192, 270.

21. Melisse, "De mens als beeld van God," 193, 204, 206.

22. Angelika Berlejung, "Geheimnis und Ereignis: Zur Funktion und Aufgabe der Kultbilder in Mesopotamien," in *Die Macht der Bilder* (ed. Marie-Theres Wacker and Günter Stemberger; JBTh 13; Neukirchen-Vluyn: Neukirchener Verlag, 1999) 109–43, here 109–11.

23. Melisse, "De mens als beeld van God," 206–7.

24. Berlejung, "Geheimnis und Ereignis," 141–42; Jill Middlemas, *The Divine Image: Prophetic Aniconic Rhetoric and Its Contribution to the Aniconism Debate* (FAT 2/74; Tübingen: Mohr Siebeck 2014) 28, 43.

25. Melisse, "De mens als beeld van God," 209.

26. See, e.g., Phyllis A. Bird, "Theological Anthropology in the Hebrew Bible," in *The Blackwell Companion to the Hebrew Bible* (ed. Leo G. Perdue; Oxford: Blackwell, 2001) 258–75, here 259–61.

27. Silvia Schroer, *In Israel gab es Bilder: Nachrichten von darstellender Kunst im Alten Testament* (OBO 74; Freiburg, Switzerland: Universitätsverlag; Göttingen: Vandenhoeck & Ruprecht, 1987) 12–13.

against the background of this image ban. The text makes clear that the image of God is no longer formed by a wooden or metal statue, but by a human: a human is the image of God. Here again it is clear that a *beth essentiae* is meant in the Genesis text: God creates the human as God's image. To criticize the worship of idols, P uses the word צלם because this word refers to idols (the first form of use) as well as to the tradition of worshiping these images in Israel before the exile and in surrounding cultures before, during, and after the exile. As the image of God, the human represents God on earth, through whom the human has received the task to subdue the earth and rule over all the animals (Gen 1:28). This representative function is a consequence of being the image of God.[28]

■ III. The Word דמות in Genesis 1:26–27

The word דמות can profile a "resemblance" against the base "to be similar to," a "being" against the base "specific form," and a "two- or three-dimensional representation" against the base "specific form."[29]

1. In the first form of use, the word דמות indicates that there is an agreement between two things (profile: "resemblance"). This similarity, however, is partial (base: "to be similar to"). The word דמות does not indicate the point of similarity. The language user knows what the point of similarity is; so, it is presumed and does not need to be mentioned in the context. The word דמות can be translated by "similarity," but the translation "likeness" is also possible.[30]

2. In the second form of use, the word דמות indicates a being seen in a vision. The translation "form" is adequate.[31]

3. In the third form of use, the word דמות refers to an image. The similarity between these different uses is that there is always an incompleteness involved. The similarity that is profiled (first use of the word) is partial: something resembles something else, but never entirely. This also applies to the form (second form of use): it partly has the appearance of

---

28. For an overview of arguments why the representative function is not, in itself, the meaning of the fact that the human is the image of God, but the consequence of it, see Melisse, "De mens als beeld van God," 113–23, 273–74.

29. The first form of use can be found in Isa 13:2–5; 40:12–26; Ezek 1:2–28c (vv. 5b, 10a, 13a, 16b, 22a, 26a, and 26c); 10:1–22; 23:1–20; Ps 58:2–6; Dan 10:4–21. The second form of use can be found in Ezek 1:2–28c (vv. 5a, 26c, 28c); 8:1–4. The third form of use is present in 2 Kgs 16:1–18; 2 Chr 4:1–6.

30. Melisse, "De mens als beeld van God," 242–46, 250–52.

31. Ibid., 243, 255–56.

something from ordinary life, because otherwise it cannot be understood and described, but it never coincides with it. It can be seen only in a vision. The image (third form of use) represents something else, but does not fully match it either.[32]

4. Finally, there is a fourth form of use, which can be found in Gen 5:1–5 (twice) and 1:26. A "form or feature" is profiled against the base "the trajectory of the temporal relation," namely, God.[33] As we study these verses in more detail, it becomes apparent that the word דמות is used here in the same way as in the first form of use. The feature that is profiled consists of a similarity: it is a feature of man to resemble God, the trajector. This similarity, however, is partial; there is always a difference between the human and God.[34]

The word דמות is used in Gen 1:26–27 in combination with the word צלם to indicate that, because the human is the image of God, there is a resemblance between them. The preposition -כ, which is used in combination with the word דמות, expresses that a similarity is present, whereas the word דמות emphasizes that this similarity is partial. The word צלם makes it clear that this is a physical similarity; the human being represents the divine as an image. Just as a cult image represents the appearance of the deity it represents, so the human represents God. It should be noted that the text is primarily concerned with the fact that the human is the only permitted image of God and thus takes over the place of the cult image.

IV. THE WORD εἰκών IN COLOSSIANS

Now that the meaning of Gen 1:26–27 has been made clear, we can look at Colossians. Paul and his students, that is, the readers of the letter, are familiar with Genesis and its meaning, allowing Paul to allude to this text.[35] In Col 1:15, Christ, referred to in v. 13 as the son of God's love, is

---

32. Ibid., 244, 258–59. Both by using the word צלם and through the word דמות, an image can be indicated. The difference, however, is that the word צלם refers to an image with a certain power of presentation, whereas the word דמות lacks this aspect.

33. In Gen 5:3 an aspect referring to the notion "son" is profiled against the base "the trajectory of the temporal relationship."

34. Melisse, "De mens als beeld van God," 244, 248, 261.

35. The scope of this contribution is the Greek text of Colossians and its allusions to Genesis. Whether the people of Colossae were familiar with a Hebrew text of Genesis or its translation in the Septuagint—or another Greek version—and whether this affects their interpretation of the text, are subjects for further research. A topic

described as the εἰκών of the invisible God, the firstborn of all creation. Thus, two names are given to Christ, the second name being an adjustment to the first name. Colossians 3:9 says that the Colossians have taken off the old man with his deeds, and they have put on the new man. According to v. 10, this new man is being renewed according to the εἰκόνα of God, who created the new man.[36]

In 1:15, the word εἰκών profiles a "characteristic or feature" against (part of) the base "a certain relationship with a specific person." This "person" is God. In 3:10, the word εἰκών is used in the same way. It refers to 1:15, where Christ is at issue: he is the εἰκών of (the invisible) God. In both verses "creation" is the domain.[37]

Since, in combination with the word εἰκών, the domain "creation" is touched upon, Paul's readers can make a link with Gen 1:26–27. The word צלם is used in 1:27 in the same way as the word εἰκών is used in Colossians: both words profile a characteristic or feature, and the base of both words is a relationship with God. Paul therefore chooses the word εἰκών and, by emphatically mentioning the concept of creation in the context, he wishes to teach his students, the Colossians, something about Christ. The meaning of Genesis 1 about humans is thus incorporated and reworked into a message about Christ. This meaning of Genesis 1 consists of three elements, as shown above. First of all, the word צלם expresses the belief that God should not be worshiped by means of a wooden or metal statue; the human being is meant as God's statue. Second, since the human is the image of God, the word צלם expresses that a material image with a certain appearance is meant. The human has a body; and since the human is a physical being, the human is the image of God. Third, the human represents God on earth. The human is God's representative.

These elements can be found in Colossians as well, specifically in 1:15. This usage fits within the cognitive worldview of that time. As was the case at the time Genesis was committed to writing, the worship of

---

within this research would be the interpretation of the Hebrew preposition -ב, which is understood not as a *beth essentiae* but as a *beth normae*. Consequently, it is translated as κατά: humans were created "in the image of God." See Helmut Merklein, "Christus als Bild Gottes im Neuen Testament," in Wacker and Stemberger, *Die Macht der Bilder*, 52–75, here 49; Michael Wolter, *Der Brief an die Kolosser, Der Brief an Philemon* (Ökumenischer Taschenbuch-Kommentar zum Neuen Testament 12; Gütersloh: Gütersloher Verlagshaus; Würzburg: Echter, 1993) 59–61.

36. Melisse, "De mens als beeld van God," 334, 632–33, 636.

37. Ibid., 342–44, 355–56. In order to map fully the meaning of the word εἰκών within the New Testament, all the pericopes in which this word is used should be analyzed syntactically, semantically, and cognitively. This will enable the interpreter to determine what the word can profile in relation to which base and within which domains. In this essay, I focus only on Colossians.

cult images was rejected by Jews, as it would later be by Jewish Christians and by Christians too. They lived in the Greco-Roman culture in which images were made and worshiped.[38] Although the Colossians accepted the production of statues and images as art, they continued to follow the ban on cult images.[39] This is in line with 1:15, where Paul states that Christ is the only image of God. This implies that other gods and images of these gods may not be worshiped and that even God may not be worshiped by means of a cult image.[40]

Christ is described as an image of the invisible God. The word ἀόρατος ("invisible") is also used in Rom 1:20; Col 1:16; 1 Tim 1:17; and Heb 11:27. Christ, as the image of God, makes the invisible God visible. On the basis of Gen 1:26–27, it can be said that Paul may be speaking here of a physical similarity between Christ and God. The Greco-Roman culture contains various examples of cult images that physically represent the person being depicted. For example, there were statues of the emperor and coins with his image in use then.[41]

It has already been mentioned that in Col 1:15 the title "firstborn of creation" is an adjustment to the title "image of the invisible God." Because of their close connection, the second title given here to Christ explains the first. Being an image of God results in being the firstborn of creation. Next, vv. 16–18a explain what it means to be the firstborn of creation. These verses describe the reign of Christ: in him, through him, and for him everything was created, and he is the head of the body of the *ekklēsia*.[42] The third aspect of the Genesis text that the image represents, namely, the one who is depicted, thus comes to the fore in these verses.[43]

Colossians 3:10 repeats that Christ is the image of God. The Colossians have taken off the old man (3:9) and put on the new man. This new man is being renewed in knowledge. In the light of Gen 1:26–27 the verb

---

38. William E. Dunstan, *Ancient Rome* (Lanham, MD: Rowman & Littlefied, 2011) 5.

39. See, e.g., Jason von Ehrenkrook, *Sculpting Idolatry in Flavian Rome: (An) Iconic Rhetoric in the Writings of Flavius Josephus* (EJL 33; Atlanta: Society of Biblical Literature, 2011) 63, 78, 83–89, 90–92; Helen K. Bond, "Standards, Shields and Coins: Jewish Reactions to Aspects of the Roman Cult in the Time of Pilate," in *Idolatry: False Worship in the Bible, Early Judaism and Christianity* (ed. Stephen C. Barton; London: T&T Clark, 2007) 91–93, 104–6.

40. Melisse, "De mens als beeld van God," 368.

41. Ibid., 369; Bond, "Standards, Shields and Coins," 91–93.

42. Patzia, *Ephesians, Colossians, Philemon*, 32; Joseph Pfammatter, *Epheserbrief, Kolosserbrief* (NEchtB 10, 12; Würzburg: Echter, 1987) 63; Josef Ernst, *Die Briefe an die Philipper, an Philemon, an die Kolosser, an die Epheser* (RNT; Regensburg: Pustet, 1974) 166.

43. Melisse, "De mens als beeld van God," 303, 370–71.

ἀνακαινόω ("to renew") can be understood as a re-creation. The new human, like the old human, was created by God, but something is done to the new human that did not happen to the old human: the new human is continually renewed εἰς ἐπίγνωσιν ("in knowledge"). The phrase εἰς ἐπίγνωσιν means that knowledge is achieved; the new human possesses knowledge. This knowledge is κατ᾽ εἰκόνα τοῦ κτίσαντος αὐτόν ("according to the image of its creator"). The preposition κατά indicates a similarity: the renewal in knowledge has the aim of becoming equal to the image of God, namely, Christ. In this manner, one can act in the right way. This correct way of acting is further explained in 1:12–17.[44] Colossians 1:9–10 already emphasizes the importance of this topic: it contains the wish that the Colossians be filled with the knowledge of God's will, so that they live a life worthy of the Lord, bear fruit in all good deeds, and grow in the knowledge of God.[45]

In sum: Paul uses the prior knowledge of his hearers of Gen 1:1–2:3 to make clear who Christ is: the one and only image of God, who makes God visible in a physical form and represents God on earth. The Colossians become equal to Christ in knowledge, so that they can act rightly.[46] The meaning of Genesis and the cognitive worldview in which the text

---

44. For the prepositions εἰς and κατά, see also Gerald L. Stevens, *New Testament Greek Primer* (Cambridge: Lutterworth, 2009) 131–33; Walter Bauer, Kurt Aland, and Barbara Aland, eds., *Griechisch-deutsches Wörterbuch zu den Schriften des Neuen Testaments und der frühchristlichen Literatur* (6th ed.; Berlin: de Gruyter, 1988), s.vv. εἰς and κατά; BDF §§208, 224; Max Zerwick and Mary Grosvenor, *A Grammatical Analysis of the Greek New Testament* (5th ed.; SubBib 39; Rome: Gregorian & Biblical Press, 2010) 60. Cf. Michael Dübbers, "Christology and Existence: A Study of the Intention of the Letter to the Colossians" (Ph.D. diss., Eberhard-Karls-Universität); James D. G. Dunn, *The Epistles to the Colossians and to Philemon: A Commentary on the Greek Text* (NIGTC; Grand Rapids: Eerdmans 1996); Allan R. Bevere, *Sharing in the Inheritance: Identity and the Moral Life in Colossians* (JSNTSup 226; Sheffield: Sheffield Academic Press, 2003) 174.

45. Patzia, *Ephesians, Colossians, Philemon*, 22.

46. Melisse, "De mens als beeld van God," 376. Several exegetes believe that the transformation described in Col 3:10 presupposes the fall of humanity and that the image of God in human beings, damaged or lost due to the fall, is now restored. However, this does not fit with either the Genesis text or Col 3:10. Genesis 3:22 does not narrate that the human is no longer the image of God. On the contrary, in Gen 9:6, the human is mentioned again as made as the image of God. From Col 3:1–17 it cannot be deduced that the human was no longer the image of God. In the description of the old human there is no reference to Genesis. The idea of a/the "fall" is a later theological interpretation, which can be found, for example, in Irenaeus, but plays no role in Col 3:10. See Gunnlaugur A. Jónsson, *The Image of God: Genesis 1:26–28 in a Century of Old Testament Research* (ConBOT 26; Stockholm: Almqvist & Wiksell, 1988) 12–13.

originated constitute the cognitive worldview of the readers of the letter regarding the worship of cult images.

V. Concluding Remarks

This essay shows that Paul, as teacher in Col 1:15; 3:10, activates specific prior knowledge in his students—the readers of the letter—especially prior knowledge about Gen 1:1–2:3. Paul does this by using the word εἰκών in relation to the domain "creation." In this way, he hopes to make his readers sensitive to his message about Christ. In this teaching, the original meaning of the Genesis text, which focuses on the human, is applied to Christ in such a way that it fits with the cognitive worldview of the time. In Gen 1:26–27, the human is described as an image of God. In Col 1:15; 3:10, this title is reserved for Christ. He is the image of God; and God should therefore not be worshiped by means of a cult image. As the image of God, Christ makes God visible in physical form and represents God on earth.

10

Moses Our Teacher:
Moses as a Model for Rabbinic Teaching

Leon Mock z"l

This contribution will focus on a couple of rabbinic texts that give different pictures of Moses as a teacher. After all, Moses is the only biblical figure who, next to his first name, gets the extra Hebrew title רבינו ("our Teacher, our Master").[1] These texts will be analyzed in relation to how the rabbis see teaching. Issues such as the concrete organization of formal education among the rabbis in antiquity and late antiquity, the extent to which literacy was spread among the population of Israel and among which social strata, or the question of the function of written texts in the rabbinic period—although important—will not be discussed here. Interpreters like Shmuel Safrai, Meir Bar-Ilan, Catherine Hezser, Martin Jaffee, and others have written about this in detail.[2]

---

1. For the English Talmudic texts, the Soncino edition was used.
2. See, e.g., Shmuel Safrai, "Education and the Study of the Torah," in *The Jewish People in the First Century: Historical Geography, Political History, Social, Cultural and Religious Life and Institutions* (ed. Shmuel Safrai and Menahem Stern; 2 vols.; CRINT 1.2; Assen: Van Gorcum; Philadelphia: Fortress, 1987) 945–70; M. Bar-Ilan, "Illiteracy in the Land of Israel in the first centuries C.E.," in *Essays in the Social Scientific Study of Judaism and Jewish Society, Volume II* (ed. Simcha Fishbane, Stuart Schoenfeld, with Alain Goldschläger; New York: Ktav, 1992) 46–61; Martin S. Jaffee, *Torah in the Mouth: Writing and Oral Tradition in Palestinian Judaism, 200 BCE–400 CE* (Oxford: Oxford University Press, 2001); Catherine Hezser, "Private and Public Education," in *The Oxford Handbook of Jewish Daily Life in Roman Palestine* (ed. Catherine Hezser; Oxford: Oxford University Press, 2010) 465–81. For the relationship between written texts and orality see also Catherine Hezser, "Jewish Literacy and the Use of Writing in Late Roman Palestine," in *Jewish Culture and Society under the Christian Roman Empire* (ed.

■ I. Torah Study as the Highest Goal

In later rabbinic Judaism, Torah study is one of the most important religious activities—and, according to some, even the highest goal. Besides "learning to do" (*m. Avot* 6.6) there is "learning with the purpose of teaching" (*m. Avot* 6.6)—but the highest goal is perhaps "learning for the sake of learning" (לשמה), with no purpose other than fulfilling the divine commandment to study the Torah.[3] Anyone who reads the Bible will see that knowledge of the commandments of the divine covenant and of the divine laws is certainly mentioned as important, but not necessarily in the way that they were shaped in the rabbinic world of late antiquity. Deuteronomy, in particular, considers the transmission of the covenant stories and the contents of the Torah to future generations to be important.[4] For this reason, the biblical stories and characters in the rabbinic Midrash are often viewed through this later rabbinic lens, so that doctrines, rabbinic courts (*sanhedria*) and scribes are read in. Thus, patriarch Abraham knew the rabbinic commandments,[5] Jacob learned in the teaching house of Shem and Eber, and King David regularly consulted the Sanhedrin.[6] That is why the prophet Moses was made the rabbinic teacher Moses, with whose revelation the rabbis would be directly connected through their transmitted oral teaching (*m. Avot* 1.1).[7]

Richard Kalmin and Seth Schwartz; Interdisciplinary Studies in Ancient Culture and Religion 3; Leuven: Peeters 2003) 149–95; Carol Bakhos, "Orality and writing," in Hezser, *Oxford Handbook of Jewish Daily Life*, 482–99.

3. See, among others, Maimonides, *Ch. Talmud Torah* 3.10 on the prohibition of taking pleasure from Torah study.

4. See, e.g., Deuteronomy 6; 31:9–13.

5. *B. Yoma* 28b (Eruv Tavshilin allowing cooking on Yom Tov before Shabbat); *Bereshit Rabbah* 63.10 as an exegesis on Gen 25:27 about the tent in which Jacob stayed, as opposed to Esau, the man of the field. That tent, of course, is the Beth Midrash of Shem and Eber.

6. *B. Ber.* 3b: "A harp was hanging above David's bed. As soon as midnight arrived, a North wind came and blew upon it and it played of itself. He arose immediately and studied the Torah till the break of dawn. After the break of dawn, the wise men of Israel came in to see him and said to him: Our lord, the King, Israel your people require sustenance! He said to them: Let them go out and make a living one from the other. They said to him: A handful cannot satisfy a lion, nor can a pit be filled up with its own clods. He said to them: Then go out in troops and attack [the enemy for plunder]. They at once took counsel with Ahithofel and consulted the Sanhedrin and questioned the Urim and Tummim...."

7. See, e.g., Catherine Hezser, *The Social Structure of the Rabbinic Movement in Roman Palestine* (TSAJ 66; Tübingen: Mohr Siebeck, 1997) 457–59.

■ II. MODEL I: MOSES TEACHES TORAH TO THE ENTIRE NATION OF ISRAEL

The first text I will discuss presents Moses as the teacher of the whole nation of Israel (or just the men?), teaching mainly orally. It is a rabbinic representation of what Moses's teaching looked like in the desert period—but may be primarily a representation of elements of rabbinic teaching in antiquity/late antiquity. The text comes from *b. Erub.* 54b and I will discuss it in smaller text elements. The text opens (element A) with the question what Moses's teaching looked like and gives the origin of this:

> A. Our Rabbis taught: What was the order of learning? Moses learned from the mouth of the Almighty.

The Hebrew here has סדר משנה, *seder Mishna*, which can be translated as the order of learning (the root is after all ש-נ-ה). At the same time, it confirms the dogma that Moses's teaching is of divine origin. The emphasis on the fact that Moses himself learned from the mouth of the Almighty (Hebrew גבורה) also underlines the oral character of the teaching. In his commentary on this passage, Rashi interprets *seder Mishna* explicitly as the oral teaching. Thus, the entire passage would be explicitly about the oral teaching and not the written Torah.[8] From a rabbinic point of view this may not be an illogical conclusion, since there is no mention of a written text, and according to the Talmud the written Torah may not be recited only orally (without reading from a text).[9]

After Moses learned directly from God, his brother Aaron was taught first:

> B. [Then] Aaron came in and Moses taught him his lesson. Aaron sat down on Moses' left side.

Aaron sits on Moses's left side, although one would expect him to sit on the right—after all, the right side is usually considered more important. However, according to Rashi, sitting or walking on the right next to your

---

8. Rashi on *b. Erub.* 54b: כיצד למדו ישראל תורה שבעל פה, "How Israel Learned the Oral Torah."

9. See *b. Git.* 60b: "R. Judah b. Nahmani the public orator [meturgaman] of R. Simeon b. Lakish discoursed as follows: 'It is written, "Write thou these words" [Exod 34:27] and it is written, "For according to the mouth of these words"' [Exod 34:27]. What are we to make of this?—It means: The words which are written thou art not at liberty to say by heart, and the words transmitted orally thou art not at liberty to recite from writing."

teacher is respectful only if there is also someone present on the left who is the lowest in rank.[10]

The next to be taught are the sons of Aaron, Eleazar and Itamar:

> C. [After this] Aaron's sons came in and Moses taught them their lesson. His sons left [after this] [from before Moses]: Eleazar took his place on Moses' right and Ithamar on Aaron's left. R. Judah said: Aaron had always sat on Moses' right side.

Surprisingly, in this first variant, Eleazar is seen as more important (he may sit on Moses's right) than his own father Aaron—an illogical conclusion according to Rabbi Judah. Hence, the latter states that Aaron always sat to the right of Moses, from the very beginning. The next step is to teach the elders (זקנים), who have an important position of authority in the Bible, already in the stories about the people of Israel in Egypt.[11]

> D. [After this] the Elders came in and Moses taught them their lesson. When the Elders left [Moses's field of vision], all the people came in and Moses taught them their lesson. So, the result was that Aaron [heard] the lesson four times, his sons three times, the Elders twice, and all the people once.

In this—at first sight—somewhat hierarchical system, the people are taught last. A hierarchy indeed, but one that includes everyone and excludes no one. Remarkable here is also the important function of the priests as teachers—in other rabbinic traditions this role is minimized (see *m. Avot* 1:1).[12]

After this cycle (elements A–D) is completed, the different actors have heard the lesson an unequal number of times, depending on their hierarchical position. The next steps are aimed at making this difference disappear:

> E. Now Moses departed and Aaron taught them [the people] the lesson [literally: his lesson, as he heard it the first time]. After this, Aaron made way, and his sons taught them [the people] the lesson [literally: their lesson]. His sons made way, and the Elders taught them [the people] the lesson [literally: their lesson]. Now everyone had [heard the lesson] [at least] four times.

---

10. Rashi on *b. Erub.* 54b: המהלך לימין רבו הרי זה בור, וכל שכן יושב בזמן שאין שני לישב בשמאל, "The one who moves to the right, many say, is an idiot, and even more so, sitting at a time when there is no one to sit on the left."
11. See, e.g., Exod 3:16; 12:21; Deut 21:2–3; Josh 24:1, 31.
12. In the historical chain of tradition mentioned there, the priests do not even appear anymore: Moses–Joshua–The Elders–Members of the Great Assembly, etc.

138   Models of the Teacher

In E something happens that was already visible in A—the roles of teacher and pupil change. A teacher is himself first a pupil, just as Moses was first a pupil and God his teacher. Now Aaron, Eleazar, Itamar, and the elders also become students and teachers. Now each of them must teach the people until everyone reaches the minimum number of four.

■ III. From Biblical Times to the (Rabbinical) Present

So far, the Talmudic fragment aims to give a truthful account of the biblical past. From this past, the focus now shifts to the present, to what can be learned for the teacher–student relationship from this biblical example.

> F. Based on this, R. Eliezer said, A man is obligated to teach his students [the material] at least four times. And we can deduce this on the basis of a kol vachomer [a fortiori argument]: if Aaron who learned directly from Moses—and Moses from the Almighty—had to do it like this [hear the lesson four times], how much more than an ordinary [הדיוט, from Greek ἰδιώτης] pupil who receives instruction from an ordinary person.

So, the conclusion is that a teacher must teach new material to the pupil at least four times, otherwise the basis for further study will not be laid. Apparently, the assumption is also that most students have enough with these four times. But has the teacher fulfilled his duty? According to Rabbi Akiba not necessarily:

> G. R. Akiba says: How do I know that a teacher [literally: man] should teach his student until he has [really] taught him? For it is said, "and teach the sons of Israel" [Deut 31:19]. And how do I know [that the teacher should continue], until it comes out of their mouths in a proper order? For it is said, "Put it into their mouths" [Deut 31:19]. And how do I know that he must show him [the pupil] the reasons? For it is said, "and these are the ordinances of law which you shall present to them" [Exod 21:1].

Rabbi Akiba states that these four times of teaching the student is only a minimum. This does not mean that the student has in fact mastered what he learned. In Hebrew it says, actually, that the teacher must continue to teach until the student has learned.[13] Then, according to Rabbi Akiba—obviously following Moses's example—the teacher must continue his teaching until the student can articulate what he has learned flawlessly.

---

13. רבי עקיבא אומר: מניין שחייב אדם לשנות לתלמידיו עד שילמדנו, "Rabbi Akiba says: The minyan is that a person is obligated to change for his student until he teaches us."

Finally, the teacher must make clear to the pupil the reasons for a certain matter, the justification for the subject matter taught.[14] Only when all these conditions are met, one can speak of learning, according to Rabbi Akiba.

IV. MODEL II: LEARNING IN INTIMATE CONTEXT

The second model focuses on the intimate teacher–pupil relationship, ideally in a one-on-one setting. The ideal model here is the way Moses learned from God. This model is found in the *Sifra* on Lev 1:1 – *Dibura deNedaba* 1 (sub sec. 1 and 2). This exegesis is best known from the Rashi commentary on Lev 1:1, and it is this fairly literal rendering by Rashi that is used below. The *Sifra* opens by stating that every time there was a speaking of God to Moses, it was preceded by a calling of God to Moses. This as a sign of love:

> A. Every "speaking" [וידבר], "saying" [ויאמר] or "commanding" [צו] was [by God] always preceded by [calling] [Moses by his name].[15]

The *Sifra* adds that Moses's name was then pronounced twice—"Moses, Moses"—followed by the "here I am!" (הנני).[16] The central idea here is that communication between teacher and student should be done in love. However, calling Moses by name occurred only when divine speaking followed in which new learning was given:

> B. ... One might think that [Moses] was also called at the interruptions [the breaks between topics in divine speaking] [and the conversation then continued]. Therefore, it says, "And He spoke" [to Moses, Lev 1:1] prior to the speaking there was the calling, but not at the breaks.[17]

These periods of pauses between divine speaking had a didactic purpose that is so much truer in the "normal" teacher–student situation:

> C. And what was the function of these interruptions? To give Moses a space for reflection between sections and between substantive details [of

---

14. This following Rashi's explanation on the words of Rabbi Akiba on *b. Erub.* 54b: ללמדו, לתת טעם בדבריו בכל אשר יוכל, ולא יאמר: כך שמעתי, הבן אתה הטעם מעצמך. אשר תשים לפניהם – ולא כתיב אשר תלמדם – צריך אתה לסדר ולשום לפניהם טעם המיישב תלמודם, "To teach him, to give a reason for his words in every way he can, and he should not say: Thus I heard, you are the reason for yourself. Whatever you put before them – and it is not written that you will teach them – you need to arrange and put before them a reason that will satisfy their learning."
15. Rashi on Lev 1:1.
16. *Sifra* (Weiss edition), *Dibura deNedaba* 1.1–10, 11. See also Exod 3:4.
17. Rashi on Lev 1:1; and *Sifra, Dibura deNedaba* 1.1–8.

a passage]. A fortiori then, this certainly applies to an ordinary person receiving instruction from an ordinary teacher [see also above].[18]

The *Sifra* and Rashi continue with an account of the divine voice that was audible in the tent of meeting. However, this could be heard only by Moses, not others—confirming the intimacy of the teaching situation:

> D. To him [אליו]: this excludes Aaron. . . . One might think that surely, they [the Israelites] would hear the calling [of God to Moses] [but thus not the content of the speaking]. For that, it says "to him" [אליו – where it could also theoretically have said לו]: only Moses heard it, but all Israel did not.[19]

Sifra (and Rashi) continues with another exposition of the divine voice. The fact that it was not heard by anyone except Moses was not due to its low intensity; on the contrary, God's voice shatters the cedars of Lebanon (Ps 29:5).[20] Finally, the *Sifra* reports that Moses must reassure Israel that his divine teaching comes solely because of Israel herself. The teacher must never forget his calling to the collective:[21]

> E. . . . as follows, saying [לאמר]: [God said to Moses:] Go and tell them [the Israelites] words of persuasion [namely,] "Because of you he speaks to me." For we find, after all, that all thirty-eight years in the desert, when the Israelites were wandering around as outcasts—from the sin of the spies—the divine speaking was no longer with Moses. As it is written, "And it was then that of the people all the warriors had died, and the Eternal One spoke to me" [Deut 2:16–17]. Only then was the divine speaking addressed to me.[22]

■ V. MODEL III: THE MYSTICAL TEACHER

In this model, the teacher has at his disposal mystical skills that enable him to "ascend" to heavenly regions and "descend" again to earth with

---

18. *Sifra, Dibura deNedaba* 1.1–9.
19. Ibid., 1.2–1.7–8.
20. Ibid., 1.2–10 and Rashi on Lev 1:1: "This teaches us that the [Divine] voice stopped and did not project itself beyond the Tent [of Meeting]. One might think that this was because the voice was low. Scripture therefore says, '[And when Moses came into the Tent of Meeting, he heard] the voice' [Num 7:89]. What is the meaning of 'the voice' [with the definite article]? It is the voice referred to in Psalms [29:4–5]: 'The voice of the Lord is in strength; the voice of the Lord is in beauty. The voice of the Lord breaks cedars.' If so, why does it say, '[and the Lord spoke to him] from the Tent of Meeting'? [To inform us] that the [divine] voice stopped."
21. On the will of rabbis in the first centuries of the era to actively share their knowledge with the public, see Hezser, "Social Structure of the Rabbinic Movement," 100–104.
22. *Sifra, Dibura deNedaba* 1.2–13.

knowledge gained. Or at least to provide on earth a kind of mini-revelation.[23] A good example of this is a Talmudic passage in b. Shab. 88b–89a. In it, we are told how Moses ascends to heaven prior to the Revelation and there is confronted by hostile angels who do not want God to give the Torah to flesh and blood, to mortal humans—in other Midrash stories, too, the angels are negative toward humanity.[24] Moses even has to fear for his life because of "the fiery breath" of the angels. This excerpt bears similarities to mystical texts in Talmud and Hekhalot literature. There, the mystic ascends to heaven and must fear all kinds of dangers, including angels. With proper preparation and mystical knowledge, the mystic manages to make the journey and return safely to earth.[25] After God offers protection to Moses, Moses must answer the angels:

> A. Lord of the World! The Torah that You give to me—what is written in it? "I am the Eternal your God who brought you out of the land of Egypt" [Exod 20:2]. Did He say to them [the angels], "Did you then descend into Egypt; were you slaves of Pharaoh? Why should the Torah belong to you?" And, what else is written in it: "You shall have no other gods" [Exod 20:3]—do you then live among peoples who worship other gods? And, what else is written in it: "Remember the day of the Sabbath to keep it holy" [Exod 20:8]—do you then work so that you should rest? . . . And, what else is written in it: "You shall not murder; you shall not commit adultery; you shall not steal" [Exod 20:3–15]: is there then jealousy among you, is the Evil Tendency to be found among you?"

Moses manages to convince the angels and they give him "gifts"—esoteric knowledge:

> B. Immediately, the angels agreed with the Holy One—praised be He [to give the Torah to man], as it is said, "O Eternal One, our Lord, how glo-

---

23. See the story about Jochana ben Zakai in b. Ḥag. 14b: "Our Rabbis taught: Once R. Johanan b. Zakkai was riding on an ass when going on a journey, and R. Eleazar b. 'Arak was driving the ass from behind. [R. Eleazar] said to him: Master, teach me a chapter of the 'Work of the Chariot' [Merkavah]. He answered: Have I not taught you thus: 'Nor [the work of] the chariot in the presence of one, unless he is a Sage and understands of his own knowledge'? [R. Eleazar] then said to him: Master, permit me to say before thee something which thou hast taught me. He answered, Say on! . . . Forthwith, R. Eleazar b. 'Arak began his exposition of the 'work of the Chariot,' and fire came down from heaven and encompassed all the trees in the field; [thereupon] they all began to utter [divine] song . . . ."

24. See, e.g., *Midrash Genesis Rabbah* (Vilna edition) 8.5, in which angels oppose the creation of man.

25. See, among others, Ithamar Gruenwald, *Apocalyptic and Merkavah Mysticism* (1980; repr., AJEC 90; Leiden: Brill, 2014). On the passage from b. Shab. 88b see, e.g., 125–26, and on the parallel passages in rabbinic literature and the theme of the hostile angels, see n. 45.

rious is Your Name on all the earth" [Ps 8:10]. . . . Immediately each angel became a friend of Moses [literally: beloved] and gave him something. As it is said, "You went up to heaven and took booty there. You took gifts [to distribute] among men" [Ps 68:19]—as a reward that you [Moses] were called "man" [אדם] by them, you took gifts. The Angel of Death gave him something. For it is said, ". . . and then he put incense on it and made atonement for the people" [Num 16:47], and it is said, "and he stood between the dead and the living, and the plague ceased" [Num 16:48]. If he had not told him [Moses], how did he know [that incense stops the plague]?

Moses even manages to overcome death through knowledge given to him by the Angel of Death. Interesting here is the parallel exegesis on the same Psalm text in Eph 4:7–8, where it is applied to Jesus and believers reap the benefits of this in the form of grace (and the Holy Spirit).[26]

■ VI. Conclusion

This post has described three models related to the teaching of Moses as imagined by the rabbis. While these models are distinct, as shown above, they are not necessarily mutually exclusive. Rather, they are complementary—a teacher may adopt a particular model depending on the physical situation and on the student. From one-on-one teaching with a beloved star pupil in which depth and personal attention are central, to a kind of lecture for the collective. And for a very select few, there is the mystical model in which the initiate gains access to esoteric knowledge. A skillful and authoritative teacher masters these three models and knows how to use each one in the right way, tailored to the situation. Just as Moses did. Thus, at least in a metaphorical sense, the important teachers are extensions of him [Moses] in every generation.[27]

---

26. See also Augustine, *Exposition on Psalm 68* (trans. J. E. Tweed; NPNF First Series, ed. Philip Schaff; Buffalo: Christian Literature Publishing, 1888), vol. 8 (online: *New Advent*; ed. Kevin Knight; http://www.newadvent.org/fathers/1801068.htm; accessed December 12, 2024), paragraph 22.

27. *Tikkunei Zohar, Tikkun* 69, ואתפשטותיה הוא בכל דרא ודרא, "and its extensions are in every generation." In some editions: *Tikkunei Zohar* 114a: ואתפשטותיה דמשה בכל דרא ודרא, "the extensions of Moses are in every generation."

11

"Are We to Turn and All Listen to Her?"
Mary Magdalene as Contested Teacher from the *Gospel of Mary* to *Mary Magdalene* (Garth Davis, 2018)

Caroline H. C. M. Vander Stichele

One of the most well-known women from the Gospels, apart from Jesus's mother, is Mary Magdalene, although in the New Testament her role is rather limited. She appears at the end of the Gospels as one of the women visiting Jesus's tomb (Matt 28:1; Mark 16:1, 9–10; Luke 24:10; John 20:1–18).[1] In the Gospel of John, she is the only one to receive a message from the risen Christ for his apostles: "But go to my brothers and say to them, 'I am ascending to my Father and your Father, to my God and your God'" (20:17). Mary delivers this message faithfully, and that is the last thing we hear of her in the New Testament.[2]

It is, however, not the end of her story, which continued well beyond the New Testament. Her reputation grew, albeit in different directions. In the Western tradition she became identified with other female characters from the New Testament, such as the sinner in Luke 7:37–50 and the

---

1. The Gospel of Luke is the only one that mentions her earlier in the Gospel. In Luke 8:2 she is introduced as "Mary, called Magdalene, from whom seven demons had gone out" (NRSV), together with other women who supported "them" (Jesus and the Twelve) out of their own means (v. 3). The reading in the text of NA[28] has "them" (αὐτοῖς), but a variant reading has the singular "him" (αὐτῷ). In that case, the women provide financial support for Jesus only.

2. For a discussion of her role in the canonical Gospels, see Edmondo F. Lupieri, "The Earliest Magdalene: Varied Portrayals in Early Gospel Narratives," in *Mary Magdalene from the New Testament to the New Age and Beyond* (ed. Edmondo F. Lupieri; Themes in Biblical Narrative 24; Leiden: Brill, 2020) 11–25.

woman caught in adultery in John 8:3–11, but also with later characters, such as the desert mother Mary of Egypt.[3] Later legends were recorded by Jacobus de Voragine in his *Legenda Aurea*, which dates from the thirteenth century. It includes Mary's journey to Marseilles in France, where she started preaching to people sacrificing to idols: "She came forward, her manner calm and her face serene, and with well-chosen words called them away from the cult of idols and preached Christ to them. All who heard her were in admiration at her beauty, her eloquence, and the sweetness of her message."[4] This is one of the instances in which Mary Magdalene is portrayed as teacher. Another, much earlier text in which that is also the case is the extracanonical *Gospel of Mary*, where she is instructing the apostles after the resurrection.[5]

In what follows, I take a closer look at the way in which Mary is depicted in this Gospel and the way in which the apostles respond to her message. In the second part of this essay, I fast forward to the twenty-first century and discuss the portrayal of Mary Magdalene in two films. The first one is *Mary* (2005) from Abel Ferrara, the second *Mary Magdalene* (2018) from Garth Davis. I will argue that in both cases the depiction in these films of Mary Magdalene as a teacher has been inspired by the *Gospel of Mary*.

3. The conflation of Mary Magdalene with the sinful woman from Luke 7 can be traced back to the patristic era. See Amanda Kunder, "The Patristic Magdalene: Symbol for the Church and Witness to the Resurrection," in Lupieri, *Mary Magdalene from the New Testament*, 105–27. For the conflation with Mary of Egypt, see Barbara Baert, *Maria Magdalena: Zondares van de Middeleeuwen tot vandaag* (Cahier 4; Gent: Museum voor Schone Kunsten Gent, 2002) 17–20, 77–78; and Ann-Sophie Lehmann, "Maria Magdalena und die feministische Kunstgeschichte," in *Doing Gender in Medien-, Kunst- und Kulturwissenschaften: Eine Einführung* (ed. Rosemarie Buikema and Kathrin Thiele; Gender-Diskussion 23; Berlin: LIT, 2017) 159–77, here 169. For the legend of Saint Mary of Egypt, see Jacobus de Voragine, *The Golden Legend: Readings on the Saints* (trans. William Granger Ryan; 2 vols.; Princeton, NJ: Princeton University Press, 1993) 1:227–29.

4. Jacobus de Voragine, *Golden Legend*, 1:374–83, here 376–77.

5. Trent A. Rogers notes that a distinction should be made between the canonical Gospels and narrative expansions that feature Mary Magdalene as witness of the resurrection and Gnostic texts in which Mary Magdalene appears as "ideal dialogue partner, revealer of gnosis, and spiritual consort of the Lord" ("The Apocryphal Magdalene: Expanding and Limiting Her Importance," in Lupieri, *Mary Magdalene from the New Testament*, 26–49, here 26 n. 3. See also Caroline Vander Stichele, "Talking Nonsense? The Disciples' Response to the Women in Luke 24:1–22 and Other Early Christian Texts," in *Themes and Texts in Luke-Acts: Essays in Honour of Bart J. Koet* (ed. Bert Jan Lietaert Peerbolte, Caroline Vander Stichele, and Archibald L. H. M. van Wieringen; Studies in Theology and Religion 31; Leiden: Brill, 2023) 241–56.

■ I. Teaching the Apostles

The *Gospel of Mary* is an early Christian text that was unknown until the end of the nineteenth century. It was found in a codex containing four works written in Coptic. The codex itself was bought in Egypt in 1896 and taken to Berlin, hence its name Papyrus Berolinensis (BG 8502). Due to a series of misfortunes, however, it took until 1955 for it to be published. The Coptic manuscript itself dates from the fifth century, but the content is clearly older, as other evidence, in the form of two small Greek papyri fragments (*P.Oxy.* 3525 and *P.Ryl.* 463), makes clear. These fragments cover parts of the text in the Coptic manuscript and can be dated to the third century. Unfortunately, no textual evidence covers the full story. From the Coptic text only pages 7–10 and 15–19 have survived, and the Greek papyri merely cover a few lines of the text, barely enough to map some of the differences between the extant Coptic version and the Greek fragments. The existence of these fragments, however, makes it possible to surmise that this Gospel was originally written in Greek during the second century.[6]

Notwithstanding the fact that the text has been only partially preserved, its overall structure is clear. The current text starts in the middle of a dialogue between the Savior and Peter (7:4–9:4). It is followed by the departure of the Savior (9:5) and the distressed reaction of his disciples (9:6–11). Mary comforts the disciples (9:12–23), and Peter invites her to tell them what the Savior has revealed to her (10:1–6). Mary's lengthy reply extends from 10:7 to 17:9, but unfortunately a substantial part of her speech (pages 11–14) is missing. It is followed by a discussion between Andrew, Peter, and Levi about the trustworthiness of her words (17:10–18:21), by the observation that they start to go out to teach and preach (19:1–2), and finally by the identification of the text as the *Gospel of Mary* (19:3–5).

As this overview makes clear, the text that has been preserved consists mostly of direct speech embedded in a narrative framework,[7] but apart from the characters involved it remains unclear where this scene

---

6. Christopher M. Tuckett, *The Gospel of Mary* (Oxford Early Christian Gospel Texts; Oxford: Oxford University Press, 2007) 3–12. The translation used in what follows is that of Tuckett.

7. A more detailed discussion of this framework can be found in Judith Hartenstein, *Die zweite Lehre: Erscheinungen des Auferstandenen als Rahmenerzählung frühchristlicher Dialoge* (Texte und Untersuchungen zur Geschichte der altchristlichen Literatur 146; ; Berlin: Akademie, 2000) 142–52.

takes place.[8] Moreover, the identity of the one called "the savior" is not revealed.[9] These characteristics play an important role in the discussion about the genre to which this text belongs. As already noted above, the title attributed at the end of the text itself is that of Gospel (π[εγ]αγγελιον). This designation is in line with what the Savior himself orders his disciples to do before he leaves (8:21–22: "Go then and preach the gospel of the kingdom") and what Levi repeats at the end (18:18–19: "Let us preach the gospel, not laying down any other rule or other law beyond what the Saviour said").

Nevertheless, the comparison with other early Christian texts has led to a variety of genre attributions, most of them based on the dialogical character of the text, such as *Dialogues of Jesus with His Disciples after His Resurrection*, or *Gnostic Dialogues*.[10] In her discussion of the genre issue, Sarah Parkhouse observes that genre labels are tentative at best, because they highlight certain issues but obscure others. "The confusion that the *Gospel of Mary* causes about where it belongs demonstrates that texts cannot be pigeonholed. The *Gospel of Mary* is a gospel, a (revelation) dialogue, a dialogue gospel, and an apocalypse."[11] Like other dialogues, it features Jesus instructing his disciples before his final departure. Some of these dialogues also include women. This is notably the case in the *Gospel of Thomas*, the *Wisdom of Jesus Christ*, the *Dialogue of the Savior*, and the *Pistis Sophia*.[12] In all these texts Mary Magdalene is explicitly mentioned and, in some cases, even plays a prominent role, but no parallel exists for her role in the *Gospel of Mary*, where she takes over Jesus's role as a teacher after his departure.[13]

---

8. This information may have been included in the missing pages from the beginning of the document.

9. Other designations that appear in the text are "blessed one," "lord," and "son of man." It is clear, however, from the context and the other characters involved that all these titles refer to the resurrected Christ. The same identification as "savior" also appears in other apocryphal dialogues between the risen Christ and his disciples featuring Mary Magdalene, such as the *Wisdom of Jesus Christ* (NHC III,4; BG 8502,3) and the *Dialogue of the Saviour* (NHC III,5). See further James M. Robinson, ed., *The Nag Hammadi Library in English* (3rd rev. ed.; Leiden: Brill, 1988) 220–55.

10. See the overview in Sarah Parkhouse, *Eschatology and the Saviour: The Gospel of Mary among Early Christian Dialogue Gospels* (SNTSMS 176; Cambridge: Cambridge University Press, 2019) 27.

11. Ibid., 37.

12. For a detailed analysis of Mary's role in these writings, see Silke Petersen, *Zerstört die Werke der Weiblichkeit! Maria Magdalena, Salome, und andere Jüngerinnen Jesu in christlich-gnostischen Schriften* (NHMS 48; Leiden: Brill, 1999) 94–194, here 102–4.

13. See Petersen, *Zerstört die Werke*, 139: "Die Einzigartigkeit des EvMar besteht

This teaching role can be seen in all the scenes after Jesus's departure. Mary first addresses the despairing disciples, called "her brothers," with the words: "Do not weep and do not grieve nor be irresolute, for his grace will be wholly with you and will protect you. But rather let us praise his greatness, for he has prepared us and made us into human beings" (9:14–20). Then Peter addresses Mary saying, "Sister, we know that the Saviour loved you more than the rest of women," and he invites her to share with them "the words of the Saviour which you remember, which you know but we do not, and which we have not heard" (10:1–6). Mary accepts the invitation and tells them that she has seen the Lord in a vision and shares the conversation that she had with him about this experience. Unfortunately, the text breaks off in the middle of the Lord's reply, because the following pages 11–14 are missing. The text resumes in the middle of a report about what can be called the journey or rise of the soul.[14] When she has finished her report, Mary falls silent, "since the Saviour had spoken with her up to now" (17:8–9).

The response of the disciples to her message is mixed. The first one to react is Andrew, who expresses his doubts, saying, "I, myself do not believe that the Saviour said this. For these teachings [ⲚⲒⲤⲂⲞⲞⲨⲈ] seem to be giving different ideas" (17:13–15).[15] Notwithstanding his critical attitude, Andrew nevertheless identifies Mary's words as teaching and thus recognizes her role as teacher. Peter supports his brother and equally raises doubts, but in his case they relate to Mary: "He did not speak with a woman without our knowing, and not openly, did he? Shall we turn around and all listen to her? Did he prefer her to us?" (17:18–22). Mary is shocked and starts weeping, asking him, "My brother Peter, what do you think? Do you think that I thought this up in my heart, or that I am lying about the Saviour?" (18:2–5). At this point Levi intervenes and comes to her support, asking Peter, "if the Saviour made her worthy, who are you then to reject her? Certainly, the Saviour knows her very well. That is

---

darin, dass Maria ... in einer Rolle auftritt, die sonst nur Jesus zukommt: Sie tröstet, ermutigt und belehrt die JüngerInnen."

14. As Karen King notes, such accounts were widespread in late antiquity (*The Gospel of Mary of Magdala: Jesus and the First Woman Apostle* (Santa Rosa, CA: Polebridge, 2003) 72–76.

15. The Rylands Papyrus (*P.Ryl.* 463) includes the reply of Andrew, but a corresponding word for "teachings" is missing. The (reconstructed) text has δοκει γ[αρ ετε]ρογνωμονειν τη εx[ε]ιν[ου ενv]νοια (2:9–11). See Tuckett, *Gospel of Mary*, 112. The (reconstructed) Coptic text also includes "to teach" ([ⲈⲦⲢⲈⲨⲦ]ⲀⲘⲞ) at the end of the Gospel in 19:2: "and they began to go out [to pr]oclaim and to preach" (translated by Tuckett as "proclaim" [*Gospel of Mary*, 103]), but King translates "to teach" (*Gospel of Mary of Magdala*, 18). P.Ryl. 463 only has "to preach" (κη[ρυσ][σειν, 22:15–16).

why he loved her more than us" (18:10-15).[16] He then summons the other disciples to go preach the gospel, and that is what they end up doing.[17]

In the *Gospel of Mary*, it is Mary Magdalene who teaches the apostles words from the Savior that they do not know.[18] Her lengthy speech reveals things that were hidden from them so far (10:8).[19] This gives her a prominent and unique position among the disciples, but their reaction is mixed. Andrew identifies what she said as "teachings" (17:14), but he has his doubts about their content, which is unfamiliar to him. Peter's doubts relate to the trustworthiness of the teacher, who is a woman.[20] Levi, on the contrary supports her with reference to the authority of the Savior, who considered her worthy, and summons them to do as the Savior instructed and preach the gospel.[21]

---

16. A shift takes place here, insofar as Peter recognized earlier that Jesus loved Mary more than other women (10:3), while Levi states here that Jesus loved her more than all of them (18:14–15).

17. Only Levi is mentioned in *P.Ryl.* 463 (22:15).

18. As Hartenstein notes, in the *Gospel of Mary* two characters are presented as teaching the disciples (*Die zweite Lehre*, 129). In the first part it is Jesus; in the second part, Mary. In both cases, however, the actual teaching is presented as that of Jesus. In the first case he is teaching the disciples himself; in the second case he is teaching indirectly through Mary. See also King, *Gospel of Mary of Magdala*, 30.

19. The extent to which the *Gospel of Mary* can be qualified as gnostic is a debated issue. See Esther A. de Boer, *The Gospel of Mary: Beyond a Gnostic and a Biblical Mary Magdalene* (JSNTSup 260; London: T&T Clark, 2004) 27–34. On the usefulness of the category "Gnosticism" more generally, see Antti Marjanen, ed., *Was There a Gnostic Religion?* (Publications of the Finnish Exegetical Society 87; Helsinki: Finnish Exegetical Society; Göttingen: Vandenhoek & Ruprecht, 2005).

20. Other texts in which Peter appears as Mary's antagonist are the *Gospel of Thomas* (114) and *Pistis Sophia* 36:72. See further Petersen, *Zerstört die Werke*, 163–88. According to Cambry G. Pardee, "The Gospel of Mary is the only one among these three conflict texts in which the quarrel between Mary and Peter is likely a literary or symbolic allusion to an historical conflict between Petrine (proto-orthodox) Christianity and opposing (heterodox) Christianities" ("The Gnostic Magdalene: Mary as Disciple and Revealer," in Lupieri, *Mary Magdalene from the New Testament*, 50–78, here 73). Douglas M. Parrott observes that disciples mentioned in the *Wisdom of Jesus Christ*, notably Philip, Matthew, Bartholomew, and Mary, are portrayed as Gnostic and "contrasted with some regularity, and in various ways, with 'orthodox' or 'orthodox turned gnostic' disciples (principally, Peter and John)" ("Eugnostos the Blessed [III,3 and V,1] and The Sophia of Jesus Christ [III,4 and BG 8502,3]," in Robinson, *Nag Hammadi Library in English*, 221).

21. The association between Mary and Levi also appears in other extracanonical texts. See Petersen, *Zerstört die Werke*, 165–67.

In sum, Mary's prominent role in the *Gospel of Mary* (and other apocryphal texts) signals her importance and elevated status for particular groups of Christians, but that this role was contested is also apparent from the texts in question. As Cambry Pardee points out, the *Gospel of Mary* thus serves both an apologetic and a polemical end.[22] Her gender is a returning issue in this context. Other evidence for the contested nature of her and other women's authority to teach can also be found in the *Didascalia Apostolorum*, dating from the third century:

> For He, the Lord God, Jesus Christ, our Teacher, sent us the Twelve to instruct the People and the Gentiles; and there were with us women disciples, Mary Magdalene and Mary the daughter of James and the other Mary; but He did not send them to instruct the people with us. For if it were required that women should teach, our Master Himself would have commanded these to give instruction with us.[23]

That Mary Magdalene is mentioned first signals her importance in an ongoing debate about women's role as teacher. The *Gospel of Mary* serves as evidence of this role as well as of the resistance to it.

The publication of this Gospel in 1955 has contributed to a renewed interest in and rehabilitation of Mary Magdalene. Numerous scholarly and popular publications have seen the light ever since and visual artists, including filmmakers, have also picked up on that. A notable case is Dan Brown's successful novel *The Da Vinci Code* (2003) and the film based on that novel, which came out in 2006. Other examples are Abel Ferrara's film *Mary* (2005), and Garth Davis's *Mary Magdalene* (2018). In what follows I focus on these two films.

■ II. Mary Magdalene in Film

Mary Magdalene made her entrance in film already in the silent film era, first in scenes related to the passion and later in full-fledged Jesus films. Most often the traditional image of Mary Magdalene as woman of ill repute was simply reproduced in these films, but a shift can be noticed in

---

22. See Pardee, "Gnostic Magdalene," 74.
23. R. Hugh Connolly, *Didascalia Apostolorum: The Syriac Version Translated and Accompanied by the Verona Latin Fragments, with an Introduction and Notes* (1929; repr., with a foreword by K. C. Hanson and an introduction by Dom Aidan Bellenger; Eugene, OR: Wipf & Stock, 2010), 133. See also Rogers, "Apocryphal Magdalene," 33.

the twenty-first century.²⁴ The two films under discussion here have in common that Mary Magdalene plays an important role. As I will show in what follows both also draw on the *Gospel of Mary* for the way in which they represent Mary as a teacher in her own right. That is most explicitly the case in the first film, entitled *Mary* (2005).²⁵

Mary (2005)

In Abel Ferrara's film *Mary*, the story of Mary Magdalene is embedded in a present-day narrative featuring the following characters: an actress, Marie Pavesi (played by Juliette Binoche); a film director, Tony Childress (Matthew Modine); and a TV-host, Theodore Younger (Forest Whitaker). Younger is presenting a TV show entitled "Jesus: The Real Story," in which he interviews several (nonfictional) religious experts.²⁶ Marie Pavesi for her part plays the role of Mary Magdalene in a film, entitled *This Is My Blood* directed by Tony Childress.

Mary starts with a scene from this film (*This Is My Blood*), notably the discovery of the empty tomb by two women, one of them Mary Magdalene. The scene is filmed from inside the tomb. The women push away the stone and enter the cave. They look around and weep. There are two other characters in the tomb, dressed as angels. One of them asks, "Woman, why are you weeping?" Mary replies, "They've taken away my lord. I don't know where they've laid him." The angel replies, "Why do you search the living among the dead?" Mary turns around and sees Jesus, who stands outside looking in from behind the stone, which is only

---

24. For a discussion of Mary Magdalene in Jesus films, see Adele Reinhartz, *Jesus of Hollywood* (Oxford: Oxford University Press, 2007) 125–49. For a discussion of the representation of Mary Magdalene in three twenty-first century films, see Caroline Vander Stichele, "Mary Magdalene in Motion," in *Recent Releases: The Bible in Contemporary Cinema* (ed. Geert Hallbäck and Annika Hvithamar; Bible in the Modern World 15; Sheffield: Sheffield Phoenix, 2008) 93–114. The three films discussed are: *The Passion of the Christ* (Mel Gibson, 2004), *Mary* (Abel Ferrara, 2005), and *The Da Vinci Code* (Ron Howard, 2006). See also Caroline Vander Stichele, "Mary Magdalene Portrayed on the Silver Screen," in *Mary Magdalene: Chief Witness, Sinner, Feminist* (ed. Lieke Wijnia; Zwolle: Waanders; Utrecht: Museum Catharijneconvent, 2021) 26–31.

25. The film did not really make it in mainstream cinema, in part because it never came out on DVD in the United States. See Erica-Lyn Saccucci, "From Disciple to Deviant: The Magdalene in Contemporary Popular Film," in Lupieri, *Mary Magdalene from the New Testament*, 318–36, here 331.

26. The interviewees are Amos Luzzatto (president of the Union of Italian Jewish Communities), Ivan Nicoletta (Benedictine monk), and Jean-Yves Leloup (theologian). Elaine Pagels also makes an appearance (in a documentary about the apocryphal Gospels that T. Younger watches in the studio).

partially rolled away. They look at each other. He says, "Mary" (offscreen), she replies "Rabbouni!" She runs to him, but he raises his hand and says, "Do not hold on to me for I have not yet ascended to the Father. But go to my brothers and tell them I am ascending to My Father and your Father, to my God and your God." The scene ends with a close-up of Mary's face looking at him with wide-open eyes. This scene, largely based on John 20, introduces both Mary Magdalene and Marie Pavesi, the actress who plays that role in *This Is My Blood*.[27] The character of Mary is thus foregrounded from the very beginning, and her unique role as both witness and messenger of the resurrected Jesus Christ is stressed. This role is expanded further in the rest of the film with material from the *Gospel of Mary*, which results in an elaboration of her activity as teacher of the disciples of Jesus.

In the following scene of Ferrara's *Mary*, an argument takes place between Tony and Marie. They are to fly back to New York, but Marie refuses to come along. Instead, she decides to leave for Jerusalem.

One year later in New York, Theodore Younger is attending the screening of Childress's film for the invited press. We now see a different scene from *This Is My Blood*, again featuring Marie as Mary Magdalene. The scene shows several men, gathered in a dark room. We hear someone say, "How are we to go among the unbelievers to announce the Gospel of the Kingdom of the Son of Man?" The scene is interrupted by a shot of two women outside hurrying through a small alley. The same voice continues, "They didn't spare his life, eh Peter?" Mary enters the room when he says, "Why should they spare ours?" She replies, "Do not remain in sorrow and doubt. For His Grace will guide you. . . ." She embraces the speaker and continues, ". . . and comfort you. Instead let us praise His greatness for He has prepared us for this. He is calling upon us to become fully human." Another man (Peter) addresses her and says, "Sister, we all know that the Teacher loved you differently from other women. Tell us whatever you remember about words that he told you, that we did not hear." Mary replies, "I will now speak about that which you haven't heard. . . ." This scene is a faithful rendition of the dialogue from the *Gospel of Mary* mentioned earlier (in this case 9:7–10:23).

Although it is never explicitly mentioned, most scenes from *This Is My Blood* in *Mary* are in fact based on the *Gospel of Mary*. The translation used here and in other cases is that of Jean-Yves Leloup, who is moreover

---

27. The scene is also informed by the parallel versions of the empty tomb story in the other Gospels. In Matthew, two women visit the tomb (28:1), and in Luke 24:4 the women see two men in the tomb who ask them, "Why do you look for the living among the dead?" (24:5).

interviewed halfway through the film in Theodore's show and says that Mary Magdalene can speak and teach like a man.[28] One remarkable feature of Leloup's translation is that the Coptic word ⲡⲥⲱⲣ, which means "the savior" is consistently replaced with "Teacher" in the text and the film. As a result, the focus shifts from Jesus's salvific role to his identity as teacher. This also has consequences for the representation of Mary when she delivers the words of Jesus to her.

After a close-up from Theodore at the screening of *This Is My Blood*, the film fragment continues with the response of the disciples to the words that Mary just spoke. Here, the argument between Andrew, Peter, Mary, and Levi from *Gos. Mary* 17:11–18:12, discussed earlier in this essay, is reproduced. The scene ends with a close-up of Mary's face. Later in *Mary*, other fragments of Mary's speech appear as well. One scene from *This Is My Blood* covers *Gos. Mary* 15:1–8; another scene at the very end of *Mary* covers a selection of verses from *Gos. Mary* 10:14–16; 16:14–16, 19, 21–22; 17:1–6. As a result, both the character and words of Mary are foregrounded.[29]

The image of Mary as teacher and guide for the distressed disciples in the *Gospel of Mary* in her own right recurs in the present-day story, where Marie plays a similar role for Theodore/Ted, who seeks her help in times of trouble. In a phone interview with Ted, she explains that she felt inspired by Mary Magdalene to leave her job to go on a spiritual journey. The difference between Marie and Ted is also reflected on the visual level. The color associated with Mary is a warm dark red, while the color associated with Ted is dark blue. Ted is also, quite literally, in the dark, insofar as scenes that feature him in the first part of *Mary* are shot inside and/or at night. In this way, they reflect his state of mind. Marie, on the contrary, appears most often outside and is associated with religious places in Jerusalem and rituals such as the Jewish Passover meal.

In *Mary*, the antagonistic attitude of Peter toward Mary in the *Gospel of Mary* is reflected in the attitude of Tony toward Marie. Tony has a rather high idea of himself. He played the role of Jesus in his own film,

---

28. Jean-Yves Leloup, *The Gospel of Mary Magdalene* (trans. Joseph Rowe; Rochester, VT: Inner Traditions, 2002). This English translation is based on the original French translation from the Coptic text by Jean-Yves Leloup, *L'évangile de Marie: Myriam de Magdala* (Paris: Albin Michel, 1997).

29. The only other speech included from *This Is My Blood* is delivered by Jesus at the foot washing and is based on his farewell speech in the Gospel of John (chaps. 14–16). Among the people present is Mary Magdalene. She is the only woman included in this scene of *This Is My Blood*.

This Is My Blood, because "I'm a good actor and I couldn't find anyone else better than me to play the part." He is also impulsive and has a hard time accepting Ted's appreciation for Marie, but he undergoes a change of heart at the end of *Mary*, when he says, while watching Mary's speech in his own film: "It's not what you see with your eyes, it's what you see with your heart."

The image of Mary Magdalene in *Mary* is strongly informed by the *Gospel of Mary*. She appears not only as a witness to the resurrection but also as a source of spiritual wisdom for those around her. Her relevance is not limited to the disciples in *This Is My Blood* but includes her representative, Marie, as well as Theodore Younger and Tony Childress, the two male protagonists in *Mary*. As a result, her influence and inspiration are not restricted to the past but extend well into the present.

Mary Magdalene (2018)

The second film under discussion here is entitled *Mary Magdalene* and is fully devoted to her character and role in the story of Jesus's earthly life. She is introduced in the film before Jesus himself appears on the scene. Their first encounter is when he is called in his capacity as healer to deliver her from the demon that is supposed to possess her because she refuses to marry. Jesus, however, declares, "There is no demon here."[30] Mary decides to follow Jesus but receives a mixed response from his disciples. She is welcomed by Judas, but met with resistance from Peter, who fears that "she will divide our community." The antagonism of Peter comes to a climax at the end of the film when Mary visits the apostles after she has met the resurrected Jesus.

Mary is self-confident, she confronts Peter, she stands her ground, she does not avert her eyes, and she tells the apostles, "I will be heard." After leaving them she meets Jesus once more at the tomb. While these meetings with Jesus are clearly based on John 20, the confrontation with Peter is informed by the *Gospel of Mary* (17:18–22).[31]

---

30. The reference here is clearly to Luke 8:2. For a more extensive discussion of this scene, see Caroline Vander Stichele, "Lovers or (Just) Friends? Mary Magdalene in the Gospel of John and in Film," in *The Ties That Bind: Negotiating Relationships in Early Jewish and Christian Texts, Contexts, and Reception History* (ed. Esther Kobel, Jo-Ann Brant, and Meredith J. C. Warren, in Collaboration with Andrew Bowden; LNTS 660; London: T&T Clark, 2023) 161–71.

31. Nick Hasted mentions that Helen Edmundson, one of the script writers, consulted the *Gospel of Mary*. See Nick Hasted, "Mary Magdalene and Christian Cinema's Resurrection," *The Independent*, March 15, 2018 (online: https://www.independent

This film does not reproduce the speech of Mary from the *Gospel of Mary* nor the responses of Andrew and Peter, as is the case in *Mary*, but the idea of a confrontation between Mary and Peter is preserved and developed throughout the whole film. In this film, however, Mary is determined to get her message across. Her response to Peter contains elements of Jesus's own teaching earlier in the film, more specifically, his appeal to "become like children" in Magdala and the importance of forgiveness in Cana. Mary also confronts Peter with the same question Jesus asked a woman in Cana: "How does it feel to carry that anger around in your heart? Does it lessen as the days go by?" In this final confrontation with Peter, their different views on the kingdom surface. Mary tells the disciples, "The Kingdom is not something we can see with our eyes. It is here within us." Peter, however, counters her: "Every man in this room is his rock, his church, upon which he will build his glorious new world, with *one* purpose and *one* message...." Mary replies, "Your message. Not his." Peter sighs and tells her, "You have weakened us, Mary. You have weakened him." As a result, Peter is made to represent a patriarchal view of the kingdom/church over against Mary, whose view aligns with the *Gospel of Mary*. The fact that Peter is played by Chiwetel Ejiofor, a well-known black actor, who adopts an African accent here, is very unfortunate and highly problematic.[32]

The film ends with the following statement:

> According to Christian Gospels, Mary of Magdala was present at both Jesus' death and burial; and is identified as the first witness to the resurrected Jesus. In 591, Pope Gregory claimed that Mary of Magdala was a prostitute, a misconception which remains to this day. In 2016, Mary of Magdala was formally identified by the Vatican as Apostle of the Apostles—their equal—and the first messenger of the resurrected Jesus. This film is inspired by the story of Mary Magdalene. While artistic license has been taken, we believe that this film is true to the essence, values and integrity of Mary and her story. The biblical story of Mary Magdalene can be found in the Gospels.

.co.uk/arts-entertainment/films/features/mary-magdalene-film-rooney-mara-joaquin-phoenix-religion-a8258036.html; accessed July 21, 2022).

32. See also the critical remarks about ethnicity and gender in Steven D. Greydanus, "Through Other Eyes: Point of View and Defamiliarization in Jesus Films," in *The T&T Clark Handbook of Jesus and Film* (ed. Richard Walsh; London: T&T Clark, 2021) 77–87, here 86; and, in the same volume, Michelle Fletcher, "Seeing Differently with *Mary Magdalene*," 55–65, here 61; see also Grace Emmett, "'You Weakened Him': Jesus's Masculinity in *Mary Magdalene*," *Religion and Gender* 10 (2020) 97–117, here 105 n. 20 (online: De Gruyter Brill, https://doi.org/10.1163/18785417-01001009; accessed December 18, 2024).

This statement reveals the intention of the film to correct the traditional representation of Mary Magdalene and to restore "her spiritual authority," as co-script-writer Philippa Goslett put it.[33] In this case, however, this happens at the expense of Peter, who is her antagonist throughout the film, from their first encounter to their last. As a result, the conflict in the *Gospel of Mary* and other texts is played up.

■ III. To Conclude

The shift that has taken place in the representation of Mary Magdalene signals a change in the interpretation of her role and reflects a reappraisal of her character that is largely informed by apocryphal early Christian traditions as well as, I would argue, changing gender roles in society. Both films under discussion here show the same interest: to present a different picture of Mary Magdalene from the one that was dominant in the past. In both cases the *Gospel of Mary* played an important role in this shift. As a result, Mary Magdalene is not portrayed simply as disciple of Christ but as teacher of his disciples as well. Her authority is, however, not taken for granted, as the antagonism between Peter and Mary in the *Gospel of Mary* and the two films under discussion makes clear. Mary Magdalene may well appear as teacher, but she is a contested one regardless.

33. See Hasted, "Mary Magdalene."

12

Job's Best Pupil:

An Exploration of Gregory the Great as Teacher

ARNOLD A. M. SMEETS

Gregory the Great (ca. 540–604) did not opt for rhetoric and teaching. As a true son of Rome, he preferred the public cause. But there was always a deep longing for the monastic, contemplative life: a life in seclusion from the world, dedicated to Scripture reading and prayer. He struggled with it all his life. The fact that Gregory the Great deserves a place in this collection on models of the teacher has everything to do with this struggle. His longing for *contemplatio* seemed an impossibility because of his involvement in worldly *actio*. Eventually he discovers a way out by relating the two to each other. Gregory succeeded in transforming the tense opposition between rest and action into a dynamic of complementarity and reciprocity. The source of *contemplatio* thus gave his urge for action a profound depth and urgency. It was the foundation of his spirituality. The elaboration and especially the propagation of it made Gregory the Great a spiritual leader—and one with great impact, especially once he held Peter's seat as pope and bishop of Rome.[1]

In this contribution I want to explore the model of teaching of Gregory the Great. I will consult the American Gregory expert George Demacopoulos, director of the Orthodox Christian Studies Program at

---

1. On Gregory the Great, see Robert A. Markus, *Gregory the Great and His World* (Cambridge: Cambridge University Press, 1997); and Carole Straw, *Gregory the Great: Perfection in Imperfection* (Transformation of the Classical Heritage 14; Berkeley: University of California Press, 1988). Still relevant is Claude Dagens, *Saint Grégoire le Grand: Culture et expérience chrétiennes* (Paris: Cerf, 1977; repr., 2014).

Fordham University. He recently published a biography of Gregory the Great. As part of this study, I also include his research into models of spiritual leadership in the early church.[2] Demacopoulos's biography aims to show that the ascetic and pastoral theology of Gregory the Great determined his actions as pope and influenced how he governed the Church of Rome. In the study of spiritual guidance, Gregory the Great is positioned at the end of a development that, Demacopoulos considers, begins with Athanasius of Alexandria. The sixth century manifests the phase in which clerical models of pastoral care and monastic models of spiritual guidance became more and more interwoven. The unique contribution of Gregory the Great to this development is, in the view of Demacopoulos, an "ascetization" of the pastor. Made wise by his own struggle with ambition and vocation, only the ascetic attitude to life, as practiced in the monastery, proved to be a useful anchor and beacon for beneficial action in the world, including guiding the flock of the faithful. And Gregory could not do without working in the world. He was too much of a Roman to keep himself secluded in a desert or behind the safe walls of a monastery, but above all too much of a Christian to be deaf to the mystery of the salvation of Christ and the double commandment of the Gospel.

In the following four sections I want to follow Demacopoulos's argument and map out the Gregorian model of teaching. I will start with a short sketch of his life, in which Gregory's conversion experience is central. In his case "conversion" meant the decision to withdraw from the world and become a monk. In the second section I will discuss the importance of the monastic context for the development of the spirituality of Gregory the Great and his vision of pastoral care and spiritual guidance. Gregory's commentary on the biblical Book of Job (*Moralia in Iob*) is the hallmark of his vision. The third section will cover the more immediate context of his commentary, explaining what Gregory learned from reading and studying Job and how he became, so to speak, Job's best pupil. Section IV provides the profile of the ideal spiritual leader or pastor, and the last section will offer a final instance of Gregorian wisdom, namely, that any leader, and any teacher, should remember to be a pupil as well.

---

2. See George E. Demacopoulos, *Five Models of Spiritual Direction in the Early Church* (Notre Dame, IN: University of Notre Dame Press, 2007); and idem, *Gregory the Great: Ascetic, Pastor, and First Man of Rome* (Notre Dame, IN: University of Notre Dame Press, 2015).

I. Gregory the Great: A Brief Biography

In traditional iconography, Gregory the Great is depicted with a dove on his shoulder. It symbolizes the Holy Spirit, who whispers to him the words that he writes down himself or dictates to one of the papal clerks. It represents the authority that has always been attributed to his words. For those who want to see it, the iconography represents the source of the spirituality of Gregory the Great. In any case, his spirituality was deeply lived and authentic.[3]

He was born and raised a Roman. His family was Christian, influential, and prosperous, with real estate in the city and several estates in Sicily, which Gregory later incorporated into the Petrine patrimony. After a thorough education and training, he held important official positions in the Eternal City. He was *quaestor* (official responsible for finances), *praetor* (official with judicial and other governmental responsibilities), and finally, in the years 573–574, *praefectus urbis*, or Prefect of the City. As prefect, he was responsible for the Senate, for the water and food supply, as well as for the city's defenses. The office made him a powerful man; a public figure—and this in turbulent times, when a great deal of leadership was required. After his term as prefect he fled, in his own words, naked from the shipwreck of this life to the safe harbor of the monastery. It is a final chord of a long period of doubt and wrestling. About twenty years later he wrote in an exceptionally personal letter about what made him dissatisfied in his early years:

> I had, in fact, indefinitely put off the grace of my conversion after having been filled with the desire for heaven and had decided it was better to remain clothed in worldly apparel. It had already been shown me that I should want to love eternity, but longstanding habits had gained the upper hand, keeping me from altering my way of life. Although my mind still urged me to love the present life only in an external fashion, many influences springing from my worldly concerns began to oppress me so that I was detained there, no longer only externally but mentally as well, which is far worse. At last, in my anxiety to avoid all this turmoil,

---

3. Deep-felt spirituality and involvement in the church were a family tradition. Gregory's father was *defensor*, and he had three religious aunts. One of his ancestors was Pope Felix III (r. 483–492) and probably Pope Agapetus I (r. 535–536). See Markus, *Gregory the Great*, 8–14; and Barbara Müller, *Führung im Denken und Handeln Gregor des Grossen* (Studien und Texte zu Antike und Christentum 57; Tübingen: Mohr Siebeck, 2009) 11–26.

I sought the safe harbor of the monastery, having left behind all that belongs to the world, as I then vainly supposed, and I escaped the shipwreck of this life unclothed.[4]

The mistake Gregory mentions refers to the hard fact that his monastic peace was disturbed when he was called to be a minister of the church. He would undoubtedly have experienced it as a "cruel disturbance."

The quotation from the famous letter sketches the history of a conversion. Gregorius longs for the grace of conversion but continues to live and work in the world (wearing "worldly apparel"). He finds a certain balance, but, in the end, one that does not work. The worries become too much, and ultimately his soul has no defense. Then, when he was around the age of thirty-five, his radical decision of the flight to the monastery follows. He had searched and now found the peace and quiet of a life dedicated to prayer and the study of the Bible. The period of Gregory's monastic retreat—he would later repeatedly call it the happiest time of his life—turned out to be relatively short-lived. It was inevitable that the fact of the conversion itself would prove to be a link in the continuity of his career. Moreover, no matter how much he mourned the loss of contemplative peace and seclusion in sermons, letters, or prologues, it is just so that Gregory the monk never turned his eyes away from the world. And before he realized it, he found himself again in the world, when Pope Pelagius II ordained him a deacon in 579 and soon after sent him as his *apocrisiarius* on a diplomatic mission to Constantinople. After his return in 584/585, Gregorius lived for a few more years in his monastery, acting as Pelagius's minister, until his elevation to the papacy in September 590.[5]

---

4. Gregory the Great, *Ep. ad Leandrum* 1.1, in *S. Gregorii Magni, Moralia in Iob* (ed. Marci Adriaen; 3 vols.; CCSL 143, 143A, 143B; Turnhout: Brepols, 1979–1985] 1:1): "(Q)uoniam diu longeque conversationis gratiam distuli et postquam caelesti sum desiderio afflatus, saeculari habitu contegi melius putavi. Aperiebatur enim mihi iam de aeternitatis amore quid quaererem, sed inolita me consuetudo devinxerat, ne exteriorem cultum mutarem. Cumque adhuc me cogerent animus praesenti mundo quasi specie tenus deservire, coeperunt multa contre me ex eiusdem mundi cura succrescere, ut in eo iam non specie, sed, quod est gravius, mente retinerer. Quae tandem cunta sollicite fugiens portum monasterii petii et relictis quae mundi sunt, ut frustra tunc credidi, ex huius vitae naufragio nudus evasi." English translation from Gregory the Great, *Moral Reflections on the Book of Job* (trans. Brian Kerns; 6 vols.; Cistercian Studies Series 249; Collegeville, MN: Liturgical Press for Cistercian Publications, 2014–2022) 1:47. The letter is known as the dedicatory letter of the *Morals on Job*, addressed to Leander of Seville.

5. Müller, *Führung im Denken*, 23–26, 66–68.

The conversion experience is the key to understanding Gregory the Great. The monastery proved to be a fertile ground for the further development of an authentic and swirling spirituality.

■ II. Gregory: A Monk in Rome

Already in Classical philosophical schools it was an experienced teacher who helped the student on the path of reflection to a better and deeper understanding of not just himself but also of the world and the cosmos. This model was given a new life in the Christian monastic traditions, where the teacher, father, or abbot, bore the responsibility for the spiritual guidance of the monks of the community. The path of reflection was replaced by the path of asceticism, and the focus on the individual was shifted to the soul. The urgency of spiritual guidance lay in the spiritual battle for the sake of the salvation of souls, against worldly temptations and, above all, against the almost inexhaustible tricks of the ancient enemy, the devil.[6] It was not ordination, as in the tradition of the clerical church, but the deeply lived ascetic attitude that gave the teacher the competence of spiritual guidance. It was on this basis that the teacher was given authority and inspired confidence, and his exhortations for the life of souls, or the exercises of detachment he offered, were adopted as wise counsel for imitation. Like no other, the teacher saw through and inspired the disciple to fight his own spiritual battle. Every good spiritual director needed "discernment" (*discretio*): the gift of sharp insight into a person's character and personality. In this way, the spiritual director could give advice in relation to a precise measure, sometimes directly and—if it was more prudent—indirectly and discreetly.[7] Subsequently, the "competence of regulation" (*condescensio*) was indispensable: on the basis of his insights, the spiritual director was able to deviate from the prescribed admonitions and punishments.[8] Although the monastic model

---

6. Demacopoulos, *Five models*, 9.
7. Ibid., 11: "For some ascetic authors such as Antony, discernment was a tool sought by a monk for his own enlightenment. In the context of spiritual direction, however, it was the key supernatural gift that enabled effective guidance. Discernment empowered the elder to recognize demons and angels and to understand the spiritual challenges of his disciples. It was believed that individual monks had specific needs. According to Basil, the discerning elder would offer the precise admonition and/or instruction that could lead his disciples to salvation."
8. Demacopoulos, *Five Models*, 12.

of spiritual leadership was interwoven with the internalization of spiritual combat, the body was considered not only as a target but also as a shield and weapon. The spiritual guidance of the teacher concerning the practice of asceticism—rules concerning eating, sleeping, praying, and working—and "humility" (*humilitas*) edified the pupil and thus strengthened his soul in resisting temptations and seductions.

In 574/575 Gregory the Great entered this tradition. In fact, he founded the monastic community himself in the house where he grew up on the Caelian Hill in Rome, pleasantly situated overlooking the Palatine Hill and what is now the plain of the Circus Maximus. In the monastery where he entered, he—the founder and financier—became not an abbot but a simple monk. He devoted himself to the study of God's Word and subjected himself to a strict asceticism, a practice that undermined his health. Here he experienced the value of the monastic learning model of the experienced spiritual director and the learning disciple.

The new monastic community placed itself under the patronage of the apostle Andrew. It was a deliberate and programmatic choice—not only because of the central significance of an active charity in the cult around Andrew, but also because Andrew stood for conversion and for the proclamation of Truth.[9] After all, Andrew was the elder brother of the first among the apostles. It was he who proclaimed the truth to Peter. The monastery, about halfway between the Vatican Hill and the Lateran complex, grew into a hotspot of religious inspiration and a think tank of mostly young and talented monks.[10] Under the watchful eye and guidance of the apostle Andrew, who was addressed in prayer as *praedicator et rector*, Gregory the Great's thinking gained spiritual depth and urgency.[11] In the safe harbor of the monastery, Gregory was given the building blocks for the way out of his earlier experience. His predicament consisted in the fact that his "long-standing habits" had tied him up so tightly that he could not change or improve his ways and was held "no longer only externally but mentally as well."

In Gregory's spirituality, *conversio*, in addition to an ultimate formative experience, became a battle cry and an indication of the basic structure of the Christian life. As such, conversion made it possible to live a lifestyle in the world without being chained to the secular. It was helpful that the contemplative was "seeing with other eyes": don't just look at

---

9. Müller, *Führung im Denken*, 31–39.
10. Ibid., 31–40.
11. Ibid., 35 n. 56, referring to a prayer of Saint Andrew's feast in the Gregorian *Liber sacramentorum*.

reality with the eyes of your body but see with the eyes of your mind the truth of God's involvement in the history of the world and people's lives. This "seeing," ultimately the grace of a *visio Dei*, puts reality into perspective as a specific, spiritually charged spatiality for human action.[12] Gregory the Great's commitment was to make use of that spatiality—or to have it made use of—insofar as persuasive pastoral exhortations to the faithful entrusted to him were successful. In a sense, it is a question of shaping or transforming human freedom into action as a facilitation of salvation history.

The French bishop and church historian Claude Dagens speaks of Gregory's years of silent preparation.[13] In this phase, Dagens includes the period of his stay in Constantinople. Far away from the monastery on the Caelian Hill, Gregory started working there on his commentary on Job (the "dark book of Job," he complains; but eventually writes thirty-five books full of commentary). The conferences he held for some fellow brothers and interested members of the court and imperial family were a welcome contemplative counterbalance to the hustle and bustle of diplomacy and political scheming as the pope's representative.[14] In the *Moralia in Iob*, Gregory developed the thoughts and arguments that he would later sharpen and translate into actions as pope. The continuity and coherence of his spiritual ideas become clear in the letters he wrote after his elevation to the papacy and are, for example, also evident in the reflections in the *Liber regulae pastoralis*, which Gregory wrote as a more concise tractate on the themes and topics he developed in his opus magnum.[15]

---

12. The structure of conversion can be seen as a dynamic of, first, a profound internal reflection (*intus*; *contemplatio*) distancing oneself from the world and its appearances, which then leads to a purified engagement with the world (*foris*; *actio*). The result of *contemplatio* is a spiritual knowledge of God's intentions and sacred history. What is seen in contemplation (the *visio Dei*) touches the soul and thus puts it into motion, leading to an inspired acting in and for the world, without the attachment to wealth and glory.

13. Claude Dagens, "Grégoire le Grand avant son pontificat: Expérience politique et expérience spirituelle," in *De Tertullien aux Mozarabes: Mélanges offerts à Jacques Fontaine, à l'occasion de son 70e anniversaire, par ses élèves, amis et collègues* (ed. Louis Holtz and Jean-Claude Fredouille; 3 vols.; Collection des études augustiniennes: Série Antiquité 132; Paris: Institut d'études augustiniennes, 1992) 1:143–50.

14. Müller, *Führung im Denken*, 99–106; Katharina Greschat, *Die Moralia in Iob Gregors des Grossen: Ein christologisch-ekklesiologischer Kommentar* (Studien und Texte zu Antike und Christentum 31; Tübingen: Mohr Siebeck, 2005).

15. Greschat, *Die Moralia in Iob*, 252–53.

III. Learning from Job

Moralia in Iob is a fine example of monastic study in which Gregory teaches what he learned while studying Job and contemplating its deeper meaning. He did so "on the job," as it were, also in the sense that Gregory reflected in his expositions on Job on his own struggle for some kind of balance between his longing for contemplation and his duties in and for the world and its affairs as representative of the pope.

He addressed his audience as *rectores* or *praedicatores*, the learned elite with responsibilities in the church and thus the world.[16] They had the responsibility of participating in God's plan for humankind and were given their power and authority to proclaim the Truth and to act and guide Christ's church in turbulent times. And, yes, the task was a heavy burden and sometimes a predicament, and not all were up to the task. Job was the prototype of the righteous sufferer and no doubt someone the *praedicatores* and *rectores* could relate to. For them, and for Gregory himself, it was important to realize that Job was tested by God and that he passed the test and was rewarded for it.[17]

But Job meant so much more. He was not only exemplary in how any human should relate to God, but allegorically Job's suffering mirrored that of Christ and of Christ's church through the ages. On a deeper, allegorical level, the Book of Job disclosed the pitfalls and dangers that tested the spiritual resilience of the *praedicatores* and *rectores* as depending on God's *providentia*, which made clear that, ultimately, all will be well. The allegorical reading made it possible to recognize in Job's wife and in his friends those who opposed the *divina providentia*: those who held on to worldly riches and glory, the arrogant, and the heretical Thus, it opened the perspective on how to live well: learning from Job was a lesson in imitating Christ and a call to that imitation.[18]

Gregory's stay in Constantinople proved to be a time of spiritual growth. He could not refuse the call to serve the interests of the Church of Rome at the imperial court in Constantinople, albeit not without some

---

16. Ibid., 28–30; Demacopoulos, *Gregory the Great: Ascetic*, 58–59. In the *Regula pastoralis* the common term is *rector*; in *Moralia in Iob* Gregory refers to the leading elite as *praedicatores*.

17. Greschat, *Die* Moralia in Iob, 46. Gregory saw Job, in line with tradition, as an *athleta Dei* in his battle with the devil and as an *exemplum patientiae*.

18. Greschat, *Die* Moralia in Iob, 71–75; see also the final chapter with a summary, 243–55.

grumbling and complaining. Once there, the invitation to comment on the Book of Job made it possible for Gregory, as clearly as God's Word would allow, to understand how important and meaningful it was to use the spiritual insights of contemplation for the service of one's neighbor.[19] Job gave Gregory an appealing argument—no doubt causing some unease among his audience of high-ranking officials and members of the imperial family—against riches and snobbery and for the importance of "humility" (humilitas) as the center of the ascetic attitude to life.[20] In the wake of his comments and contemplations, Job became more and more a figure of inspiration and identification. Job became the paradigm of his thinking, and Gregory became Job's best pupil.

▪ IV. Learned in Job

In the *Moralia in Iob*, Gregory develops his spirituality of conversion into a pastoral pedagogy. In his model, the teacher is the shepherd (*pastor*) of the soul, responsible for a community of the faithful. With his allegorical reading of Job, Gregory sketches the profile of the ideal spiritual director and formulates the necessary competencies, which will enable him to be helpful in promoting the spiritual growth of the souls entrusted to his care. The modern distinction between pastoral care and spiritual direction is foreign to him. Both belong together and strengthen each other.[21] According to Gregory the Great, "pastoral care" (*cura pastoralis*) is an art, "the art of arts," quoting Gregory Nazianzen (*ars est artium regimen animarum*, "the government of souls is the art of arts"). For, while in sickness, we consider it normal to consult only a competent and experienced physician, how much more so should one look for an even better trained and experienced shepherd to care for one's soul: "who does not realise that the wounds of the mind are more hidden than the internal wounds of the body."[22]

---

19. Demacopoulos, *Gregory the Great: Ascetic*, 59.
20. Müller, *Führung im Denken*, 99–106.
21. Demacopoulos, *Gregory the Great: Ascetic*, 53–54.
22. Gregory the Great, *Regulae pastoralis* 1.1 in Grégoire le Grand, *Règle pastorale* (trans. Charles Morel; introduction, notes, and index by Bruno Judic; critical text by Floribert Rommel; 2 vols.; SC 381–382; Paris: Cerf, 1992; repr., 2017) 128: "Quis autem cogitationum vulnera occultiora esse nesciat vulneribus viscerum?" English translation from St. Gregory the Great, *Pastoral Care* (trans. Henry David; Ancient Christian Writers 11; New York: Newman, 1978) 21.

The ideal *pastor* is someone who, from a deeply lived contemplative and ascetic attitude to life, takes on the spiritual and pastoral burden of responsibility in and for the world. After all, what is the point of keeping the inspiration of contemplation to oneself? Gregory had experienced at first hand how this was a way to ground firmly his commitment to the world and at the same time to give his urge to act in the world a spiritual stability. With his actions, the shepherd enters the world—a turbulent sea with dangerously high waves. The ascetic attitude to life functions as an anchor—but also as a shield against the temptations of power, prestige, and authority. Moreover, the ascetic attitude guarantees the authenticity and reliability of the shepherd, who not only preached the Truth but also lived it, because without the latter, you put the salvation of the flock at stake:

> There are some who investigate spiritual precepts with great care but trample on what they analyse by the way in which they live. Hastily, they showcase what they have learned, not by practice, but through reading. And the very words they preach they impugn by their habits, just as when a shepherd walks on steep hills, the flock follows him to the precipice.[23]

The rector's responsibility concerned the faithful placed under his care. Gregory emphasized that every community had a great internal variety—in itself, a great challenge. Every individual had his or her own unique spiritual gifts, opportunities, and challenges; was sensitive to specific vices; and possessed unique talents for certain virtues. To illustrate: in book 3 of the *Regulae pastoralis*, Gregory the Great discerns no fewer than seventy-two types of personalities, in both their positive and negative determinations, and includes tailor-made pastoral advice for each category.[24]

In line with tradition and learning from Job, Gregory emphasizes the importance of *discretio* and *condescensio* for the *rector* or *preadicator*. In their mutual coherence, they outline the pedagogical route of spiritual guidance.[25] It is crucial to discern between true and feigned virtues or,

---

23. Gregory the Great, *Regulae pastoralis* 1.2 [SC 381:134]): "Et sunt nonnulli qui sollerti cura spiritalia praecepta perscrutantur, sed quae intellegendo penetrant, vivenvo conculcant; repente docent quae non opere, sed meditatione didicerint; et quod verbis praedicant, moribus impugnant. Unde fit ut cum pastor per abrupta graditur, ad praecipitium grex sequitur." English translation as quoted in Demacopoulos, *Five Models*, 132.

24. Demacopoulos, *Five Models*, 130; idem, *Gregory the Great: Ascetic*, 24.

25. On *discretio*, see Demacopoulos, *Five Models*, 135; and idem, *Gregory the Great: Ascetic*, 72–73. Straw describes discernment as the ability to see the secrets

even better, between a virtue and a vice that presents itself as a virtue, like a wolf in sheep's clothing. Using his discernment, the pastor could provide the client with a deep sense of "self" and be able to encourage a movement of the soul (leading to the *actio* of corporal good works). To complete the spiritual guidance, the rector should be able to know which rules were applicable, but especially how the regular provisions and guidelines could best be used and applied to an individual's soul in a specific situation—or not. In the eyes of Gregory the Great, spiritual direction is a matter of a *longue durée* and lasting commitment. Gregory makes the comparison between spiritual growth and that of a tree, which grows year after year and reaches maturity.[26]

The eschatological perspective of Gregory's spirituality gives his guidance not only a pastoral but also a salvific sense of urgency. The End approaches. Just watch and see the signs in nature and history. The awareness that time is pressing makes one gloomy, but appropriately gloomy: it is also a means to an end, namely, to strengthen the call to repentance. Typical—and pastorally helpful—is the fact that Gregory does not share Augustine's pessimistic view of humanity. Free will offers possibilities and opportunities for any human initiative in the unfolding of God's gifts of grace. Should his *discretio* have given him reason to do so, Gregory was willing to underline the importance of good works in such a way that his client would have no choice but to take courage and indeed to start the work for the salvation of her or his soul.[27]

The pastor is understood by Gregory as a contemplative preacher, a hybrid figure, grafted onto the structure and mission of conversion.[28] Grounded in an attitude of contemplation, the ascetic voluntarily enters the world to engage with the spiritual growth of the faithful. It is his task and duty to guide the souls of those entrusted to his care.

The ideal type of pastor is, of course, a reflection of Gregory's own conception of his pastoral tasks and drive. In his sermons and personal letters, he reaches out to the faithful, encouraging them and is always able to strike the right tone, sometimes strict, sometimes praising, to keep them on the path to eternal salvation. At the same time, he showed himself to be a competent manager, able to provide the means to feed the poor and support widows, a powerful leader who sent missionaries to

---

of the soul (*Gregory the Great*, 50). On *condescensio* (in Greek: *oikonomia*), see Demacopoulos, *Five Models*, 12, 135–56; and idem, *Gregory the Great: Ascetic*, 73–74.

26. Demacopoulos, *Gregory the Great: Ascetic*, 58, referring to *Moralia in Job* 22.7.16.

27. Demacopoulos, *Gregory the Great: Ascetic*, 32–35.

28. Ibid., 59.

faraway Kent to proclaim the true faith, and someone who resolutely dealt with heretics and abuses.[29]

■ V. How the Preacher Should Return to Himself

In both the *Moralia in Iob* and the *Regulae pastoralis* Gregory rounds off his reflections with a "return to oneself."[30] Anyone who has ever overwhelmed an interested audience with his or her compelling argument knows the uplifting feeling of sheer adrenaline. How much satisfaction does it give the teacher to see her or his pupil pass an exam? But, Gregory warns, one should realize that there are many examples where "the greatness of one's virtues was the cause of one's downfall." It is therefore necessary and beneficial that, when the "abundance of virtues" flatters us, "the eye of the soul turns its gaze to its imperfections and, for its own salvation, casts itself to the ground."[31] The soul of the *praedicator* or *rector* carries the responsibility not to fall into the trap of pride—and place himself at an unbridgeable distance from the faithful entrusted to his care. This makes the "return to self" essential. Only a renewed contemplative retreat enables one to focus one's competences again and again on the well-being of a soul, the same soul that earlier one had encouraged to walk upwards along the path toward salvation.

---

29. Markus, *Gregory the Great*.
30. Gregory the Great, *Regulae pastoralis* 4 [SC 381] 534: "Peractis rite omnibus qualiter praedicator ad semetipsum redeat, ne hunc vel vita vel praedicatio extollat." English translation from Davis, *Pastoral Care*, 234: "How the preacher, when he has done everything as required, should return to himself, to prevent his life or preaching from making him proud." Also Gregory the Great, *Morales sur Job* 35.49 (texte critique by Marc Adriaen; SC 538; Paris: Cerf, 2010) 378: "Expleto itaque hoc opere, ad mihi uideo esse redeundum." English translation from Kerns, *Moral Reflections on the Book of Job*, 6:536: "And so the work is done, and I can see that it is incumbent upon me to return to myself."
31. Gregory the Great, *Regulae pastoralis* 4.73–75 [SC 381] 538: "Unde necesse est ut cum virtutum nobis copia blanditur, ad infirma sua mentis oculos redeat, seseque salubriter deorsum premat." English translation from Davis, *Pastoral Care*, 237.

13

Francis of Assisi:
Teacher as Model

WILLEM MARIE SPEELMAN

When Francis preaches to the birds, he teaches them nothing more than that they should praise and love the Lord, because he has created them like birds; he tells them to be birds.[1] At first this seems a very minimal doctrine, but in fact Francis testifies here to a new and, as it turns out later, very influential vision of nature.[2] In a certain sense Francis was a teacher, but in a special, humble sense—for he did not want to be called a teacher—Francis followed the footsteps of Jesus Christ, his Lord and Teacher. If we want to investigate in which sense Francis was a teacher, we will have to start with a description of the teachership of Jesus. In relation to Jesus, Francis will be the model of the disciple who, because he knew his Lord and Teacher, also knew his works, including the Scriptures. Finally, I would like to discuss briefly, what this can mean

---

1. Thomas of Celano, *The Life of St. Francis*, 58 [further 1Cel 58)] in *Francis of Assisi: Early Documents*, vol. 1: *The Saint* [further FAED 1] (ed. Regis J. Armstrong, J. A. Wayne Hellmann, and William J. Short; New York: New City Press, 1999) 234–35; see also *I Fioretti: The Little Flowers of Saint Francis*, 16 [further Fior 16] in *Francis of Assisi: Early Documents*, vol. 3: *The Prophet* [further FAED 3] (ed. Regis J. Armstrong, J. A. Wayne Hellmann and William J. Short; New York: New City Press, 2001), 593–94. These sources are available online at https://www.franciscantradition.org/early-sources (accessed March 19, 2020).

2. *Om de hele wereld: Inleiding in de franciscaanse spiritualiteit* (ed. Willem Marie Speelman, Gerard Pieter Freeman, and Jan van den Eijnden; 2nd ed.; Heeswijk: Berne Media 2015) 141–53.

for recent educational issues, examining the role of the teacher, of encounter, and of contemplative learning.

■ I. Jesus, "Lord and Teacher," as a Model for the Religious Teacher

When we describe the teaching of Jesus, we do not come up with a description of his teaching and how he conveyed it to his disciples. For Jesus did much more than that: in a short period of time of about three years, he changed the lives of his disciples completely and permanently, and he sent them out to continue his own mission.[3] His teaching is literally "education," from the Latin *e-ducere* ("to lead out").[4] Jesus led his disciples—and, through them, all of his followers—out of the old world into a new reality. The teaching of Jesus is dominated by this vocation and mission, from which the typical characteristics of his teaching also flow.

Vocation and Mission

Jesus was called to proclaim the kingdom of God in word and deed as the Son of God. His calling is prepared by John the Baptist (Mark 1:2–8); when Jesus is baptized by him, he hears his calling as the Son of God (Mark 1:10–11). According to Matt 3:2; 4:17, Jesus's conversion is the same as that of John: "Repent, for the kingdom of heaven has come near."

The moment Jesus begins to preach, he calls his disciples. This seems to happen without much deliberation. Mark 1:16–20 describes how Jesus walked by the sea, saw some fishermen at work, and said, "Come, follow me. I will send you out to fish for people." The other disciples also meet Jesus on the way. Though it seems that the disciples were chosen quite randomly, it is much more important that Jesus gathers the Twelve around him. They must follow him in every way—almost like children imitating their model—to become partakers of his being, life, and mission. Only in this way could they share in the mystery of God's kingdom: by being it, living it, and "e-ducating" it themselves.[5] The vocation and mission of his disciples were thus integrally part of Jesus's own mission.

---

3. Robert E. Coleman, *The Master Plan of Evangelism* (1964; repr., Grand Rapids: Revell, 2010) 34.

4. See Bert Roebben, "Living and Learning in the Presence of the Other: Defining Religious Education Inclusively," *International Journal of Inclusive Education* 16 (2011) 1–13, here 5.

5. Keith Ferdinando, "Jesus, the Theological Educator," *Themelios* 38 [2013] 360–

Learning as Appropriation

The Gospels pay little attention to the long learning process that Jesus himself underwent. Mark and John begin their Gospel when Jesus is already thirty years old; only Matthew and Luke give him the opportunity to be a child and grow up. Luke writes that, after three days of searching, his parents found him in the temple sitting among the teachers, listening to them, and asking them questions (Luke 2:46). He was twelve years old. Could we find traces of his learning process in the following years? I think that the story in which he asks his disciples "Who do people say I am? And who do you say I am?" (Matt 16:13–19) might provide such a trace. This story indicates that Jesus appropriated the Jewish writings in full, that he felt personally addressed by them, and that he read them from the perspective of his mission. The Jewish Scriptures formed his identity as if they were his "mother," just as he called God his Father (Luke 2:49). The formation of Jesus's identity is a trace of his personal appropriation of his tradition, and his question is in how far the people and his disciples recognize him.

To clarify the process of personal appropriation, I would like to refer to the description of the child's natural learning process by Maurice Merleau-Ponty.[6] This phenomenologist describes in detail how a child bodily develops relationships with others,[7] and only through them with himself. Merleau-Ponty notices how important the face is in this process. It begins by the child following its mother through bodily imitation, and thus making its "own" movements. Gradually the child learns that he is the agent and owner of those movements. After a while, a transition takes place, in which the bodily dimension mirrors itself in the face of another

---

74, here 367): "He obliged those of his hearers (as well as later readers) who wanted to understand his message to engage deeply with what he said. They had to make a mental and spiritual effort to penetrate the surface and grasp the deeper levels of meaning; indeed, they had in a sense to become part of the story and find their own place within it. Only through such a profound engagement did real understanding become possible. Such a requirement also meant that 'those on the outside' stayed there."

6. Maurice Merleau-Ponty, "The Child's Relations with Others," in *The Primacy of Perception: And Other Essays on Phenomenological Psychology, the Philosophy of Art, History and Politics* (Northwestern University Studies in Phenomenology and Existential Philosophy; Evanston, IL: Northwestern University Press, 1964) 96–155.

7. I prefer to use the word "bodily" instead of "physical," to indicate that this is not about a physical matter, but about sensing, experiencing, and acting, about the feeling of presence and recognition—in short, about the *living* body. See Willem Marie Speelman, "Bodily Presence. A Franciscan Vision," *Studies in Spirituality* 24 (2014) 179–204.

child and in that mirror dissects the space of the "I" as the "double" of his bodily self. The child learns to understand that the other is an "I," and, on the basis of the mutual relationship, recognizes himself also as an "I" (my "I" comes later). The process ends, if it succeeds, in another unity, in which the differences are overcome in love.

Although Merleau-Ponty's analysis concerns a small child and not a twelve-year-old, and although the relation to Scripture is different from the relation to a real mother, the model may be helpful to describe the process of personal appropriation. It begins as a communion in which differences are not really developed yet. Then the child notices that he is actually the agent of his own conduct. Then he develops his own identity in the face of a peer, and finally there is another, different communion. Merleau-Ponty does not explicitly address the question to what extent the "I" of the other continues to play a role in my worldview and my perspective on reality. Not being familiar with any research on this specific question, I would expect the mutual relationship to continue to play a role here. In this mutual relationship, it is to be expected that both poles can adopt each other's vision. I can see the world and myself through your eyes, as it were. In this way I can become a model for myself as an imitator. And in Paul's words I can even say that it is not I who live, but you who live in me (Gal 2:20). When Jesus asks the question concerning his identity in Matt 16:13–16 (cf. Mark 8:27–30; Luke 9:18–20) and the answers refer to the Jewish Scriptures, Jesus has *bodily* formed his identity in relation to God, the "I" of the Scriptures. It is God who gives Jesus his identity. This, by the way, contrasts sharply with his fellow villagers' misunderstanding of him (Mark 6:1–4).

Note that the consequence of this appropriation of the "I" of the Scriptures is, that Jesus's identity is in resonance with the identities mentioned: Elijah, Jeremiah, John the Baptist, and in resonance with the identities of his disciples. Jesus is a continuation in the most original way of the mission of his predecessors, and his disciples are, each in an authentic way, a continuation of Jesus's mission. Keith Ferdinando observes that Jesus, after his recognition by Peter, tells what is foreseen about him as Messiah (Matt 16:21). But this prospect is also a prophecy concerning the disciples: following him means that they must take up their own cross (Matt 16:24; Phil 3:10).[8] This radical personal engagement characterizes the teaching of Jesus, who sends his disciples out "to fish for people." People will only allow themselves to be "caught" as followers of Jesus if

---

8. Ferdinando, "Jesus, the Theological Educator," 363.

those who fulfill this task also embody the reality of which they speak, as Jesus did.⁹

An All-Embracing Form of Teaching

Just as Jesus appropriated his tradition, so his disciples will have to appropriate Jesus. The natural learning model, as described by Merleau-Ponty, is so intimate that it must lead to a select group. Jesus forms a core group of twelve men who have responded to the call "Follow me." And just as they give themselves to Jesus, so Jesus gives himself to them. For three years they experience everything he goes through: how he eats, sleeps, prays, preaches, heals. And by following him narrowly and bodily—like an infant following his mother—the disciples are transformed into who they are in the eyes of the Lord. At the same time the individual disciples are transformed into a community that has the closeness of family ties, a brotherhood.[10] Thus, the disciples learned not only from Jesus but also from each other, in the context of their relationships and interactions (cf. Matt 23:8).[11] Finally, it is only in this strong communion that the disciples can become the unique individuals that they are.

Ferdinando mentions two typical characteristics of Jesus's teaching,[12] which I would like to summarize and to which I will add a third, *a bodily learning model*. First, Jesus taught on occasion, as a *response* to a situation or a question. As he was walking through his environment, people came to him, and he met their needs and responded to their questions. His teaching was rooted in the bodily reality of their everyday life. And he always pointed to the coming of the kingdom of God in *this* situation. Thus, he opened the minds of his listeners every time the opportunity arose. Second, Jesus taught with *stories*. He invited his listeners to identify with the movement of the story, which, because of its enigmatic character, revealed a deeper meaning. In this way he invited the listener to

---

9. Ibid., 365.
10. Brotherhood is based on the sharing of the same nourishment ("mother"); cf. the Latin *companion*, which comes down to "having shared the same bread." See Jean-Luc Nancy and Sarah Clift, "Fraternity," *Angelaki* 18 (2013) 119–23.
11. Wim Weren stresses the importance of "horizontal relationships" as opposed to the "vertical" responsibility (*Matteüs* [Belichting van het Bijbelboek; 's-Hertogenbosch: KBS, 1994] 98–99). The brotherhood of disciples, however, is based on their shared relationship with the one Lord. Interestingly, the word *fraternitas* in late antiquity expresses not only mutual (horizontal) relationships but also a common goal. See Théophile Desbonnets, *From Intuition to Institution: The Franciscans* (Chicago: Franciscan Herald Press, 1988) 60.
12. Ferdinando, "Jesus, the Theological Educator," 366–67.

determine his or her own position: What would I do in such a situation? Third, and this is what I would like to add, Jesus taught in *gestures*. By bringing in outcasts, healing the sick, freeing those who were possessed, and raising the dead, he taught that God's kingdom is a gift of grace to all who open themselves to it. Gestures are examples of behavior that opens up a deeper sense of reality, and by doing so brings a new reality nearer.[13] But because the meaning of the gesture is a communicative one, his actions were not aimed at immediately destroying all mechanisms of expulsion, disease, possession, and death. Thus, through bodily imitation of their Lord and Teacher, his disciples learned to understand the situation as the place where the kingdom of God is coming, to transform themselves into a new people in this situation, and to continue Jesus's mission.[14]

Mission of the Disciples

At the beginning Jesus called his disciples with the words "Follow me." A learning path that begins with a vocation to follow will inevitably result in a mission of the followers, for in following their Teacher, they will end up calling others to follow. At an early stage, Jesus sends his disciples two by two to continue his mission (Mark 6:7–13). The impossible task for people to cast out demons and raise the dead is, according to Luke 9:1, a trace of the power Jesus gives to his disciples. When they do this, they transcend their own humanity, and he works through them. With this delegated acting, Jesus presents himself operating through, with, and in his disciples, which is a gesture confirmed at the end of the Gospel of Matthew in 28:19–20 and in the mission of his Spirit in Acts 2:1–13. Jesus becomes what Henk Schoot calls an "inner teacher," who will guide their speaking and observing, thinking and doing from now on.[15] However, the mission is still part of the learning process: after a while the apostles

---

13. An analysis of the gesture is given in Giorgio Agamben, *Karman: A Brief Treatise on Action, Guilt, and Gesture* (Meridian; Stanford, CA: Stanford University Press, 2018). For a Franciscan approach, see Willem Marie Speelman, "Pope Francis and Francis of Assisi: Men of Gesture," *Franciscan Studies* 78 (2020) 275–88. For a theatrical approach, see Antonio Attisani and Jane House, "Franciscan Performance: A Theatre Lost and Found Again," *Journal of Performance and Art* 25 (2003) 48–60.

14. Ferdinando, "Jesus, the Theological Educator," 362: "His explicit intention was for them to become like him . . . (Luke 6:40). Accordingly, Jesus's pedagogy was highly relational, reflective of the fundamentally relational nature of the truth which he incarnated in his own person."

15. Henk J. M. Schoot, "Lerend leiderschap: Augustinus en Thomas over de leraar," in *De volgeling die voorgaat: Leiderschap in het licht van Franciscus van Assisi* (ed. Krijn Pansters; Nijmegen: Valkhof, 2014), 128.

return to tell Jesus what they have been doing (Mark 6:30). After that the story of Jesus continues, because he will have to do and undergo everything that has been written about him.

How Did Jesus See Himself as a Teacher?

In Gospel texts like Matt 23:8–11 and John 13:13–15, Jesus calls himself a teacher who is a servant. According to recent distinctions, however, I would rather see him as a *spiritual* leader rather than a *servant*.[16] What matters to Jesus is not so much the internal organization of his "circle of doctrine," "school," or "church," as the *mission* of that church. In that mission there is only one who sends—God; all others are sent. In the same way there is only one Lord and Teacher; all the others are pupils, brothers, and sisters. This means that all masters, all fathers, all teachers are led by one Lord, who teaches them and whom they serve. The paradoxical position of Jesus, as teacher and servant, points to a model that, on the one hand, is the center of the learning process and, on the other hand, is rather a gateway to the true center: God.

■ II. Francis of Assisi: A Follower Who Became a Model

As mentioned above, the life of St. Francis is characterized by following in the footsteps of Jesus (1 Pet 2:21). With this nonintellectual, bodily imitation, he takes up the position of Jesus's disciples. For example, he felt personally addressed when he heard the Gospel according to which the Lord sent out his disciples to preach, and immediately began to do what he had heard.[17] In this paragraph I will describe how Francis's teaching in many ways resembles that of Jesus, and how Francis intends to be an exemplary disciple among the disciples. Francis was—in resonance with Jesus's words in Matt 23:8—brother with his brothers and allowed himself to be moved, not only by the Lord but also by his brothers and sisters.[18]

---

16. Francoise Contreras, "Servant and Spiritual Leadership Theories: Are They Two Different Notions?," *Journal of Human Values* 22 (2016) 202–8. Although the author does not give a final answer, it seems that the *servant leader* is more concerned with the relations within the organization, whereas the *spiritual leader* is focused on the mission of the organization.

17. 1Cel 22 in FAED 1:201–2.

18. In this, Francis seems close to what philosophers of education like Martin Buber, Simone Weil, and Martin Heidegger called an "aporetic experience." N. Tubbs comments: "[A]n experience of the relation between teacher and student where

A Life of Conversion

The fact that Francis was a disciple rather than a teacher stems from the beginning of his conversion. In his *Testament* he says that he used to live in sin.[19] And although it is true that he must have been a nice and courteous young man,[20] at some point in his life he did not feel at home in his world anymore. Because he saw no way out, not even a religious one, he decided to leave the world, waiting for God to show him what to do. This question, what God wanted him to do, guided Francis for the rest of his life.[21]

The lifelong quest for what he had to do also characterizes the story of his vocation. When he felt that he did not correspond well with his world, Francis first went after his dream: to become a knight. But an inner voice told him that he had to return to the place where he belonged: "and what you are to do will be told to you."[22] Furthermore, it is told that once back in his native region, riding on horseback in the neighborhood of Assisi, he saw a leper. He heard an inner voice that made him get off his horse to meet the man.[23] He remembers this encounter in his *Testament* as the decisive moment of his conversion.[24] Later, when he had left the world but did not yet know what to do, he heard the voice of the Lord speaking to him from the crucifix of San Damiano: "Francis, don't you see that my house is being destroyed? Go, then, and rebuild it for me."[25] And immediately Francis started restoring the church of San Damiano. His

---

individuality or identity is in some sense lost to and re-formed in their encounter. This re-formation can be called spiritual for it seems to transcend each individual person and to have a significance beyond each of them, a 'beyond' that can be said, at least to begin with, to be an experience of unity over separation" ("The Spiritual Teacher," *Journal of Philosophy of Education* 39 [2005] 287–317, here 288).

19. *Testament*, 1 in FAED 1:124 [further Test 1].

20. H. Nolthenius, *Een man uit het dal van Spoleto: Franciscus tussen zijn tijdgenoten* (Amsterdam: Querido, 1988), 106.

21. Francis formulates this question in different ways: in a dream (*The Legend of the Three Companions* [further 3Comp] 6, in *Francis of Assisi: Early Documents*, vol. 2: *The Founder* [further FAED 2] [ed. Regis J. Armstrong, J. A. Wayne Hellmann, and William J. Short; New York: New City Press, 2000] 71); through a biblical oracle (3Comp 28–29 in FAED 2:85–86); by asking his brothers and sisters to pray for him (Fior 16 in FAED 3:591–94); and even by saying to an angry leper (Fior 25 in FAED 3:607–9): "I'll do whatever you want."

22. 3Comp 5–6 in FAED 2:70–71.

23. 3Comp 11 in FAED 2:74.

24. Although he (Test 2 in FAED 1:124) describes it as an encounter with more than one leper: "And the Lord Himself led me among them and I showed mercy to them."

25. 3Comp 13–14 in FAED 2:76.

companions write that Francis did not yet realize that the Lord's assignment to restore his house was more extensive than the restoration of that little church. Because of this, the reaction of Francis becomes somewhat naive. But in this "naivety" his actions became a meaningful gesture: touched and directed by the Lord's speaking, he immediately got going, and the bodily change this movement brought about nourished his self-awareness.[26] Thus he received the Lord's commission as his life task; in the process he would find out how far this life task would reach.

We followed three moments of Francis's vocation and conversion: return to where you belong to hear what to do; get off your horse to meet the outcast; and when you hear what to do, start doing it without delay. The last phase in his vocation characterizes the story in which he heard, during a Mass, the Gospel in which Jesus sends his disciples two by two to preach the gospel. His reaction was remarkable. He immediately shouted, "This is what I want to do with all my strength."[27] As if he knew inwardly what he had to do but needed the confirmation of the Gospel. Later, when the first brothers joined him, he opened the Gospel book, found the same text, and indeed went with his brothers two by two, without taking anything with him, to bring peace to every house where they were to be received. And when they returned from their mission, they, like the disciples of Jesus, retreated for a moment to rest and reflect again on their vocation. For Francis and his brothers, these retreats were indispensable. Francis even longed for a hermit's existence and wrote a *Rule* for it.[28] But the retreats also led to a form of life.

How Learning Led to a Life Form

Jesus chose his disciples without paying attention to criteria such as intelligence, origin, and status. He met them on the way and asked them to follow him. While following in his footsteps (1 Pet 2:21), the Twelve were transformed into a community. Francis did not choose his brothers; they came to him—or, in his own words, they were given to him.[29] Again, however, apart from the Catholic faith, no criteria were used in the admission of the brothers.[30] More than Jesus, Francis was concerned and

---

26. Cf. the theory of Antonio Damasio (*The Feeling of What Happens: Body, Emotion and the Making of Consciousness* [London: Vintage, 2000]), about which I will speak later.
27. 3Comp 25 in FAED 2:84.
28. *Rule for Hermitages* in FAED 1:61–62.
29. Test 14 in FAED 1:125.
30. 1Cel 31 in FAED I:209–10. Such openness is not originally Franciscan; it has already been described in the eleventh century. See Mirko Breitenstein, *Das Noviziat*

involved with the brotherhood. And more than Jesus, he learned from his brothers. The community became, as it were, his body and identity.[31] When, at the end of his life, Francis felt the tensions within the brotherhood, he personally suffered.[32] In fact, however, these were the growth spurts of an initial *communitas* as described by the anthropologist Victor Turner, in which a diverse but strongly sensed community is turning into a regular order.[33] The redemption from Francis's personal suffering came from the Lord himself, who reminded him that the brotherhood belonged to the Lord alone and that Francis had his own mission.[34] We will come back to this.

A community develops a form of life of its own accord, something inaccurately referred to today as a "lifestyle."[35] Not much is clear from the Gospels about the form of life of Jesus and his disciples, apart from that through a bodily learning process they were transformed into the "new Adam": Jesus. Together they were transformed into a new community and, at the same time, into the unique individuals that they were. In much the same way, through bodily imitation, Francis and his brothers were transformed into a new religious order.[36] But Francis was much more concerned than Jesus was with the formation of the brotherhood and the development of their form of life. In the yearly chapters, he and his brothers laid down their form of life in a *Rule* by mutual agreement. This was done in a way that tells us something about Francis's teaching, namely, that he allowed himself to be corrected by his brothers. After the brothers had been sent out two by two (see Mark 6:7–13), they came back at regular intervals to tell what they had done and what they had experienced (Mark 6:30). In the beginning, this happened once or twice a year, on Pentecost and Michaelmas (September 29) at a chapter in

---

im hohen Mittelalter: Zur Organisation des Eintritts bei den Cluniazensern, Cisterziensern und Franziskanern (Vita Regularis 38; Münster: Lit, 2008) 420–29.

31. Willem Marie Speelman, "Brother Sun, Sister Moon: Franciscan Identity as a Brotherhood of Virtues," *ET Studies* 9 (2018) 273–88.

32. Speelman, *Om de hele wereld*, 225–26.

33. Victor Turner calls Francis and his brotherhood an example of this *communitas* in relation to the hierarchical structure of the church (*The Ritual Process: Structure and Anti-Structure* [Ithaca, NY: Cornell University Press, 1969] 141).

34. Thomas of Celano, *The Remembrance of the Desire of a Soul*, 158 [further 2Cel 158] in FAED 2:231–393.

35. Lifestyle is related to image, how one wants to be seen, whereas the form of life is at the same time more bodily and is aimed at the inner life of the brotherhood.

36. In 2Cel 188 Francis focuses on this bodily imitation—"follow my footsteps"—by resigning as minister general of the order. He gives himself as an example in opposition to "the examples of the ancients" (Augustin, Bernard, and Benedict).

Portiuncula.³⁷ Like new thoughts from a living conversation, experiences led to new forms of conduct which were discussed in these chapters. Thus, the experience of the brothers grew into a life form of the brotherhood. That explains why there are various editions of the *Rule of the Friars Minor*, and why this *Rule* is still seen as a stage in the infinite growth and adaptation of the Franciscan life form.³⁸

Thus, Francis learned by listening and doing and by listening again. But in this communicative process, he always kept or sought contact with his Lord and Teacher. He regularly retreated into a cave or hermitage to connect with his vocation. You could say that meeting and contemplation were two important pillars of his learning process. And it was this learning process that he showed his brothers as a living example. The study of the Holy Scriptures, if you can call it a study, was never without the living practice in which the one mirrored the other. Francis appropriated the Scriptures in a very personal way. He felt personally addressed by them and called to realize them in his own life. We will discuss this as a contemplative reading, in which knowing the Author goes together with recognizing the Author in the works. The works reveal themselves in the living practice of Francis and his brothers, rather than in reading about the great deeds of others.³⁹

A Bodily Form of Learning

Just as Jesus did not go around proclaiming a doctrine, but the coming of the kingdom of God, so Francis did not go around proclaiming a new doctrine, but a new form of life. The content of his sermons is unknown and, according to sources, was focused not so much on well-considered wordings as on the eloquence of his gestures.⁴⁰ Francis went among the

---

37. As is reported by Jacques de Vitry in his letters (see FAED 1:583). See also David Flood, *Frère François et le mouvement franciscain* (Paris: Ouvrières, 1983) 96–100.

38. See Desbonnets, *From Intuition to Institution*; David Flood and Thaddée Matura, *The Birth of a Movement: A Study of the First Rule of St. Francis* (Chicago: Franciscan Herald, 1975); S. Verheij, *Naar het land van de levenden: Regel van Franciscus van Assisi voor de minderbroeders* (Nijmegen: Valkhof, 2007).

39. *Assisi Compilation*, 103–7 [further AC 103–7] in FAED 2:207–10. In AC 105 Francis says, "A person is only as learned as his actions show; and a religious is only as good a preacher as his actions show."

40. J. Hoeberichts, "Franciscus' visie op 'leven volgens het model van het evangelie,'" *Franciscaans Leven* 88 (2005) 98–112; Gerard Pieter Freeman, "Minderbroeders, boeteprediker: Een antwoord aan Jan Hoeberichts," *Franciscaans Leven*, 88 (2005) 113–15. Michael W. Blastic shows that the friars' preaching was very popular and very close to the daily life of those who listened to them ("Preaching in the Early Franciscan Movement," in *Franciscans and Preaching: Every Miracle from the Beginning*

people and did what in his eyes every creature should do: be as you have been created; do not try to be more than a creature; and love and praise the Lord as a creature.[41] And just like Jesus, Francis placed the emphasis on salvation, true joy, and life.

Further, in the form of his proclamation, the characteristics of Jesus's proclamation—within the living situation, with stories, and through gestures—were recognizable. That the brothers told *stories* is obvious. Most of what is known of Francis and his brothers has been handed down in stories. And their sermons too included many stories with "examples" (*exempla*), perhaps sentimental to our ears, which called the listeners to another, more penitential conduct. An example of such an *exemplum* can be found in Francis's *Earlier* and *Later Admonition and Exhortation*, where in scents and colors it is explained how a miser dies and goes to hell.[42] Theological issues are not discussed, but rather the life of the people and how they can find the good life. There are also many examples of *gestures*, such as the "sermon" that Francis gave to the Sisters in San Damiano, which consisted of sprinkling himself with ashes and reciting the Psalm *Miserere Mei* (Psalm 51).[43] Another example is that Francis gave away an expensive Gospel book to a poor woman.[44] Furthermore, Francis took every opportunity of *the living situation* to get more deeply engaged in the form of life with his brothers. One example is the story of the brother who could not sleep because he was fasting so fanatically that he did not give his body what it needed.[45]

He who seizes the opportunity in his teaching will be open to outside influences, the context in which he tries to shape his life. And because the world in the thirteenth century—the rising monetary economy and citizenship, the free cities, the hierarchic organization of the church, the new poverty—changed drastically,[46] Francis and his brothers had to adapt their way of life to the new era. It became a crisis for the brotherhood and for Francis, in which they tried to maintain the original charisma within

---

of the World Came about through Words [ed. Timothy J. Johnson; Medieval Franciscans 7; Leiden: Brill, 2012] 13–40, here 33).

41. Cf. his model for preaching in his *Earlier Rule* (RegNB 17:3 and 21:1–9 in FAED 1:75 and 78).

42. *Earlier Exhortation* in FAED 1:41–44; *Later Admonition and Exhortation* in FAED 1:45–51. The Latin abbreviations are EpFid I (*Epistola ad Fideles*) and EpFid II.

43. 2Cel 157.

44. 2Cel 91.

45. AC 50 in FAED 2:149–50.

46. Giacomo Todeschini, *Franciscan Wealth: From Voluntary Poverty to Market Society*, trans. Donatella Melucci (St. Bonaventure, NY: Franciscan Institute, 2009) 12.

the structure of a regular order, in the context of the new world in which the Franciscans received an important pastoral task.[47] The "spiritual lay brothers" had the feeling that a new generation of brothers, the ordained members, were adapting too much to the demands of the world, and in fact led the brotherhood back into the reality that Francis and the first brothers had forsaken.[48] I cannot describe this struggle here, but I would like to note that Francis and his closest brothers resisted with their bodies and lives the demise of what they remembered as the original world-forsaking community.[49]

The Testament of St. Francis: An Attempt to Preserve the Bodily Form of Imitation

As an exemplary disciple of Jesus, Francis became a model for those who followed him. Although he had already withdrawn in 1220 from the position of general minister of the Order, Francis used his charismatic authority to preserve the original "spirit of prayer and devotion" in the brotherhood.[50] A circle of close followers supported him in this. They were sometimes referred to as "spirituals" or "lay brothers." In one of the collections of stories they explicitly call themselves *nos qui cum eo fuimus*, "we who were with him."[51] This is of course a significant statement, namely, that they (and not the others) were the true followers of him, and through him, of Jesus. There is a tendency, even now, to take sides with these lay brothers, "poor of spirit," who preserved Francis's original spirituality. But Francis tried not to take sides with one group or against the other, by which he would inadvertently have clung to the divisions. On the contrary, he tried to endure the pain of division in his own brother-

---

47. Franciscans not only taught against heresies (Breitenstein, *Das Noviziat im hohen Mittelalter*, 420), but they were especially valued as confessors in a world that longed for a holy life. See Sylvain Piron, "Présentation," in *Pierre de Jean Olivi: Traité des Contrats* (ed. and trans. Sylvain Piron; Bibliothèque Scolastique 5; Paris: Les Belles Lettres, 2012) 40.

48. Laurentio C. Landini, *The Causes of the Clericalization of the Order of Friars Minor, 1209–1260, in the Light of Early Franciscan Sources* (Chicago: Pontificia Universitas Gregoriana, 1969).

49. Despite the discussions and struggles in the first generations of the brotherhood, I tend to say that the brothers succeeded. See Willem Marie Speelman, "Franciscan *usus pauper* as the Gateway Towards an Aesthetic Economy," *Franciscan Studies* 74 (2016) 185–205, here 187–88.

50. Jacques Dalarun, *Gouverner, c'est servir: Essai de démocratie médiévale* (Paris: Alma) 2012, 373: "Directeur spirituel, le Frère par excellence, la référence. Il renonce au pouvoir et accroît son autorité. Il déborde l'institutionnel par le spirituel."

51. These stories were collected in the *Assisi Compilation*, in FAED 2:111–230.

hood, and, in enduring this tension, to accept the different views within the one brotherhood. Francis chose to preserve the original charism of the brotherhood *by adapting* his order to the new circumstances. In his *Testament*, we can unravel how he appeals to this original charism and to the demands of the new age.[52]

In his *Testament*, St. Francis emphasizes to the new generation of priest-brothers that everything is given to him by the Lord: his penitential life, his reverence for the churches in this world as the site of Christ, his ability to see the Son of God even in sinful priests and theologians, the brotherhood and the Gospel as a model of life, the peace of the Lord, and finally the *Rule* and his *Testament*. In the same document, however, Francis stresses to the spiritual lay brothers that they must remain within the obedience of the regular and ecclesiastical order.[53] And what goes for the brothers also goes for Francis himself: he will try to hold out in the face of tension between the world-forsaking *communitas* and the ecclesiastical order in the world.

Did Francis See Himself as a Teacher?

Francis undeniably saw himself and his friars as examples, and he was certainly a spiritual teacher, but he was so in the manner of a disciple.[54] Francis followed Christ, his Lord and Teacher, whom he heard speaking in his inner being.[55] Like Jesus, Francis saw himself as a servant, as he shows in his *Admonitions*, a servant of the Lord.[56] And in the perspective of his dealings with the tensions within his brotherhood, we can say that Francis indeed followed Jesus as a *suffering* servant. By bearing the divisions as if in his own body, he preserved the Spirit of unity and communion in which, according to his closest brothers, he was confirmed by the Lord.[57]

---

52. AC 106 in FAED 2:210–13. See Mark Weaver, "The Testament and the Fractured Fraternity of Francis," *Greyfriars Review* 10 (1996) 269–82.

53. Respectively Test 2–3, 4–5, 6–13, 14, 23, 39 and Test 25, 27, 28, 30, 31, 32, 33, 35, 36, 37, 38 in FAED 1:124–27.

54. RegNB 4:6 in FAED 1:66; Test 21 in FAED 1:125.

55. 1Cel 25 in FAED I:204.

56. In his *Admonitions* (in FAED I:128–37) Francis elaborates the life of a true servant of the Lord. For an analysis, see Edith van den Goorbergh and Theo Zweerman, *Was getekend: Franciscus van Assisi; Aspecten van zijn schrijverschap en brandpunten van zijn spiritualiteit* (Scripta Franciscana 5; Assen: Van Gorcum, 2002) 37–61; English translation: *Respectfully Yours, Signed and Sealed, Francis of Assisi: Aspects of His Authorship and Focuses of His Spirituality* (St. Bonaventure, NY: Franciscan Institute, 2001).

57. AC 112, in FAED 2:219–20.

III. THE CONTEMPORARY DEMAND FOR RELIGIOUS LEARNING

When we ask about the question of Franciscan teaching for our time, we have to take into account the current religious context. That context is first and foremost that in our secularized culture there exists a varied religious landscape. The variation is formed not only by different religions within, for example, a school class, but also by the fact that the faithful are related in various ways to their religion. On the one hand, there are many people who, due to a lack of religious formation and thus a lack of a religious language, have to develop forms of expressing themselves in order to relate to the religious sphere. On the other hand, there are also many people who feel at home in traditional religious institutions and use the traditional language in relation to the same questions. In such a multiform context, young people in particular, seem to be able to mirror each other, which creates something like "spontaneous" interreligious learning. However, it seems that young people are not so much looking for the right religion as for a respectful, authentic life of their own.[58]

In this context, the question of the value of Franciscan teaching forces us to reflect on the real mission of religious education. I think that a Franciscan teacher would focus on the growth of the student's self in the world, which, in Franciscan terms, is at the deepest level a community sharing in the divine creation. The growth of the self goes together with the development of a form of life in which everything is a divine gift, with universal brotherhood as a most precious one. If we can share in this mission, we may highlight some recent educational issues from a Franciscan perspective. Then we will see an inner teacher light up, who takes shape in encounters, who makes himself known in everyday events, in stories, and in gestures.[59]

I would like to dwell briefly on three recent educational positions: the spiritual teacher (Nicolas Tubbs), learning through encounter and the

---

58. *Handboek Jongeren en Religie: Katholieke, protestantse en islamitisch jongeren in Nederland* (ed. M. van Dijk-Groeneboer; Almere: Parthenon, 2010) 210–21.

59. Schoot, "Lerend leiderschap," 128. In discussion with Augustine's *De Magistro*, Henk Schoot speaks of "Christ as *inner teacher;* He is the *summus magister* who supports the student from within in his or her learning process" (my translation). This approach is known as the "illuminatio-theory." The Socratic approach also describes an inner teacher, which Socrates calls *daimonion*. See Angelo Caranfa, "Silence as the Foundation of Learning," *Educational Theory* 54.2 (2004) 211–30, here 213–14.

competence to deal with people of other religions (Bert Roebben), and the importance of contemplation and action (Fran Grace).

Servant-Teaching

Nicolas Tubbs poses the question of the relationship between the pupil and the teacher and describes in particular Martin Buber's educational theory.[60] He paints the spiritual teacher as someone who can be both master and servant, teacher and pupil. The spiritual teacher works with "inclusion," that is, the ability to take the point of view of the other (the pupil) as if it were his own. Because he also sees himself through the eyes of the pupil, "inclusion" makes the spiritual teacher extremely vulnerable. At the same time, the teacher becomes an inevitable model for the pupil in all his or her actions. Not that the pupil also practices "inclusion," because then the student would stop being a pupil and would become a friend. It is rather the spiritual teacher who is both teacher and pupil, and thus embodies a commitment. In the classroom this relationship has its own form, namely, from center to periphery. As the center of the learning process, the spiritual teacher is focused not so much on the pupil as on the example of the learning process: he acts for how he stands in the world and deals with what happens to him. In this way the teacher teaches as if he were not a teacher but a pupil who forms life in the beings of his pupils.

What remains undiscussed in the approach of Tubbs is the question of what the spiritual teacher focuses on. The term "spiritual" is defined as that which transcends the individual person, and which would be "at least to begin with" an experience of oneness. But as personal as Buber's I–Thou relationship is, so the teacher's inspiration and destiny in this approach seem impersonal. What transcends the individual person is, according to Buber, a Thou, that is to say, a personal relationship. It follows almost inevitably from Tubbs's description of the spiritual teacher, that he is directed by an inner teacher. The learning process is an inner process in which the teacher—as if he were a doctor or a farmer—creates the conditions under which the pupil can learn. In this sense, the teacher is a servant of the inner teacher, who enlightens the mind from within.

Learning by Meeting

Of course, with an inner teacher we do not think of a kind of homunculus that speaks from the heart to the pupil. It may very well be that the inner

---

60. Tubbs, "Spiritual Teacher," 287–317.

teacher is the voice of the one who gave the pupil a mission, and at times is still heard. Through this mission the pupils can be so deeply connected with him or her that they can see through his or her eyes, as it were, and act with his or her gestures. Listening to the voice of the inner teacher can take shape in encounters. It can also be the case that encounters between students establish or reenact a teacher–pupil relationship.

In the context of students of different abilities and different religions, Bert Roebben describes learning through encounters, which, after Mary Boys, he also calls "learning in the presence of the (religious) other."[61] Pupils can learn from each other precisely because of their differences, as long as they experience each other's presence and dare to meet each other in their shared vulnerability.[62] From Francis we can learn that the teacher can be an exemplary student in this horizontal process. It is obvious, however, that this activity is not always free of conflict; we have heard of teachers who, confronted with the vulnerability of their pupils, avoid discussing difficult issues. But learning by meeting is a good way to overcome these confrontations, by transforming them into encounters. Encounters were the engine of Francis's spiritual life, including the difficult encounters like those with the sultan.[63] But also here, in Francis's encounter with the sultan, faith in the other person's faith is the precondition of the conversation. One must dare to show one's vulnerability and one's orientation toward the good, the shared good. According to Roebben, the teacher plays a central role in this, offering the opportunity to meet but also setting the goal.

Learning in the presence of the other thus evokes three bodies: the first pupil, the other pupil, and the teacher. The teacher connects the learners to each other and to a common goal. To this end, it is needed that he or she attunes himself or herself to the inner teacher of the pupil, becoming an embodiment of it. It is a paradox that, on the one hand, the teacher is the center of the learning process and, on the other hand, he or she is not actually the center: there is another center, which is the inner teacher. With reference to Francis, the teacher is in fact a model pupil,

---

61. M. C. Boys, "Learning in the Presence of the Other," *Religious Education* 103 (2008) 502–6.

62. Roebben, "Living and Learning," 1: "We become learners through the encounter. We receive our identities in the encounter. The experience of otherness interrogates learners mutually about their autonomy to, their relationship with and their knowledge about each other—about what they have to offer to one another."

63. See J. Hoeberichts, *Francis and Islam* (Quincy: Franciscan Press, 1997); also Paul Moses, *The Saint and the Sultan: The Crusades, Islam, and Francis of Assisi's Mission of Peace* (New York: Doubleday Religion, 2009).

who through his or her exemplary obedience to the inner teacher shows the pupils where the source is, and how they too can draw from it.

Contemplative Learning, Active Learning

Encounters bring about changes in the students. Antonio Damasio describes how the self, as a nuclear consciousness, awakens and is shaped by the changes that someone experiences in his or her body. Second, he argues that an "other self," the autobiographical consciousness, will process these changes narratively into a story of one's own life.[64] Back to the learning situation: if a pupil experiences changes in him- or herself because of these encounters, he or she needs time and space to process the experiences into a personal story. That is why a moment of contemplation, alone or together with others, is an important element in the learning process. Fran Grace distinguishes "third person learning," in which content is central, "second person learning," in which mutual communication is central, and "first person learning," in which personal processing is central.[65] The last mentioned requires a safe, quiet, secluded—"sacred"—space in which the teacher and pupils can be humble and vulnerable.[66] We see this in both Jesus and Francis: they and their disciples regularly withdrew in order to be able to focus on their (shared) inner teacher. This inner teacher took shape in the silence, in prayer, and in mutual conversation.

Both Jesus and Francis show us, in addition to something like contemplative learning, a more active form of learning: they learned by gestures. Merleau-Ponty showed us, and this has been confirmed by Damasio, that the original learning is, first, a bodily experience. It is like learning language, which is primarily an imitation of movements, rhythms, sound sequences, and only in the second instance—also through bodily experiences—a matter of meanings. It is good when pupils receive practical assignments that will allow them to actively experience what it means to help others, to follow them, and to work together. Learning to think and learning to see are essentially the same process as learning to walk.

---

64. Damasio, *Feeling of What Happens*, 16–17.
65. Fran Grace, "Pedagogy of Reverence: A Narrative Account," *Religion & Education* 36.2 (2009) 102–23.
66. Caranfa develops a Socratic educational theory, in which silence—that is, the silent listening to the inner voice—is approached as a source of self-knowledge and as a way to bring this self in an attentive relationship with the object of knowledge ("Silence as the Foundation of Learning," 211–30).

Mission as a Perspective of Learning

It is not self-knowledge that is the ultimate goal of learning, but the ability to meet with the world, with others, and with God.[67] The content of teaching, including the minimum attainment levels, is therefore nothing more than a trace of encounters. This trace has been drawn to lead to new encounters. The ultimate goal is, however, that pupils are sent out to create the conditions in the world for the coming of the good life. The mission itself, the feeling of being sent, is a trace of the inner teacher, who has nestled himself in the shape of a teacher or another pupil or a disclosure of something in the heart of the pupil, and who directs his or her actions as another voice. The awakening and shaping of the student's self and the ability to receive that other voice are practiced in a personal learning process that, in stories and gestures, in silence and encounter, opens the door to a new reality in which life is good.

67. K. M. Fischer, "Look before You Leap: Reconsidering Contemplative Pedagogy," *Teaching Theology & Religion* 20.1 (2017) 4–21.

14

Magisterial:

Thomas Aquinas as Teacher

Henk J. M. Schoot

At the time when the first universities were founded in Europe, the Order of Preachers—Dominicans—also saw the light of day (1216). The development of the university and the evangelical movement of mendicant brothers, to which the Dominicans belonged together with the Franciscans, went hand in hand. Thus, the four Dominican *studia generalia* in fact formed the theological faculties of the universities of Paris, Bologna, Padua, and Montpellier. The friars thus acquired an important role in the development of new learning, and Thomas Aquinas (1225–1274) was a pioneer in this: as a student as well as a master (*magister*) and as (co-)founder of new studies in Cologne (under the leadership of Albert the Great †1280), Rome, and Naples.[1] The almost fifty years of his life were dedicated to education: from his oblation in the Benedictine Abbey of Monte Cassino; through his student days at the young universities of Naples and Paris and the new *studium* of the Dominicans in Cologne; to his professorship in Paris, his teaching assignments in Italy and again as a professor in Paris; and finally, to end in Naples.

---

1. Detlef Rohling, *Omne scibile est discibile: Eine Untersuchung zur Struktur und Genese des Lehrens und Lernens bei Thomas von Aquin* (Beiträge zur Geschichte der Philosophie und Theologie des Mittelalters 77; Münster: Aschendorf, 2012) III. Rohling discusses the most important literature on the subject (9–16). For reflections on education in the Dominican tradition, see Sister Matthew Marie Cummings and Sister Elizabeth Anne Allen, eds., *Behold the Heritage: Foundations of Education in the Dominican Tradition* (Tacoma, WA: Angelico Press, 2012), also with a contribution by Vivian Boland on Thomas and education.

Thomas's teachership was mainly shaped by the lectures he gave, the disputes he held, the sermons he delivered, and the books he wrote. Of course, this teaching practice also required Thomas to think about teaching and education as such. Of all the medieval theologians, he is the only one to have written a *quaestio disputata* on the subject, *De Magistro*.[2] Thus, we are dealing both with philosophical and theological reflection on being a teacher and with books and college notes in which that reflection is applied.

This subject, therefore, covers an enormous field of research, with many possible topics and questions. In my contribution I will try to point out and elaborate on a few details: (1) Thomas's care for clearly structured and summarizing texts, (2) the way in which he implements this in texts about teaching, (3) in which he makes the learning process of the pupil central, and (4) for which Christ as teacher is the guiding principle.

■ I. SHORT AND CLEAR

In the prologue to the *Summa theologiae* (*STh*), Thomas Aquinas employs the expression *ordo disciplinae*. These words indicate what we can call the "learning process" of the pupil. You can teach and you can learn; if you teach, you are a teacher, and if you learn, you are a student or a pupil. Thomas here calls the teacher *catholicae veritatis doctor*, "teacher of Catholic truth," while the student is referred to as "beginner" (*incipiens*), "novice" (*novitius*), and "advanced" (*provectus*). So, Thomas states that a teacher is dealing not only with advanced students but also with novices. It is precisely these beginners he has in mind when writing his *Summa theologiae*, he says. In this book he wants to explain what belongs to the Christian religion in a way that fits the formation of beginners. Thomas gives three reasons why a separate kind of book is needed for this. First of all, beginners are hindered by a multitude of useless issues, articles, and arguments in existing different writings. We may therefore expect that such elements will be lacking in this text. Second, learners are expected to learn the necessary things by explaining a passage or by arguing, but the method that is appropriate for this differs from the method that is appropriate for the learner's learning process. It is not the book to be commented upon, which was not written for teaching, or the dispute, that should be the starting point, but the *ordo disciplinae*, the learning process of the pupil.[3]

---

2. Rohling, *Omne scibile est discibile*, 17.
3. Besides "science," discipline also means learning from the pupil. A clue to this is a statement by Aristotle in the first book of the *Posteriora Analytica*, which Thomas

And, third, there is too much repetition, which results in boredom and confusion. We may therefore expect that this too is not discussed in the *Summa theologiae*. The motto is literally *"breviter ac dilucide,"* short and clear. Thomas wants to follow the example of Aristotle and Pseudo-Dionysius in this.[4]

Thus, Thomas shows himself as a theologian with a very practical side. As a master it is his task "to read" (*legere*), that is to say, to explain and comment on important books from the tradition while reading; "to debate" (*disputare*), in other words, to discuss philosophical and theological questions, to weigh up arguments for and against, and to formulate his answer; and "to preach" (*praedicare*), that is, to address the university and the religious community during eucharistic celebrations, vespers, and on special occasions.[5] But Thomas does not, therefore, consider it his task only to read, debate, and preach, but also to summarize and explain to beginners the most important questions of the faith.

Thomas energetically carries out this part of the task of teacher (*catholicae veritatis doctor*) as he sees it. It seems that his experiences as a

---

(*STh* I, q. 117, a. 1) quotes in his question about education and the acquisition of knowledge: "Omnis doctrina et omnis disciplina ex praeexistenti fit cognitione" ("All teaching and all learning proceed from previous knowledge"). Cf. *QD* [*Quaestiones Disputatae*] *De Veritate* q. 11, a. 1 ad 3. In his commentary on this, Thomas (*Expositio in I Post. An.* 1, 9) explicitly states that *doctrina* stands for the teaching of the teacher, and *disciplina* for the acquisition of knowledge by the pupil: "Nomen autem doctrinae et disciplinae ad cognitionis acquisitionem pertinet. Nam doctrina est actio eius, qui aliquid cognoscere facit; disciplina autem est receptio cognitionis ab alio" ("The terms 'teaching' and 'learning' pertain to the acquisition of knowledge. For teaching is the action of one who causes another to know something, while learning is the reception of knowledge from another"). See also *STh* II–II, q. 16, a. 2. Thus, most existing modern translations of *ordo disciplinae* do not satisfy: "wetenschappelijke volgorde" ("scientific order," Dominicanen [Dutch and Flemish], 1927), "the order of the subject matter" (Fathers of the English Dominican Province, 1920), "planvoller Ordnung" (Deutsche Thomas-Ausgabe, 1934), "l'ordre de la discipline" (Les Editions du Cerf, 1984); but see "sound educational method" (Blackfriars, 1964), "the order of learning" (A. J. Freddoso, New English Translation, available online, http://www3.nd.edu/~afreddos/summa-translation/TOC.htm). See also *QD De Veritate* q. 11, a. 1 and *STh* III, q. 9, a. 4 ad 1 on *inventio* and *disciplina*.

4. After all, in two other places in his work Thomas also speaks about this "learning process." In his commentary on Aristotle's *De sensu et sensato* (tr. 1, l. 9, n. 2) he explains the order of treatment, namely, taste first and only then smell, from the learning process of the listener or reader. For man knows taste rather than smell. And also, Pseudo-Dionysius (*In Divinis Nominibus* 2,2) proceeds in such a way, that he starts with the things that are clearer, to go from the knowledge of those things to other things of which the knowledge still has to be acquired.

5. Jean-Pierre Torrell, *Initiation à saint Thomas d'Aquin: Sa personne et son oeuvre* (new ed.; Paris: Cerf, 2015) chapter V.

teacher in the Dominican convent of Orvieto (1261–1265), where he taught those brothers who had not received an education at the higher Dominican schools (*Studium generale* or *Studium provinciale*), are at the basis of this educational innovation. Such brethren had above all to learn to preach and to hear confession, but the theological overview and theological foundation were lacking. Literature suggests that when Thomas was commissioned from 1265 to set up a school for Dominicans in Santa Sabina, Rome, he not only began to write the *Summa theologiae* there, but also used it in his teaching.[6] Moreover, this conception of his task as a teacher fits in with what he was doing before. After all, there are many more of his writings that are introductory and summary in character. Think, for example, of the *Summa contra gentiles* and the *Compendium theologiae*. So we may conclude that we are dealing here with a task that Thomas took very much to heart. And it is precisely here that the student's learning process is central, so we may equally conclude that it is precisely this learning process that Thomas took to heart.[7]

■ II. Short and Clear about Education

The difference between a short treatise aimed at the pupil and a text representing a dispute—that is, a text that highlights a question from all sides—is clearly apparent when we place the *Summa theologiae* next to the *Quaestiones Disputatae De Veritate*. Let's take the text that deals with the question of whether one human being can teach another. *STh* I, q. 117, a. 1 contains 1,125 words; *De Veritate* q. 11 (titled *De Magistro*) a. 1

---

6. Leonard E. Boyle calls the Roman *studium* a *studium personale*, says Torrell (*Initiation*, 191; see also 193). Torrell is of the opinion that it is precisely the concern for the education of the friars that made Thomas write his most important work: "C'est finalement à son souci d'éducateur que l'on doit la Somme de théologie qui devait immortaliser sa renommée" (231). It could be the reason why he discontinued his second commentary on Petrus Lombardus's *Sentences*, suggests Adriano Oliva ("La Somme de théologie de Thomas d'Aquin: Introduction historique et littéraire," *Chôra: Revue d'études anciennes et médiévales* 7–8 [2009] 217–53, here 226).

7. It is unclear whether the *Epistola de modo studendi* (Letter about the way of studying) really is from Thomas's hand. But at least the first lines fit very well with what we have seen as Thomas's vision on the learning process of students. After all, the author says to Johannes, the addressed student, that he "should not jump into the sea immediately, but should prefer narrow streams, because it is precisely through easier things that you can reach the more difficult ones." We recognize Thomas's *ordo disciplinae*. The letter can be found in S. Thomae Aquinatis, *Opuscula Theologica*, vol. 1 (Rome: Marietti, 1954) 451.

contains 3,502 words. In the *Summa* Thomas treats four arguments and gives one *sed-contra* argument. In *De Veritate* he treats as many as eighteen arguments and gives seven *sed-contra* arguments.[8] So in the *Summa*, Thomas has cut down many trees, making the forest visible again.

From both texts, however, it immediately becomes clear that these treatises are not only based on a search for understanding the possibilities of education. Both texts give a prominent role to Jesus's statement in Matt 23:8, 10, in which he forbids the disciples to strive to be called "rabbi": "You have only one master [*magister*], and you are each other's brothers and sisters.... Do not be called teacher [*magister*] either, for you have only one teacher [*magister*], Christ."[9] Thomas's commentary on the Gospel of Matthew has been handed down to us in two separate lecture dictates, which were not reviewed by Thomas, and of which the second is clearly of inferior quality to the first; for example, it is much shorter. If we are going to count words here, we will have to interpret it cautiously. The four verses in question receive a commentary of 736 words. In the *Summa*, on the other hand, 119 words are spent on this Scripture text, and in *De Veritate*, 152. If one takes into account that, on the one hand, Leodegarius of Besançon, who is the author of this part of the lecture-dictate, has been rather summary and, on the other hand, that there is more to these four verses than just the role of the teacher, the main line is clear: with respect to the genre of Bible commentary, in which the magister "reads" the text, the *Summa* is also clearly concise.

The fact that the treatment in the *Summa* is thus short, clear, and concise, does mean that the reader of that text must be wary. And that is very applicable here. After all, whoever reads Thomas's answer to the first argument in the *Summa*, can easily, especially if hindered by prejudice, conclude that Thomas simply gets rid of it and only pays lip service to the traditional, Augustinian view that "divine enlightenment" (*illuminatio*) is necessary for the transfer of knowledge. The prejudice is that Thomas follows in Aristotle's footsteps to such an extent that this would be an insufficiently realistic view for him. We will, however, first take a

---

8. The *Summa theologiae* is made up of *quaestiones*, usually consisting of several articles (*articulus*) that are familiar with the structure of a medieval dispute, but do not reflect it: first, a question is formulated to which an affirmative or negative answer is possible; then arguments (*obiectiones*) are listed for either confirmation or denial; then there are opposing arguments (*sed-contra*), which are almost always authority arguments and thus borrowed from Scripture or the Fathers of the Church or the philosophers. Thomas gives his answer (*responsio* or *corpus articuli* or *solutio*), and concludes with answers to the arguments or considerations with which he started.

9. Two different Greek words in Matt 23:8, 10, respectively διδάσκαλος (v. 8) and καθηγητής (v. 10), are translated by the Vulgate with one word: *magister*.

closer look at what Thomas actually says in the *Summa*, and on the basis of a comparison with the texts from *De Veritate* and his commentary on Matthew, we can conclude that this is precisely the reason for respecting each person's own learning process: it is an internal intellectual light of a person that can only acquire knowledge itself, and it is God who is the creator of that light.

As is to be expected, Thomas links a biblical with a patristic and a philosophical line. The biblical line is Jesus's seemingly negative talk about teachers: no one should place himself above anyone else, we are all brothers and sisters, and only Christ is a teacher; and whoever is the greatest will be the servant. The patristic line is the line of Augustine, who struggles with the question of how he can explain that a person acquires knowledge, for example, a language. On the one hand, people need signs, in order to be able to teach any reality to others; but, on the other hand, people need knowledge of that reality, in order to understand the meaning of signs. Augustine sometimes speaks with confidence about this process, but sometimes he is also skeptical about what people can teach to other people, and then appeals to Christ as an internal teacher.[10] The third line touches on Augustine's, but is more philosophical in nature, because it corresponds to a problem of Averroës (Ibn Rushd, 1126–1198) and of those whom Thomas calls the "Platonians." Averroës solves the problem of the transfer of knowledge by positing a "common sense," the *intellectus possibilis*, to all people; education then consists of teaching one person to teach the other, to order one's sensory perceptions in such a way that the knowledge that one already has in potential, as it were, comes to the surface. For Platonians, knowledge is a form of participation in eternal ideas, and knowledge transfer consists in the teacher teaching pupils what the pupils should already know from memory, were it not for the fact their physicality prevented them from doing so. Thomas vigorously rejects both ideas and chooses the approach he recognizes in Aristotle. Thomas summarizes:

> An important comparison is made between the teacher and the doctor. The doctor treats a sick person and makes him healthy again. But in fact it is the sick person himself who becomes healthy, and the doctor only helps, by doing what human nature does to the sick person himself, to remove the cause of the illness. And so it is also true for the teacher that he is not a direct cause, but only an outside help. Just as internal nature is the main cause of healing, so internal intellectual light is the main cause of knowledge. (*STh* I, q. 117, a. 1 ad 1)

---

10. The more trusting or encouraging line can be found in Augustine's *De catechizandis rudibus*, and the more skeptical in *De Magistro*.

And therein lies, precisely, the answer to the question of whether one can teach someone else without assuming something that belongs only to God, the reason why Christ might have said that no one should be called a rabbi or a teacher. Thomas's answer is that a teacher does not claim the role of God, any more than a doctor does; both are merely outside help; however, God is the source both of the inner nature (of a sick person) and of the inner intellectual light (of a student), and on this basis, God may be called both the healer of all diseases (Ps 103:3) and the one who gives knowledge to humans (Ps 94:10). All things are shown to us through the light of God's countenance shining upon us (Ps 4:7).

In the whole of the *Summa* article, this answer to the first argument is the only part that has a clear theological character.[11] One might therefore be tempted to take Thomas's answer as a superficial reference to God's all-causality, which has little to do with the problem at hand here. Does his reasoning not apply to everything that could be called second causes, because God is always the first cause? Even if it is builders who build a house, it is in vain if it is not God who builds the house, to give another biblical example (Psalm 127). But with a look at the other texts from his commentary on Matthew and *De Veritate*, we have to say that things are not like that for Thomas.

Before we do that, we should first let Thomas talk about what a teacher does when passing on knowledge (*STh* I, q. 117, a. 1). Even if the teacher is just an assistant, just a servant, just an outside helper, how does that help take place? Every human being has at his disposal an internal principle of knowledge. Thomas calls this the "light of the active mind" ("intellectual agent"). Through this principle a human being knows the universal principles of all kinds of knowledge in a natural and immediate way. He who acquires knowledge himself applies these principles to individual cases, the experience of which is provided by the senses and stored in memory. Thus, he who provides himself with knowledge goes from the known to the previously unknown. He who teaches does not lead himself, but the pupil from what he knows to what he does not know. Thomas quotes Aristotle: "All teaching [*doctrina*] and all learning [*disciplina*] arise from pre-existing knowledge." The teacher leads the student from the known to the unknown in two ways. First, by providing tools or aids that the student can use for knowledge acquisition—for example, by offering less-universal propositions than the first principles, on which the student can form an opinion with the help of his existing knowledge; or by giving concrete examples, things that seem to be or are opposite, so that

---

11. Except that Paul is invoked as proof of the conviction that one person can teach another, because he himself says so in 1 Tim 2:7 (*sed-contra*).

the learner is taken by the hand (manual instructor) on his way to the truth of something he did not yet know. Second, the teacher teaches by strengthening the student's mind. The pupil's mind is strengthened when he gains a better understanding of the ordering of principles and conclusions. This is the strengthening of logical insight, which is applied to a certain field of knowledge. In all this it is obvious that in the learning process the pupil is central for Thomas and not so much the teacher. It is the student who either "acquires knowledge himself" (*inventio*) or "acquires knowledge himself with the help of a teacher" (*disciplina*). The teacher is the help, who can assist logically or substantively. But it is always the student who acquires knowledge, who is central.

■ III. THE LEARNING PROCESS OF THE STUDENT IS CENTRAL

As promised, we now turn our attention to the other two texts from the commentary on Matthew and from *De Veritate*. We do this to discover whether there is indeed a connection between a Thomas who focuses on the learning process of the pupil and a Thomas who attributes the acquisition of knowledge mainly to the inner divine teacher.

The central word that Thomas places above his interpretation of Matthew 23 is "justice." Jesus and the scribes and Pharisees are engaged in a battle of words that, according to Thomas, is about the latter knowing themselves to be provoked by the honor shown to Christ and the wisdom he shows—and here, in particular, the iniquity of which he accuses them. More specifically, it is about the desire to hold positions of dignity, for example, in the church, while those who teach and those who lead should not rule but serve. And that is why this is specifically about the name "*magister*"and the name "father," for it is up to the former to instruct, says Thomas, and up to the latter to govern.

"Let yourself not be called a rabbi, for you have but one master" (Matt 23:8). That one master (*magister*) is God, says Thomas. What, according to Thomas, does Jesus want to say here now? That the title "master" really belongs only to the one who has his teaching of himself and did not receive it from others, and not to the one who passes on to others what he himself has received. Only God, therefore, is a teacher in the true sense of the word, and all other teachers are teachers only by virtue of the "service" (*ministerium*) they perform. The difference between the two ways of being a teacher is the difference between authority and humility. If you seek authority, then you place yourself in the position of God, and that is exactly what Jesus forbids here.

But perhaps there are teachers who think the success of their teaching depends solely on themselves. Thomas, however, makes short work of that (#1849). If that were true, then such a person should be able to give his teaching to whomever he wants. But it is obvious that he cannot, for, as Thomas says, only God enlightens the heart within. I do not think it is on the grounds of piety that Thomas says this. He simply observes a fact, namely, that no teacher can ensure that a student learns what the teacher would like him to learn. The teacher may want that, but the actual acquisition of knowledge is beyond his power. He just has to wait and see. He is, and here comes the same example again, as a doctor who wants to heal a sick person, but who has to wait and see whether the human nature of the sick person does what he wants. The doctor only stands on the sidelines and administers certain aids from the outside. And just as healing belongs to the human nature of the sick person, so the acquisition of knowledge belongs to the natural mind that is each person's own. Only God is entitled to work on the intellect, so only God is "master" in the true sense of the word.[12]

So, in the Bible commentary Thomas uses his understanding of teaching to explain why Jesus says that there is only one teacher, and that people should not be called (in this way) teachers. In this commentary it becomes clear that there is no reason to suppose that Thomas sees the acquisition of knowledge as an autonomous human matter. On the contrary, all learning presupposes the internal work of God. Teaching is a divine matter, and that is why it is so important that teachers do not place themselves in the position of God.

In *De Veritate*, as we saw, Thomas needs fewer words. The second *sed-contra* argument simply says that the fact that God is Father to all does not exclude that a man can truly be called a father, and that this also applies to naming a man a teacher. The answer to the first objection in fact boils down to the same thing. Thomas quotes the comment that the prohibition pronounced by Jesus should not be understood as an absolute prohibition. It is forbidden to call a human being a teacher in the way that God is a teacher, namely, the one to whom the principality of teacher belongs. For the things we hear from human beings, we must consult the divine truth which Thomas says speaks in us through the "impression" (*impressio*) of his likeness through which we can judge all things. God created humans in the divine image and likeness, and through this the

---

12. In #1852, Thomas explains why Christ calls himself the sole teacher of the disciples. He does so, says Thomas, because he is the Word, and therefore it is his own to teach, and because it is his mission (as the only one who has become man) to make God (whom no man has seen) known; so Christ is called teacher both according to his divine and to his human nature.

divine truth speaks in us, and a person is able to acquire knowledge and to judge.[13] So this applies to a person as a human being. He does not have to become someone else, would that be possible; no, he has to be himself and thus come to knowledge.

I have come to the conclusion, based on Thomas's commentary on Matthew and on *De Veritate*, that Thomas's text from the *Summa* cannot be regarded as a text of someone who easily gets rid of and explains the success of the learning process by appealing to God as internal teacher, but who is, rather, more interested in a purely natural explanation of the acquisition of knowledge. On the contrary, Thomas regards knowledge acquisition primarily as something done by the student himself, and in which the teacher plays only a secondary role; the respect for the student's learning process is due precisely to the fact that the student in this way is an image of God, and in himself hears the divine truth speak as it were.[14] Thomas himself puts this theory of the educational process into practice by taking the learning process of the pupil as a starting point in the *Summa theologiae*. Thomas's theory and practice agree with each other.

■ IV. CHRIST AS TEACHER

Let's return to the prologue to the *Summa theologiae*. As we saw, Thomas there speaks about himself and other teachers as *catholicae veritatis doctor*. The Latin word used here is *doctor*, and that word is also considered by Thomas as one of the names given to Christ in the New Testament.[15] Christ is the teacher whose task it is to proclaim a new doctrine, a new *doctrina*. The commentaries Thomas wrote on the Gospel of Matthew and on the Gospel of John make it very clear that Thomas sees the proclamation of this new doctrine as the first and very essential part of sal-

---

13. *QD De Veritate* q. 11, a. 1 ad 1; just before this, at the end of the response, Thomas speaks in similar terms of the light of reason inspired by God, which is a parable of the uncreated truth reflected in humanity.

14. *De Veritate* q. 11, a. 1 ad 1: "Quasi in hominum sapientia spem ponentes, et non magis de his quae ab homine audimus divinam veritatem consulentes, quae in nobis loquitur per suae similitudinis impressionem, qua de omnibus possumus iudicare" ("It would be as if we put our hope in the wisdom of men, and did not rather consult divine truth about those things which we hear from man. And this divine truth speaks in us through the impression of its likeness, by means of which we can judge of all things").

15. See Henk J. M. Schoot, *Christ the 'Name' of God: Thomas Aquinas on Naming Christ* (Publications of the Thomas Instituut te Utrecht 1; Louvain: Peeters, 1993) 79.

vation, the grace that signifies his incarnation.[16] It is clear Thomas recognizes the teacher in Christ. However, he not only recognizes that teacher role, but he also sees it as exemplary. He sees his own role as teacher as an extension of that of Jesus, without immediately saying or claiming it so explicitly.[17] We can illustrate this by looking at the way Thomas explains Jesus's conversation with the Samaritan woman (John 4:1–42).[18]

John tells in his fourth chapter how Jesus returns from Judea to Galilee and comes through Samaria on that road. Near the city of Sichar, the weary Jesus sits down at the well of Jacob and asks a Samaritan woman to give him something to drink. Then a conversation unfolds between Jesus and the woman about "living water." The disciples return from buying food in the city and the woman goes into the city to tell who it is she has spoken to, and many Samaritans come to faith.

From the beginning, Thomas makes it clear that he regards what Christ is doing here as authoritative teaching. The fact that he sits down at the source indicates the authority of the one who teaches, speaking as someone who possesses power (#564). The doctrine or teaching he gives is the "teaching of the spiritual water" (*doctrina de aqua spirituale*, #620). The evangelist, Thomas says, tells Christ's spiritual doctrine (#575). This spiritual doctrine can be summarized as: ask Jesus, and he will give you living water. At the end of his conversation with the Samaritan woman, Jesus reveals himself to her as the Messiah, as the Christ. "That is I who speak to you" (John 4:26). This concludes Thomas's second lectio (*In John* 4:2). But not until he has explained the "way of working" of Jesus. Jesus did not reveal himself as the Christ at the very beginning of the conversation, but he brought her "step by step" (*paulatim*) to the knowledge of himself

---

16. Relevant issues in the *Summa* about this are III, q. 7 (the grace of Christ), q. 9 (the knowledge of Christ) and especially q. 42 about the doctrine of Christ. For the Bible commentaries, see Pawel Klimczak, *Christus Magister: Le Christ maître dans les commentaires évangéliques de saint Thomas d'Aquin* (Studia Friburgensia n.F. 117; Fribourg: Academic Press, 2014).

17. However, it is contained in what Thomas learned from Augustine, namely, that all Christ's actions are instructive for us. Torrell recognizes in Thomas's work an omnipresence of Christ as the absolute model of Christian life (*Initiation*, 368).

18. For the commentaries on the Gospels of Matthew and John, I use the recent editions of The Aquinas Institute from Lander, Wyoming: Saint Thomas Aquinas, *Commentary on the Gospel of Matthew* (trans. Jeremy Holmes and Beth Mortensen; Latin/English Edition of the Works of St. Thomas Aquinas 33, 34; Lander, WY: Aquinas Institute, 2013); Saint Thomas Aquinas, *Commentary on the Gospel of John* (trans. Fabian R. Larcher; Latin/English Edition of the Works of St. Thomas Aquinas 35, 36; Lander, WY: Aquinas Institute, 2013) [further abbreviated as *In John*]. The numbers in the references correspond to paragraph numbers in the commentary.

and thus revealed himself at the right moment. Thomas then quotes Prov 25:11: "He who speaks the right word at the right time is like golden apples on silver bowls." He contrasts the Samaritan with the Pharisees, who also questioned Jesus. The Pharisees, however, did so to put him to the test, but the Samaritan to learn from him. She learns from him the lesson of salvation, in which Jesus follows the path from what is known to the woman to what is unknown to her. He goes from the water that you can drink and taste, to the spiritual water that you can only know and desire. From praying on Mount Gerizim to praying in spirit and in truth. From Jesus as prophet to Jesus as Messiah. We recognize the method Thomas himself advocates in his *Summa theologiae*: a learning process in which the known is the starting point to get to know the unknown; and the person of Christ himself is the culmination of this process.

For the teaching that Jesus gives here, it is essential that it takes place within the framework of a conversation, a dialogue. Jesus asks questions and gives answers, and the Samaritan asks questions and gives answers. The initiative comes from Jesus. He gives, says Thomas, knowledge of the good (that he wants to give), of the question for that good and of the giver (#579). And it is up to the woman to follow and answer the steps taken by the teacher, for it is this knowledge that leads to the desire for grace. And so she takes the spiritual doctrine of Jesus, asks for that grace and shows herself to be an excellent disciple who, Thomas says explicitly, takes up the ministry of apostle.[19]

Christ the teacher is thus, in a certain sense, the example for Thomas. In a certain sense, of course, this is because Thomas is very conscious of the fact that there is no other teacher like Christ who is the teacher of teachers. Christ has not only been sent as man to proclaim and teach the God whom no one has seen, but is also the Word of God, and on both these grounds speaks of himself as the one and only teacher, says Thomas in his commentary on Matthew. In addition, the incarnate teacher who is Christ, is exalted above the teaching role of Thomas himself. After all, Thomas writes books, but Christ did not, precisely because he was a very excellent teacher. In the third part of the *Summa* Thomas formulates this fascinating question: "Why did not Jesus leave any writings behind?"[20]

---

19. *In John* 4, l. 3, 624: "Officium apostolorum annuntiando assumentis" ("By what she said to her people, she was taking on the role of an apostle").

20. This contribution deals primarily with the distinction between oral and written teaching, which is different from the distinction between primary and secondary teaching roles. The former falls within the scope of secondary teacher role but, in the case of Christ, it transcends that distinction.

(*STh* III, q. 42, a. 4). Surely there would have been something to be said for that. After his death one could have remembered his teachings through his writings. And the Old Law, the Old Testament, which is, after all, a foreshadow of Christ, has been written down. Now, in the eyes of some, there remains grave doubt as to whether the disciples who wrote about him did not make him greater than he was, as Augustine says. Had he written himself, some would have accepted it more easily, and Christ would not have given rise to error, but offered a way of faith. These are the considerations that Thomas incorporates into the objections, but he tries, as usual, to find reasons for the absence of these writings. I will mention two of the three arguments Thomas puts forward. He says that Christ, as the most exalted teacher, is also entitled to the most exalted way of learning, and that is that he presses his teaching upon the hearts of his listeners, that he speaks to their hearts. Like Pythagoras and Socrates, Jesus needed no scripture to reach his hearers. Written doctrine is of a lower order than oral teaching. Direct, oral teaching takes precedence over indirect, written teaching. In addition, the second argument is that Jesus's teaching was so exalted that it could not be contained in letters; if Christ had entrusted his doctrine to writing, people would think that his doctrine would not be higher than what is contained in writing. Both arguments are extremely interesting. Indeed, the first implies that even if one is dealing with a human teacher, who is thus secondary to the human learning process, teaching can indeed speak to the hearts of people and take on an inner form. The distinction between primary and secondary teaching roles must therefore not be reduced to an absolute contrast between internal and external teaching. The second ground marks a radical difference between the holy Scriptures of fundamentalists and non-fundamentalists. Non-fundamentalists believe that the written testimony is secondary to the life and works of Jesus, and it does not coincide with them. Those who study the Scriptures about Jesus are therefore aware that the authority with which Jesus himself taught is of a different order from the authority of the testimony.

The internal teacher role also comes back in a different way in the answers to the arguments (*ad* 2). Certainly, the Old Law is written and perceptible to the senses, but Christ's teaching, which is the law of the spirit of life (Rom 8:2), was to be written—not with ink, but with the Spirit of the living God, not on tablets of stone, but on the tablets of the fleshly hearts, as Paul says in 2 Cor 3:3. You might think that when Thomas speaks about the proclamation of Jesus directly to the hearts of his audience, he means only the listening disciples of the time, but this last thing, he says, applies to disciples of all times. Of course, we have thus left the terrain of the earthly Jesus. Jesus writes, not in writing but on people's hearts, and through the Spirit he is the (inner) teacher *par excellence*.

V. CONCLUSION

Of course, there is much more to write about the role of teacher of Thomas Aquinas than I have been able to do here. For example, the study of Thomas's systematic works is of great importance for the interpretation of his role as teacher, and so is the study of his understanding of *sacra doctrina*, for the concept of *ordo disciplinae* has to do not only with the learning process of the pupils, but also with the logical arrangement of the matters being taught. More recently, Thomas's sermons have received a lot of attention as well as his explanations about the (intellectual) virtues, and this also forms part of his teaching role. The way in which Christ is a teacher and an example for Thomas, is another subject that has received a lot of attention recently and will receive even more attention under the influence of the increased interest in Thomas's Bible commentaries.

But for now it is important to see how much Thomas, as a *magister*, wants to follow the example of Aristotle and Pseudo-Dionysius and respect the student's learning process. It is not about the teacher; it is about the student and what the student has with and from God. The teacher will focus on the learning process of the student because that is the only way he can help the student, and so he respects what God enables the student to do. Thus, the teacher follows Christ, the teacher *par excellence*, and Thomas shows himself *doctor ecclesiae*.[21] To repeat what was said above: teaching is a divine matter; and that is why it is so important that teachers do not place themselves in the position of God.

---

21. Pope Pius V proclaimed Thomas *Doctor Ecclesiae* in 1568. See also Pope Pius XI's encyclical of 1923, six hundred years after Thomas's canonization by Pope John XXII. Pius XI (*Studiorum Ducem*, 10) proclaims Thomas *Doctor Communis* or *Universalis*: "A person can derive more benefit from his books for a year than from contemplating the teaching of others throughout his life."

15

The Conversation as a Space of Teaching:

Pastoral-Communicative Situations within Prison Chaplaincy

Renilde G. W. M. van Wieringen

A man in his thirties sits with a chaplain in the chaplaincy of a prison.

Man: That verdict was so disappointing. They really only considered the victim. Who is thinking about me?

Chaplain: Do you understand why the victim is being considered?

Man: The point is that no one considers me.

Chaplain: I am here with you. And speaking from within our faith, I can also tell you that God is with you.

Man: That may be true, but I don't really experience it that way. The only party to be satisfied here is the victim.

Chaplain: Do you think he really is satisfied? That he is happy about everything that has happened?

Man: Not really. But it's not like I can turn back the clock. Of course, he is experiencing a lot of hardship right now, but so am I. I am just as much a victim of the whole affair, even though nobody seems to notice that.

Chaplain: What is the worst thing for you in this situation?

Man: The worst thing is that I lose everything. I lose my house, my work, and my friends. I can't stand it anymore. How can I ever come back from this?

■ I. A Case from Pastoral Theology

This is a case from the chaplaincy department of a prison.[1] Someone asking for pastoral guidance and a prison chaplain are having a conversation. How does pastoral theology help a teacher to understand a case like this?

Pastoral theology is about the human being in his or her entirety. Traditionally, the language of "body and soul" was used to refer to the whole person. In pastoral theology, the whole human being is addressed. However, this does not only concern the person as an individual, but also includes the perspective of a person in relation to other people. These relationships become visible on occasions of contact. In these moments, communication is the supporting element, and therefore it is of the utmost importance. People communicate with one another. They talk to each other. They send each other messages. They make video calls to one another. They write letters. They make phone calls. They text. And they send emails.

In chaplaincy work, having a pastoral conversation is one of the chaplain's tasks. Chaplains talk with people. This can be in a group or one on one. Through the pastoral conversation, the chaplain can aid the church member, and the church member may feel that they are being listened to and that what they say matters.

There is a reason a pastoral conversation is called a "conversation."[2] A conversation can be defined as the contact between two people in which communication is central. In other words, a conversation concerns human beings. Sometimes we communicate without other people. In that case, we are satisfied to communicate with models or computers. In some cases, due to the progress of technology and the acceptance of models, people are no longer needed. Traffic lights, for example, are excellent replacements for traffic control. However, when the doctor spends more time looking at a computer screen than at us patients, we do find it annoying—especially when the doctor has a negative message to communicate.[3] In that case, we want to be able to look the other person

---

1. For an important collection of articles about prison chaplaincy, see Ryan van Eijk, Gerard Loman, and Theo W. A. de Wit, eds., *For Justice and Mercy: International Reflections on Prison Chaplaincy* (Centrum voor Justitiepastoraat; Tilburg: Wolf Legal Publishers, 2016).

2. Richard Riess defines communication: "Mit 'Kommunikation' wird das komplexe Beziehungssystem bezeichnet, das Menschen miteinander verbindet" (*Seelsorge: Orientierung, Analysen, Alternativen* [Göttingen: Vandenhoeck & Ruprecht, 1978] 8).

3. This despite the fact that algorithms and statistical models are sometimes

in the eye, to ask questions and express our feelings. In other words, there is a desire for personal nearness. We want to be able to relate to someone else.

There is also a good reason a pastoral conversation is called "pastoral." Chaplains will have to "do something" with the story they are told and with the questions they face, because they commit themselves to humankind from the perspective of the kingdom of God. Indeed, chaplains are called and sent by the church. From this understanding of their role, they will want to try to be close to people and to get in touch with them.

Chaplains have very few material means. They can offer some tangible items such as a Bible, rosary beads, a holy picture, or a booklet specifically published for the target audience, such as the prison diary. It may well be that the person who contacts a chaplain would like to have those things. These things may also be an incentive for a conversation or for praying together. This brings me straight to the chaplain's less tangible baggage, because the person addressing the chaplain often has an idea (however vague) about said chaplain. The chaplain "is of the church," "is religious," "does not report," "can listen well," "is someone with whom you can share you story," "will pray for you," and "knows beautiful and inspiring biblical stories." In other words, the chaplain is known as someone who dedicates time and space to someone else in such a way that the other person knows they are being heard.

Being heard does not mean that the chaplain's interlocutor benefits from constantly receiving hmm-hmm answers from the chaplain. The effective chaplain will also steer the conversation by asking questions, giving feedback, and by suggesting reasons why the client should do one thing or refrain from another. When the chaplain carries out his or her role in that way, he or she is acting as a teacher does.

When and how may the chaplain fulfill the role of a teacher in a pastoral conversation? This central question may be approached from several angles. Classically, this is done from a systematic-theological perspective. A text-analytical one is also a possibility. Both lead to profound and mutually supportive answers. I would first like to illustrate this method by taking an example from the theology of creation. This choice functions as an instance of a systematic-theological approach.

---

simply better at assessing a medical situation then a human doctor. In the late 1990s, Brendan Reilly experimentally proved that the Goldman algorithm was 70 percent more accurate at recognizing patients with heart attacks than the human doctors at Cook County Hospital. See Malcolm Gladwell, *Blink: The Power of Thinking without Thinking* (New York: Back Bay Books, 2005) 126–36.

Then, I will pay attention to the domain-analytical angle, as an example of the second approach. Finally, I will link these two ways of considering the role of a teacher.

■ II. THE APPROACH FROM THE BIBLICAL THEOLOGY OF CREATION

Although the person asking for pastoral guidance may not say so, the effective chaplain will be convinced that they see the other person as they are, namely, created in the image and likeness of God.[4] According to the story in Genesis 1, a human being is distinguished from other animals, because he or she was created not "according to his kind," but rather, "according to his image,"[5] As a result, the purpose of being human does not lie primarily in the continuation of his species, but in being the image of God. It is not in the human being per se that the goal of being human is situated. The purpose of being human transcends the human being and resides in the relationship which, both individually and collectively (God creates "him" as "them"; see Gen 1:27), comes from God and may be assumed to exist between the human being and God.

Being created in the image and likeness of God means that the human being is created for relationship. God does not enter into a relationship with humanity, because a human being is able to enter into a relationship with the other. A human being is called to enter into a relationship with God and may enter into relation with other humans, because God has entered into relation with the human race. In addition, from the point of view of the story of creation, the other is just as much created in the image of God as he or she is. This means that all people are equal. The effective chaplain will want to live up to this equality in the pastoral conversation.[6] The chaplain's communicative skills determine whether and to what extent he or she will succeed in this.

---

4. For pastoral theology, the view of Abraham J. Heschel in *God in Search of Man: A Philosophy of Judaism* (New York: Farrar, Straus & Cudahy, 1955) is very valuable, because of its communicative elements that God is the one addressing the human being.

5. See Gen 1:21, 24, 25 vs. Gen 1:26–27. Also compare these to Gen 5:1–3. See also Hans Walter Wolff, *Anthropologie des Alten Testaments* (Gütersloh: Gütersloher Verlagshaus, 2010) 229–37.

6. See also John Cooper, "The Pastoral Approach in Prison Chaplaincy," *Contact* 32 (1970): 20–27.

From the theology of creation, it can be established that God is the one who has primarily entered into a relationship with humanity. As a "derivative" of this, people can enter into relationship with one another. This not only means that people are primarily equal among themselves, but also that the guiding role lies fundamentally with the God who creates.

God is the first to give commands: "become numerous," "subdue the earth," and "rule over the fish, the birds, and the crawling animals" (Gen 1:28). God is the first to explain: "you may not eat from that tree, because . . ." (Gen 2:16–17). God is the first to ask questions, even though God knows the answers (Gen 3:9–13). The human has gone wrong, so God the teacher wants the human to be taught again and to learn. God does so by asking the human questions. This means that the human has to reflect in order to find the way back. God as a teacher is also punitive. God is clearly not the teacher who approves of everything (Gen 3:14–24).

The fact that God is the first to enter into communication and to use educational techniques such as giving instructions, explaining, asking questions, and punishing means that God is the first teacher. God is the primary teacher, and so the chaplain is a teacher in a derivative sense. There is the option that members of the church congregation—created, just like the chaplain, in God's image and likeness—may also carry out teaching functions. In this way, they can provide the chaplain with a perspective on his or her actions that the chaplain had never seen before.

III. The Text-Analytical Approach

Traditionally, pastoral theology has employed the kerygmatic approach, which refers to the classical view of the preaching task of the chaplain, including individual pastoral conversation.[7] The therapeutic and hermeneutic approaches emerged from the 1980s onwards. The therapeutic approach focuses on the reception of psychoanalysis, in particular. Other psychological intervention techniques can also be received. The therapeutic approach is not particularly descriptive; rather, it is about pastoral interventions.

---

7. For the chaplain as the one with listening skills, especially from a Buddhist perspective, see also Josiah N. Opata, *Spiritual and Religious Diversity in Prisons: Focusing on How Chaplaincy Assists in Prison Management* (Springfield, IL: Charles C. Thomas, 2001).

The hermeneutic approach, on the other hand, focuses on the life story. It is indeed a narrative approach, but without the use of narratology as is commonly used in biblical studies. From the beginning of this century, the evidence-based approach has been added to their number, in which making pastoral activities measurable is central. In the case of all these approaches, there is actually no insight into how to analyze a verbatim report (or nowadays possibly also an audio recording and/or video recording). It is precisely for this reason that the reception of biblical scholarly approaches is of great importance for pastoral theology. A literary pastoral theology is necessary to remain primarily descriptive and to best serve, in my case, the individual pastoral conversation. This is precisely how full justice can be done to both dialogue partners and, therefore, to the role of the chaplain as a teacher.

The chaplain can gain better insight into the way he or she communicates by writing down his or her conversations and evaluating them. A conversation can even be illustrated and examined diagrammatically. I have developed a method for this,[8] based on the literary method of domain analysis, which is used in biblical exegesis as well.[9]

In this method a text is visualized by means of boxes called domains. In this literary method, the text in its entirety is the basic domain and the domains of the speakers in the text can be represented as embedded domains. This diagrammatic analysis can also be done, and if necessary, adapted with the pastoral conversation. The pastoral conversation in its entirety is the basic domain. It contains the chaplain's speaker domain and the interlocutor's speaker domain. These domains are located next to each other in the basic domain.

New domains can also arise in a speaker's domain if the opinion, view, or statement of a third part is communicated, whether it is elaborated or not.

---

8. See my dissertation on this topic: Renilde G. W. M. van Wieringen, "Gaande het gesprek: Domeinanalytische benadering van het individuele pastoraal gesprek" (Ph.D. diss., Utrecht, 2004; online https://pure.uvt.nl/ws/portalfiles/portal/680728/Gaande.pdf).

9. See in particular José Sanders, "Perspective in Narrative Discourse" (Ph.D. thesis, Katholieke Universiteit Brabant, 1994; Tilburg s.a.; and, for biblical exegesis, see A. L. H. M. van Wieringen, "Isaiah 12,1–6: A Domain and Communication Analysis," in *Studies in the Book of Isaiah: Festschrift Willem A. M. Beuken* (ed. J. van Ruiten and M. Vervenne; BETL 132; Leuven: Peeters, 1997), 149–72; A. L. H. M. van Wieringen, *The Implied Reader in Isaiah 6–12* (BIS 34; Leiden: Brill, 1998) and the (complex) domain-analytical schemes they contain.

Basic domain
| Speaker domain of the client | Speaker domain of the chaplain |

When someone speaks, he or she speaks in their speaker domain, which is an embedded domain in the basic domain. When a person is silent, they are silent in their speaker domain and part of their speaker domain in the diagram is empty.

New domains can also arise in a speaker domain if the opinion, view, or statement of a third part is communicated, whether it is elaborated or not.

With the help of such a domain analysis, the chaplain can see whether he or she is fulfilling the teaching role and, if so, when and how they are doing it.

■ IV. DOMAIN-ANALYTICAL SCHEME OF THE CASE

The conversation between the man asking for pastoral guidance and the chaplain in the case above looks like this:

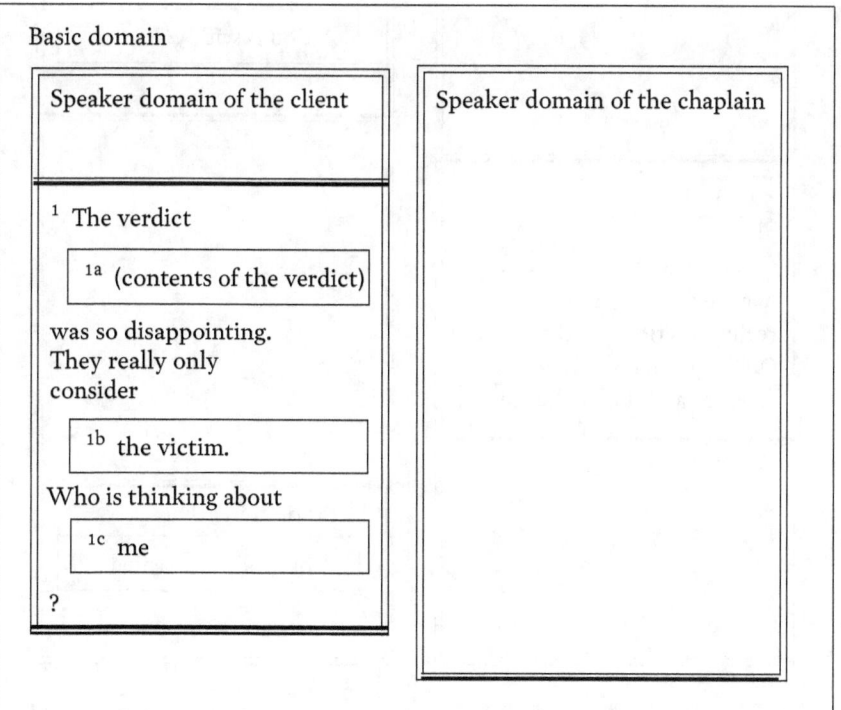

¹ Do you understand

    ¹ᵃ why

        ¹ᵇ the victim

    is being considered

?

² The point is that no one considers

    ²ᵃ me

.

² I am here with you. And from our faith I can also tell you that

    ²ᵃ God is with you

.

³ Right,

    ³ᵃ that

may be true, but I don't really experience it that way. Only one person can be satisfied and that is the victim.

³ Do you think that

    ³ᵃ he really is satisfied

?

³ᵇ That he is happy

³ᶜ with everything that has happened

?

4

⁴ᵃ Not really.

But it's not like I can turn the clock back. Of course, he is experiencing a lot of hardship right now, but so am I. I am just as much a victim of the whole affair, even though nobody seems to notice

⁴ᵇ that

.

⁴ What is the worst thing for you in this situation?

⁵ The worst thing is that I lose everything. I lose my house, my work, and my friends. I can't stand it anymore. How can I ever come back from this?

■ V. Domain Analysis of the Pastoral Conversation: First Teaching Moment

What the chaplain says and how he or she directs the conversation becomes visible in the domains and thus reveals how the chaplain's performance can be understood from a teacher's point of view. In this context, I am going to analyze the conversation that has been shown. I wonder what moments of teaching occur and what they look like.

At the start of the conversation, the client brings three items into the speaker domain 1: the court ruling, the court's consideration for the victim, and the client's lack of thought about him. This is the information the chaplain receives, and it is concise. The content of the decision is unknown. The embedded domain is empty.

The chaplain knows who it is who is being considered, namely, the victim. This is the content of the second embedded domain. The chaplain sees the content of the first two embedded domains as identical, as the words alone indicate.

The third embedded domain of the client containing the word "me" contrasts with this picture. In this way, the man puts himself in opposition to what he says. He stands in opposition to the court ruling and to the victim.

The chaplain poses a question in his speaker-domain that connects with the second issue raised by the man. On the one hand, the chaplain takes over the domain structure of the interlocutor, but, on the other hand, he also works with it. The chaplain places the entire item in an embedded domain. This new embedded domain depends on the verb "to be considered."

The chaplain here is the teacher who wants to make something clear to the other, namely, that the victim is being looked at and that there is a good reason why this is so. Does the man understand that the victim is being looked at? This is what the chaplain focuses on here. The chaplain tries to persuade the client to answer this question, not by rejecting the way the client sees things but by placing them in a new embedded domain.

■ VI. Domain Analysis of the Pastoral Conversation: Second Teaching Moment

The client focuses on the fact that he feels alone. He says that nobody thinks about him. In his second domain, too, "me" is found in an embedded domain. The difference between this point and the first part of the domain is that this embedded domain is the only embedded domain. The speaker emphasizes the fact that he is on his own. He is alone. That's what he faces.

Indirectly he answers the chaplain's question. He neither denies nor confirms the importance of paying attention to the victim, but he replaces the embedded domain about the victim with an embedded domain about himself. This replacement evokes the suggestion by the parallelism between "victim" and "me": the man sees himself as a victim (as well). The chaplain acts in a relativistic way. He does this not by discussing the suggestiveness of the embedded domain of the other in his second speaker's domain, but by linking the being-alone to the concrete here and now. The man is not alone at the moment. The chaplain is with him. They are together. What is more, the chaplain broadens the not-being-alone by pointing out the presence of God in the life of the man, in a general sense, without linking it to the concrete here and now.

The chaplain as a teacher expands the classroom here, as it were. The man is not alone at the moment. The chaplain is also there. And you can even say that God is there. By introducing this element, the chaplain takes on the corrective role of the teacher, on the one hand, and, on the other hand, the chaplain is a fellow pupil who points out that there is another who is not as present in the way that the pupils themselves are, but who is nevertheless there.

The chaplain brings God into the conversation. At least, he can do that, he says. He can say that God is with the chaplain. The embedded sphere in the speaking domain of the chaplain, which is itself formed by the construction of being able to say something, is indeed filled. However, God has not been given God's own domain in the speaking domain of the chaplain. God is introduced, but God remains hidden. By claiming that you can say something, that something has already been said. In this way, the chaplain takes on a restrained role as a teacher, offering an option, an opportunity. It is up to the interlocutor to seize the opportunity or not.

The teaching material that the chaplain introduces is spiritual. Experiencing the presence of God in your life is a subject that the teacher-chaplain can convey to another person by speaking about it. In other words, this happens when the subject matter is effectively conveyed to the student. A modern-language teacher will ask his or her student to learn words because he or she hopes that the student will use this material in their life. If you learn something about God's presence, there is also the pedagogical aim of the one who taught you that it will have some effect on your life.[10]

---

10. Henry J. M. Nouwen describes how encountering Rembrandt's painting

Spiritual material becomes tangible for a student who seeks to see things from a spiritual perspective or to adopt spiritual attitudes or practices in their life. Examples of spiritual attitudes and practices include meditation, prayer, and reading from the Holy Scriptures.[11] These activities can be practiced in the pastoral conversation. In this case, the chaplain begins by communicating statements about the proximity of God. It remains to be seen whether the client will pick up on these lines of thought and how the chaplain will be able to develop things from that point.

The chaplain speaks of God "from within our faith." The use of the first-person plural possessive pronoun *us* is ambiguous, because it may be used in an inclusive or an exclusive manner. If used inclusively, the person addressed is also involved. In this case, both parties are embraced.

This mutual involvement can be either factual or evocative. The chaplain can use the word to draw our attention to the fact that the client is also a believer, as this may have already been discussed in an earlier conversation. The chaplain then determines what both parties already know. However, what is important at this moment in the pastoral discussion is that what may be already known to both is spoken about again and thereby receives new emphasis. Although the chaplain corrects the other's opinion that no one is thinking of him, this remark is more a reminder of what both interlocutors already know than it is an actual correction.

It is also possible that the chaplain uses the word "us," even during this pastoral discussion, to refer to the congregation from which he has been sent. The word "us" does not refer only to the chaplain and the client, but it also has the effect of supporting the chaplain's own pastoral activity. The use of the word relates to the congregation that supports him and his pastoral work. In this way, the chaplain indicates not only that he is doing what the client believes he is lacking, but also that the chaplain's ecclesial community may be relied on for continuous similar support. The chaplain is not so much the presence of a single person, as he is the representative of a community.

The expression "from our faith" can also relate to the content of the tradition of faith in which care for prisoners is continuously present. For example, there are several passages in the Bible in which someone who is detained, whether justly or unjustly, asks to be remembered. Joseph, for

---

Return of the Prodigal Son became an encounter with the biblical story and changed his life: "That encounter turned out to be the beginning of my own return" (*The Return of the Prodigal Son: A Story of Homecoming* [New York: Doubleday, 1994] 134).

11. Compare: Communauté de Taizé, *En ton amour je me confie: Méditer la Bible dans le silence, le partage et le chant* (Taizé: Ateliers et Presses de Taizé, 2003).

example, asks the cupbearer to think of him (Gen 40:14). Remembering someone means keeping them in the picture. This alone can make Joseph feel supported in the difficult situation in which he finds himself. Joseph asks his companion to remember him on his release and return to normal life.

▪ VII. Domain Analysis of the Pastoral Conversation: Third Teaching Moment

This theme of being remembered features in the embedded domain of the chaplain in the third section. The client's "That may well be so" clearly refers to the chaplain's assertion that God is with you. The chaplain returns to the activity of teaching and the role of teacher. He resumes this role without speaking explicitly about the presence of God. Through domain analysis, the chaplain can become aware of this detail. God may be present as the Absent, but the client speaks namelessly about God and God's presence (or absence) and then moves on to another topic.

It is up to the teacher-chaplain to gently reintroduce this theme. This can be done, for example, by returning to this material at the end of the conversation and by asking the client to think about the theme of God's presence in the client's life and about his response to it.[12]

Another possibility is to return to the theme in a subsequent conversation. The chaplain will not want to act as a reticent teacher, but as someone who will make the material about God's presence more explicit. The chaplain can do this, for example, by allowing God to speak in his domain. For instance, when the chaplain says, "God says: 'I'm with you,'" then God speaks through the chaplain's domain. This awareness makes the subject matter more direct. The same effect may be achieved by the attitudes and practices recommended by the chaplain, namely, to pray, to meditate, or to read from the Bible. In that way, there is the possibility that God is given God's own domain in the pastoral discussion.

Next, the client returns to the victim and thus moves from his first speaking domain to the second embedded one. In response, the chaplain asks two questions. Both questions are about the victim. They are interesting because the chaplain talks about everything that has happened. In this way, he fills out the victim-filled embedded domain raised by the

---

12. In this homework assignment, the chaplain is in line with the teaching material and with the pastorant's world of experience; see also Fred A. J. Korthagen, Jos Kessels, Bob Koster, Bram Lagerwerf, and Theo Wubbels, *Linking Practice and Theory: The Pedagogy of Realistic Teacher Education* (New York: Routledge, 2019).

client. The chaplain does not talk about the victim specifically in relation to the verdict (the details of which are not mentioned), but in relation to everything that has happened, of which the judgment is only a part.

In this way, the chaplain wants to make two things clear to the client. First, the chaplain wants the client to look at another person, in this case the victim. Second, he wants to make it clear that the other person is not elated by what has happened. After all, he is a victim. And if the client suggests that it is nice to be a victim and that he envies that position, he needs to bear in mind that it is not such a desirable thing. He could gain an insight into this position from the part of the conversation where he presents himself as a victim.

It would be easy for the chaplain to advise the client against seeing himself as a victim, but the chaplain does not do so. He teaches through questions. He helps the other by using embedded domains in his questions. The first of these focuses on the verb "to think." The main question is not about the victim, but about the client: What does he think? There are two embedded domains linked to this activity of thinking. The second is elliptically dependent on the verb "to think." The two embedded domains are parallel in terms of content: being satisfied and being happy. Both activities are implicitly attributed to the victim. The chaplain uses the anonymous personal pronoun "he."

The two embedded domains form a climax in relation to each other. This climax is reached by the presence of an embedded domain in the second embedded domain. While in the first one, this would have been an option on the basis of the expression "satisfied with," the new embedding follows in the second instance only with the help of the phrase "happy with." Semantically, the climax is evoked by the chaplain's expanding the conversation from the issue of satisfaction, the client's expression, to include the notion of happiness. A victim may still be satisfied with the judgment, but they cannot possibly be happy with everything that has happened.

The content of the first embedded domain in the fourth speaker domain of the client shows that the chaplain's teaching material has been successfully shared. A shift has occurred. The man understands that the victim now has a lot of trouble. At first, he considered the victim to be satisfied. They are now, at least, both victims.

The learning, however, is modest. The chaplain sought embedded domains that relied on the activity of thinking. However, there is no embedded domain in the client's reaction. In other words, no embedded domain for the learned material shows that a partial recognition of the position of the victim has been achieved. On the other hand, the present embedded domain is intended for the victim's own situation, although a shift has taken place with regard to the content. Whereas, in the first and second speaker domains, this embedded domain was still filled with the self, the content is now an abstract one that concerns not so much the entire person of the client as his perceived misery.

The client has taken a step forward with the help of the teaching devices the chaplain has offered with embedded domains through the medium of questioning. Being a victim is not a good thing, for anybody, himself included. He experiences the content of this teaching material firsthand. He is just as much a victim as the other. But nobody notices that.

■ VIII. Domain Analysis of the Pastoral Conversation: Fourth Teaching Moment

In his previous section, the client says he is now in a lot of trouble. With this indication of time, he no longer speaks in a general temporal sense, as in his first speaker's domain. There he used no time determination. His misfortunes, however, are related to the concrete here and now. In fact, he makes the same movement as the chaplain did in his second speaker domain. His own here and now is central. The focus is no longer on his perception of the victim's current situation.

This shift offers the chaplain the opportunity to ask about the worst of the client's many misfortunes. The client is, clearly, in a bad situation. He considers himself the victim. The chaplain can now ask him what he feels so bad about.

The chaplain's question cuts both ways. The moment the client answers this question, he can no longer say that nobody sees his misery. He is now allowed to say what is so bad about his situation. As a result of what has happened, someone has asked him about his troubles. Maybe those who see his pain are few, or maybe one even. But at least that is one more than the number he stated originally.

In the fifth speaker domain, the man answers. He mentions many things, all of which he will lose. He wonders how he can ever recover. Thus, he confirms the chaplain's role as a teacher. So far, he has made progress in learning by way of responding to the chaplain's domains. At this stage, he is the one who is asking the question. But there is something else of significance here. In this question there is a trace of wanting to escape from his misery. On the one hand, he can't take it anymore but then, on the other hand, he talks about wanting to get back on his feet, even though he has no idea yet how to do it. This means that he positions himself as a learner in relation to the teacher chaplain.

■ IX. EMBEDDED TEACHERHOOD

Using the exegetical approach of domain analysis in relation to the pastoral interview, I examined both speaker domains. In this investigation I have mainly described the teaching role of the chaplain. Furthermore, both the theology of creation and the domain analysis show that the chaplain is not the only one who carries out the role of teacher or performs actions of a teacher.

The pastoral encounter is created incrementally by both the chaplain and the client. As teacher, the chaplain will realize he is enabled to be close to his interlocutor. There is a reason for the speaker's column of the chaplain being placed beside the speaker's column of the client in the diagram. This is a fact that must be kept in mind during the whole conversation.

Perhaps this fact seems self-evident: if there are two people talking to each other, there are also two columns. But the client needs something more to make the column his own. The good chaplain will not appropriate the other's column. The parts of the client's speaker should be formed by himself, both in terms of structure and content, as he judges fit. The successful chaplain will be alert to this. The chaplain who derives his teaching material for the other only by repeating that of his speaker's domain, including the corresponding domain structure, is a teacher-chaplain who usurps the other's domain. Sometimes this kind of teaching is necessary. The modern language teacher who wants to convey a row of irregular verbs to the student hopes that the latter will absorb the teacher's speaking domain completely. The teacher succeeds when the student makes the information his own. This model does not apply to the pastoral conversation.

If, in a pastoral interview, the embedded domains of the chaplain are literally taken over by the client, it remains to be seen whether there is freedom in the learning situation.[13] This does not happen here. Nevertheless, the chaplain has transferred material that the man has picked up.

---

13. H. W. Stone, "Does Freedom Exist between This Person and Me?," in *Theological Context for Pastoral Caregiving: Word in Deed* (ed. H. W. Stone; Religion, Ministry & Pastoral Care; London: Haworth Pastoral Press, 1996) 33–38, here 33.

The chaplain made particular use of questioning.¹⁴ The conversation included four embedded domains of the chaplain. Four questions occur in three of these four domains. The chaplain's first question is in response to the client's first field of speech, which ends with the question "Who is thinking of me?" The question is a complex paradox. Anyone who poses this question to another expects attention to be paid to him. The chaplain does not answer the question. The theme will be discussed a little later in the discussion, but by then the communicative situation will have changed. At that point, the client utters the observation that no one is thinking about him. This is followed by the only non-inquiring part in the chaplain's speaking domain. It is here that the chaplain introduces God into the conversation. He is convinced of God's presence. He can say that. He believes that God is there for the client also. This faith has permeated the chaplain, who formulates it as a free choice for the man to accept or reject. At this moment in the conversation, the client does not reject the chaplain's religious conviction, but he indicates that his experience is different. The questions posed by the chaplain initiate a learning process whereby the client makes a shift in his questions from "Who is thinking about me?" to "How can I ever recover from this?"¹⁵ Such a shift carries with it the movement from "What action is being performed by another person?" to "What activity can I undertake myself?" In the client's first question, he is central as the object. He is the powerless lonely victim whose role is to wait and see whether he is being thought of. In the question of how he can ever recover, he is the subject.

In the first question, "Who is thinking of me?," the client is in an embedded domain through using the word "me." There is no embedded domain in the second question of how he will recover. The client has come to the surface. Apart from the fact that a good chaplain will not appropriate the other's speaking domain, there is something else that he or she will be aware of. The chaplain is part of a larger whole. From the perspective of creation theology, it is taken for granted that both are

---

14. Asking questions is one of the teacher's competencies in participant-oriented communication. See also Helena Pedrosa-de-Jesus, Sara Leite, and Mike Watts, "'Question Moments': A Rolling Programme of Question; Opportunities in Classroom Science," *Research in Science Education* 4 (2016) 1–13; Hanna Roose, "Educational Perspectives on Questions in Biblical Texts," in *Asking Questions in Biblical Texts* (ed. Bart J. Koet and Archibald L. H. M. van Wieringen; CBET 114; Leuven: Peeters, 2022), 355–63.

15. Anselm Grün calls a change of perspective that does not involve coercion and that the person in question fully supports a *"Verwandlung"* (*Verwandlung: Eine vergessene Dimension geistliches Lebens* [Mainz: Matthias-Grünewald, 1993] 7). When one is forced to change, a change becomes a *"Veränderung."*

created in God's image and likeness and that, primarily, it is God who is the teacher.

In visualizing the conversation in domains, the entirety of the conversation is the basic domain. In this fundamental domain the actors act. They are therefore not the owners of the basic domain. This insight also applies to the chaplain's teaching. The chaplain is not the one who carries the entire conversation. Each speaker has his or her own domain of speakers and exercises responsibility in this area. For example, the chaplain is responsible for his or her domain contents and domain structures. With these as support, he tries to assist the client. He is also responsible for ensuring that he does not own the other person's speaker domain.

The speaking domains are held together by the basic domain. Without the latter, there is no conversation. In other words, the basic domain is the framework in which the conversation happens and develops.

The basic domain is therefore relational. The chaplain can be a teacher because there is someone for whom he can be a teacher. If the chaplain wants to be able to transmit subject matter, listen, speak, ask questions, summarize, and give feedback, then the chaplain must be in relation to someone else.

The genre of conversation means that there is no prescribed text. How long the speaking domains in a basic domain remain together depends, in part, on the chaplain's communication skills. With the help of domain analysis, the result of the chaplain's teaching may be identified. The client has made a shift from object to subject in response to the chaplain's questions. From a domain technical point of view, a change is deemed to have taken place from the hidden to the accessible person of the client.

These results can influence the continuation of the pastoral discussion. The presence of God has not yet been discussed. The man has not questioned this subject matter, but he has not yet reached the level where he can affirm this. The experience that God is with you presupposes closeness. Because of the nearness of the chaplain, the client has become more subject for himself. The possible continuation of this could be that the client will also experience God as near in his life and thus will increasingly become the subject in his own domain.

■ X. To Conclude

Pastoral theology has a lot to learn from biblical studies, at a methodical and theological level. As far as the methods of pastoral theology are concerned, I have shown in my contribution that a literary approach appears to be essential. It provides access to a descriptive understanding of the various aspects that play a role in pastoral care. I have shown this in this contribution, which is based on the domain analysis for the individual pastoral conversation.

When one uses this domain-analytical method, the different roles within the individual pastoral conversation can be further highlighted. In this contribution, I have done this specifically for the teaching role of the chaplain. This becomes visible in many layers of the conversation, not by the chaplain becoming some kind of a schoolmaster, but by the more and less embedded communication from the chaplain to the client. The chaplain appears to always be also a teacher in his conversations.

16

A Passover Gone Wrong:

BioShock Infinite as a Teaching Model of Critical Religious Appropriation of the Bible

FRANK G. BOSMAN

> If the Prophet had just purged the vipers of the Orient, but not suffered the sacrifice of his beloved, it would have been enough.
>
> If the Prophet had just suffered the sacrifice of his beloved, but not expelled the Vox Populi, it would have been enough!

The last words of Preacher Witting's sermon echo through a slightly flooded church. Candles burn, devotees pray at the shrines of their Lady, stained-glassed windows project the images/imaginings(?) of holy men, proselytes prepare themselves to receive their initiation by being submerged into the waters of redemption, an unseen choir sings the Christian hymn "Will the Circle Be Unbroken?," and the walls are covered with inspirational quotations evoking the language of pastures, salvation, and paradise.

The religious paraphernalia, welcoming the player of the game *BioShock Infinite* (2013) to the floating city of Columbia, are unmistakably Christian in origin and inspiration, but its content is certainly not.[1] The stained-glass windows portray the three Founding Fathers of the United States of America, holding a sword, a key, and a scroll, respectively. The shrine is of the Lady Comstock, deceased wife of "Father Comstock," the self-proclaimed prophet of Columbia. And the blind preacher is baptizing his

---

1. *BioShock Infinite* (PC, PlayStation 3, Xbox360, OSX, Linux, Switch), Irrational Games (2K Games) 2013.

catechumens "in the name of our Prophet, in the name of our Founders, in the name of our Lord!"

Columbia's theology is a complex mixture of Christianity, American exceptionalism, and religious and racial xenophobia.[2] Amid this theological inferno, the player, as detective Booker DeWitt, has to find a way to enter the flying city of Columbia to rescue a certain girl with the name Elizabeth. And the only way to enter is to let DeWitt be baptized by this Columbian variant of your average-day preacher, eager to collect as many souls as he can get his hands on. However, even before this strange "forced baptism," the attentive gamer will be already alerted by the "rhythm" of Witting's sermon (see quotation above). It follows a pattern A-B/B-C/C-D/ . . . , praising the goodness of the Prophet Comstock.

Witting's sermon evokes direct associations, both in content and poetic form, with the Hebrew *Dayenu* ("it would have been enough for us") song, an integral part of the Haggadah, the ritual-liturgical complex that has been celebrated by Jews on Pesach for centuries: "If He had killed their firstborn but had not given us their money, it would have been enough for us! / If He had given us their money but had not split the sea for us, it would have been enough for us . . ."[3] When studied in more detail, the game and the song share a deep and fundamental intertextual relationship, not only with each other but also with the biblical Book of Exodus. And to complicate things even more, *BioShock Infinite*'s appropriation of the *Dayenu* song is (predominantly) based on a specific Christian interpretation of the Exodus texts that inspired the song, especially in the context of the initiation sacrament of baptism.

However, does this theology hold? In popular culture, people will sometimes use "the duck test" as a form of abductive reasoning: If it looks like a duck, swims like a duck, and quacks like a duck, then it probably is a duck.[4] In the case of *BioShock Infinite*, the question is, If it looks like the

---

2. Frank G. Bosman, "Accept Your Baptism, and Die! Redemption, Death and Baptism in Bioshock Infinite," *Gamenvironments* 6 (2017) 100–129; Bosman, "The Lamb of Comstock: Dystopia and Religion in Video Games," *Online* 5 (2014) 162–82; Erik Kain, "BioShock Infinite Refunded on Religious Grounds," *Forbes*, April 17, 2013 (online, http://www.forbes.com/sites/erikkain/2013/04/17/bioshockinfinite-refunded-onreligious-grounds; accessed June 18, 2020); Jan Wysocki, "Critique with Limits: The Construction of American Religion in BioShock Infinite," *Religions* 9.5 (2018) 150.

3. Heinrich Guggenheimer, *The Scholar's Haggadah: Ashkenazic, Sephardic, and Oriental Versions* (Northvale, NJ: Jason Aronson, 1998) 54.

4. Robert A. Palmatier, *Speaking of Animals: A Dictionary of Animal Metaphors* (Westport, CT: Greenwood Press, 1995) 127.

Bible, and sounds like the Bible, and appropriates biblical notions, could you call it "biblical"? In this contribution, I will present an analysis of these complex intertextual and intermedial relationships between game, song, and written text, to understand the (presumed unintentional) educational value of the game, with regard to the theory and practice of appropriation of biblical source material in contemporary cultural objects. Essentially, what can we "learn" from the game, with regard to the appropriation of the Bible and biblical notions in modern contexts?

Intertextuality is a form of synchronic literary analysis focusing on the relationships between different texts, enlarging the concept of "text" from traditional exclusively written forms to all possible cultural expressions, like films and digital games.[5] The related term "intermediality" denotes the crossing-over of a narrative complex between different mediums, in our case, between written texts and digital games.[6] And, last but not least, the concept of (cultural) appropriation—"appropriation that occurs across the boundaries of cultures"—draws attention to the potential problematic nature of the cultural borrowing between different cultural groups.[7]

In this contribution, I define video games as digital, interactive, playable, narrative texts.[8] As a text, a video game is an object of interpretation; as a narrative, it communicates meaning; as a game, it is playable; and as a digital medium, it is interactive in nature. The close reading of *BioShock Infinite* is done by playing the game itself (multiple times), including all possible (side) missions, in what is known as the game-immanent approach.[9] The sequence of texts is discussed and analyzed according to a method of literary archaeology, in which the narrative analysis of successive generations of intertextual relationships concerning a specific topic, topos, or idea is done in reverse chronological order. In this case, this means that I will start with the game, followed by the song and the biblical text.

---

5. Julia Kristeva, *Desire in Language: A Semiotic Approach to Literature and Art* (New York: Columbia University Press, 1980).

6. Lars Elleström, "The Modalities of Media: A Model for Understanding Intermedial Relationships," in *Media Borders, Multimodality and Intermediality* (ed. Lars Elleström; London: Palgrave Macmillan, 2010) 11–50.

7. James Young, *Cultural Appropriation and the Arts* (New Directions in Aesthetics 6; London: Blackwell, 2008) 5. For biblical appropriation, see Archibald L. H. M. van Wieringen, "Psalm 65 as Non-Appropriation Theology," *Bib* 95 (2014) 179–97.

8. Frank G. Bosman, *Gaming and the Divine: A New Systematic Theology of Video Games* (Routledge New Critical Thinking in Religion, Theology, and Biblical Studies; London: Routledge, 2019) 38–43.

9. Bosman, *Gaming and the Divine*, 43–51.

■ I. *BioShock Infinite*: A Heterodox Passover

BioShock Infinite is a first-person shooter developed by Irrational Games and published by 2K Games, released for PC, PlayStation 3, Xbox360 and OSX in 2013, and for Linux in 2015. *BioShock Infinite* is the third installment in the series, preceded by *BioShock* and *BioShock 2*, which share the same narrative multiverse as *Infinite*, but not the same storyline.[10] The original *BioShock* and *BioShock Infinite* share their director, Ken Levine, while part 2 of the series was directed by Jordan Thomas.

Levine self-identifies as a cultural, not a religious, Jew, which did not prevent his religio-cultural heritage from seeping into his art, much to his own surprise. Game critic and self-identified cultural Jew Cody Mello-Klein wrote about Levine after the two met in Boston: "Although Levine never set out to make a game about Jewish identity, his own family history and upbringing inevitably infused BioShock's world. He wrote what he knew."[11] In the same interview, the game director admitted, "I don't think I was conscious of how Jewish it was until afterwards." As Mello-Klein and Levine himself, on multiple occasions, have argued, the story of *BioShock* is filled with secular Jews. Levine: "BioShock 1 is about Jews. I'm a Jew. If you think about it, Andrew Ryan, Sander Cohen, Tenenbaum, they're all Jews."[12] Even the philosophical background of the original *BioShock* is based on the ideas of the Russian-American philosopher Ayn Rand, who was also of Jewish descent.[13]

BioShock Infinite takes on another ideological battle, not against Objectivism as its processor deed, but against American exceptionalism and its sermonized traits of racism, sexism, and xenophobia. Levine hit a

---

10. *BioShock* (PC, PlayStation 3, PlayStation 4, Xbox360, Xbox1, OSX, iOS, Switch), 2K Boston/2K Australia (2K Games) 2007; *BioShock 2* (PC, PlayStation 3, Xbox 260, OSX, Switch), 2K Marin (2K Games) 2010.

11. Cody Mello-Klein, "BioShock's Jewish roots run deep," *Kotaku*, July 10, 2018 (online, https://kotaku.com/bioshocks-jewish-roots-run-deep-1827482206; accessed June 18, 2020). See also Mike Futter, "Faith in Rapture – Ken Shares Thoughts on Creating Authentic Diversity," *Game Informer*, April 9, 2009 (online, https://www.gameinformer.com/b/features/archive/2015/04/09/faith-in-rapture-ken-levine-shares-thoughts-on-creating-authentic-diversity.aspx; accessed June 18, 2020).

12. Quoted in Paul Tamburro, "Ken Levine Defends BioShock Infinite's Most Controversial Scene," *Mandatory*, September 15, 2016 (online, https://www.mandatory.com/culture/1117863-ken-levine-defends-bioshock-infinites-controversial-scene; accessed June 18, 2020).

13. Ben Murnane, *Ayn Rand and the Posthuman: The Mind-Made Future* (London: Palgrave Macmillan, 2018) 133–60; Bosman, *Gaming and the Divine*, 162–66.

soft spot for sure, since the infamous Stormfront forum scourged it for its supposed hate of "white America": "The Jew Ken Levine is making a white-person-killing simulator."[14]

Even though *Infinite* is not as "Jewish" as *BioShock* was according to its own director, the second game is also influenced by Judaism. Not only does Witting's sermon intimate the Jewish *Dayenu* song, as I will discuss in detail below, but also the game itself was released on March 26, 2013, that is, Nisan 15, 5773, on the Jewish calendar, the day of Pesach, the liturgically correct context of the song.

The game follows the story of Booker DeWitt, a former soldier and Pinkerton agent, who—in an allohistorical version in 1912—is tasked to rescue Comstock's daughter Elizabeth, who is, in fact, his own daughter from his original timeline within the multiverse. The story of the game is too complicated to address here fully, but for now the important thing is to understand that Booker DeWitt and the Prophet Zachary Comstock are one and the same person, but in different timelines.[15] After he was traumatized by his own involvement in the massacre at Wounded Knee on December 29, 1890, DeWitt meets Preacher Witting somewhere in 1891 or 1892 proclaiming forgiveness and performing baptisms in a river.[16]

Here the timeline splits. In one timeline, DeWitt accepts baptism and becomes the Prophet founding his own semi-Christian religion, while in the other Booker refuses to be baptized, ending up as an emotionally and financially broken man with a deceased wife and a missing daughter. DeWitt-turned-Comstock from timeline #1 buys/steals the infant daughter of DeWitt from timeline #2 through a dimensional wormhole. The reason that the older Witting in 1912 does not recognize the older DeWitt at the baptism in Columbia is that the older preacher is not only blind, but in his timeline, DeWitt became Comstock.

In Witting's sermon, when entering the slightly flooded church in order to pass through the rest of Columbia, the player overhears the tri-

---

14. Evan Lahti, "Interview: Ken Levine on American History, Racism in BioShock Infinite: 'I've always believed that gamers were underestimated,'" *PC Gamer*, December 13, 2012 (online, https://www.pcgamer.com/bioshock-infinite-interview-ken-levine-racism-history/; accessed June 18, 2020); see also Jim Sterling, "Racists Call BioShock Infinite a White-Killing Simulator," *Destructoid*, December 14, 2012 (online, https://www.destructoid.com/racists-call-bioshock-infinite-a-white-killing-simulator-240586.phtml; accessed June 18, 2020).

15. Bosman, "Accept Your Baptism, and Die!," 106.

16. Rani-Hendrik Andersson, *The Lakota Ghost Dance of 1890* (Lincoln: University of Nebraska Press, 2008).

umphs of DeWitt-cum-Comstock being praised (for the sake of convenience, I have numbered the stanzas):

(1) And every year on this day of days, we recommit ourselves to our city, to our Prophet, Father Comstock. We recommit through sacrifice, and the giving of thanks, and by submerging ourselves in the sweet water of baptism.
(2) And lo, if the Prophet had struck down our enemies at Wounded Knee, and not railed against the Sodom beneath us, it would have been enough.
(3) If the Prophet had just railed against the Sodom beneath us, but not accepted the three golden gifts of the Founders, it would have been enough.
(4) If the Prophet had just accepted the three golden gifts of the Founders, and not prayed for our deliverance, it would have been enough.
(5) If the Prophet had only prayed for our deliverance, and not led us to this New Eden, it would have been enough.
(6) If the Prophet had just led us to this New Eden, and not purged the vipers of the Orient, it would have been enough.
(7) If the Prophet had just purged the vipers of the Orient, but not suffered the sacrifice of his beloved, it would have been enough.
(8) If the Prophet had just suffered the sacrifice of his beloved, but not expelled the Vox Populi, it would have been enough!

The pattern is clear:

If A but not B, it would have been enough.
If B but not C, it would have been enough.
If C but not D, ...
If D but ...
If E ...

The emerging into the "sweet water of baptism" is performed not so much as a way of initiating—although DeWitt's later baptism is certainly considered by Witting as such—but to give continuous grace to Comstock: it is "re-commission," a repeatable act of sacrificing oneself to the Prophet (1). The form in which this re-commission takes place is a lengthy praise of the Prophet's wonderous deeds for the benefit of his beloved people. Witting evokes the massacre at Wounded Knee, but instead of expressing sadness and shame, he identifies the Native Americans as "the enemies" (2), even though remorse drove the younger DeWitt to Witting's first baptism, splitting the timeline between DeWitt-Comstock and DeWitt-detective.

Next, Witting glorifies the highlights of Columbia's rise, only understandable to the educated player, probably the one who has already played the game to the end at least once. In 1893, Comstock launches the floating city of Columbia, a marvel of modern technology, at the (historical) Chicago World's Fair. The fair is often associated with the rise of American exceptionalism, the idea that America holds an exceptional position among the nations.[17] This notion has rather strong religious overtones—God has given America this position in the world, culminating in the notion of the United States as "a shining city on the hill." The phrase stems from Matthew 5:14 and entered American politics in 1630, when the Puritan leader John Winthrop gave a sermon aboard the ship Arbella for the soon-to-be Massachusetts colonists.[18] After Comstock involved the massive weaponry of Columbia in the (historical) Boxer Rebellion (1901), the US Congress, initially supporting Comstock's project financially and politically, disavows the Prophet.[19] Columbia and its founder disappear in the skies.

The "vipers of the orient" is a racial slur referring to the Chinese forces in the Boxer Rebellion (7) and the "New Eden" the Prophet has led his people to is a reference to Columbia itself as a haven for white supremacists (6). Columbia does employ the "services" of supposed *Untermenschen* like the Irish, the Mexicans, the Native Americans, and people of color, but only to perform the lower-grade tasks typically associated with immigrant and minority workers (see image 1). The "Vox Populi," Latin for "the voice of the people," is a reference to a violent emancipation movement within Columbia fighting for equal rights for all citizens (8).

Columbia's ideology is dualistic in nature (3): all inside the "shining city of the hill" are the chosen ones, while those outside this "New Eden" are disqualified as "the Sodom below," evoking the fate of the biblical

---

17. Deborah L. Madsen, *American Exceptionalism* (1998; repr., Edinburgh: Edinburgh University Press, 2009); Ben Zimmer, "Did Stalin Really Coin 'American Exceptionalism,'" *Slate*, September 27, 2013 (online, https://slate.com/human-interest/2013/09/american-exceptionalism-neither-joseph-stalin-nor-alexis-de-tocqueville-coined-the-phrase-that-is-now-patriotic-shorthand.html; accessed June 18, 2020).

18. Michael Rosano, John Winthrop, John Cotton, and Nathaniel Niles, "The Basic Principles of Puritan Political Thought," in *History of American Political Thought* (ed. Bryan-Paul Forst and Jefferey Sikkenga; Applications of Political Theory; Lanham, MD: Lexington Books, 2003) 25–43.

19. Diana Preston, *A Brief History of the Boxer Rebellion: China's War on Foreigners, 1900* (London: Robinson, 2002).

IMAGE 1. Promotional material for *BioShock Infinite*, criticizing the xenophobic dimension of the fictional, in-game religion of Comstock. Credit: Irrational Games/2K Games 2013.

cities of Sodom and Gomorrah (Genesis 18–19). The "gifts of the founders" given to and accepted by Comstock (4) are references to America's Founding Fathers George Washington (1732–1799), Benjamin Franklin (1706–1790), and Thomas Jefferson (1743–1826), who are worshiped as the "Three Saintly Founders," and whose statues, paintings, and depictions in stained-glass windows can be found across Columbia. They can be recognized by their attributes: a sword, a key, and a scroll respectively, all—apparently—given to Comstock.

When Witting is ready with his sermon-cum-litany, or when the player enters through the circle of catechumens surrounding the preacher, a new (heavily scripted) sequence is initiated. Witting stands in the shallow waters of a giant baptismal font. The catechumens are dressed in white robes, folding their hands in prayer. Above Witting, a sign is placed: "This path of forgiveness is the only way to the city." Behind the preacher a small passage is seen, at whose end light shines through (see image 2).

Witting hears (he is blind after all) the newcomer approaching: "Is it someone new? Someone from the Sodom below? Newly come to Columbia to be washed clean, before our Prophet, our Founders, and our Lord?" After DeWitt bluntly asks passage to the city, Witting rebukes him: "Ha ha! Brother, the only way to Columbia is through rebirth in the sweet waters of baptism. Will you be cleansed, brother?" DeWitt accepts

IMAGE 2. Witting urges Booker DeWitt to let him be baptized in order to be able to enter the city of Columbia. Credit: Irrational Games/2K Games 2013.

reluctantly, and the player has no choice but to proceed through the game and then press the appropriate button—"Accept baptism."[20] The crowd cheers: "Praise the Lord!" Witting grabs DeWitt's arm forcibly, draws him into the font and says solemnly: "I baptize you in the name of our Prophet, in the name of our Founders, in the name of our Lord! And make him born again in the bosom of Columbia!" Witting pushes DeWitt under water for a couple of seconds, but when he coughs while submerged, the preacher is not convinced the baptism worked: "I don't know, brothers and sisters, but this one doesn't look clean to me." DeWitt is put under water again, loses consciousness and reawakens after an

---

20. In 2013, a Christian video game player by the name of Breen Malmberg asked and (allegedly) received a refund from game platform Valve for his copy of the game *BioShock Infinite*. Malmberg's letter to Valve is quoted on Kotaku.com: "I wish to return/exchange this game [*BioShock Infinite*] for steam credit or refund on the grounds that I cannot play it.... At the very beginning of the game there is a section of the game that is so offensive to my religious beliefs that I cannot proceed with it any further.... The player is forced to make a choice which amounts to extreme blasphemy in my religion (Christianity) in order to proceed any further—and I am therefore forced (in good conscience) to quit playing and not able to experience approx. 99% of the content in the game." See Patricia Hernandez, "Some Don't Like BioShock's Forced Baptism: Enough to Ask for a Refund," *Kotaku*, April 4, 2013 (online, https://kotaku.com/some-dont-like-bioshocks-forced-baptism-enough-to-as-473178476; accessed June 18, 2020).

immeasurable amount of time in a garden with the statues of the Three Founding Fathers in front of him: the passage to the city lies now open to him.

Eventually, DeWitt manages to free Elizabeth (his own daughter Anna) from Comstock. Elizabeth is called "the Lamb of Comstock" in Witting's timeline, both a reference to the lamb's blood on the doorposts protecting the Israelites from the angel killing Egypt's firstborn, and to the image of the *Agnus Dei*, the "Lamb of God" as a reference, in Christian tradition, to the suffering Christ. At the end of the game, DeWitt willingly lets himself be drowned by multiple versions of Elizabeth/Anna from various timelines, since his death at Witting's River, just after Wounded Knee, is the only way to prevent all the atrocities to come from it. Elizabeth is the angel of death, DeWitt's firstborn, closing the waters of the Red Sea/immersion in baptism erasing him from existence. And by accepting his violent death, DeWitt becomes the savior he always was meant to be.

■ II. The *Dayenu* Song: A Praise of Passover

The *Dayenu* is part of the Passover songs, used in the seder ritual, the festive meal associated with the Jewish festival of Passover. After the "sanctifying of the day" (*Kaddesh*), the "washing of the hands" (*Urchatz*), the "dipping of the greens/vegetables" (*Karpas*), and the "breaking of the Matzah" (*Yahatz*), the "story of the redemption" (*Maggid*) follows.[21] The *Dayenu* is part of this story of redemption, although it has been qualified as an optional, but old, addition.[22] It is a communal praise of the glory of God, who has bestowed so many blessings on his chosen people.[23] The poetic rhythm suggests that, if God had done only one of these wondrous things, it would have been enough to be eternally thankful and grateful. But God did not do just one thing but fourteen things, all of which are proclaimed "to have been enough for us" in and of themselves. Although there are slight differences between the various traditions, Heinrich

---

21. Joseph Tabory, *JPS Commentary on the Haggadah: Historical Introduction, Translation, and Commentary* (Philadelphia: Jewish Publication Society, 2008) 45–48.
22. Guggenheimer, *Scholar's Haggadah*, 308–9.
23. Eric Werner, "The Tunes of the Haggadah," *Studies in Bibliography and Booklore* 7.1/4 (1965) 57–83.

Guggenheimer provides us with the following English translation (again, I have numbered the stanzas for the sake of convenience):[24]

(i) For how many [Y: doubled and redoubled] supernatural good things are we indebted to the Omnipresent One [Y: praise to Him]?

(ii) If He had led us out of Egypt but had not punished them, it would have been enough for us!

(iii) If He had punished them but not [Y: passed judgment on] their idols, it would have been enough for us!

(iv) If He had [AS: punished; Y: passed judgment on] their idols but had not killed their firstborn, it would have been enough for us!

(v) If He had killed their firstborn but had not given us their money, it would have been enough for us!

(vi) If He had given us their money but had not split the sea for us, it would have been enough for us!

(vii) If He had split the sea for us but had not let us pass on a dry path, it would have been enough for us!

(viii) If He had let us pass on a dry path but had not sunk our enemies in the sea, it would have been enough for us!

(ix) If He had sunk our enemies in the sea but had not provided for our needs in the desert for forty years, it would have been enough for us!

(x) If He had provided for our needs in the desert for forty years but had not fed us on Manna, it would have been enough for us!

(xi) If He had fed us on Manna but had not given us the Sabbath, it would have been enough for us!

(xii) If He had given us the Sabbath but had not brought us before Mount Sinai, it would have been enough for us!

(xiii) If He had brought us before Mount Sinai but had not given us the Torah, it would have been enough for us!

(xiv) If He had given us the Torah but had not brought us into the Land of Israel, it would have been enough for us!

(xv) If He had brought us into the Land of Israel but had not built for us the Chosen Temple, it would have been enough for us!

---

24. Variations in the text between traditions are indicated separately between square brackets: A is Ashkenazic and Y is Yemenite. See Guggenheimer, *Scholar's Haggadah*, 54–56.

When the *Dayenu* is compared to Witting's sermon in *BioShock Infinite*, the intertextual correlations appear quite clearly. Apart from the clear structural similarity—A-B/B-C/C-D/ . . .—the Prophet Comstock is substituted for the God of Israel. The massacre from Wounded Knee (2) is connected with the destruction of the Egyptian army (ix); the provision of the New Eden (6) with the gift of the Land of Israel (xv); the submerging in the sweet waters of baptism (1) with the passing of the Reed Sea on a dry path (viii); and defeat of the Sodom below (3) with the judgment passed on the Egyptians (iii); and, last but not least, the three golden gifts (4) are equated with the manna (x), the sabbath (xii), and the Torah (xiv).

The intertextual relationship between the song and the game is one of reversal. In *BioShock Infinite*, the object of the praise is an "idol," a human who is thought to be a godhead, while the God of the *Dayenu* song is the exact opposite, and who is praised exactly for destroying the Egyptian idols (iv). The God of the Jewish song is praised because he has liberated an enslaved people from foreign oppressors, preventing them from reaching their God-given land where they belong. Comstock does the opposite: instead of liberating "his people," he is locking them up in their self-chosen isolation "in the clouds," far away from the "real" world below. *Dayenu* brings people from captivity into the free world; Comstock brings people from the free world to derailed utopia with its invisible walls. Whereas the Hebrew *Dayenu* is a Passover song of praise, the *BioShock Infinite*'s *Dayenu* reflects a heterodox Passover.

■ III. The Book of Exodus: The Liberation of a People

As Witting's sermon from *BioShock Infinite* has an intertextual relation with the *Dayenu* song, so does the song have one with its biblical source material, especially the Book of Exodus. The song takes a little liberty in the sequence of events described in Exodus, but that is probably due to its poetic genre. If we take Exodus as our point of departure, we can group the *Dayenu* stanzas into four groups: (A) God's actions while the people are still in Egypt, (B) God's actions on the flight from Egypt, (C) God's action in the desert, and (D) God's action when arriving in Israel (See table 1).[25]

---

25. For the structure of the Book of Exodus, see especially Christoph Dohmen, *Exodus 1–18* (HTKAT; Freiburg: Herder, 2015) 64–67. For a detailed commentary, see Thomas B. Dozeman, *Commentary on Exodus* (Eerdmans Critical Commentary; Grand Rapids: Eerdmans, 2009).

TABLE 1. Overview of the Stanzas of the *Dayenu* Song vis-à-vis Its Source Material from Exodus (and Other Biblical Books)

		Exodus
A: In Egypt		
iii	God punishes Egypt (ten plagues)	7:14–11:10
v	God kills Egypt's firstborn	11:1–10
iv	God passes judgment over Egypt's idols	12:12
B: Flight from Egypt		
ii	God leads his people out of Egypt	12:33–41
vi	God gives his people Egyptian gold	12:36
vii	God splits the Reed Sea	14:16–21
viii	God lets his people pass through the sea	14:22
ix	God sinks the Egyptian army	14:27–28
C: In the Desert		
x(a)	God takes care of the people's needs in the desert I (water)	15:22–27
xi	God provides manna	16:1–8
x(b)	God takes care of the people's need in the desert II (meat)	16:8–21
xii(a)	God gives the sabbath	16:22–36
x(c)	God takes care of the people's need in the desert III (rock)	17:1–7
xiii	God brings the people to Mount Sinai	19:1–25
xiv	God gives the Torah ("the Ten"/"Exodus"/ "Tanak")	
	The Ten Commandments	20:1–26
	Various ordinances	21:1–23:9
	Cultic regulations	
	Concerning the sabbath and the land	23:10–13
	Concerning the three national feasts	23:14–19
	Concerning the ark of the covenant	25:1–27:21
	Concerning the Temple service	28:1–30:38
	Concerning the craftsmen	31:1–11
xii(b)	God gives the sabbath (again)	31:12–18
	The golden statue	32:1–35
	Moses intercedes	33:1–23
	Replacement of the tablets	34:1–9
	Renewal of covenant	34:10–35
	Sabbath emphasized	35:1–9
	Tabernacle workmen	35:10–19
	Offerings to God	35:20–35
	The building of the sanctuary	36:1–38:31
	Priestly garments	39:1–43
	The construction of the tabernacle	40:1–38

D. In Israel

xv(a)	God brings the people to Israel	Joshua/Judges
xv(b)	God builds his temple	1 Kings 6 / 2 Chronicles 3–4

As we can see, some *Dayenu*-praised divine interventions are summaries of multiple instances. The "providing for our needs in the desert for forty years" (x), for example, can be split up into three instances: providing water (15:22–27), providing meat (16:8–21), and again providing water, now from a rock (17:1–7). Even the gift of manna could also be incorporated, but it is praised separately in the song (xi). The gift of the sabbath is given twice in Exodus (16:22–36 and 31:12–18), while the song unites them (xiii). And, of course, while all stanzas are based on passages from Exodus, the occupation of the land of Israel and the construction of the First Temple are found in Joshua and Judges, and in 1 King 6 and 2 Chronicles 3–4 respectively.

While the *Dayenu* praises God for the gift of the land of Israel (xv), the song does not explicitly include praise for the building of the Temple, partly because it would break the rhythm of the stanzas. But there are other reasons to consider. Diachronically, one could argue that the Temple did not exist in the desert, while all the other "things" God is praised for, did. That is also why the *Dayenu* does not include in its glorification of God's deeds the erecting of the tabernacle in Exodus 40: God's temporary and conveyable resting place on Earth is superseded by the construction of the Temple of Jerusalem, an event the song does mention and even closes with. Another option is that, since the Temple does not exist anymore, praising God for it does not fit easily into the celebrational sphere of the Haggadah. From a more synchronic point of view, however, one could argue from all those "things" that the Temple is not placed into the hands of the people, that is, not entirely, signifying the eternal and principal "otherness" of God's dwelling place on this earth.

The fourteenth stanza praises God for the gift of the Torah. In the context of the *Dayenu*, this phrase could have five concentrically enlarging meanings: (1) the Ten Commandments, (2) all the regulations and ordinances given to the people in the Book of Exodus, (3) as a *pars pro toto* for the Pentateuch, or (4) as a *pars pro toto* for the whole Tanak, or (5) even as encompassing the idea of "oral Torah." The song text itself does not exercise any pressure on either of these reading options.

Chapters 32–40 of Exodus are also missing from the *Dayenu* text. Again, a possible reading option is that the events described in these chapters are not very "festive": the chapters relate the people's transgression of God's commandment (the construction of the golden idol) and all the efforts on the part of God and Moses to repair the stressed relationship.

If the intertextual relationship between the song and the game is of a destructive kind—Witting is reversing the message of the song, as discussed above. The relationship between the song and the biblical text is of a more constructive kind. The praises of the song echo the stories of Exodus, even though the song is somewhat selective in what it chooses to praise and what to omit. If the people in the desert were prone to complain about their situation to Moses and God, and if they were even capable of beginning to worship an idol, the text of the song is, without doubt, subversive. It stresses time and time again, how great God has been to the people, and how benevolently God has bestowed his boons for his chosen ones.

■ IV. COMPLEX APPROPRIATIONS: WHO IS APPROPRIATING WHAT?

The intertextual relationship between the three texts—the game, the song, and the Bible—is complex. The relation between the Exodus text and the *Dayenu* is a constructive one. The poet echoes the text of Exodus. The relation between the song and the game, however, is a destructive one, since Witting is reversing the message of the song to fit his own exclusivist theology. The relationship between the Exodus text and *BioShock Infinite* is even more complicated, because of the twofold appropriation the game exercises (see table 2).

TABLE 2. The Multiple Layers of Appropriation in *BioShock Infinite*'s Baptism Scene

Texts	Medium	Appropriation Primary	Appropriation Secondary
Exodus	Book	...	...
Dayenu	Song	Exodus	...
Witting's baptism	Game (aesthetics)	Christian baptism	Exodus
Witting's sermon	Game (rhetoric)	*Dayenu*	Exodus

To understand what is happening in the game in terms of appropriation, we have to differentiate between two narrative layers within *BioShock Infinite*'s baptism scene as described in full detail earlier in this contribution. Rhetorically, Witting is appropriating the *Dayenu* song. Witting's sermon follows the Jewish song in poetic structure and—even if not so tightly—in its content. But aesthetically, Witting is appropriating the Christian ritual of baptism. The whole interaction between DeWitt and Witting is concentrated in the former being baptized by the latter, while standing in a giant baptismal font witnessed by a multitude of catechumens dressed in white.

In the context of this aesthetic appropriation of the Christian ritual of baptism, it is important to note, even though this contributes only more to the complexity of the scene itself, that within Christian theology, the biblical imagery of the passage through the Reed Sea has been appropriated as a forerunner of Christian baptism itself. The crossing of the Israelites through the Reed Sea to escape from their former lives as slaves is reinterpreted as foreshadowing the catechumen's crossing through of the waters of baptism, shedding his old life that was formerly ruled by slavery to sin.[26]

Thus, the multiple levels of appropriation are as follows: First, here, the Book of Exodus is not appropriating anything.[27] Second, the *Dayenu* song reinterprets the story of Exodus in the light of praise for God's glorious deeds in the liberation of the people from Egyptian slavery to entry into the promised land, while at the same time excluding some painful elements from the journey through the desert and from the destruction of the Second Temple.

Third, the game appropriates two things directly or primarily, and two indirectly or secondarily. As stated above, Witting, in his sermon, reinterprets praise for the God of Israel from the song in "Comstockian" terms, twisting its original message of praise of God into exaltation of an "idol," namely, the Prophet Comstock himself. But in the imagery of the whole game scene, Witting is also reinterpreting the Christian ritual of baptism, changing its universal claim of salvation for all into a "ticket" to enter the separatist and racist "paradise" of Columbia.

---

26. Robin Margaret Jensen, *Baptismal Imagery in Early Christianity: Ritual, Visual, and Theological Dimensions* (Grand Rapids: Baker Academic, 2012).

27. That is, of course, not completely true, since Exodus also knows a complex Redaktionsgeschichte. See Suzanne Boorer, "Sources and Redaction Criticism," in *Methods for Exodus* (ed. Thomas B. Dozeman; Methods in Biblical Interpretation; Cambridge: Cambridge University Press, 2010) 95–130. This consideration, however, falls outside the boundaries of this contribution and the research detailed in it.

However, Witting is also appropriating Exodus twice: once through the reinterpretation of the *Dayenu* song *and* once through reinterpretation of Christian baptism. In both words and images, Witting is destroying Exodus's original message of liberation for the many and transforming it into a select society focused on race and social class. If, in Exod 12:38–39, "a mixed multitude went up" with the Israelites, "along with flocks and herds" and started to bake the dough of unleavened bread too, thus sharing in Israel's liberation from slavery, Witting is the gatekeeper of an exclusive, "members-only" religious club, for which many request membership while only few are admitted.

▪ V. THE GAME AS MODEL OF THE ROLE OF TEACHER

Let us return to "the duck test," mentioned at the beginning of this contribution, and its application to *BioShock Infinite*'s appropriation of the Bible and of biblical language and images. If it looks like the Bible, and sounds like the Bible, and appropriates biblical notions, could you call it "biblical"? The answer supplied by the game is a resounding no. Witting's sermon seems biblical, but it is not so. Witting celebrates a Passover gone wrong. Exodus portrays the meal as the ultimate moment of liberation from Egyptian slavery, the start of their long journey to the land promised to them by God.[28] And the *Dayenu* echoes this sentiment. Witting's Passover leads people not into freedom but into captivity, that is, under the "spell" of the Prophet Comstock. And even though we can be quite sure that Levine's product was never intended for or designed to be what one could call an "educational game," *BioShock Infinite* teaches its player three important things, all related to the use and abuse of the Bible and its strong cultural anchorage.

First, at a conceptual level, *BioShock Infinite* shows its gamers the difference between intertextuality and appropriation.[29] Intertextuality

---

28. For the characteristics of the Passover meal, see also Archibald L. H. M. van Wieringen, "Meal in Bible and Liturgy," *Orientis Aura: Macau Perspectives in Religious Studies* 1 (2016) 118–30.

29. Theoretically, a distinction must be made between the text-external and text-internal reader-cum-player. Because I am focusing on the text-internal communication of the game, I do not discuss the quality or quantity of individual players who might or might not understand the game's complex intertextuality. For more methodological issues about the difference of text-internal and text-external readers, see the handbook Frank G. Bosman and Archibald L. H. M. van Wieringen, *Video Games as Art: A*

is, by and from itself, a descriptive term focused on pointing to relationships between "texts." Appropriation, however, is a notion that sensitizes people to the problematic nature of specific forms of reusing culturally determined rhetoric and aesthetic. Intertextuality can be done better or worse, only in the technical sense that one text can convey other texts that it is (indirectly) quoting.

Appropriation can be done better or worse in a very real sense; that is, it can be conceived of as benign or violent. There is technically nothing wrong with the intertextual relationships between book, song, and game—these relationships simply *exist*—but in terms of appropriation, the reinterpretation of Exodus in the *Dayenu* is of another category than *BioShock*'s Witting's reinterpretation of the *Dayenu*, the Christian ritual of baptism, and the Exodus text that lies behind those two.

Second, at the level of semantics, *BioShock Infinite* teaches its gamers the difference between two kinds of liberation. The liberation spoken of in Exodus, the Passover song, and the Christian baptism are of a universal kind. Everyone can be liberated as long as one abides by God's commandments. Everyone can become a member of the chosen people, as long as one "walks the walk" with it. The liberation Witting is suggesting is, however, precisely of the opposite nature. In Columbia only white people are welcome, excluding perceived *Untermenschen* like Mexicans, Native Americans, Roman Catholics, and people of color. Liberation for Witting is not for all, but only for the happy few.

Third, at the level of hermeneutics, *BioShock Infinite* teaches its players that the duck analogy is a dangerous one. Not everything that sounds like a duck is a duck per se. Not everything that sounds biblical is from the Bible. Not everyone who proclaims liberation is a savior. One can copy the form of a religious text—as Witting imitated the *Dayenu*—or one can take over the Christian ritual of baptism, as the same Witting did with DeWitt, but as long as the message conveyed in these texts and rituals is not accounted for, both are rendered cold and dead. The original Passover, told in Exodus and praised in the *Dayenu*, went well and saved many people, just like Christian baptism brought many to salvation too.

Witting's Passover only imprisoned people, in their own utopia, in their own thoughts of exclusivism and racial purity, and in the City of Columbia, which reveals itself slowly but inevitably to the gamer as a new form of slavery instead of the liberation it promised to those who sought it. The game implicitly judges Witting as a false teacher, who superficially

---

Communication-Oriented Perspective on the Relationship between Gaming and Art (Video Games and the Humanities 12; Berlin: De Gruyter Oldenbourg, 2023).

clothes his xenophobic message in the disguise of Jewish and Christian texts and customs regarding a universal liberation. The game itself gives a strong warning to its players to identify such an abuse of Jewish and Christian texts and customs, making the game into a teacher figure. The character Witting as a false teacher, preaching racism, xenophobia, and exclusion, is contrasted by the game itself as a good teacher, who reveals Witting's true ideological face and values. *BioShock Infinite* teaches its players to shun such false teachers, to think critically about what they teach, and to rebel against it.

Witting is really a blind teacher. The game makes that crystal clear.

17

Epilogue:

Non scholae, sed vitae discimus

Bénédicte Lemmelijn

The prologue to this book started with a title inspired by Seneca's famous saying: "We do not learn for school, but for life." I take this saying up once more in this epilogue by way of an *inclusio*: "Non scholae, sed vitae discimus" (*Lucil.* 17–18.106.12). It is a short sentence with deep meaning. It seems to reflect or meta-reflect on the aim and goal of learning. Seneca's saying even seems rooted in some kind of disappointment about the reality he observes. It denies something that seems to be taken for granted, but pushes it further to an apparently less evident reality.

■ I. THE AIM OF LEARNING

In our days also, the same questions could arise when we look around. Is it merely our own ambition that strives for more knowledge or perfection? Do we aim at more scientific research in our faculties to acquire a higher place in the rankings? Do we stimulate our students to study more intensely to be the "best" or at least to become "better" than others? Is it our desire for competition to know more than others? Do our students, even those having chosen to study theology, mainly learn for grades and marks and brilliant certificates in order to gain coveted positions in the inner world of the academy? Is that the reality that is fulfilling our desires?

Seneca already noticed that all of that does not make education valuable. What then makes education worth striving for? It is as simple as it is fundamental. It is about its relevance in and impact on our lives: *vitae discimus* .... Ultimately, we learn with a view to becoming intrinsically rich human beings, and consequently, we teach in order to form critically thinking human persons. People who will be able to put themselves at the disposal and service of their fellow human beings, to all those entrusted to them one day, to create opportunities, in turn, to develop themselves and flourish in a world that always transcends us. Or in Martha Nussbaum's words, quoted in the prologue to this book: "to become critical thinkers and to become empathetic and democratically minded citizens."

■ II. THE ATTITUDE OF TRUE LEARNING

It should indeed be that intrinsic aim that moves us forward to learn more deeply and to teach constructively. Moreover, learning implies a specific disposition. Even more, the desire really to learn implies several fundamental qualities. First, it has to do with true openness of mind. Second, it involves modesty. And, third, it allows for self-criticism. An openness of mind is needed in order even to enable oneself to ask questions, to be open to new perspectives, to question one's own lens. All of that implies modesty. Disciples know that they do not know. They want to know more. They wish to understand by learning and to learn by listening. All of that implies, in turn, listening to a teacher whom the disciple respects and trusts as someone knowing more, being wiser, showing the way or demonstrating the method, passing on both ancient tradition and new insights synergically synthesized. And indeed, all of that presupposes the ability to question oneself, to be open to self-criticism, to search for nuanced answers, even if that means the letting go of the "fit for one and for all" easy solutions.

In the Bible, good teachers and true disciples are characterized by the same qualities and realities. This volume has shown how both literary characters and historical figures function as teachers as well as how texts themselves or even other means can take over the role of a teacher.

Turning to Jesus himself, depicted regularly as a "rabbi," a teacher, and his apostles being characterized as disciples, or his audience described as people listening to his words and wisdom, we can indeed observe that the same fundamental disposition applies. Whether it is the crowd listening to him at the shore of the Sea of Galilee or Nicodemus at night listening to his wise words, it is about deep learning. It is about an openness of mind to allow a new perspective to enter. It is about the modesty to let oneself be corrected. It is about opening one's eyes, literally or figuratively, to new paths to follow and new choices to make.

■ III. THE SCRIPTURES AS A TEACHER

Taking one step further, beyond Jesus, it is evident that the Scriptures themselves function as a teacher, even to Jesus himself. If the editors of this book state in their introduction that, very fundamentally, the biblical teacher is the one who "actualizes the Scripture(s)," then indeed, that is exactly what Jesus does when he confronts the ancient prescriptions of the Torah with his actual reality. When he opposes the old sayings with his own "but I say," when he reinterprets and corrects the rules that the scribes have made out of living narratives that were meant to create life.

Indeed, we observe that the biblical text reinterprets itself in changing new contexts. The message of proto-Isaiah is very different from that of Trito-Isaiah: evolving from warning to an almost utopian hope and promise. Even the Ten Commandments, depicted as written on stone, present themselves in two different versions and are alluded to in quite a number of differing ways.

Since the Bible as a true teacher reinterprets and actualizes itself, the same need for reactualization of those living Scriptures forms the way forward for those of us who read it today as a source of inspiration in our lives. And it is here that "exegesis" comes in. It is needed, first and foremost, so that the readers of the Bible may become conscious that this book, as a true teacher, is also a strange teacher, from strange times and odd places. It is only when we allow ourselves really to consider that notion that we can create the conditions for this biblical teacher to reinvent itself again and again. This is true, especially today when we still face the same so-called "existential" questions about life and death, love and pain, illness and pleasure, vulnerability and fragility about which the Bible talks.

■ IV. EXEGESIS AS A TEACHER

Precisely in the context of exegesis, it could be tempting to look for ready-made answers in that old book: to open the recipe book and to look for what we want to find there. The word "Bible" can sound very familiar to us. In effect, it is very much the foundation of our Judeo-Christian faith. Yet the Bible is first and foremost a strange book. Only when we are fully aware of that reality, will we be able to look for ways in which the Scriptures can still mean something in our lives.

A look at some aspects of this "strangeness" will illustrate the difficulties and will ultimately help us to transcend them. And here we meet another "teacher," in and through the development of (historical-critical) exegesis. A few observations that seem almost basic today are, in fact, essential and worth repeating succinctly.

Although in religious language we sometimes say that a text from the Bible "addresses" us, nothing could be further from the truth. None of us is "addressed." No text in the Bible is addressed to people of the twenty-first century. No reader today is part of the original living world of the biblical authors. When the prophets speak of apostasy and injustice, they are addressing the Israelites of the first millennium BCE. And when Paul writes a letter to the Corinthians, he is not speaking to people in Western Europe in the twenty-first century. As an example, take the case of a letter read by someone other than the addressee who does not immediately understand what it means. We need background information to be able to interpret what we are reading. This is also true when reading biblical texts.

Second, none of the books in the Bible is written in a modern, living language. Biblical literature is written in Hebrew, Greek, and Aramaic. Whoever wants to read the text in its original form is confronted with a serious barrier. Learning a biblical language is not easy: the language system is very different and the vocabulary is sometimes really unclear. In this context, we often rely on translations. But anyone who has ever tried to translate a text (let alone a poem) knows that every translation involves choices and interpretations, both in terms of grammar and language structures and in terms of content. The French saying "traduire, c'est trahir" is very clear: to translate is to betray. When the contemporary reader attempts to interpret the biblical text on the basis of a translation, we face interpretation in a double degree. The translation itself is already interpretation, and the reader, in turn, reinterprets that interpretation.

Third, there is a huge cultural and chronological gap between the original writers and readers of the biblical texts and the readers of the twenty-first century. The living world of the biblical texts is that of the ancient Near East: a predominantly patriarchal culture without women's emancipation, without globalization, mostly strongly agriculturally oriented and following the rhythm of the seasons. Slavery was accepted, medicine undeveloped, mortality high, and life expectancy low. This cultural gap implies that the biblical text, when read by contemporary readers, needs historical-cultural clarification. Moreover, the cultural gap is inevitably linked to a huge chronological gap that exists as a result of the many centuries that have passed since the emergence of the biblical texts. If one were to read a newspaper article from 1950, it is far from easy to understand immediately what the editor is getting so worked up about, if one does not have any sense of the situation current at the time. Between the origins of a majority of biblical texts and today, the gap is not seventy years, but more than two millennia! If we add to this that the biblical texts were not all created in the same period, should it surprise us that it is necessary to find out the historical context of each text individually? Since exegesis has taught us that the Bible is not a history book but rather religious literature that favors proclamation, any account of so-called historical events should be interpreted with serious caution.

And there is even more to worry about, when discussing a fourth aspect. When we think of the Universal Declaration of Human Rights, it is immediately clear that this is a document that came about as the result of a growth process, in which the text took shape through the work of various authors and/or editors. In parallel, most probably, no Old Testament book was written by a single author. If the Book of Isaiah in its three major sections echoes situations between the eighth and sixth centuries BCE, it may soon be clear that no single historical person Isaiah could have lived so long that he would have written it all down himself. Rather, the present form of the book is the result of a very complex and lengthy process of editing, rewriting, updating, and supplementing—in short, of reactualization. The Bible reflects cultural and theological thought from different periods, which, moreover, was written down by various authors over different centuries in a collection of books, many of which were repeatedly edited and reactualized, and subsequently transmitted in different text versions.

Fifth, there is no actual autograph of any of the biblical books. Moreover, the oldest complete Hebrew text of the Old Testament dates only from around the year 1000 of our era. In addition, in the second half of the twentieth century, numerous ancient, albeit mostly fragmentary, manuscripts of the biblical text were found, of which the Dead Sea discoveries are the most important. The biblical texts found among the Dead Sea Scrolls date from the third century BCE to the first century CE. Some of these texts contain a textual version that differs in important ways from the above-mentioned Hebrew text. In some cases, this is due to deliberate reinterpretation and, once again, to reactualization. In other texts, the variations are simply based on mistakes in copying. One thing is clear, however: the biblical text we usually use or refer to, is not "the" text but "a" text. This awareness alone may keep us from perceiving the text as an "absolute" in a fundamentalist way.

Finally, the Bible may be counted among the classics of world literature. It is literature on general human themes and existential issues for all times. However, the Bible possesses an extra dimension: it functions within a community of faith. Therein, the Scriptures have somehow acquired divine authority in such a way that they are considered "Holy Scripture." That fact implies that when one interprets biblical texts, one joins a long line of teachers who have sought to understand and explain the text. On the one hand, this offers an advantage, as many of the problems have already been noticed and possible solutions have already been explored. On the other hand, this tradition history should not be stultifying. Readers today must dare to let go of this age-old tradition, to create space for other, new, legitimate interpretations and new actualizations.

Thus, facing this "strange" phenomenon of biblical tradition immediately reveals its own ongoing process of interpretation, reinterpretation, and actualization. It is precisely that process that the present editors emphasize in their introduction to this book as being a fundamental quality of a teacher.

■ V. The Attitude of True Teaching

The Bible itself in its inner-biblical exegesis, as well as the development of exegetical approaches to its interpretation and reactualization, can function as "teachers" in the process of our gaining an understanding of this ancient tradition of existential reflection and deep faith. Beyond any historicization or fundamentalist affirmation of the biblical narratives—denying the aspects described above—it is precisely these kinds of observations that have been at the heart of historical-critical exegesis. The result was that the Bible was no longer characterized as an objective report of historical facts, but rather as a faithful reflection on the realities in which it emerged and with which it deals.

At the beginning of the twentieth century, exegetical scholarship demonstrated conclusively that biblical narratives could no longer be interpreted as objective eyewitness accounts of historical facts. On the contrary, the texts that paint a picture of how Israel fared are theological texts that have undergone a long and complicated process of development. The Bible is primarily literature that seeks to proclaim rather than to describe. Consequently, anyone who wants to engage honestly with the Bible must distinguish between historical reality and its theological interpretation, reinterpretation, and actualization, even within the Bible itself. What is important is the deeper message that the biblical authors wanted to convey about what was at stake in their historical communities.

When the texts are taken seriously in this way, it is not about trying to prove the Bible's right in historicization or fundamentalism, but rather it is about critically interpreting historicity in and through biblical narratives in the context of an understanding that conceives of the Bible first and foremost as developed religious literature. However, this insight is itself the result of a gradual understanding that marked the evolution of biblical scholarship. Progressively, the emphasis and focus shifted from the history *behind* the text to the history *of* the text. In particular, the origin and development of the text itself in its multiple origins and complex editorial layering as well as its own phases of inner-biblical reinterpretation and actualization became the object of study. In this development, one sees a further shift that no longer places the development of the text at the center of attention. Instead, that place is occupied by the relevance and theological meaning of the final text. Admittedly, this too must always be done in awareness of the fact that this so-called final text is a developed text. The final text is a complex literary composition, but it has by no means suddenly fallen out of the blue.

In conclusion, if the Scriptures reveal themselves as "teachers" in actualizing and reactualizing their central messages, and if current exegesis has demonstrated that the Scriptures did so time and again within their changing contexts, we can observe that the fundamental attitude of true teaching corresponds to the same qualities that we described above as the essence of true learning: openness of mind, modesty, and self-criticism. The teacher too, like the disciple, should keep an open mind to observe, understand, and interpret an ever-changing reality. This includes a willingness to reconsider truths and values in changing contexts. Teachers should be modest in not defining their own truths as ultimate. And, in doing so, they should be ready to develop a nuanced and critical attitude toward the content of their own teaching.

If inner-biblical reinterpretations and the development of exegesis have taught us one thing, it is that our insights do indeed change and develop. In other words, our evolving contexts reveal new aspects, and our "knowledge" of transcendent reality, which is ultimately God, cannot be captured in any single human answer. It is in the light of that understanding that we may claim that we do not learn for school, but for life. We do not study the Bible merely for the sake of the academy and science. Rather, we may remind ourselves that the Bible consists of the real reflections and the deep faith of living people, each in the context of their own life's realities. These are shared with people of today who live in ever-changing contexts, each with its own particular complexity and sensitivities. Let true learning be guided by true teaching: open minded, modest, and self-critical.

Index of Ancient Sources

Hebrew Bible
Genesis
1:1–2:3	12, 38, 123, 126, 133, 204				
1:21	204
1:24	204
1:25	204
1:26	129
1:26–27	123–26, 128–31, 133, 204
1:26a	126
1:26b	123
1:27a	123
1:27	126, 130, 204
1:27b	123
1:28	46, 128, 205
2:2	91
2:16–17	205
3:9–13	205
3:14–24	205
3:22	132
5:1–3	204
5:1–5	126, 129
5:3	129
7:2–3	91
9:1–7	126
9:6	132
18–19	227
25:27	135
40:14	213
41:53	91
49:28	90

Exodus
2:16	91
3:4	139
3:16	137
7:8–12	99
7:14	21
7:14–11:10	232
11:1–10	232
12:12	232
12:15–20	91
12:21	137
12:26–27	2
12:33–41	232
12:38–39	236
12:36	232
13:8–10	2
13:14	2
14:16–21	232
14:22	232
14:27–28	232
15:22–27	232–33
16:1–8	232
16:8–21	232–33
16:22–36	232–33
17:1–7	232–33
18	117
18:20	113, 117
19:1–25	232
19–40	9
20:1–17	9
20:1–26	232
20:2	141
20:3	141
20:8	141
20:17	10
21:1	138
21:1–23:9	232
23:10–13	232
23:14–19	232
24	9
25:1–27:21	232
25–31	9
28:1–30:38	232
28:28	59
31:1–11	232
31:12–18	232–33
32:1–6	9
32	232
32–40	233
33	232
34:1–9	232
34:10–35	232
35:1–9	232
35–40	9
35:10–19	232
35:20–35	232
36:1–38:31	232
39	232
40	232

Leviticus
1:1	139–40
14	91
18:3–4	113
20:23	113
25	91
25:39	35
26:21	113
26:23	113
26:27	113
26:40	113

Numbers
15:38	59
16:47	142
16:48	142
17:16–17	90
21:6–9	47
33:9	90
33:50–56	126

Deuteronomy
1:6b–4:40	9
1:23	90
2:16–17	140
5	9
5:1	9
5:1b–28:68	9
5:21	10
5:33	113
6–11	9
6:20–21	2
8:6	113
10:12	113
11:22	113
12–28	9
17:18	9
19:9	113
21:2–3	137
21:10–14	11
22:13–19	11
24:1–5	11
31:2b–6	9
31:7b–8	9
31:10b–13	9
31:14b	9
31:16b–21	9
31:19	138
31:23b	9
31:26–29	9
32	9
33:2b–29	9
34:10	9

Joshua
3:12	90
4:1–8	90
4:2	90
24	94
24:1	137
24:31	137

Judges
19:29	90

1 Samuel
6:1–11	126–27

1 Kings
4:29	92
6	233
6:11	113

2 Kings
11:1–20	126
16:1–8	128
17:13	34
19:28	46

2 Chronicles
3–4	233
4:1–6	128
23:1–21	126
33:11	46

Nehemiah
9:7–57	94

1 Maccabees
2:50	69
6:44	69
7:41	21

2 Maccabees
8:19	21
15:22	21

Psalms
1:1	112
4:7	193
7:16	3
8:10	142
26:1	113
26:3	113
26:11	113
29:5	140
39:2–7	126
58:2–6	128
68:19	142
69:26	90
73:13–20	126
78	94
94:10	193
103:3	193
105	94
109:8	90
119:1	113
119:3	113
127	193
128:1	113
135:8	21
136:10	21

Proverbs
2:16–17	3
5:1–23	3
6:24	3
7:5	3
8:1–9:12	3
8:9	58
9:13–18	3
26:27	3
31:1–9	3

Ben Sira
1:11–30	60–61
2:6	113
2:15	113
6:13–31	57
6:18	56, 58
6:18–22	57–58
6:18–37	56–57
6:19	58
6:22	57–58
6:22–23	57
6:23	57
6:23–31	57–58
6:30b	59
6:31b	59
6:32–37	57, 59–60
6:34	56
24:19–22	58
24:30–33	51
27:5–6	57
33:16–18	51
34:17	54
35:14	54
38:24–39:11	51
41:14	54
42:5	54
42:8	54
44–50	52

45:12	59	11:10	26	40:1	25, 30
48:22	113	11:11–16	26	40:1–11	24, 28
50:27	50, 52, 54	11:16	26	40–66	18, 23, 28–30
51:13–20	55	13–14	26–27	40:4	28
51:13–30	54, 56	13–23	26	40:12–26	128
51:23	53–54	13:2–5	128	49	28
51:29	54	15–19	26	49:6	28
51:30	55	19:1–15	27	49:22–23	28
		19:16–25	27	50:4	18
Isaiah		19:21	27	50:10	18
1–39	18, 30	19:22	27	53:1–11a	18
1:1–8	15	19:23	27	53:7–8	98
1:1–31	14	19:24–25	27	53:10	18
1:2–4	15	20	26	54:13	18
1:2–8	16	21:1–10	26	54:17	18
1:5–7	15	22	26	60	28
1:8	16	23	26	60:3	28
1:9–10	15–16	24–35	26–27	60:4	28
1:11	15–16	25:6	27	60:10	28
1:17a	14–15	25:7	27	60:12	29
1:18	16	25:8	27	60:14	28
2:2	25–26	25:6–10	27	60:16	29
2:2–5	25–30	25:9–10	27	63:7–64:12	18
2:3	25	36–37	20, 24	66:18	29
2:4	25	36–39	23	66:18–21	29
2:5	25	36:2	20	66:20	29
6–12	17, 26	37:1	21	66:20b	29
7:1–17	19–20, 22–24, 26	37:14	21	66:20e	29
7:2	19	37:30	20		
7:6	24	37:36	21	**Jeremiah**	
7:9b	19–20, 25, 29	37:37	21	8:17	47
7:10	20	37:38	21	16:16	46
7:12	19	38	21–22		
7:14	26	38:1–8	23	**Ezekiel**	
7:14–15	19, 24	38:7–8	22	1:2–28c	128
7:16–17	19	38:9	22–23	1:5a	128
7:17	24	38:9–20	22	1:5b	128
8	17–18	38:10–14	22	1:10a	128
8:1–2	17	38:15–20	22	1:13a	128
8:11	17	38:20b	22	1:16a	128
8:12	17	38:21	23	1:22a	128
8:16	17	38:21–22	23	1:26a	128
8:18	17	39	23–26, 30	1:26c	128
8:23a–9:6	26	39:6	24	1:28c	128
10:5–19	27	39:6–8	25	7:10–22	126
10:15	27	39:7	24	8:1–4	128
11:1–9	26	39:2	24	10:1–22	128

Ezekiel (cont.)

11:20	113
16:1–19	126
20:5–40	94
23:1–20	126, 128
29:4	46

Daniel

2:24–35	126
3:1–30	126
3:19	126
7	63, 65–67, 70, 74
7:13	65
10:4–21	128

Hosea

14:9	113

Amos

1:1	33
1:2	33
2:4	33–34
2:4–5	32
2:6	35
2:6–13	32
2:6c–8b	34
2:7	35
2:8	35
2:10	32
2:12	34, 36
3:3	32
3:9–10	32
3:12	41
4:1	46
4:1g	41
4:2	42
4:3	42
4:4–5	32, 42
4:4–11	38
4:6c	40
4:6–11	40
4:8d	40
4:9c	40
4:10d	40
4:11e	40
4:13	37–38
5:3	40
5:4	40
5:7	32
5:8	39
5:8–9	37–38
5:10	32
5:12	32
5:16b–17a	40, 47
5:18–20	42
5:18d–e	46
5:19	46–47
5:20	46
5:21–23	32, 42
5:21–27	126
5:27a	40
6:1–2	43
6:7b	40
6:8e	40
6:11–12	40
6:14	40
7:2	47
7:3	40, 47
7:5	47
7:5c	44
7:6	40, 48
7:10–17	32, 47
7:12	36
7:13	36, 44
7:15c–d	36, 44
7:16c–d	44
7:17	47
8:7–8	32
8:11c–f	40
9	44
9:2–4	44
9:3	47
9:5–6	37, 39

Habakkuk

1:15	46

Malachi

4:5	73

New Testament
Matthew

3:2	169
4:17	169
5:14	226
5–7	78
9:20	90
15:14	98
16:13–19	170–71
16:24	171
23	194
23:8	172, 191, 194
23:8–11	174
23:10	191
28:1	143, 151
28:19–20	173

Mark

1:1–8:21	71
1:2–8	169
1:10–11	169
1:21	85
1:27	85
2:10	66–67
2:28	66–67
5:25	90
5:42	90
6:1–4	171
6:7–13	173
7:1–23	113
8:22–10:52	68, 71
8:27–30	71, 171
8:31	66–67, 71, 73, 75
8:32	66
8:32–33	71
8:34–38	71
8:38	66–68
9:2–8	71
9:5	73
9:9a	72
9:9	66, 68, 72–73
9:9–13	63–64, 71–73, 75
9:9b	72
9:10	72
9:11	72
9:12a	72, 74
9:12	66, 68–69
9:12b	72
9:13	72
9:14	72
9:31	66, 69, 71

Index of Ancient Sources 251

9:32–37	71	5:17–26	82	12:16–21	84
9:41–49	71	5:22	82	12:24	84
10:32–34	71	5:23	82–83	12:25	84
10:33	66, 69	5:34	82	13:2	84
10:35–41	71	6:1–11	82	13:6–9	84
10:45	66, 69	6:2	83	14:3	84
11:1–16:8	71	6:3–4	83	14:7–10	84
12:28–34	78	6:6	98	15:3–7	78
13:26	66, 70	6:6–11	83	15:8–10	78
14:21	66–67, 70	6:7	83	15:11–32	78
14:41	66–67, 70	6:8	83	16:1–13	78
14:56–57	94	6:13	90	17:5	90
14:62	66, 70	6:16	90	18:18–19	84
14:67	66	6:20–38	78	18:31	90
16:1	143	6:20–49	82	20:1	84
16:9–10	143	6:39	82, 98	20:1–7	84
		6:40	86	20:2	84
Luke		6:41	82	20:21–23	84
1–2	78	6:42	82	22:3	90
1:3–4	88	6:46	82	22:14	90
1:5–25	78	7:19	83	22:20	94
1:18	81	7:36–50	82	22:31	93
1:26–38	78	7:39	82	22:31–32	101
1:34	82	7:40	83	22:32	101
1:43	82	7:42	82	23:34	95
1:57–80	79	7:44	82	23:46	95
2:1–40	79	7:49	83	24:4	151
2:22	79	8:1	90, 95	24:5	151
2:23	79	8:2	143, 153	24:10	90, 143
2:24	79	8:3	143	24:13–35	84, 98
2:27	79	8:25	83	24:14	85
2:39	79	8:30	83	24:15	85
2:40	79	8:42–43	90	24:17	85
2:40–52	12, 76, 80	8:45	83	24:19	85
2:41	79	9:1	90	24:19–24	86
2:41–45	79	9:9	83	24:45–49	102
2:41–52	79	9:10	90	24:47	100
2:42	79, 90	9:12	90	24:48	92
2:43	81	9:18	83		
2:46	81, 170	9:18–20	171	**John**	
2:46–47	80	9:20	83	4:1–42	197
2:46–49	82	13:10–17	82–83	8:3–11	144
2:47	80–81	10:13–15	83	10:13	98
2:48	82	10:15	83	13:13–15	174
2:49	80, 82	10:26	98	14–16	152
2:52	79	12:14	84	20:1–18	143
4:16–30	98	12:15	84	20:17	143

Index of Ancient Sources

Acts
1:2	90	6:1–6	89	13:6–12	93, 101
1:5	97	6:1–7	117	13:10	113
1:5–22	94	6:2	90	13:12	97
1:8	90, 100, 102	6:3	92	13:48	97
1:14	100	6:4	92, 100	14:4	90
1:14–20	90	6:6	90	14:8–10	93, 101
1:15–26	90	6:7	93	14:14	90
1:17	100	6:8	95	14:22	101
1:21–22	90, 102	6:8–8:2	93	15:2	90
1:22–23	105	6:14	94	15:4	90
1:26	90, 93, 100	7–8	89	15:6	90
2:1–4	97	7:57	94	15:7–11	101
2:1–13	173	7:58	101	15:22	90
2:14–36	94	7:58–60	95	15:23	90
2:28	113	8:1	90, 95, 101	15:35	105
2:37	90	8	93, 97	16:4	90
2:38–41	97	8:3	95	16:15	97
2:41	97	8:3–14	97	16:17	113
2:42	90, 100	8:5	95, 101	16:33	97
2:42–44	94	8:6	100	18:11	105
2:43	90	8:7	100	18:24	106
2:46	100	8:9	100–101	18:25	113
2:47	93	8:10	100	18:26	113
3:1–10	93, 101	8:11	100	19:1–7	93
3:12–26	94	8:12	99, 101	19:2–7	97
4:4	93	8:12–13	97	19:8	101
4:8–12	94	8:13	95–96, 100	19:9	113
4:21	94	8:14	90	19:11–12	93, 101
4:32–37	94	8:14–17	97	9:23	113
4:33	90	8:14–24	93	19:23–40	93, 101
4:35	90	8:15	97	20:9–10	93, 101
4:36	90	8:17	97	20:25	101
4:37	90	8:20	101	21:8	89, 91, 93
5	94	8:21	100	21:8–9	103
5:2	90	8:24	101	22:4	113
5:12	90	8:26–39	97	22:16	97
5:12–16	93, 101	8:30	98	22:20	94
5:14	93	9:2	113	24:14	113
5:16	93	9:4	93	24:24	113
5:18	90	9:17–18	97	28:23	101
5:29	90	9:27	90	28:31	101
5:39	94	9:36–41	93, 101		
5:40	90	9:43	101	**Romans**	
6	95, 97	10	101	1:20	131
6:1	91, 93	10:44–48	97	2:21	107
6:1–3	93	11:1	90	8:2	199
		12:6–10	93, 101	16:1	91

Index of Ancient Sources

1 Corinthians	
1:10	109
1:10–11	120
1:10–17	108
1:10–26	106
1:10–4:21	108
1:12–4:21	120
1:18–25	108
1:26–31	108
2:1–5	108
2:6–16	108
3	108
3:1–4	106, 108
3:1–4:21	106
3:5	108
3:5–8	108
3:5–9a	106
3:5–17	108
3:9	108
3:9b–17	106
3:18–23	108
4:1–2	106
4:1–5	108
4:6	106, 108
4:6–13	108
4:7	108
4:7–13	108
4:10	109
4:11	109
4:14	109
4:14–15	106
4:14–21	108
4:15	109
4:16	106, 109
4:17	12, 106–11, 113–14, 117–18, 121
4:18	108
4:19	108
5:1	115
5:2	108
7:3–6	115
7:10–11	116
7:12–16	115–17
7:14	116
8:1	108
9:9–10	115
10:1–11:1	120
10:6–11	120
10:24–29	115
10:33	120
11:7	107
11:23	109
11:23–25	118
13:4	108
14:16	115

2 Corinthians	
1:19	118
3:3	199

Galatians	
1:1	107
1:12	107
1:13	107
1:14–15	121
1:15–16	121
2:20	171

Ephesians	
4:7–8	142
4:21	107

Philippians	
3:10	171

Colossians	
1:1	122
1:9–10	132
1:12–17	132
1:13	129
1:15	12, 122–23, 129–31, 133
1:16	131
1:16–18	131
2:6	114
2:18	108
3:1–17	132
3:9	130
3:10	12, 122–23, 130, 132–33

1 Timothy	
1:17	131
2:7	105, 107, 193

2 Timothy	
1:11	105, 107

Hebrews	
11:27	131

1 Peter	
2:21	174

Revelation	
7:17	98

Dead Sea Scrolls	
2Q18 [2QSir]	57
4QMMT	117

Old Testament Pseudepigrapha
1 Enoch

37–71	63

New Testament Pseudepigrapha
Acts of Paul and Thecla

16–17	106

Gospel of Mary

7:4–9:4	145
8:21–22	146
9:5	145
9:6–11	145
9:7–10:23	151
9:12–23	145
10:1–6	145, 147
10:7–17:9	145
10:14–16	152
15:1–8	152
16:14–16	152
16:19	152
16:21–22	152
17:1–6	152
17:8–9	147
17:10–18:21	145, 152
17:13–15	147

254 Index of Ancient Sources

Gospel of Mary (cont.)
17:14	148
17:18–22	147, 153
18:2–5	147
18:10–15	148
18:14–15	148
18:18–19	146
19:1–2	145
19:3–5	145

Josephus
Vita
7–12	8

Rabbinic Literature
Genesis Rabbah
63.10	135

Mekilta de-Rabbi Yishmael
Yitro 2	117

Mishnah
Avot
1:1	137
6:6	135

Pesaḥim
10:5	3

Qiddushin
2:1	116
3:12	116
Yoma 28b	135

Pirqei Avot
1:1	91
2:1	113
2:9	113

Sifre Leviticus
Dibura deNedaba
1	139
1.1–8	139
1.1–9	140
1.1–10	139
1.11	139
1.2–13	140

Talmud Bavli
Baba Batra
60b	119

Berakot
3b	135
62a	78

Baba Meṣiʿa
30b	117
59	120

Erubim
54b	136–37, 139

Giṭṭin
60b	136

Ḥagigah
14b	141

Shabbat
88b–89a	141

Tikkunei Zohar
69	142
114a	142

Tosefta
Soṭah
15.10	120

Ancient World
Plato
Phaedrus
274b–275a	5

Seneca
Ad Lucilium
17–18.106.12	2, 239

Christian World
1 Clement
5:5–7	106

Clement of Alexandria
Paedagogus
10.84	61
10.85	61
10.87	61

Compilatio Assisiensis
50	179
103–7	178
105	178
106	181
112	181

Francis of Assisi
Regula non bullata
(Earlier Rule)
4:6	181
17:3	179
21:1–9	179

Testament
1	175
2	175
2–3	181
4–5	181
6–13	181
14	176, 181
21	181
23	181
25	181
27	181
28	181
30	181
31	181
32	181
33	181
35	181
36	181
37	181
38	181
39	181

The Legend of the Three Companions
5–6	175
6	175
11	175

Index of Ancient Sources

13–14	175
25	176
28–29	175

Gregory the Great
Ep. ad Leandrum

1.1	159

Moralia in Job

22.7.16	166
35.49	167

Regula Pastoralis

1.1	164
1.2	165
4	167

Jacobus de Voragine,
Golden Legend

1:227–29	144
1:374–83	144

John Chrysostom
Homilies

15	119

Pseudo-Dionysius
In Divinis Nominibus

2,2	189

Tertullian
Adversus Marcionem

4.2.4	106

Thomas Aquinas
In John

4, l. 3, 624	198

Questiones De Veritate

q. 11, a. 1	189–90
q. 11, a. 1 ad 1	196
q. 11, a. 1 ad 3	189

Summa Theologiae

I, q. 117, a. 1	189–90, 193
I, q. 117, a. 1 ad 1	192
II–II, q. 16, a. 2	189
III, q. 7	197
III, q. 9	197
III, q. 42	197
III, q. 42, a. 4	199
III, q. 9, a. 4 ad 1	189

Verbum supernum prodiens

1–6	69

Thomas of Celano
Vita Prima

22	174
25	181
31	176
58	168

Vita Secunda

91	179
157	179
158	177
188	177

Ugolino Brunforte
I Fioretti: The Little Flowers of Saint Francis

16	168, 175
25	175

Index of Modern Authors

Ackroyd, Peter R., 21
Adams, E., 64
Agamben, G., 173
Aland, Barbara, 132
Aland, Kurt, 132
Albertz, Rainer, 17
Allen, Elizabeth A., 187
Andersen, Francis I., 38, 41–42
Andersson, Rani-Hendrik, 224
Assmann, Jan, 9
Attisani, A., 173

Bacher, Wilhelm, 112
Bakhos, C., 135
Bakker, Cok, 122
Bakon, Shimon, 43
Bar-Ilan, Meir, 134
Barrett, C. K., 111
Barth, Markus, 123
Barton, John, 43, 45
Barton, Stephen C., 114–15, 119
Bauer, Susan W., 7
Bauer, Walter, 132
Bautch, Richard J., 3
Beck, Martin, 47
Beentjes, Pancratius C., 56–60, 78
Beer, Georg, 3
Beetham, Christopher A., 123
Begg, Christopher T., 23
Bellenger, Aidan, 149
Berlejung, Angelika, 127
Beuken, Willem A. M., 18, 206
Bevere, Allan R., 132
Beyerle, S., 64
Billerbeck, Paul, 81
Bird, Phyllis A., 127
Blanke, Helmut, 123
Blastic, M. W., 178

Boer, Esther A. de, 148
Böhmisch, F., 56
Bokser, Baruch M., 3
Bond, Helen K., 131
Boorer, Suzanne, 235
Bormann, Lukas, 123
Bosman, Frank G., 16, 221–24, 236
Boyd, William, 5
Boyle, L., 190
Boys, Mary C., 184
Breitenstein, Mirko, 176, 180
Brenner, Athalya, 11
Brinkhof, Joke H. A., 89, 99
Buber, Martin, 174, 183
Bulkeley, Tim, 43
Byrskog, Samuel, 6, 77

Cadbury, Henry J., 93
Callaham, Scott N., 15
Caranfa, A., 182
Carroll, Mark D., 41–43
Casey, Maurice, 64
Cassuto, U., 10
Chronis, H. L., 64
Ciampa, Roy E., 111
Civil, M., 4
Clift, Sarah, 172
Coleman, Robert E., 169
Collins, John J., 50, 65
Communauté de Taizé, 212
Connolly, R. Hugh, 149
Contreras, Francoise, 174
Cooper, John, 204
Copenhaver, Martin B., 81
Cotton, John, 226
Couey, J. Blake, 37
Cranfield, C. E. B., 68
Crenshaw, James L., 53

Index of Modern Authors

Cummings, Matthew M., 187
Cuyckens, Hubert, 124

Dagens, Claude, 156, 162
Dalarun, Jacques, 180
Daube, David, 81, 117
Davies, G. I., 17
Deissmann, Gustav A., 105
Demacopoulos, George, 156–57, 160, 163–66
Dempsey, Carol J., 45
Dempster, Stephen G., 41
Denning-Bolle, Sara J., 3
Desbonnets, Théophile, 172, 178
Deutsch, C., 54
Di Lella, Alexander A., 60
Dijk-Groeneboer, Monique van, 182
Dijkstra, Meindert, 41
Dohmen, Christoph, 2, 9–10, 231
Donahue, John R., 63
Dozeman, Thomas B., 231
Dübbers, Michael, 132
Dunn, James D. G., 64, 73–74, 132
Dunstan, William E., 131
Dutch, Robert S., 106

Ebner, Martin, 61
Edzard, Lutz, 15
Egger-Wenzel, Renate, 60
Ego, Beate, 61
Ehrenkrook, Jason von, 131
Eijk, Ryan van, 202
Eijnden, Jan van den, 168
Elleström, Lars, 222
Emmett, Grace, 154
Ernst, Josef, 131
Evans, Craig A., 67

Fabien, Patrick, 89, 100
Ferdinando, Keith, 169, 171–173
Fischer, K. M., 186
Fishbane, Michael, 8
Fitzmyer, Joseph A., 68, 79–80, 86, 88, 91
Fleming, Daniel E., 43
Fletcher, Michelle, 154

Flood, David, 178
Fohrer, Georg, 56
Freedman, David Noel, 38, 41–42
Freeman, Gerard Pieter, 178
Frilingos, Chris A., 80
Futter, Mike, 223

Garrett, Duane A., 34–35
Garroway, Kristine Henriksen, 2
Geeraerts, Dirk, 124
Georges, Tobias, 11–12
Gerhardsson, Birger, 6, 118
Gillihan, Yonder M., 115–116
Gladwell, Malcolm, 203
Goorbergh, E. van den, 181
Görg, Manfred, 17
Gould, Ezra P., 68
Grace, Fran, 183, 185
Gregg, Brian H., 65
Gregory, Brad S., 104
Greschat, Katharina, 162–163
Greydanus, Steven D., 154
Grosvenor, Mary, 132
Gruenwald, Ithamar, 141
Grün, Anselm, 217
Guggenheimer, Heinrich, 221, 229–30
Guyette, Fred, 35

Hadjiev, Tchavdar S., 44–45
Hanson, K. C., 149
Hardmeier, Christoph, 20
Harper, William R., 42
Harrington, Daniel J., 68
Harrington, Wilfrid J., 68
Hartenstein, Judith, 145, 148
Haspecker, Josef, 60
Hassell Bullock, Clarence, 45
Hayes, John H., 33
Heidegger, Martin, 174
Heilmann, Jan, 6
Henderson, Suzanne W., 66
Héring, Jean, 111
Hernandez, Patricia, 228
Heschel, Abraham J., 204
Hezser, Catherine, 134–35, 140
Hisley, Jennifer, 8

258 Index of Modern Authors

Hoeberichts, Jan, 178, 184
Hooker, Morna D., 64
Hubbard Jr., Robert L., 41

Jaffee, M. S., 134
Jemielity, Thomas, 42
Jenni, Ernst, 126
Jensen, Robin M., 235
Jonge, Henk Jan de, 79–80
Jónsson, Gunnlaur A., 132

Kain, Erik, 221
Kaiser, Otto, 17
Kaufmann, S. A., 9
Kearns, Conleth, 57
Kelber, Werner H., 6, 62
Kempler, Toni, 8
Kessels, Jos, 213
Kilgallen, John J., 80
King, Edmund J., 5
King, Karen, 147–148
Klauck, Hans-Josef, 100
Klimczak, Pawel, 197
Koet, Bart J., 1, 73, 77–79, 94, 99, 111, 114, 120–21
König, Eduard, 3
Konkel, A. H., 38
Korthagen, Fred A. J., 213
Koster, Bob, 213
Kramer, Samuel N., 8
Kristeva, Julia, 222
Kunder, Amanda, 144
Kunz-Lübcke, Andreas, 2
Kynes, Will, 12

Lafferty, Theresa V., 43
Lagerwerf, Bram, 213
Lagrange, Marie-Joseph, 80
Lahti, Evan, 224
Landini, Laurentio C., 180
Lehmann, Ann-Sophie, 144
Leite, Sara, 217
Leloup, Jean-Yves, 150–152
Lemaire, André, 6
Lenhardt, Pierre, 110
Lévi, Israel, 54

Linville, James R., 45
Lupieri, Edmondo F., 143–44, 148, 150
Lux, Rüdiger, 2

MacKenzie, R. A. F., 53
Madsen, Deborah, 226
Maier, Christl M., 3
Malbon, Elizabeth S., 63, 65
Malina, Bruce J., 69
Malley, Edward J., 68
Mamahit, Ferry Y., 45
Marböck, Johannes, 57
Marcus, Joel, 63, 65
Marjanen, Antti, 148
Markus, Robert A., 156, 158, 167
Matura, Thaddée, 178
Mays, James L., 41–42
Melisse, Cornelia J. M., 15, 123, 125–132
Mello-Klein, Cody, 223
Merklein, Helmut, 130
Merleau-Ponty, Marcel, 170–172, 185
Meyers, Carol, 3
Middendorp, Theophil, 52
Middlemas, Jill, 127
Moessner, David P., 93, 101
Möller, Karl, 38–39, 41–42
Moses, P., 184
Murnane, Ben, 223
Murphy, Cullen, 3
Murphy, Roland E., 3, 68

Nahkola, Aulikki, 46
Naluparayil, J. C., 64
Nancy, Jean-Luc, 172
Neirynck, Frans, 107
Neumann-Gorsolke, Ute, 126
Niles, Nathaniel, 226
Noble, Paul R., 36
Nogalski, James D., 47
Nolthenius, Hélène, 175
Nouwen, Henry, 211
Nussbaum, Martha C., 2, 11, 77

Ó Floinn, Gearard, 70
Oliva, Adriano, 190
Ong, Walter J., 7

Opata, Josiah N., 205
Osten-Sacken, Peter von der, 110
Otto, Eckart, 2, 10–11

Paas, Stefan, 38
Palmatier, Robert, 221
Pardee, Cambry G., 148–149
Parkhouse, Sarah, 146
Parrott, Douglas M., 148
Patrick, Brian C., 8
Patzia, Arthur G., 123, 131–32
Pedrosa-de-Jesus, Helena, 217
Peterlevitz, Luciano R., 35
Peters, Norbert, 53, 61
Petersen, Silke, 146, 148
Peursen, W. Th. van, 54
Pfammatter, Joseph, 131
Pieper, Josef, 4–5
Pinker, Aron, 35
Piron, Sylvain, 180
Plöger, Otto, 3, 56
Plummer, Alfred, 80–81
Preston, Diana, 226
Prince, Deborah T., 81
Puech, Émile, 55

Rastoin, Marc, 93
Reimer, Andy M., 100
Reinhartz, Adele, 150
Renz, Thomas, 34
Reymond, Eric D., 54–55
Riesner, Rainer, 77, 79
Riess, Richard, 202
Roberts, J. J. M., 43
Robson, Eleanor, 4
Roebben, Bert, 169, 183–84
Rogers, Jesse, 57
Rogers, Trent A., 144, 149
Rohling, Detlef, 187–88
Rohrbaugh, Richard L., 69
Rommel, Floribert, 164
Roose, Hanna, 217
Rosano, Michael, 226
Rosner, Brian S., 111

Saccucci, Erica-Lyn, 150
Sacks, Jonathan, 76

Safrai, Chana, 104
Safrai, Shmuel, 110, 112, 134
Safrai, Zeev, 104, 115, 121
Sanders, E. P., 105
Sanders, José M., 206
Schart, Aaron, 38, 43
Schmitt, Hans-Christoph, 17
Schneider, Wolfgang, 14
Schnügel-Straumann, Helen, 10
Schoot, Henk J. M., 173, 182, 196
Schrage, W., 119
Schröder, Bernd, 79
Schroer, Silvia, 127
Schröter, Jens, 64–65
Seitz, Christopher R., 23
Shirley, S., 104
Short, William J., 168, 175
Shupak, Nili, 3
Shveka, Avi, 35
Sikkel, Constantijn, 15
Smend, R., 52–53
Smit, Joop F. M., 93, 108
Smith, Claire S., 105, 109–10
Smith, Gary V., 41–42
Snaith, John G., 53
Sneed, Mark, 12
Snyman, S. D. (Fanie), 33
Speelman, Willem Marie, 168, 170, 173, 177, 180
Spencer, F. Scott, 89, 100
Spinoza, Baruch, 104–105
Stadelmann, Helge, 50
Sterling, Jim, 224
Stevens, Gerald L., 132
Stone, H. W., 216
Stowers, Stanley K., 111
Strack, Hermann L., 81
Straw, Carole, 156, 165
Strousma, Guy G., 6–7
Sumney, Jerry L., 123

Tabory, Joseph, 229
Talstra, Eep, 14–15
Tamburro, Paul, 223
Taylor, John R., 124–125
Taylor, Vincent, 69

Tesch, Katja, 61
Thompson, John M., 3
Thumpanathu, Bincy Thomas, 31
Todeschini, Giacomo, 179
Tomson, Peter J., 107, 110, 115, 117
Torrell, Jean-Pierre, 189–190, 197
Tropper, Amram, 118
Tubbs, Nicolas, 174, 182–183
Tuckett, Christopher M., 64, 67, 145, 147
Tull, Patricia K., 21
Turner, Victor, 177

Van Segbroeck, Frans, 107
Vander Stichele, Caroline, 144, 150, 153
Vanlier Hunter, Austin, 42
Venter, Pieter M., 45
Verheij, S., 178
Vermeylen, Jacques, 10
Viberg, Åke, 41–42, 45, 47
Vielhauer, P., 69
Von Dobbeler, Axel, 89, 100

Waever, Mark, 181
Wakely, Robin, 35
Watts, John D. W., 37
Watts, Mike, 217
Wayne Hellmann, J. A., 168, 175
Weil, Simone, 174
Weinrich, Harald, 14
Weiss, Johannes, 110–11

Weren, Wim, 172
Werner, Eric, 229
White, Benjamin L., 107, 117
White, Devin L., 105–106, 115
Whybray, R. N., 55
Wieringen, Archibald L. H .M. van, 1, 6, 15–21, 24–27, 29, 33, 35–36, 46, 206, 222, 236
Wieringen, Renilde G. W. M. van, 206
Wilgus, Blair J., 41–42
Williamson, Hugh G. M., 17
Winthrop, John, 226
Wöhrle, Jakob, 34
Wolde, Ellen J. van, 124
Wolff, Hans Walter, 204
Wolter, Michael, 130
Wood, Joyce R., 38
Wright, Benjamin G., 57, 61
Wubbels, Theo, 213
Wuellner, Wilhelm, 107
Wypadlo, Adrian, 69
Wysocki, Jan, 221

Yarbro Collins, Adela, 65, 67, 74
Young, James, 222

Zapff, B. M., 54
Zerwick, Max, 132
Zimmer, Ben, 226
Zweerman, Th., 181

Personalia

PANC C. BEENTJES is Professor Emeritus of Old Testament at the Tilburg School of Catholic Theology.

FRANK G. BOSMAN is Assistant Professor for Cultural Theology at the Tilburg School of Catholic Theology.

JOKE H. A. BRINKHOF is a biblical scholar, formerly Lecturer of Old and New Testament at Fontys University of Applied Sciences, Henge-lo/Amsterdam, the Netherlands.

BART J. KOET is Professor Emeritus of New Testament at the Tilburg School of Catholic Theology and a deacon of the Diocese of Haarlem-Amsterdam.

CORNELIA J. M. MELISSE is Lecturer of Biblical Hebrew at the Tilburg School of Catholic Theology and a teacher of religion at the Onze Lieve Vrouwelyceum, Breda.

LEON MOCK was Assistant Professor of Judaica at the Tilburg School of Catholic Theology and a rabbi.

BÉNÉDICTE LEMMELIJN is Professor of Old Testament at the KU Leuven and a member of the Pontifical Biblical Commission.

GEARARD Ó FLOINN is Associate Professor in Religious Education and Religious Studies in the Froebel Department of Education, Maynooth University.

HENK J. M. SCHOOT is Professor Emeritus of Theology of Thomas Aquinas at the Tilburg School of Catholic Theology and a deacon of the Archdiocese of Utrecht.

ARNOLD A. M. SMEETS is Lecturer of Patristics and Coordinator of the Impact and Post-Initial Education Programme at the Tilburg School of Catholic Theology.

WILLEM MARIE SPEELMAN is Professor of Franciscan Spirituality, Theology and History at the Tilburg School of Catholic Theology and Director of the Franciscan Study Centre.

BINCY THOMAS THUMPANATHU is Lecturer of Old Testament at the Salesian Institute of Religion, Keezhmadu, Pontifical Institute of Theology and Philosophy Alwaye and Carmel Jyothy Vidyabhavan, Kerala, India, and a member of the Congregation of the Mother of Carmel.

CAROLINE H. C. M. VANDER STICHELE is Professor of New Testament at the Tilburg School of Catholic Theology.

ARCHIBALD L. H. M. VAN WIERINGEN is Professor of Old Testament at the Tilburg School of Catholic Theology and a priest of the Diocese of Haarlem-Amsterdam.

RENILDE G. W. M. VAN WIERINGEN is a pastoral theologian working as a prison chaplain, and an artist.

www.ingramcontent.com/pod-product-compliance
Lightning Source LLC
Chambersburg PA
CBHW071247230426
43668CB00011B/1623